# REASSESSING THE NUREMBERG MILITARY TRIBUNALS

# War and Genocide

**General Editors:** Omer Bartov, Brown University; A. Dirk Moses, European University Institute, Florence/University of Sydney

In recent years there has been a growing interest in the study of war and genocide, not from a traditional military history perspective, but within the framework of social and cultural history. This series offers a forum for scholarly works that reflect these new approaches.

*"The Berghahn series* Studies on War and Genocide *has immeasurably enriched the English-language scholarship available to scholars and students of genocide and, in particular, the Holocaust."*—**Totalitarian Movements and Political Religions**

# REASSESSING THE NUREMBERG MILITARY TRIBUNALS

*Transitional Justice, Trial Narratives, and Historiography*

Edited by

Kim C. Priemel and Alexa Stiller

berghahn

NEW YORK · OXFORD

www.berghahnbooks.com

Published by
Berghahn Books
www.berghahnbooks.com

**Library of Congress Cataloging-in-Publication Data**

Reassessing the Nuremberg military tribunals : transitional justice, trial narratives, and historiography / edited by Kim C. Priemel and Alexa Stiller.
    pages cm. -- (Studies on war and genocide ; volume 16)
  Includes bibliographical references and index.
  ISBN 978-0-85745-530-7 (hardback : alk. paper) -- ISBN 978-1-78238-667-4 (paperback : alk. paper) -- ISBN 978-0-85745-532-1 (ebook)
  1. Nuremberg War Crime Trials, Nuremberg, Germany, 1946-1949. 2. Nuremberg Trial of Major German War Criminals, Nuremberg, Germany, 1945-1946. 3. War crime trials--Germany--Nuremberg--History--20th century. 4. International criminal law--History.
  KZ1178 .R43 2012
  341.6/90268

2012030494

**British Library Cataloguing in Publication Data**

A catalogue record for this book is available
from the British Library.

Printed on acid-free paper.

ISBN: 978-0-85745-530-7 hardback
ISBN: 978-1-78238-667-4 paperback
ISBN: 978-0-85745-532-1 ebook

# Contents

# LIST OF FIGURES AND TABLES

*೮ঙ্গৈ৸*

## Figures

## Tables

# LIST OF ABBREVIATIONS

*⊂8ƒ8⁓*

| | |
|---|---|
| AdeF | Archives de France, Paris |
| AFP | Alexander Family Papers, Boston |
| AGWAR | Adjutant General, War Department |
| AOF | Archives de l'occupation française, Colmar |
| APD | Alexander Papers Durham, North Carolina |
| BArch | Bundesarchiv (German Federal Archives), Berlin |
| BArch-MA | Bundesarchiv-Militärarchiv (Military Archives), Freiburg |
| BBF | Benjamin B. Ferencz Collection |
| BDC | Berlin Document Center |
| BJO | Barbarossa Jurisdiction Order |
| CCL 10 | Control Council Law No. 10 |
| CLL | Cornell Law Library, Ithaca, NY |
| CSDIC | Combined Services Detailed Interrogation Centre (UK) |
| CULS-ADLL | Columbia University Law School, Arthur Diamond Law Library |
| DNTC | Donovan Nuremberg Trial Collection |
| EDC | European Defense Community |
| FBI | Federal Bureau of Investigations |
| FEA | Foreign Economic Administration |
| FIAT | Federal Intelligence Agency, Technical (under G-2, SHAEF) |
| Gestapo | Geheime Staatspolizei (Secret State Police) |
| GPO | General Plan Ost (General Plan East) |
| HICOG | High Commission for Germany |
| ICC | International Criminal Court |
| ICTR | International Criminal Tribunal Rwanda |
| ICTY | International Criminal Tribunal for the Former Yugoslavia |
| IMT | International Military Tribunal *and* Trial of the Major War Criminals before the International Military Tribunal, Nuremberg , November 14, 1945– October 1, 1946 ("Blue Series") |
| JAG | Judge Advocate General |
| JCC | Jewish Claims Conference |
| JRSO | Jewish Restitution Successor Organization |
| LoC | Library of Congress, Washington, DC |
| LRTWC | Law Reports on Trials of War Criminals |
| MMP | Papers of Michael A. Musmanno, Duquesne University, Pittsburgh, PA |

| | |
|---|---|
| MT | The Nuremberg Medical Trial 1946/47. Transcripts, Material of the Prosecution and Defense. Related Documents, Microfiche Edition |
| NA (PRO) | National Archives (formerly Public Records Office) of the United Kingdom, Kew |
| NARA | National Archives and Records Administration, College Park |
| NATO | North Atlantic Treaty Organization |
| NMT | Nuernberg Military Tribunals |
| NPRC | National Personnel Records Center, NARA, College Park |
| NSDAP | Nationalsozialistische Deutsche Arbeiterpartei (National Socialist German Workers' Party) |
| NTN | Najwyższy Trybunał Narodowy (Supreme National Tribunal of Poland) |
| NYPL | New York Public Library, New York |
| NYT | New York Times |
| OCCPAC | Office of Chief of Counsel for the Prosecution of Axis Criminality |
| OCCWC | Office of Chief of Counsel for War Crimes |
| OKH | Oberkommando des Heeres (High Command of the Army) |
| OKW | Oberkommando der Wehrmacht (Wehrmacht High Command) |
| OLG | Oberlandesgericht (Higher Regional Court) |
| OMGUS | Office of Military Government, United States |
| OSS | Office of Strategic Services |
| POWs | Prisoners of war |
| R&A | Research & Analysis Branch, OSS |
| RCPE | Royal College of Physicians Edinburgh |
| RFSS | Reichsführer SS |
| RG | Record Group |
| RHJ | Robert H. Jackson Papers, LoC, Washington, DC |
| RKF, RKFDV | Reichskommissar für die Festigung deutschen Volkstums (Reich Commissioner for the Strengthening of Germandom) |
| RSHA | Reichssicherheitshauptamt (Reich Security Main Office) |
| RuSHA | Rasse- und Siedlungshauptamt der SS (Race and Settlement Main Office of the SS) |
| SA | Sturmabteilung |
| SD | Sicherheitsdienst (Security Service) |
| SED | Sozialistische Einheitspartei Deutschlands (Socialist Unity Party of Germany) |
| SHAEF | Supreme Headquarters Allied Expeditionary Force |
| Sipo | Sicherheitspolizei (Security Police) |
| SPD | Sozialdemokratische Partei Deutschlands (Social Democratic Party of Germany) |
| SS | Schutzstaffel |
| StAN | Staatsarchiv Nürnberg |
| TWC | Trials of War Criminals before the Nuernberg Military Tribunals under Control Council Law No. 10 ("Green Series") |
| UFA | Universum Film Aktiengesellschaft |
| UNA | United Nations Archives, Geneva |
| UNESCO | United Nations Educational, Scientific and Cultural Organization |
| UNWCC | United Nations War Crimes Commission |
| USFET | US Forces, European Theater |
| USHMM | US Holocaust Memorial Museum |
| VoMi | Volksdeutsche Mittelstelle (Ethnic German Liaison Office) |
| WVHA | Wirtschafts-Verwaltungshauptamt (Economic and Administration Main Office) |
| ZASF | Zentrum für Antisemitismusforschung (Center for Research on Antisemitism), Berlin |

# Foreword

⟡ ℰ𝒮𝒮 ⟶

### Michael R. Marrus

This book addresses German war crimes trials that need a higher profile in our understanding of how the Allies contended with the defeat of the Hitlerian regime in 1945. The twelve trials of German war criminals held under American auspices in Nuremberg, conducted between October 1946 and April 1949 following the verdict of the four power International Military Tribunal (IMT), have struggled to find their identity and their place in historical discourse ever since their last verdict was handed down in 1949. Unlike the IMT, the trials in question have suffered from historiographical neglect. Nomenclature itself has been part of the problem, and what these trials have been called has been a matter of confusion. History has generally designated the IMT trial as *the* Nuremberg Trial, and representations are often accompanied with the now-familiar iconography: Courtroom 600 in the Nuremberg Palace of Justice, with the chief Nazi defendants, most prominently Hermann Göring, in the dock. Commentators and students alike regularly confuse this "Nuremberg Trial" with the "Nuremberg Trials," in the plural. Telford Taylor, chief prosecutor in charge of the twelve trials, wrote an excellent book on the proceedings against the "major German war criminals" at Nuremberg before the IMT and titled his book, erroneously, *The Anatomy of the Nuremberg Trials*, inexplicably using the plural. In his volume, Taylor referred to "Nuremberg" as "the first Nuremberg trial." Adding further to the confusion, the latter was designated at the time, and is still occasionally referred to, as the "Göring trial," using the name of the lead defendant among the 23 accused. As Taylor told his readers, he intended to write a description of the "subsequent trials," "presided over by American judges applying international laws of war," but unfortunately he never did so. And so we have no explicit correction of this point by the person who perhaps had the most authority to do so. As a result, those who do not get beyond Taylor's title may perhaps be forgiven if they somehow blend the proceedings before the IMT into something loosely called "the Nuremberg Trials."

And then there are the official records: readers strolling through library stacks on the hunt for the 42 blue-bound volumes of the IMT proceedings – entitled *Trial of the Major War Criminals before the International Military Tribunal* and known as the "blue series" – may well come across 15 green-bound volumes, known as the "green series," with a deceptively similar title, *Trials of War Criminals before the Nuernberg Military Tribunals, Under Control Council Law No 10*, and not immediately know how to distinguish between the two. It is the latter that record the proceedings that are the subject of this book.

Terminological imprecision continues. What Taylor called the "subsequent trials" are sometimes referenced the "Subsequent Proceedings," dignified with upper case, or just generically as the "subsequent proceedings," and occasionally denoted by the courts before which the cases were heard, the "Nuernberg Military Tribunals," or NMT, specifying the city in which they were held – for whatever reason rendered as "Nuernberg," or "Nürnberg," the German rendering of the city, rather than "Nuremberg," largely reserved for the trial before the IMT. The trials are often denoted by the acronym "NMT," designating the tribunals before which the cases were heard, although the courts were actually presided over by civilian judges – and these can easily be confused with other American trials, conducted under the authority of the United States occupation forces, and which occurred elsewhere in Germany.

The essays assembled here by the diligent and thoughtful editors Alexa Stiller and Kim Priemel give us a much needed perspective on the intentions of the American trial planners, the conduct of the proceedings, and how they appeared from the vantage points of contemporaries and subsequent generations. We learn of the wide variety of defendants – industrialists, government people, the military, and diplomats. We read of both blinkered paper pushers and hard-core killers. We examine the strategies, frustrations and distractions of those who participated in the trials – judges, prosecutors, and defense attorneys. And most of all we get a selective sense, through the vast documentation associated with these trials, filling more than 300,000 pages of evidence, of the many problems associated with judging the leadership of the Third Reich.

Looking back on the work of the American organizers of the trials, I believe the essays in this book highlight a significant contribution to a worthy objective. For all of the flaws in the conduct of these proceedings, and notwithstanding their failure to live up to the more idealistic hopes at the time, the work described here sought, in the words of Telford Taylor, "the establishment of world order under the rule of law." That remains an aspiration of course, but for those who continue to seek it, the Nuernberg Military Tribunals deserve our respect and our continuing contemplation.

Massey College
September 22, 2010

# Introduction

# Nuremberg's Narratives

## Revising the Legacy of the "Subsequent Trials"

*Kim C. Priemel and Alexa Stiller*

⌒⟍⟋⌒

Less than a month after the final verdict of the Nuernberg Military Tri-bunals (NMT)[1] had been handed down in the so-called High Command Case, the departing chief prosecutor, Brigadier General Telford Taylor, wound up the four-year-long venture in a statement to the International News Service, articulating his expectations as to the legacy of the trial series. To those who thought that the war crimes proceedings, which by that time had come under scrutiny and criticism on both sides of the Atlantic, would fade into oblivion Taylor issued a stern warning: "I venture to predict that as time goes on we will hear more about Nuremberg rather than less, and that in a very real sense the conclusion of the trials marks the beginning, and not the end, of Nuremberg as a force of politics, law, and morals."[2] Although not everything did go as planned and most of the later Nuremberg trials indeed receded into prolonged obscurity, Taylor's prophecy was not wholly mistaken, and the trials would indeed show a remarkable resilience, if more indirect and implicit than had been intended, in shaping politics, law, and historiography (rather than morals). Tracing these—frequently twisted—roads of the NMT's influence and impact lies at the heart of the present volume.

Taylor's statement attested to the great ambitions entertained by the American prosecutors in preparing the NMT. The so-called Subse-

quent Trials went beyond their famous, in a malign way more glamor-
ous predecessor, the International Military Tribunal (IMT) with its cast
of high-ranking Nazis. While the IMT's ambition had been to punish
the surviving leadership of the Third Reich and put on record Nazi
criminality, the NMT, or rather their instigators, aspired to nothing
less than indicting the entire Nazi state and analyzing its workings in
an authoritative way. Structures rather than individuals, and institutional representatives rather than easily identifiable villains, were to be
publicly prosecuted, literally for everyone to see. For that reason, the
courtroom became the site of (pre)scholarly dispute over the nature of
the German dictatorship, its power structures and dynamics, and most
important of all, the highly charged issue of who was answerable for the
regime's crimes.

On the German side, the trials presented a second major stage (after
the IMT which had put the blame almost exclusively on the top level of
the Nazi leadership) in the process of coming to terms with the legacy
of guilt and the need for atonement. Not surprisingly, the defendants
rejected entirely the American reading of the Third Reich, pleading "not
guilty" both for themselves and for German society.[3] Since the different
explanations of the prosecution, the judges, the German lawyers, and
the defendants often proved to be mutually exclusive, the Nuremberg
trials rapidly turned from an effort at judicial reckoning to a forum for
protracted negotiations over history which affected political as well as
academic life in postwar Germany. A whole set of narratives of the all
too recent history emerged from the NMT trials and made their way
into historical textbooks, speeches of commemoration, and the phrasing of restitution acts. Conversely, other narratives such as victims'
accounts remained conspicuously subdued or absent. As the contributions in the present volume argue, many of these representations and
images, interpretations and legal legacies had their genesis in the NMT
rather than the IMT. Patterns and paradigms which would determine
historical research, policies of remembrance, and the evolution of international criminal law emanated from the "subsequent proceedings" and
resonate until the present day.

That these narratives have by and large escaped the attention of historical research so far is the result of two key shortcomings of the existing, in fact abundant, studies dealing with Nuremberg: firstly, there
has been too strong and exclusive a focus on the IMT at the cost of the
NMT. Without denying its merits, the IMT-centered approach has led
to a view of the Nuremberg stage which has preferred the spectacular
over the profound, the big names and the drama at the surface over
the intricate patterns and deep structures of analysis, narration, and
interpretation.[4] Secondly, the relative neglect of the NMT[5] attests to a
perspective on Nuremberg which conceives of the proceedings either as
an epilogue to the Third Reich or as the prologue of its three successor
states (and, indeed, often solely of the Federal Republic).[6] Meanwhile,

little effort has been made so far to read the trials as trials, i.e. to take seriously both the epistemological premises of judicial proceedings and the dialectical tension of the historical-political trial.

From this perspective, the trials at Nuremberg (and Tokyo) stand out as the first major manifestations of what has by now come to be known as "transitional justice," embracing the three types identified by Timothy Garton Ash as judicial trials, purges, and history lessons.[7] The NMT as a concerted—if, from the German point of view, imposed—effort to come to terms with the past pursued all three objectives by trying to bring perpetrators to justice, to eliminate them from key positions in German society, be they in the public service or in business, and to establish a comprehensive, authoritative historical narrative of twentieth-century Germany and Nazi rule.

## Transitional Justice, Trial Narratives and Historiography

Despite its recent career in academic debate, transitional justice is hardly a new concept. In fact, in his famous analysis of the political trial, first published in 1961, the American-German jurist Otto Kirchheimer paved the way towards such an understanding of justice at the intersection of history and law which to him accounted for the "peculiar dialectics" of the Allied proceedings at Nuremberg. These, he argued, had been the most important case of what he dubbed "successor justice"—a specific variant of the use of legal procedure for political ends which Kirchheimer conceptualized non-normatively and beyond the abuse of Stalinist and Nazi show trials[8]—and had thus been characterized by their "both retrospective and prospective" intentions.[9] As a former analyst of the United States Office of Strategic Services (OSS) and a close collaborator of those OSS colleagues who went on to Nuremberg, Kirchheimer's analysis not only built on first-hand knowledge, but also gave an insight into the multiple intentions of those who had done the ground work for the trial program. As a former German émigré, a well-reputed legal theoretician, and an OSS employee, Kirchheimer could lay some claim to representativeness for the members of the Nuremberg think-tank. And he was no less characteristic in his endeavor to fit the Nuremberg experience into a larger intellectual undertaking, in his case an analysis of the power and the obligations of law in the age of total war. In fact, his own academic path—first fighting Nazi Germany through analysis, and then evaluating Nuremberg's contribution to the world order of the twentieth century's latter half—was mirrored in the retro- and prospective pattern Kirchheimer found in the Nuremberg trials.

What was more, Kirchheimer tackled an issue that has been on the minds of many historians (and some lawyers) over the past decades, although the debate is nearly as old as the two disciplines: how close

family bonds between historiography and jurisprudence are, which epistemological premises they share, and how they relate to the larger categories of "truth" and "justice." These do not need to be discussed here
in detail. Suffice it to say that much of the criticism brought against the
Nuremberg trials is rooted either in misunderstandings or in the lack of
analytical rigor, or both, when it comes to differentiating between the
diverse levels on which the war crimes trials were staged.[10] Historians
have frequently criticized Nuremberg for failing to account for historical complexity and bring about adequate justice, while jurists are wary
of the historical agenda of the trials and the historians' tendency not
to appreciate the trials as legal institutions governed by established
procedures and operating their own logic.[11] The present volume avoids
both dead ends. Neither does it conceive of the law in general and the
NMT in particular as a closed system only comprehensible if placed
in the history of legal dogma, nor does it judge the trials by standards
which ignore the peculiarity of legal thought and, more importantly,
legal practice.

Instead, the contributions to this volume concentrate on another
dimension of that double tenet of transitional justice as depicted by
Kirchheimer. Its underlying contention that the successor trial as a specific legal institution shares its essentially diachronic perspective with
historical research is one easily identifiable issue at stake. Another is
the trial's quality as a tool to enquire into political issues in the broad-
est sense, i.e. a social performance which raises questions of causality,
responsibility, and legitimacy—this is the didactic quality of all criminal
trials which Lawrence Douglas has emphasized.[12] And the trial also
bears political significance in its own right and constitutes a subject of
historical study itself.[13] A third common denominator of the trial and
historical analysis will be found in the narrative as the key means of
structuring analysis. Both the legal trial and the historical study are
reconstructions of past events and therefore essentially interpretative,
leaving a residual degree of uncertainty which is reflected in historiographical *Quellenkritik* (source criticism), on the one hand, and in the
legal figure of doubt, prohibiting conviction under the Rule of Law,
on the other. Clearly, both undertakings also differ, mostly in their
consequences. Whereas the trial is "a practical enterprise," historical
investigation is essentially (though not exclusively) academic.[14] While
historiography allows for ambiguity, the judgment, in the end, will usually have to side with either of the two narratives presented.[15]

Without obscuring these differences, it is the common denomina-
tors that the present volume sets out to investigate, with the narrative
as a crucial junction. As Robert P. Burns has demonstrated for the
trial, narratives help to organize vast and complex information, lend-
ing coherence and consistency to analysis. The courtroom dynamics
are marked by a dialectical sequence of construction and deconstruc-
tion of narratives which is undertaken in turns by prosecution and

defense—in particular in the adversarial pattern of Anglo-Saxon law.[16] Thus, the trial resembles historical debate, and both forums of discussion have proven to be mutually susceptible to their respective insights. In particular, practitioners of contemporary history have made ample use of legally generated sources—interrogations, protocols of proceedings, accumulated evidence, indictments, and judgments—while lawyers have, in turn, resorted to historiographical expertise in order to interpret evidence, or as a substitute where other proof has been unavailable. There is hardly any more compelling case for this intense, often fruitful cooperation than the legal and historical investigation of the literally immense crimes of National Socialist Germany.[17]

## Early Analyses of the Third Reich and Nuremberg's Epistemic Community

In fact, the very scope of Nazi criminality and the difficulties with which the Allied—especially the distant American—prosecutors met when enquiring into the workings of the Third Reich, made them look out for structuring devices early on, and such analyses and interpretations were indeed readily available. Excavating Nazi Germany's diverse layers of power, influence, and responsibility, the task of exposing the scale of criminal deeds, and analyzing the dynamics of destruction was helped a good deal by interdisciplinary assistance provided by experts such as Otto Kirchheimer. The German lawyer was one of many émigrés who, in addition to American academics, entered the Allied services as government advisors, military and intelligence officers and who brought along a range of theoretical and methodological tools, or abstract knowledge to be turned into useful information. Jurists and philosophers, historians and economists conferred in Allied offices such as the OSS and the Foreign Economic Administration (FEA), in the Departments of War and Justice, within the Allied occupation authorities such as the Office of Military Government, US Element (OMGUS), and at Nuremberg where they formed a temporary, often pragmatic rather than principled, yet effective epistemic community.[18] Despite considerable differences in terms of their academic training and their respective ideological creeds, these people—predominantly but not exclusively men—shared a set of common objectives which were best summarized in the famous 'four Ds' of the Potsdam Agreement in August 1945: the policies of democratization, denazification, demilitarization, and decartelization were not only the lines along which Germany would have to be rebuilt, these were also the categories in which much of Nazi criminality was sorted.[19]

   As the following years of Allied occupation would show, there was less agreement on what precisely these objectives meant in practical terms between the four victorious powers as well as in their respective offices. However, in what Jeffrey Herf has called "the brief Nuremberg interregnum between the end of the war and the crystallization of the Cold War,"[20] the determination to expose the Third Reich's offences overcame these differences. What was more, there was a general agreement that only an all-embracing approach to Nazi criminality, covering all spheres of society, would do. The years 1944 to 1947 may not have been that "golden era of judicial confrontation with the Nazi past" that Herf has rather optimistically found them to be. But it was during these years that plans for Allied occupation, German reconstruction and, most of all, judicial reckoning were devised by an epistemic community, short-lived though it was, which agreed on key issues—although frequently more on the questions to be asked than on the answers to be given: which had been the most harrowing crimes, who had been the most important perpetrators, and which wrong turns Germany had taken in the preceding decades. Thus, an American penologist like Sheldon Glueck, a German lawyer and political scientist such as Franz L. Neumann, jurists Raphael Lemkin and Hersch Lauterpacht, historians Hajo Holborn and Walter L. Dorn, and economists Edward Mason and Otto Nathan, half of them European émigrés, could all agree on the salient features of National Socialist rule and modern German history: (1) a tradition of authoritarianism and militarism; (2) a corresponding lack of liberal, democratic, and free-market institutions; (3) a racialized worldview—though its genuineness was less unequivocal with Marxist analysts like Neumann; and (4) a vicious onslaught on multilateralism which was targeted by the prosecution's double construct of conspiracy and crimes against peace for which the War Department lawyer Murray C. Bernays has become famous.[21] Some of them, including Glueck, Neumann, Lemkin, and Bernays, joined the Nuremberg project in person, although the influence of their written works may have been even more profound. Glueck's articles on war crimes trials and aggressive war, Neumann's famed *Behemoth*, and Lemkin's opus magnum *Axis Rule*, in spite of the initial outsider position of its author, became set texts with the Nuremberg prosecution and helped to shape the narratives which would govern the war crimes trials at the Palace of Justice.

In his celebrated study, *Behemoth*, Neumann argued that the Nazi state was based on four pillars: the armed forces, private business, state bureaucracy, and the party (including the SS).[22] Building on this paradigm, the NMT prosecutors emphasized precisely those crimes which showed the interaction between the said groups and accordingly composed the trial series. Among the twelve trials, three proceedings targeted German industrialists (the Flick, Krupp, and I.G. Farben cases), two indicted generals and field marshals (the Hostages and High Command cases), four put SS officers in the dock (the Medical, Pohl, RuSHA, and *Einsatzgruppen* cases), and two more investigated the role of state bureaucracy (Justice and Ministries cases); the solitary case against Erhard Milch combined features of all divisions. Obviously, Taylor's Office of Chief of Counsel for War Crimes (OCCWC) applied Neumann's theoretical premises,[23] but there were also limits to the transformation of the abstract concept into judicial practice. The prosecutors made use of Neumann's study only to a certain degree both for practical reasons and the fact that other ideas resonated in the concept of the twelve trials as well.

Among those influential ideas was Sheldon Glueck's seminal study on aggressive war,[24] which may justly be described as the second set text of the Nuremberg paradigm. Glueck, who collaborated with members of both the IMT and the NMT staff, had already been a major influence on Robert H. Jackson's preparations for the four-power tribunal with its central objective of proving that the alleged "major war criminals" had been involved in the planning and waging of a war of aggression. In combination with Bernays's tactical advice to resort to the conspiracy charge,[25] the idea that "aggressive war" was the principal international crime had been ingested into the Nuremberg proceedings and had made the charge of "crimes against peace" the gravamen especially of Jackson's strategy. As a former member of Jackson's office, it is hardly surprising that Telford Taylor adopted a similar stance. However, the trials under his direction displayed a marked broadening of scope under the influence of Neumann's analysis, involving a larger group of protagonists and drawing a much more complex, institution-minded picture of the Third Reich.

Simultaneously, another important wartime study on the Nazi state gained influence among the staff of OCCWC. Raphael Lemkin's report, *Axis Rule in Occupied Europe*, and the concept of "genocide"[26] had a lasting effect on the composition of the trial series and the prosecutors' view on the Nazi crimes, serving as the third set text for the NMT paradigm.[27] The prosecution in the RuSHA, the Medical, and the *Einsatzgruppen* trials drew heavily on the "genocide" concept. It served as a prime means of describing both the dimension of the crimes and their underlying intentions, i.e. the extermination of a nation, an ethnic group, and other groups of persons. These trials formed a distinct group of "atrocity trials," although all trials featured atrocity charges which were easier to prove than the elaborate constructs of conspiracy and aggressive war. The prosecutors with Taylor leading the way saw atrocities, whether human experiments, kidnapping of children, expulsion, or mass murder, as crimes committed to achieve the aims of the "Nazi Plan."[28]

The manifest influence the members of the above epistemic community, despite all compromises, exerted on the construction of the Nuremberg paradigm and to an even greater extent on the formulation of indictments and opening statements—the prime documents to phrase the narratives and arguments which make up the "double helix" of the theory of the case[29]—betrays yet another narrative dimension, though on a meta-level of analysis. Biographical narratives are tightly interwoven with the evolution of the Nuremberg trial program and with its implementation. Kirchheimer and Neumann, Lemkin and Lauterpacht ingested their professional expertise just as much as their personal experiences into their contributions on how to bring the Third Reich to justice. It was not by accident that it was Lemkin and Lauterpacht who, having lost nearly all of their families to Nazi murder, helped the largely unheard of categories of "genocide" and "crimes against humanity" into the courtroom.[30] Nor was it mere chance that Neumann and Kirchheimer, both students as well as critics of Carl Schmitt, found their legal concepts soon engaging those of their former mentor, most notably in a rehearsal of *"Behemoth vs. Leviathan."*[31]

## The Nuremberg Trials and their Protagonists

Whereas personal experience and professional expertise were thus infused into the shaping of the trials behind the scenes, other protagonists made a visible appearance on the Nuremberg stage, playing a crucial part in the actual dynamics of the proceedings and, not least of all, their public perception. Both IMT and NMT are most often looked at from the side of the perpetrators, and it is on them that the lights have been quite literally placed: a judicial freak show which puts on display the agents of genocide, terror, and war. However, they were but one faction implicated in shaping the trials. Others were involved, including the prosecution counsel—some of them well-known, some of them forgotten—and their large staff of analysts who never appeared in court, the defense lawyers, the judges who made a brief jump from and back into historical obscurity, and finally the witnesses, who mostly would remain nameless outside the trial transcript. Among those who formed Nuremberg's outlook and impact, the two US Chief Prosecutors in the IMT and NMT, respectively, played major roles. With their ambitious tenets—the one to outlaw aggressive war as the supreme crime once and for all, the other to provide a full, legally and historically valid analysis of National Socialism, and also thanks to their penchant for rhetorical bravado (which generations of historians have liberally and gratefully quoted from)—Robert H. Jackson and Telford Taylor left their marks on the Nuremberg scenery. Conversely, both Jackson and Taylor, although pursuing successful careers well before the war,[32] owe their share of fame to the spotlights which were directed on the Palace of Justice. It was Nuremberg which turned them—along with the British Chief Prosecutor Hartley Shawcross and the French jurist Henri Donnedieu de Vabres—into persons of historical significance and historiographical interest.

This is even truer for the second tier of officials. Prosecutors like Robert M.W. Kempner and Benjamin B. Ferencz rose to prominence thanks to their role in the trials and would build on the social capital accumulated at Nuremberg ever after. Both became public figures in the wake of the trials and used the momentum to build a career out of them, the former as the self-conscious and self-styled thorn in West Germany's *Wirtschaftswunder* society, the other as a negotiator for the Jewish Claims Conference and an untiring campaigner for the International Criminal Court.[33] In his contribution to this volume, Dirk Pöppmann shows that Kempner was not only one of the key agents in shaping the trial program, but that he also came to epitomize everything the West German public loathed about the tribunals. Although rather successful in court, Kempner was singled out by critics as the mastermind of "victors' justice" with clear implications of the stereotype of the "vengeful Jew." However, for good or ill, this negative public attention stimulated Kempner's postwar career as a prominent critic of both old and new Nazism in Germany; Nuremberg thus made the man, Pöppmann concludes.

The significance of Nuremberg as a defining moment in individual careers holds much less truth for the majority of the judges. In the *Einsatzgruppen* case, however, Judge Michael Musmanno played a larger-than-life role which brought him a fair share of public attention on which much of his later career, including as an expert witness for the prosecution in the Eichmann trial in 1961, would rest.[34] Hilary Earl shows how the interaction of courtroom adversaries fashioned individual trials' dynamics and also boosted reputations. Revisiting the *Einsatzgruppen* trial, she highlights the interplay of the three main protagonists: much of the case proceeded as a dialogue between Musmanno and Otto Ohlendorf, accounting for both the huge success of the prosecution in achieving convictions of the defendants and for the differentiated sentences, which were ultimately pronounced by the presiding judge, a declared critic of capital punishment. Despite this key role, Musmanno faded into historical oblivion after his death whereas Ferencz made a career out of his Nuremberg experience, in this respect no different from Kempner. For most of the judges, anyway, usually being older than both prosecution and defense counsel, the Nuremberg assignment remained a singular event, briefly moving them beyond the routines of their previous careers, and not all of them were too happy with their involvement afterwards.[35]

The same cannot be said for the German attorneys who, like some of their American counterparts, made good use of the career opportunities which opened up by acting on such a large stage. A great number of the Nuremberg defense counsel, as Devin Pendas's chapter highlights, specialized in "Nazi trials," often working more than once for the same client. This was the case for the industrial firms on trial in Nuremberg and their associates, many of whom faced private litigation suits once the criminal trials were closed.[36] Such follow-up proceedings provided one mechanism by which the Nuremberg debates, elaborated and modified by the courtroom personnel of defense and prosecution counsel, were transferred to other arenas and kept alive. Not least of all, the

clemency campaign itself, organized by Nuremberg's convicted defendants and their lawyers, had a major part in continuing the examination
of National Socialist criminality. Although the West German politics of
the past with their self-exculpatory dynamics clearly showed an impetus quite opposed to that originally pursued by the Allies, they may, as
Robert Moeller has recently argued, have been the prerequisite for the
more critical reflection on the breadth and scope of German responsibility which set in by the late 1960s.[37]

The public onslaught on Nuremberg, in which former defense lawyers played a crucial role, was opposed by Taylor, Kempner, Ferencz,
and their fellow prosecutors. They vigorously defended both the historical and the legal legacy of Nuremberg, choosing the same format as their
adversaries: newspaper and journal articles, books, and public speeches.
A good deal of "Nuremberg literature" for many decades was authored
by the protagonists themselves, frequently even mutually reviewing
their respective writings.[38] Thus, the Nuremberg source corpus combines the wartime and early postwar writings of the epistemic community as depicted above but also the memoirs, treatises, and essays in
historiography by prosecutors, defense lawyers, and defendants. Many
of these not only became genuine bestsellers, they also helped to spread
notions of untarnished ethics and legends of righteousness among a
larger public. This was the case with regard to the Wehrmacht. German generals' recollections of how they had remained true to the ideals
of chivalrous warfare, ignorant of the crimes of the SS, and how they
might have won the war had Hitler not interfered, were legion in the
1950s, adding up to a veritable literary sub-genre.[39]

Not all protagonists of the Nuremberg trials have been able to exert
such influence on historical research, though. In fact, the trials and their
personnel also served as multipliers for empirical flaws, analytical shortcomings, and interpretative dead-ends. Donald Bloxham has amply demonstrated the deficiencies of the trials to—literally—do justice to the
Holocaust which he traces back to the "tyranny of a construct" made up
of the charges of conspiracy and aggressive war on the one hand and the
lack of victims' testimony on the other.[40] In his chapter, Paul Weindling
saves one group of Nuremberg's protagonists from historical oblivion. By
examining the roles played by the victims of Nazi atrocities, Weindling
argues that they were, on average, much more prominent and much
more effective in the NMT than has been assumed until recently. In the
Medical trial, the victims' voices were particularly audible and gave the
proceedings a peculiar character. The prosecution strategy framed the
experiments on humans into the larger picture of Nazi war and genocide.[41] This view was accepted by the tribunal which condemned human
experiments of any kind unless there was the clear agreement of the
subject on the tenets and methods of research. This formula, known as
"informed consent," would be widely adopted by physicians and scientists and gives credit to the victims' perspective the trial assumed.

## Nuremberg's Impact on Historiography and International Law

"Nuremberg" is usually associated with the trial-by-document strategy favored by Jackson and executed paradigmatically by Ferencz in the *Einsatzgruppen* case, where the prosecution built its strategy entirely on German records.[42] However, of the NMT cases, this was a rather extraordinary example, and if the *Einsatzgruppen* trial was on the far end in that respect, the Medical trial occupied the other extreme. Interestingly, the judges in the "Doctors' trial" imposed particularly severe sentences, second only to those of the *Einsatzgruppen* verdict, which raises questions about the success of the different prosecution strategies. Another explanation for the notable severity might be detected in the physicians' failure to create a convincing image of mere, disinterested experts.

In this the doctors clearly differed from the businessmen tried in the industrialist cases. Kim C. Priemel demonstrates that the three industrialist trials at Nuremberg were at the heart of the subsequent proceedings and played a pivotal role in shaping the trial series, its prerogatives, tenets, and outcomes. The defendants were charged as officers of the leading German economic institutions, as corporate officials of their own organizations, and as individuals, thus displaying the alleged guilt of the Nazi economic *system* as a willing and enthusiastic instrument of a criminal state bent on aggressive war. In turn, the German industrialists and financiers in the dock went to great lengths to fend off these accusations. Early on, they laid claim to interpretative sovereignty over the very recent past and constructed coherent frameworks of self-perception and self-presentation. As a result, the concept of "totalitarianism" rose to prominence. It soon became *the* interpretative blueprint among German elites and turned industrialists from perpetrators into victims for the next forty years, before the onset of a renewed and critical business history in the 1990s.

Alexa Stiller's chapter deals with one of the key questions in evaluating the legacy of Nuremberg—the significance of punishment of mass violence against civilians at the NMT trials and the question of how the Holocaust was located within this phenomenon. Analyzing a wide range of trials both at Nuremberg and outside, she argues that the prosecutors and researchers used the new concept of "genocide" in order to describe the pattern of deportation, forced recruitment, coerced abortion, mass murder, and other crimes, but entertained different understandings of this term. Their usage was confined to a descriptive rather than to a legal mode, since the mandatory standard of the Genocide Convention would not be fully formulated until December 1948, i.e. well after the trials' conclusion. Therefore, Taylor's team adopted "genocide" in exactly the way Lemkin had described it in his famous book in 1944. There, Lemkin had focused on the "techniques of genocide," highlighting not only biological and physical action—as subsequently formulated by the Genocide Convention—but also political, social, economic, cultural, religious, and moral impairments on the life of a nation or a minority group. As Stiller argues in her contribution, the concept of genocide took more than one shape in the courts at Nuremberg, losing much of Lemkin's broader vision along the way, and would be linked (and limited) to the murder of the European Jews for a long time.

This restricted perception of genocide also caused considerable collateral damage, especially when it came to identifying the agents of mass murder, expulsion, and destruction. The focus on the SS as the quintessential perpetrator group assumed its distinctive shape in the Palace of Justice and went on to characterize much of early historical research, not to mention more popular pictures. The strange career of the image of the "black order," pursued in Jan Erik Schulte's chapter, owed a lot to the "institutional approach" which the Nuremberg prosecutors devised as their analytical backbone. Originally intended as a heuristic tool to allow for a structural investigation of the Nazi state and a broader, representative portrayal of the sampled defendants, the institutional approach tended to hypothesize more homogeneity than was historically accurate in organizations like the SS or collective agents such as industry, leaving little room for individual scope of action and reflection. Moreover, the notion of an all powerful SS, a state within the state, was happily seized upon by those defendants who stood to gain from such an interpretation: private businessmen who could refer to Gestapo terror as the means that had coerced them into cooperation with the regime, or Wehrmacht generals who disavowed any involvement in the mass murder of Jews, Slavs, Roma, or other "racial enemies" in the front and rear areas of the occupied territories under their command. The very success of this strategy, so the argument of Schulte goes, laid the foundations for one of the most enduring historiographical myths in the years to come: the picture of the "Black Order" as a monolithic, highly efficient organization which had been single-handedly responsible for the extermination policy both in terms of planning and executing mass murder. The Nuremberg prosecutors thus unwittingly co-authored a one-sided perspective of the Nazi state, resulting in a perception of the SS as the main, if not sole agents of racial and genocidal crimes. The success of this narrative owed a lot to its exculpatory potential as it provided a welcome alibi for the majority of West German society.

The High Command case in particular had dramatic, lasting repercussions on the way the Wehrmacht would be perceived in postwar Germany. In the courtroom, the high-ranking generals and field marshals managed to distance themselves and the German army in general from Nazi crimes.[43] The bottom line of Wehrmacht defendants in the Nuremberg trials, Valerie Hébert argues, was the affirmation of patriotic duty on the one hand and putting all blame on Himmler's troops on the other, carefully emphasizing that both spheres had had nothing in common. Such an interpretation easily met with approval by a German public where virtually everyone had either served in the army or had a relative who had done so. The often cited "clean hands" of the Wehrmacht permeated the German conscience, curtailed the *Bundeswehr*'s efforts in coming to terms with the past,[44] and provided the incentive for the highly controversial Wehrmacht exhibition, which helped to change the popular perception of the army in the late 1990s.

Historians have made their own, increasingly proficient use of Nuremberg. Much of the groundwork done in the early years of historiography on the Third Reich nearly exclusively built on the Nuremberg records, including the pioneering studies of Léon Poliakov and Gerhard L. Weinberg, Alexander Dallin and Robert L. Koehl, Raul Hilberg, Martin Broszat, and Helmut Genschel.[45] Key documents such as the Hoßbach and Wannsee protocols were introduced to historians through the editions of documents and proceedings prepared by the Nuremberg staff,[46] and debates about the binding force of the Wehrmacht's oath to Hitler or Himmler's speech at Posen originated inside the courtroom.[47] One of the key issues at stake in the *Einsatzgruppen* trial, whether or not Hitler, Himmler, or Heydrich had ordered the outright murder of Soviet Jewry in 1941, would occupy historians for decades and spark the famous Krausnick-Streim controversy.[48] However, important as they are, the focus on documents and themes has somewhat obscured the way in which concepts and ideas, interpretations and, again, narratives, sprang from the courtroom and left their mark upon historical research on the Third Reich. Among the better-known cases of such discernible impact is Hilberg's monumental study of the *Destruction of the European Jews*, with its analytical pattern of bureaucratically organized extermination which stands squarely in the tradition of Weberian theory, mediated by Hilberg's erstwhile doctoral supervisor Franz Neumann.[49]

Much of the rhetoric emanating from the Nuremberg Palace of Justice made use of visual metaphors such as the "Black Order" or the "clean hands." But images—and the moving type in particular—also played a prominent role in their own right, innovating courtroom tactics and becoming regular icons of war crimes trials such as the many charts put on display or the earphones for simultaneous translation.[50] Ulrike Weckel's analysis of cinematographic representations of and in Nuremberg thus combines two seemingly different perspectives: the use of films as evidence, dramatic peaks, and didactic tools in the proceedings as well as Hollywood re-enactments of the courtrooms proceedings which assess the success and failure of the trials. Weckel examines the uses and effects of filmic representation by comparing the actual role of documentary film in the Nuremberg trials with its fictionalized role in feature films about those trials. The chapter analyzes both American and Soviet prosecutors' motivations for introducing Allied atrocity footage (which did not depict any of the relevant defendants) and the significantly different effects of each team's film in the courtroom. While consensus on how the defendants reacted to these movies is strikingly absent among eyewitnesses, the feature film *Judgment at Nuremberg*, modeled on the "Justice case," departs from historical reality and makes one defendant confess his guilt. Weckel's contribution analyzes how the use of atrocity footage motivates this twist, and what this departure from the historical facts reveals about contemporary desire for repentance.

If the NMT provided the model for Stanley Kramer's screenplay, did they also impact on other war crimes trials, such as the Dachau tribunals, the West German proceedings, or the Eichmann Trial in 1961? Devin Pendas broadens the picture by shedding light on early German trials of Nazi crimes and by pointing to the later, spectacular proceedings such as the Frankfurt Auschwitz trial. Finding both differences and similarities, spread unevenly among trial tactics, arguments, interpretations, and consequences, Pendas casts a skeptical perspective on the fate of Nuremberg in postwar Germany. The NMT did not have the impact that was hoped for and expected by Taylor and others. They neither set an immediate and durable legal precedent nor did they decisively shape how Germans conceived of their recent history. In the longer term, however, the impact of the trial series was somewhat more significant, if indirect. German prosecutors from the late 1950s to the 1970s drew on Nuremberg evidence in preparing their cases, and more than one prominent defense attorney who rose to fame in later Nazi trials had had his first exposure to such cases before the NMT.[51]

On an international scale, the Nuremberg proceedings could hardly remain in the realm of mere academic interest. The trials had been a case of applied science and an example of progressive law in action which necessarily prompted the question of what to do with their legacy. To Lemkin, the trials had been a means rather than an end in his struggle for a universally binding ban on genocide. The declaration of the United Nations Genocide Convention in 1948 was thus his lifetime achievement, despite all the compromises along the way.[52] More problematic than the codification, though, was the implementation of the standards formulated by the UN General Assembly as well as by the Nuernberg Military Tribunals.

In particular, the ambitious aim to rule out aggressive war remains a gaping hole in the legacy of the trials. Although the formula itself can lay some claim to official consensus, it has not passed the test of time in practice. This was not lost on the Nuremberg prosecutors either. Taylor wrestled with the issue of how to bring the distinctly American part in attacking crimes against peace at Nuremberg in accordance with the wars in Korea and Vietnam, whereas Ferencz fought an uphill battle in favor of an International Criminal Court but was opposed by his own government. Others, such as John J. McCloy who had been in the camp of the trial supporters in 1944–45 and who, as High Commissioner in the Federal Republic, gave in to the German clemency campaign, grew conspicuously silent in the Cold War years.[53]

Popular narratives which draw a straight path from Nuremberg to The Hague or from the London Charter to the Rome Statute[54] are therefore misleading as they fail to notice the twisted road international criminal justice has taken since Taylor made his final closing statement in the Ministries case in 1949. Nor has the much-acclaimed IMT provided the pattern along which much of contemporary international penal law is modeled in practice. In his chapter, Lawrence Douglas sets out to show that, instead, it is the NMT with their strong emphasis on atrocities which have had a lasting influence on how crimes against humanity and war crimes are pursued. The legal pattern of the NMT rather than that of the IMT served as a model for the future development of international criminal law, in particular its practical application, and do so to the present day as the international tribunals for Yugoslavia and Rwanda, but to some extent also the Guantanamo military commissions, show. Likewise, the Medical Trial's Nuremberg Code on human experiments which has become widely accepted (if not generally adhered to) over the last seven decades is a distinct success story of the NMT.[55]

Read together, as they should be, the chapters of this book offer a comprehensive analysis of the dynamics, the narratives, and the legacy of the trials before the Nuernberg Military Tribunals. They do not merely rescue the NMT from the long shadow of the IMT but show that the later trials shaped our views of the Third Reich and the Holocaust, on the one hand, and the paths of international criminal law on the other, possibly even more so than their famous precedent. More research on the Nuremberg trials will need to be done, if we are to appreciate fully the peculiar quality of the courtroom, especially in its international form, as a forum for negotiating recent history, and as a stage for representative justice—which transitional justice always is—as it applies to collectives which are far greater than those actually present on any of the benches. In doing so, we should take heed of Lawrence Douglas's caveat: "Just as the didactic trial must struggle to do justice to history, history also takes time to do justice to the trial."[56] If the present volume contributes to such an essentially reciprocal understanding of the Nuremberg trials and their two sides, the contributors' and editors' efforts will have been worthwhile.

## Acknowledgments

This volume goes back to an international workshop organized with generous support from and held at the Center for Advanced Holocaust Studies at the U.S. Holocaust Memorial Museum in Washington, DC, in August 2008. We are most grateful for the help and support the Center's staff, in particular Suzanne Brown-Fleming, Robert Ehrenreich, and Lisa Yavnai, have given us and which laid the basis for an immensely productive workshop. We benefitted greatly from Jennifer Belmont's organizational skills and from the untiring support we received from the staff of the museum's library and archives, notably Michlean Amir and Henry Mayer. Caroline Waddell of the USHMM Photo Archives kindly made the bulk of the photographs printed in this volume available to us. Thanks for permission to use illustrations are also due to the German Federal Archives, the State Archives NRW, the Bavarian State Library, and *Der Spiegel*.

We wish to express particular gratitude to the participants of the workshop who were not only willing to commit themselves to two weeks of intense discussion and research, but also to continue this thread for another two years in preparing the present volume. We hope that the spirited atmosphere of the workshop has found its way into print. We were lucky to have additional contributions to our discussion by Suzanne Brown-Fleming, Martin Dean, Robert Ehrenreich, and Patricia Heberer, who let us benefit from their great expertise in adjacent fields and helped to clarify our analytical objectives. This is particularly true for Jonathan Bush who was a never-ending source of information on Nuremberg and its protagonists and who spared a lot of time to join the circle during these two weeks and ever since.

Extra thanks are due to Michael Marrus for kindly contributing the foreword to the present volume and to Omer Bartov and Dirk Moses, not only for including the project into the *War and Genocide* series, but also for their many helpful comments on the manuscript. That this manuscript became printable owes a lot to the painstaking efforts by Nicholas Zücker in safeguarding the necessary consistency in spelling and formatting. Alexander Watson's corrections and advice helped us to improve on the original draft of the introduction. Finally, we would like to thank the staff at Berghahn Books, in particular Ann Przyzycki DeVita, Marion Berghahn, and Mark Stanton for all their help in making a book out of a manuscript.

## Notes

1. Throughout this book, the German "Nuernberg" will only be used as part of the tribunals' official designation. The geographical and historical place is referred to as "Nuremberg."
2. Statement by Telford Taylor to the International News Service, 9.5.1949, Telford Taylor Papers, Arthur W. Diamond Library, Columbia University Law School, 5-1-1-1.
3. Only one of the 177 tried defendants in the NMT pleaded "guilty" on one single count. Ernst Wilhelm Bohle, leader of the Foreign Organization of the German Nazi Party from 1933 to 1945, entered a plea of guilty to count eight, membership in a criminal organization. To count five of the indictment in the Ministries Case, war crimes and crimes against humanity, though, Bohle pleaded not guilty. See Opening Statement for Defendant Bohle, Dr. Gombel, *TWC*, XII, 270.
4. Cf. the classic accounts: Whitney R. Harris, *Tyranny on Trial. The Evidence at Nuremberg* (Dallas, 1954); Bradley F. Smith, *Reaching Judgment at Nuremberg* (London, 1977); id., *The Road to Nuremberg* (New York, 1981); Robert E. Conot, *Jus-*

*tice at Nuremberg* (New York, 1983); Ann Tusa and John Tusa, *The Nuremberg Trial* (London, 1984); Joseph E. Persico, *Nuremberg. Infamy on Trial* (New York, 1994). Ironically, Taylor himself contributed to this misbalance by dedicating nearly all of his widely read *The Anatomy of the Nuremberg Trials* (New York, 1992) to the IMT, while never finishing a follow-up project on the NMT (we are grateful to Jonathan Bush for sharing this information).

5. The first consolidated analysis of the NMT by a legal historian has very recently been published by Kevin Jon Heller, The Nuremberg Military Tribunals and the Origins of International Criminal Law (Oxford, 2011).

6. Norbert Frei, *Adenauer's Germany and the Nazi Past. The Politics of Amnesty and Integration* (New York, 2002); Ulrich Brochhagen, *Nach Nürnberg. Vergangenheitsbewältigung und Westintegration in der Ära Adenauer* (Hamburg, 1994); Manfred Kittel, *Nach Nürnberg und Tokio. "Vergangenheitsbewältigung" in Japan und Westdeutschland 1945 bis 1968* (Munich, 2004).

7. Timothy Garton Ash, "The Truth about Dictatorship," *The New York Review of Books* 45 (1998): 35–40. For further references, see also Louis Bickford, "Transitional Justice," in *Encyclopedia of Genocide and Crimes Against Humanity*, ed. Dinah L. Shelton (Detroit, 2005), 1045–47; "Transitional Justice," in *The Oxford Companion to International Criminal Justice*, editor-in-chief Antonio Cassese (Oxford, 2009), 538–40.

8. Otto Kirchheimer, *Political Justice. The Use of Legal Procedure for Political Ends* (Princeton, 1961). This nuanced perspective is one of the many casualties of the polemic account offered in John Laughland, *A History of Political Trials. From Charles I to Saddam Hussein* (Oxford, 2008).

9. Kirchheimer, *Political Justice*, 336–38; Judith N. Shklar, *Legalism. Law, Morals and Political Trials* (Cambridge, MA, 1986), 143–48, 220.

10. Useful insights may be gained from system theory, in particular the distinction between different programs and codes of the systems science, law, and politics. Cf. Niklas Luhmann, *Law as a Social System* (Oxford, 2004); id., *Die Gesellschaft der Gesellschaft* (Frankfurt a.M., 1998), 316–20, 359–63, 481f. See also Shklar, *Legalism*, viii, 2f., who speaks of "legalism" as the "operative ideology of lawyers."

11. For general discussions, see Marc Bloch, *The Historian's Craft*, with an introduction by Peter Burke (New York, 1992), 114–19, 160; Carlo Ginzburg, *The Judge and the Historian. Marginal Notes and a Late-Twentieth-Century Miscarriage of Justice* (London, 1999), 16–18.

12. Lawrence Douglas, *The Memory of Judgment. Making Law and History in the Trials of the Holocaust* (New Haven/London, 2001).

13. Cf. Kirchheimer, *Political Justice*, 110–18, 429–31; Shklar, *Legalism*, 149–51, 194–98; Bert van Roermund, "The Political Trial and Reconciliation," *The Trial on Trial, vol. 2. Judgment and Calling to Account*, eds. Antony Duff, Lindsay Farmer, Sandra Marshall, and Victor Tadros (Oxford, 2006), 173–90, here 173f.; Devin Pendas, *The Frankfurt Auschwitz Trial, 1963–1965. Genocide, History, and the Limits of the Law* (Cambridge, 2006), 2f.

14. Robert P. Burns, *The Death of the American Trial* (Chicago, 2009), 25.

15. Again, this is more characteristic of Anglo-Saxon and especially American law than it is of continental European law, where the task of investigation is assigned to the court; cf. Robert P. Burns, *A Theory of the Trial* (Princeton, 1999), 28f., 92.

16. Burns, *Theory*, 59–61; id., "The Distinctiveness of Trial Narrative," *The Trial on Trial, Vol. 1. Truth and Due Process*, eds. Antony Duff, Lindsay Farmer, Sandra Marshall, and Victor Tadros (Oxford, 2004), 157–77. See also the collection of essays in *Law's Stories. Narrative and Rhetoric in the Law*, eds. Peter Brooks and Paul Gerwitz (New Haven, 1996), in particular Robert Weisberg, "Proclaiming Trials as Narratives: Premises and Pretenses," 61–83.

17. Dirk van Laak, "Widerstand gegen die Geschichtsgewalt. Zur Kritik an der 'Vergangenheitsbewältigung,'" *Geschichte vor Gericht. Historiker, Richter und die Suche*

*nach Gerechtigkeit*, eds. Norbert Frei, Dirk van Laak and Michael Stolleis (Munich, 2000), 11–28, here 11; Pendas, *Frankfurt Auschwitz Trial*, 142–47; cf. "Introduction," in *Vom Recht zur Geschichte. Akten aus NS-Prozessen als Quellen der Zeitgeschichte*, eds. Jürgen Finger, Sven Keller and Andreas Wirsching (Göttingen, 2009), 9–24. For an overview of the legal reckoning with Nazi crimes, though unsystematic, see Patricia Heberer and Jürgen Matthäus, "Introduction. War Crimes and the Historian," *Atrocities on Trial. Historical Perspectives on the Politics of Prosecuting War Crimes*, eds. Patricia Heberer and Jürgen Matthäus (Lincoln, NE, 2008), xiii–xxix; *Nazi Crimes and the Law*, eds. Nathan Stoltzfus and Henry Friedlander (Cambridge, 2008); *Der Nationalsozialismus vor Gericht. Die alliierten Prozesse gegen Kriegsverbrecher und Soldaten 1943–1952*, ed. Gerd R. Ueberschär, 2nd edn (Frankfurt a.M., 2000).

18. See Peter M. Haas, "Introduction: Epistemic Communities and International Policy Coordination," *International Organizations* 46 (1992): 3f.: an epistemic community is "a network of professionals with recognized expertise and competence in a particular domain and authoritative claim to policy-relevant knowledge within that domain" who share a set of normative and principled beliefs, causal beliefs, notions of validity, and a common policy enterprise.

19. See "Communiqué, 2.8.1945," *Foreign Relations of the United States. Diplomatic Papers. The Conference of Berlin (the Potsdam Conference), 1945*, vol. 2, ed. United States Department of State (Washington, DC, 1960), 1499–514.

20. Jeffrey Herf, *Divided Memory. The Nazi Past in the Two Germanys* (Cambridge, MA, 1997), 69.

21. There is abundant research on institutions such as the OSS, on wartime debates on how to try Nazi crimes, and on individual protagonists; cf. Barry M. Kātz, *Foreign Intelligence: Research and Analysis in the Office of Strategic Services 1942–1945* (Cambridge, MA, 1989); Petra Marquardt-Bigman, *Amerikanische Geheimdienstanalysen über Deutschland 1942–1949* (Munich, 1995); Arieh J. Kochavi, *Prelude to Nuremberg. Allied War Crimes Policy and the Question of Punishment* (Chapel Hill, NC, 1998); Tim B. Müller, "Bearing witness to the liquidation of Western Dasein: Herbert Marcuse and the Holocaust, 1941–1948", *New German Critique* 85 (2002): 133–64; P. M. R. Stirk, "John H. Herz. Realism and the Fragility of the International Order," *Review of International Studies* 31 (2005): 285–306; Shlomo Aronson, "Preparations for the Nuremberg Trial: The O.S.S., Charles Dwork, and the Holocaust," *Holocaust and Genocide Studies* 12 (1998): 257–81; Ernst C. Stiefel and Frank Mecklenburg, *Deutsche Juristen im amerikanischen Exil (1933–1950)* (Tübingen, 1991); *Zur Archäologie der Demokratie in Deutschland. Analysen politischer Emigranten im amerikanischen Geheimdienst, vol. 1: 1943–1945*, ed. Alfons Söllner (Frankfurt a.M., 1982).

22. Cf. Franz Neumann, *Behemoth. The Structure and Practice of National Socialism, 1933–1944* (Reprint Chicago, 2009).

23. Cf. Joachim Perels, "Fast vergessen: Franz L. Neumanns Beitrag zur Konzipierung der Nürnberger Prozesse. Eine Erinnerung aus Anlaß seines 100. Geburtstages," *Kritische Justiz* 34 (2001): 117–25.

24. Sheldon Glueck, *War Criminals. Their Prosecution & Punishment* (New York, 1944) and "The Nuremberg Trial and Aggressive War," *Harvard Law Review* 59 (1946): 396–445. Cf. Jonathan A. Bush, "The Supreme … Crime" and Its Origins: The Lost Legislative History of the Crime of Aggressive War," *Columbia Law Review* 102 (2002): 2324–423.

25. See the pioneering study by Smith, *Road*, 50–52, 61f., 75–77, 233f.

26. See Raphael Lemkin, *Axis Rule in Occupied Europe. Laws of Occupation, Analysis of Government, Proposals for Redress* (Washington, DC, 1944), 79–95.

27. For a recent appraisal of the impact of Lemkin's work, see the special issue of the *Journal of Genocide Research* 7 (2005), No. 4. Cf. Samantha Power, *"A Problem from Hell." America and the Age of Genocide* (New York, 2002); John Cooper, *Raphael*

*Lemkin and the Struggle for the Genocide Convention* (Basingstoke, 2008); *Empire, Colony, Genocide. Conquest, Occupation, and Subaltern Resistance in World History,* ed. A. Dirk Moses (New York, 2008).

28. Cf. Opening Statement of the prosecution in the RuSHA Trial, *TWC,* IV, 622–27.
29. Burns, *Theory,* 37. The two strands, narrative and argument, should not be seen as opposing forces but as mutually complementary. In fact, in trials which pursue a genuinely historiographical agenda, narrative becomes argument.
30. Smith, *Reaching Judgment,* 59; Miriam Gessler and Daniel Segesser, "Raphael Lemkin and the International Debate on the Punishment of War Crimes (1919–1948)," *Journal of Genocide Research* 7 (2005): 453–68; Martti Koskenniemi, "Hersch Lauterpacht and the Development of International Criminal Law," *Journal of International Criminal Justice* 2 (2004): 810–25; Ana Filipa Vrdoljak, "Human Rights and Genocide: The Work of Lauterpacht and Lemkin in Modern International Law," *European Journal of International Law* 20 (2010): 1184–86.
31. Cf. William E. Scheuerman, "Introduction," in *The Rule of Law under Siege. Selected Essays of Franz L. Neumann and Otto Kirchheimer,* ed. William E. Scheuerman (Berkeley, 1996), 1–25; Stiefel and Mecklenburg, *Deutsche Juristen,* 20, 89, 100f., 107–9; Reinhard Mehring, *Carl Schmitt. Aufstieg und Fall. Eine Biographie* (Munich, 2009), 314f., 380.
32. Cf. Jonathan A. Bush, "Soldiers Find Wars: A Life of Telford Taylor," *Columbia Journal of Transnational Law* 37 (1999), 675–88; John Q. Barrett, "'One Good Man': The Jacksonian Shape of Nuremberg," in *The Nuremberg Trials: International Criminal Law Since 1945,* eds. Herbert R. Reginbogin and Christoph J.M. Safferling (Munich, 2006), 129–37.
33. Benjamin B. Ferencz, *Less than Slaves. Jewish Forced Labor and the Quest for Compensation* (Cambridge, MA, 1979); Robert M.W. Kempner, *Ankläger einer Epoche. Lebenserinnerungen* (Frankfurt a.M., 1983); *Gegen Barbarei. Essays Robert M.W. Kempner zu Ehren,* eds. Rainer Eisfeld and Ingo Müller (Frankfurt a.M., 1989).
34. Cf. Hannah Arendt, *Eichmann in Jerusalem. A Report on the Banality of Evil* (London, 2006), 210–12.
35. This is particularly true for several of the NMT judges, cf. Frank M. Buscher, *The U.S. War Crimes Program in Germany, 1946–1955* (New York, 1989), 34–36; Peter Maguire, *Law and War. An American Story* (New York, 2001), 170–77, 197–200; cf. Suzanne Bellamy, *Hoosier Justice at Nuremberg* (Indianapolis, 2010).
36. Cf. Christian Dirks, "Selekteure als Lebensretter. Die Verteidigungsstrategie des Rechtsanwalts Dr. Hans Laternser," in „*Gerichtstage halten über uns selbst...*" *Geschichte und Wirkung des ersten Frankfurter Auschwitz-Prozesses,* ed. Irmtrud Wojak (Frankfurt a.M., 2001), 163–92; Kerstin von Lingen, *Kesselrings letzte Schlacht. Kriegsverbrecherprozesse, Vergangenheitspolitik und Wiederbewaffnung: Der Fall Kesselring* (Paderborn, 2004).
37. Robert G. Moeller, "The Third Reich in Post-war German Memory," in *Nazi Germany,* ed. Jane Caplan (Oxford, 2008), 246–66.
38. See, for example, Taylor, *Anatomy;* id., *Die Nürnberger Prozesse. Kriegsverbrechen und Völkerrecht* (Zurich, 1950); id., *Sword and Swastika* (New York, 1952); id., "Review: Francis Biddle, In Brief Authority (New York, 1962)," *Harvard Law Review* 77 (1963): 201–4; Robert M.W. Kempner, "The Nuremberg Trials as Sources of Recent German Political and Historical Materials," *American Political Science Review* 44 (1950): 447–59; Benjamin B. Ferencz, "Nurnberg Trial Procedure and the Rights of the Accused," *Journal of Criminal Law and Criminology* 39 (1948): 144–51; id., "Review: Drexel A. Sprecher, Inside the Nuremberg Trial: A Prosecutor's Comprehensive Account," *American Journal of International Law* 93 (1999): 760f.; id., "Review: Bradley F. Smith, Reaching Judgment at Nuremberg (New York, 1977)," *American Journal of International Law* 74 (1980): 228–30; John H.E. Fried, "Review: Benjamin B. Ferencz, Less than Slaves. Jewish Forced Labor and the Quest

for Compensation (Cambridge, MA, 1979)," *American Journal of International Law* 75 (1981): 702–4.

39. Erich Raeder, *Mein Leben*, 2 vols (Tübingen, 1956/57); Franz Halder, *Hitler als Feldherr. Der ehemalige Chef des Generalstabes berichtet die Wahrheit* (Munich, 1949); Heinz Guderian, *Erinnerungen eines Soldaten* (Heidelberg, 1951); id., *Panzer marsch! Aus dem Nachlaß des Schöpfers der deutschen Panzerwaffe* (Munich, 1956); Albert Kesselring, *Soldat bis zum letzten Tag* (Bonn, 1953); Erich von Manstein, *Verlorene Siege* (Bonn, 1955); id., *Erinnerungen* (Bonn, 1959).

40. Donald Bloxham, *Genocide on Trial. War Criminals and the Formation of Holocaust, History and Memory* (Oxford, 2001), 69–75.

41. See also Paul Weindling, *Nazi Medicine and the Nuremberg Trials. From Medical War Crimes to Informed Consent* (Basingstoke, 2004), 225–35.

42. For the use of documents in the NMT trials, see John Mendelsohn, *Trial by Document. The Use of Seized Records in the United States Proceedings at Nuernberg* (Phil. Diss., University of Maryland, 1974).

43. See Manfred Messerschmidt, "Forward Defense: the 'Memorandum of the Generals' for the Nuremberg Court," in *War of Extermination. The German Military in World War II, 1941–1944*, eds. Hannes Heer and Klaus Naumann (New York, 2000), 381–99.

44. Cf. Donald Abenheim, *Reforging the Iron Cross. The Search for Tradition in the West German Armed Forces* (Princeton, 1988).

45. Cf. Léon Poliakov, *Harvest of Hate. The Nazi Program for the Destruction of the Jews of Europe* (Syracuse, NY, 1954); Gerhard L. Weinberg, *Germany and the Soviet Union 1939–1941* (Leiden, 1954); Robert L. Koehl, *RKFDV: German Resettlement and Population Policy 1939–1945. A History of the Reich Commission for the Strengthening of Germandom* (Cambridge, 1957); Alexander Dallin, *German Rule in Russia 1941–1945* (London, 1957); Martin Broszat, *Nationalsozialistische Polenpolitik 1939–1945* (Stuttgart, 1961); Raul Hilberg, *The Destruction of the European Jews* (New York, 1961); Helmut Genschel, *Die Verdrängung der Juden aus der Wirtschaft im Dritten Reich* (Göttingen, 1962).

46. These are first and foremost the three official series, respectively labeled Blue, Red, and Green Series due to the cloth they were bound in: *Trial of the Major War Criminals before the International Military Tribunal, Nuremberg 14 Nov. 1945–1. Oct. 1946*, 42 vols (Nuremberg 1947–49); *Nazi Conspiracy and Aggression*, ed. Office of United States Chief of Counsel for Prosecution of Axis Criminality, 8 vols plus 2 suppl (Washington, DC, 1946–1948); *Trials of War Criminals Before the Nuernberg Military Tribunals under Control Council Law No. 10*, 15 vols (Washington, DC, 1949–53). In addition, there are numerous smaller editions of individual judgments, documents, etc., several of which have been compiled by prosecution and defense counsel from Nuremberg; e.g. *Das Urteil im Wilhelmstrassen-Prozess: Der amtliche Wortlaut der Entscheidung im Fall Nr. 11 des Nürnberger Militärtribunals gegen von Weizsäcker und andere, mit abweichender Urteilsbegründung, Berichtigungsbeschlüssen, den grundlegenden Gesetzesbestimmungen, einem Verzeichnis der Gerichtspersonen und Zeugen*, eds. Robert M.W. Kempner and Carl Haensel (Schwäbisch Gmünd, 1950).

47. Cf. Gerald Weinberg's reminiscences, "The Setting and Significance of the Nuremberg Trials: A Historian's Perspective," in *Nazi Crimes and the Law*, 35–41.

48. See Hilary Earl's contribution and Helmut Krausnick, "Hitler und die Befehle an die Einsatzgruppen im Sommer 1941," in *Der Mord an den Juden im Zweiten Weltkrieg. Entschlußbildung und Verwirklichung*, eds. Eberhard Jäckel and Jürgen Rohwer (Stuttgart, 1985), 88–106; Alfred Streim, "Zur Eröffnung des allgemeinen Judenvernichtungsbefehls gegenüber den Einsatzgruppen," in ibid., 107–19, id., "The Tasks of the SS Einsatzgruppen," *Simon Wiesenthal Center Annual* 4 (1987): 309–28.

49. Neumann reported on M.A. and Ph.D. theses on German history based on the Nuremberg documents which had been in progress under his supervision at Colum-

bia University. Among these announced studies were not only Hilberg's early one on the *German Civil Service and Antisemitism* but also a proposed project by Olga Lang, formerly a staff member of Taylor at the NMT, on *Genocide and the Master Race*. See Franz L. Neumann, "War Crimes Trials," *World Politics* 2 (1949): 135–47, here 145.

50. Both the main courtroom and the charts were prepared mostly by OSS staff; Report, Presentation Branch, 6.10.1945, Cornell Law Library, Donovan Nuremberg Trial Collection, Vol. XVIII, Section 58.01, http://library2.lawschool.cornell.edu/donovan/pdf/Batch_8/Vol_XVIII_58_01.pdf (accessed August 2010); Dan Kiley, "Architect of Palace of Justice Renovations," in *Witnesses to Nuremberg. An Oral History of American Participants at the War Crimes Trials*, eds. Bruce M. Stave and Michele Palmer with Leslie Frank (New York, 1998), 15–38.

51. Cf. Annette Weinke, *Eine Gesellschaft ermittelt gegen sich selbst. Die Geschichte der Zentralen Stelle Ludwigsburg 1958–2008* (Darmstadt, 2008), 17, 176f.; Rebecca Wittmann, *Beyond Justice. The Auschwitz Trial* (Cambridge, MA, 2005), 284; Hannah Yablonka, *The State of Israel vs. Adolf Eichmann* (New York, 2004) 124–28.

52. See also Cooper, *Lemkin*, and Gessler and Segesser, "Lemkin."

53. Telford Taylor, *Nuremberg and Vietnam. An American Tragedy* (Chicago, 1970); Benjamin B. Ferencz, *An International Criminal Court. A Step Toward World Peace* (Dobbs Ferry, NY, 1990 [1st edn. 1975]); id., "Defining Aggression: Where it Stands and Where it's Going," *American Journal of International Law* 66 (1972): 491–508.

54. Cf. Theodor Meron, "From Nuremberg to The Hague," in *War Crimes Law Comes of Age. Essays* (Oxford, 1998), 198–203; Hans-Heinrich Jescheck, "The General Principles of International Criminal Law Set Out in Nuremberg, as Mirrored in the ICC Statute," *Journal of International Criminal Justice* 2 (2004): 38–55; Christian Tomuschat, "The Legacy of Nuremberg", *Journal of International Criminal Justice* 4 (2006): 830–44; Andreas Zimmermann, "Das juristische Erbe von Nürnberg—Das Statut des Nürnberger Internationalen Militärtribunals und der Internationale Strafgerichtshof," in *The Nuremberg Trials*, eds. Reginbogin and Safferling, 266–76. For a critical perspective, see Annette Weinke, "'Von Nürnberg nach Den Haag'? Das Internationale Militärtribunal in historischer Perspektive", *Leipzig—Nürnberg—Den Haag. Neue Fragestellungen und Forschungen zum Verhältnis von Menschenrechtsverbrechen, justizieller Säuberung und Völkerstrafrecht*, ed. Helia-Verena Daubach (Düsseldorf, 2008), 20–33.

55. Weindling, *Nazi Medicine*.

56. Lawrence Douglas, "Perpetrator Proceedings and Didactic Trials," in *The Trial on Trial*, Vol. 2, 191–205, here 205.

## Chapter 1

# The Trials of Robert Kempner

## From Stateless Immigrant to Prosecutor of the Foreign Office

*Dirk Pöppmann*

⌒⧽§§⧼⌒

**W**hen Nuremberg trial No. 11—the so-called Ministries case or *Wilhelmstraßenprozess* against the former state secretary of the foreign office Ernst von Weizsäcker and twenty high representatives of the ministerial bureaucracy of the Third Reich—began on November 20, 1947, it soon became obvious that Robert Kempner played a key role in the prosecuting authority. At that point, he had already served as one of the most important staff members of the American Chief prosecutor Robert Jackson in the International Military Tribunal (IMT). But by November 1947 he had evolved from his role as assistant US chief counsel to that of main prosecutor in his function as the chairman of the Political Ministries Division of the Office of Chief of Counsel for War Crimes (OCCWC). In that position he was responsible for the important Case 11, in fact one of the key proceedings on whose success the American prosecution was particularly keen.[1] Although, as usual, the trial was opened by Telford Taylor, who was Chief Prosecutor in all Subsequent Proceedings, the leading part in these hearings was played by Robert Kempner, who as Taylor's deputy directed the prosecution in all but name. This constellation added an additional, controversial twist to an already highly contested trial, for Kempner had been a high official (*Oberregierungsrat*) in the police department of the Prussian Ministry of Interior and had returned from American exile in order to accuse those responsible for Nazi crimes.[2]

Kempner was not the only former German in the American prosecuting authority. Many German emigrants had been employed because of both their language abilities and their intimate knowledge of the Third Reich, but Kempner was the only one who had risen to such a high position in the OCCWC, continuing a second life in emigration which he had built for himself: within a very short period of time he had made a fantastic career in his new homeland. In fact, upon his return to Germany, Kempner's social and professional standing and his public influence had become much more significant than it had been before he had left the Third Reich. Likewise, the contrast to his position as a stateless emigrant in France who had hoped to get an entry visa into the United States could not be more striking.

This development in his professional career was extraordinary because, on the one hand, the Americans were very reluctant—perhaps with the exception of the Office of Strategic Services (OSS) under William J. Donovan's leadership[3]—to assign German emigrants to higher echelons in the war and occupation administration.[4] On the other hand, there were other highly qualified and famous academics, lawyers, and political scientists who, at least superficially, seemed even more capable than Kempner to take over prosecuting responsibilities.[5] Finally, one has to keep in mind that for the overwhelming majority of émigrés, exile meant a social decline as job qualifications or certifications were usually not accepted in the United States.[6]

Therefore, Kempner's professional rise in the United States requires explanation. Such an undertaking is necessarily complex: first, I am going to analyze Kempner's professional abilities and the requirements of the American government in order to reveal how advantageous Kempner's profile was to the Americans. Secondly, I will show the consequences of his success on his career and his specific brand of thinking. This will be done by exploring whether there was a straight line connecting Kempner's journalistic engagement for liberty and democracy in the Weimar Republic and against the seizure of power by the Nazi Party with his activities during the years of exile and as an American citizen, or whether he had to make concessions in the course of his integration into the US bureaucracy. Thirdly, I am going to tackle the question of whether or not the German émigré Kempner influenced the prosecuting authority at Nuremberg and the trials, as well as how he himself was, in turn, affected by the tenets, principles, and daily workings of OCCWC.

## Kempner's Competences, or: Being the Right Man in the Right Place at the Right Time

### Arrival and Research Associate

In the spring of 1939, Kempner and his wife were still staying in Nice. They had fled together with ten Jewish children from Florence to Nice in the summer of 1938. In Florence, Kempner had directed a boarding school after his emigration in 1936, together with his friend Werner Peiser. When the school had been closed down by the Mussolini government in support of the Nazi regime, both students and teachers had been threatened with imprisonment or deportation from Italy.[7] The Kempners had originally planned to settle permanently in France to reopen the school. In 1938 a residence permit was within reach, but by spring of 1939 the international situation had become increasingly tense so that it was no longer possible for the couple to stay. In April 1939 their application for permission to stay was rejected and he and his wife were forced to leave France.[8]

These developments did not take Kempner by surprise. Shortly after his arrival in Nice, he had evaluated further alternatives. On the one hand, he had tried to apply directly for a job overseas while at the same time renewing his mother's old contacts, who had used to be a lecturer at the Women's Medical College in Philadelphia in the late 1890s. After returning to Germany and marrying the medical scientist Walter Kempner, Lydia Rabinowitsch-Kempner had been one of the most famous researchers in the field of tuberculosis and an assistant of Robert Koch in his institute, and had established a life-long, international social network.[9] Kempner's quest for support, though unsuccessful at first, was finally rewarded when he secured help by an old acquaintance of his mother's and also by his own friend Hans Simons, the former head of the German Academy for Politics (*Deutsche Hochschule für Politik*) in Berlin and since 1934 a member of the famous University in Exile at the renowned New School for Social Research in New York.[10] Kempner knew Simons quite well as he had taught police law at the Academy for several years. Beside his full-time job as consultant in the police department of the Prussian Ministry of the Interior, Kempner had always been linked with and committed to academic circles as well as journalistic work.

This second professional pillar paid off in June 1939 when the long-awaited message that it was possible for Kempner and his wife Ruth to immigrate to the United States reached Nice: the Institute of Local and State Government at the University of Pennsylvania offered him a job as a research associate for one year with a salary of $2,400.[11] More important than this job offer was the fact that the couple were able to immigrate to America precisely at a time when it was nigh on impossible for Jewish people to get a visa.[12] On August 25, 1939, they boarded a ship in Boulogne-sur-Mer. A week later, on September 1, 1939, their vessel reached New York. Fittingly, their arrival in the New World coincided with the beginning of the Second World War. Robert and Ruth Kempner had clearly escaped at the eleventh hour.[13]

Upon his arrival, the University of Pennsylvania asked the German émigré to do a survey on the different forms of municipality and city councils. In addition, he had to lecture students who wanted to specialize in local and superior administration.[14] He worked on studies of local government and in this respect especially on the theme of "Local

Government and Defense Problems." Besides these activities, he published several essays, mainly on general problems of state administration.[15] Furthermore, he lectured on topics concerning administration and police law, thus covering a wide range of topics. Although Kempner might be considered an expert in questions of local government and administration, the American system was still unfamiliar to him. As a result, he chose to deliver comparative studies more often than not at the beginning of his American university career.

Despite these obstacles Kempner was so convinced of the importance of his work that he sent his published (and also his unpublished) papers to different government offices in order to attract their attention to his skills and expertise. At the same time he started to give talks at other institutions, and actively promoted his being invited to lectures at military academies such as West Point. Thus, in a short time, Kempner managed to make himself a reputation. However, this promising starting ground remained fragile because his academic position as an assistant and lecturer was only on a one-year basis, hence rather insecure. If he wanted to advance to a well-paid, permanent job at an American university, Kempner had to qualify as a Ph.D., preferably in Political Science.[16] But as an immigrant he faced great problems in getting accepted as a candidate, since his academic merits were mostly unknown in the United States. In the end, it was only the letter of recommendation by Harvard Professor Carl Joachim Friedrich, a pre-1933 German émigré and influential expert on public administration that paved the road to admission in November 1940. Three months later, on February 27, 1941, the "Committee on Admission to Candidacy of the University of Pennsylvania" accepted him as a Ph.D. candidate.[17] He immediately started studying and planned on finishing his thesis in the same year. From July until mid-September 1941, Kempner was granted leave from his teaching obligations at the institute. In order to maintain his means of living he was given a grant by the Carnegie Corporation and a scholarship by the Overlaender Trust in Philadelphia. But things turned out differently since Kempner was soon occupied with many other things besides his thesis, and therefore would never finish it.

Still, by the time Kempner took on the Ph.D. project, he had clearly established a foothold in American professional and public life. To that end he had benefitted from his rather prominent position in Weimar Germany and the ensuing network to which he could turn to in the 1930s, first in Europe, then in the United States. The decisive factors which not only made it possible to immigrate to the United States but also enabled Kempner to become a lecturer at an American university were the social contacts he had inherited from his family and his close friendship with the well-connected Hans Simons. Furthermore, he benefitted from the cultural resources of his education and profession. As a lecturer he had enough time to occupy himself with further issues which exceeded his academic duties but which were of crucial interest for American government offices. This suited Kempner perfectly: to the German *Oberregierungsrat*, political science had never been a theoretical discipline but essentially an affair of practical and, above all, of political importance. To Kempner, political science first and foremost meant political and democratic education.

## Working for the Department of Justice

Kempner pursued the goal of working in his old job as an official in the police and justice apparatus from the beginning of his stay in the United States. While still in France, he had written a letter to J. Edgar Hoover, the director of the Federal Bureau of Investigations (FBI). In this inquiry, he had introduced himself as an excellent police expert and—more than just slightly stretching the truth—as a "First Secretary in the Police Department of the German Home Office in Berlin." Asking if the FBI might have use for his abilities by employing him as an instructor, Kempner showed himself absolutely convinced that he could be of value to the United States because he had brought along his intimate knowledge of, and insights into, political criminality gained in his Weimar years. Those abilities, he believed, in time would become more and more important in America as well.[18] Rather than being a pessimistic evaluation of the state of American democracy, Kempner's prophecy articulated his firm belief that Nazi activity in the United States was on the rise. Despite the self-marketing interest that went along with such assessments, Kempner relied on his information about the efforts of the NSDAP's foreign organization in the United States to bring the German-Americans in line as well as on his knowledge of increasing activities of pro-German and American isolationistic groups.[19]

His application, however, had no chance of being accepted at that time. On the one hand, it was too obvious that he was hoping to attain a non-quota visa for the United States by offering his services; on the other hand, it was unlikely for the FBI to invite him to come to the United States merely on such an application; and finally, 1938 was somewhat too early to expect significant attentiveness concerning information on Nazi *Volkstumspolitik* in the United States. Upon request by President Roosevelt the FBI had just started observing the activities of American pro-Nazi groups more intensely, though without particular enthusiasm. The American public, meanwhile, still set its hopes on the traditional liberal American understanding of freedom of speech, gathering, and opinion. Even the House of Representatives seems to have been fairly skeptical of the real danger arising from Nazi attempts to undermine the state in the second half of the 1930s.[20] But Kempner's letter had not been an entire failure: whether due to his former position or to his added references, the letter had impressed Hoover so much that he personally replied in a very timely manner.[21] With contact thus established, Kempner informed Hoover about his arrival in the United States and pressed for a meeting—which Hoover indeed agreed to.[22]

Even if Kempner's dream of a job with the FBI did not come true immediately, the Department of Justice took notice of him in summer 1941. Domestic policy in the United States had changed significantly in the meantime. The struggle between the supporters and the strict opponents of a possible intervention had been intensified by the beginning of the war in Europe. Furthermore, there had arisen a manifest fear of Nazi subversive activities in the United States.[23] All emigrants from Axis Powers were now considered "enemy aliens." Because of this development, the Foreign Agent Registration Act was appended in 1940 by the Alien Registration Act (Smith Act) which was an intensification of the political criminal law. Under this act any attempt to overthrow or remove the government violently could be punished with up to ten years in jail, a verdict that also applied to the written or oral promotion of *ideas* deemed treacherous by the state. The liberal tradition of American legal thought was thus obviously violated by the Federal state, although the Smith Act was the subject of dispute from the very beginning of its existence—and so it remained, especially when it was applied in court.[24]

In June 1941 the Department of Justice tried to bring the new law into practice. The Special Assistant to the Attorney General, Albert E. Arent, accused the scientist and journalist Friedrich Ernst Auhagen of violating the Foreign Agent Registration Act. Auhagen had immigrated into the United States in 1923 and had taught at Columbia University until 1935. Since the spring of 1939 he had taken part in forming and organizing the American Fellowship Forum, a fascist-leaning organization for German-Americans. He published regularly in *Today's Challenge* and *The Forum Observer*, the newspapers of the American Fellowship Forum. He was monitored by the authorities and finally arrested and indicted by the Department of Justice in March 1941. Within the Department of Justice, it was well known that Auhagen was a rather unimportant Nazi agent, but he was chosen as an example to deter rightist academic circles.[25]

Kempner was actively involved in the trial as a hired expert-witness on German law. His task was to prove that Auhagen as an acknowledged author was necessarily a member of the German *Reichspressekammer*, a half-official office of the Third Reich, and thus had to be connected with the German Propaganda Ministry. As a consequence he was found to be a foreign agent who would have had to register himself as such in the United States.[26]

Auhagen's loss was Kempner's gain. While Auhagen was sentenced to a two-year prison term, Kempner had proven his worth as an efficient, capable authority on German law and his expertise was now demanded in numerous cases of political penal justice all over the United States. One high point of his career proved to be the preparation of the indictment against Joseph E. McWiliams and a group of 27 co-defendants in 1944, and his own spectacular appearance as a "star witness" in these proceedings. By now Nazi activities were the talk of the day all across the States, and the McWiliams case, which accused the defendants of sedition, was fiercely discussed, by some even perceived as a show trial. Kempner was in the witness box for more than 80 hours, thus occupying a major share of the trial. After the death of the sitting judge, though, the trial was finished unspectacularly by stay of proceedings.[27]

Why had Kempner been recruited as a catch-all expert by the Department of Justice? It seems plausible that his previous communication attempts now paid back. His political publications and reports which he had sent to various governmental offices had not gone unnoticed, and his job at the University of Pennsylvania had surely helped him in gaining credibility—something he alluded to himself in a letter to the Dean of the Institute. Conscious of the positive effect that teaching at a respected university had on his reputation, and therefore reflected positively on the way his 'customers' perceived him, he wanted to hold on to his academic position even though he was already working in a distinctly different professional field.[28] Furthermore, the Department of Justice was apparently short of sufficiently qualified information about the structures of the Nazi regime, so it had to resort to external expert knowledge.[29]

His affiliation with the Department of Justice was not only of great importance for Kempner and his personal career; it also marked a milestone on the road to his appointment to the Nuremberg staff of prosecution. On the one hand, he gained and confirmed the reputation of an excellent expert on Nazi Germany. On the other hand, he cooperated directly and successfully with the most important staff members of the Attorney General, including such important protagonists as Francis Biddle—who would be named a judge on the International Military Tribunal (IMT) at Nuremberg in the not too distant future—or O. John Rogge, Albert E. Arendt, and Thomas J. Dodd. The latter would become Robert H. Jackson's right-hand man in Nuremberg. Finally, Kempner became familiar with the Anglo-American system of law to an extent and from a practical side which he would have hardly reached as a university lecturer.

### Robert Kempner at the FBI

Although Kempner was sufficiently occupied with various projects for the Department of Justice, he continued seeking an opportunity to cooperate with the FBI as well, preferably through direct employment by the Bureau. Staying in regular contact with the FBI, Kempner made a new attempt at the end of 1941. Right from the start this endeavor clearly seemed more promising as he could now refer to his varied activities and experiences as an "expert witness" for the Department of Justice and thus had valuable references as proof of his expediency.[30] However, the response from the Bureau was still rather reticent. The letter confirmed that the FBI was informed of his "excellent assistance" to the Department of Justice in Washington, and expressly praised his "spirit" which was apparent in his wish to work for them. As the FBI's reply only used the dilatory phrasing that they would not hesitate to ask for his cooperation should the opportunity arise, Kempner could do nothing but wait and see, not knowing that the local representative of the FBI had sent a copy of their correspondence to J. Edgar Hoover's Washington office.[31]

It was not before long, though, that the FBI approached Kempner with a set of tasks. In January and February 1942 he was requested by the Bureau to use private contacts and make enquiries in order to draw a personal and political portrait of Edmund Stinnes, the younger son of the industrial tycoon Hugo Stinnes, who had been living in the United States since 1939.[32] Almost at the same time he was asked by the FBI for background information and an analysis of the case of Arnold Bergsträsser which was discussed vigorously in the circle of emigrants. The well-known political scientist, who had emigrated after his dismissal on grounds of his partially Jewish ancestry, was arrested twice by the FBI's Enemy Control Unit as an alleged National Socialist spy. This suspicion was by and large based on Bergsträsser's political activities at the University of Heidelberg, where he apparently had contributed to the release of a Jewish, pacifistic colleague in 1932. Furthermore, in 1933 and 1934, he had authored two articles which could be understood as supporting the National Socialist regime. In the end, though, the affair came to naught.[33]

It seems clear that from May 1942 onwards, Kempner was officially working for the Philadelphia office of the FBI as a "Confidential Informant and Special Employee." Special employment meant that he had no contractual employ; every month he had to write reports on work submitted as well as listing the actual days that he had been working for the FBI.[34] His work was confidential and subject to the utmost secrecy. He did not even mention this job in his relations with other US authorities.[35] Kempner's tasks consisted of collecting general or specific information about certain individuals, associations, and organizations, and to write reports on these, most of them dealing with German and American nationalist and fascist or National Socialist groups. Now and again his assignments would include work relating to communists, especially concerning the activities of German communists in the United States and their postwar plans. With time moving on, more and more reports on the structure of the German police force and other German offices were added to his portfolio. In 1944, with the end of the war in sight, the former employee of the Reich also worked on memoranda which dealt with possible dangers for the internal security in both America and Germany due to postwar activities of former Nazis.[36] Methodologically, these studies relied on the scrutiny of written brochures and documents, the analysis of diverse political and cultural organizations, their hierarchies and connections with National Socialist groups, the exact analysis of the position and way of thinking of suspects through interpretations of public statements, and on obtaining information via third persons.

Finally, at the beginning of September 1943, Kempner was offered a permanent, although still unusual, position with the FBI. Because of his achievements, Hoover increased his salary without any question, thereby illustrating that Kempner had become a very valuable, esteemed collaborator. The new employee meanwhile felt that it was "a great privilege to work for the Bureau" as he wrote to Hoover in a personal letter.[37] His tenacity and his activities for the Department of Justice had therefore paid off. How much Kempner valued this connection can be seen by the fact that he declined several exceptionally well-paid permanent posts with other US authorities, usually stressing the importance of his current position.[38]

## A Lifetime Struggle against the Nazi Seizure of Power?

Throughout his life, Kempner would conceive of his activities in the United States as a continuity of his commitment against the Nazi movement in the days of the Weimar Republic: there, in his two roles as a journalist and as an official in the Prussian Ministry of Interior, he had belonged to a small group of activists who had attempted to implement a more democratic system in Germany, particularly in the field of jurisprudence. Therefore he had been a member of several democratic organizations like the German Human Rights League (*Deutsche Liga für Menschenrechte*) and the Republican Association of Judges (*Republikanischer Richterbund*). During the last years of the Weimar Republic, he had focused his activities more and more on fighting the National Socialist Party's rise to power.[39]

Indeed, there is some continuity discernible, especially Kempner's main vocation: anti-Nazism. However, if the whole period of the 1920s, rather than merely Weimar's dying days since 1930, is compared with the years in exile, a telling difference between both engagements comes to the fore. In the Republic of Weimar, Kempner had fought for a democratization of the state. His struggle against the Nazis had only been one part—even if it had become the most important one with Hitler's ascent—of the general endeavor to promote social and political democratization on a broad scale. To Kempner, this had meant, among other things, the fair treatment of the German left-wing parties and intellectuals who had often been accused because of their political attitude before German courts.

In the United States, though, Kempner's political attitude changed markedly. Both branches of his work—his job at the Department of Justice and the special projects he worked on for the FBI—might be regarded as problematic in the light of his former political stance. On the one hand, he tried to protect his new home from the dangers evoked by Hitler's alleged "fifth column" and from the implementation of fascist and National Socialist ideology. On the other, the Smith Act, as well as the very expansion of the FBI in the interwar period and the accompanying infringement of civil liberties, severely curtailed the rights of precisely those immigrants to whom Kempner belonged. This was particularly manifest in the spying on German leftist and liberal artists.[40] Referring to his activity, Kempner's papers and later works do not indicate any contemplation on the legal, political, or moral problems that went along with this illiberal transformation of the American society. In the struggle against National Socialism nearly all means seemed acceptable. Kempner does not even seem to have reflected on the fact that for the FBI the left-wing groups, who were natural collaborators in the fight against Nazism, were gradually turning into objects of suspicion. As a consequence, Kempner's fight against the inhumanity of Nazism and that for liberal freedom, which had coexisted in unison, increasingly diverged from one another with the struggle against Nazism gaining the upper hand in case of conflicting priorities.

A letter from his friend Herbert Weichmann, later First Mayor of Hamburg (1965–71), clearly articulates that not all of Kempner's political friends approved of his methods, especially of the way he interrogated his friends and acquaintances about third persons. Consequently, Weichmann refused to answer any questions about Edmund Stinnes and told Kempner off for his clandestine methods: "If officials need further information, refer them directly to the State Department which has enough employees who can make an official statement about Herrn St[innes]."[41] Kempner, though, did not agree at all with Weichmann's reproach. He angrily retorted: "Unfortunately you seem to perceive here everything still in the spirit of the Paris Dossier or the Prussian police mentality." He attacked Weichmann that he obviously could not imagine that such questions might also have the function to help somebody whom the local press had written unfavorably about, possibly to get a better reputation. Opinions expressed in public speeches did not convince authorities which "are now very anxious."[42] The moral problem Weichmann had pointed out remained incomprehensible to Kempner. This blind spot might be perceived as foreshadowing some problems and criticism Kempner would face at Nuremberg.

## The Immigrant as Prosecutor—Kempner at Nuremberg

### *The Way to Nuremberg—Working with the Judge Advocate General*

On April 23, 1945 Kempner received an invitation from Adjutant General Ulio of the Judge Advocate General's Corps of the War Department to participate in a conference on war criminals.[43] By then, Kempner was well known in Washington circles: he was working for the Justice Department, for a special project in the Office of Strategic Services

(OSS)—another hot spot of German émigré activity[44]—for the Office of War Information, and for the FBI. In addition to these activities, he had sent a memorandum with a couple of suggestions on how to deal with war criminals to the Judge Advocate General (JAG) a month before the conference on his own initiative. Having thus attracted attention in these quarters as well, JAG was pleased to have recourse to Kempner's know-how. Originally, JAG was in charge of the prosecution of offenses of or against military personnel. Thus it was the objective of the War Crime Office when it was founded in October, 1944, to collect, analyze, and prepare for an indictment all proofs of cruelties, atrocities, and coercion of American soldiers. In the course of time, Kempner's task would expand to a general assistance to Robert Jackson's Office of Chief of Counsel for the Prosecution of Axis Criminality (OCCPAC).[45]

On April 25, Kempner gave a talk about the possibilities of elaborating an indictment against war criminals, but he declined an offer to permanently and immediately work for the War Crimes Office of JAG, arguing that he could not leave his important work at the Department of Justice. However, Kempner offered his help as a special adviser for particular problems on an irregular basis. More likely, though, the refusal of a post with JAG was motivated by his professional obligations for the FBI as he clearly was highly interested in the subject matter and his potential tasks at the War Crimes Offices. Yet Kempner chose a different path and informed the FBI at once that in case the Bureau would become involved in the field of war crimes prosecution, he would appreciate being entrusted with this task.[46]

Meanwhile, the Judge Advocate General accepted Kempner's offer to work intermittently in an advisory function and immediately provided him with a contract as an expert consultant. Kempner's expertise and qualifications were beyond doubt: "Dr. Kempner is considered the best qualified person available to assist the Chief, War Crimes Office."[47] Another evaluation explicitly lauded the background knowledge of the expatriate lawyer and former Prussian official:

> His background will be of the utmost value to the War Crimes Division as he is the only individual available who has such a complete and thorough knowledge of the Nazi regime, a personal acquaintance with many influential civil servants and a comprehensive knowledge of the record-keeping systems maintained by the German government.[48]

Initially Kempner's task was to write reports on the organization, the staff, and the activities of the German police and other units of the government. Furthermore, he was supposed to describe the history, the background, and the structure of the Nazi Party including its philosophy and internal structures. These profiles were to function as background information for the war crimes prosecution program.[49]

In July 1945 Kempner additionally accepted the assignment of writing forty-five biographies of leading National Socialists, considering especially their public office and party membership since 1933, and the actual competences that went with these positions. For the purely biographical parts of his dossiers, he mostly built on reports compiled by the OSS. For the more specific questions about the subjects' respective functions and their positions in the hierarchy of the Third Reich, Kempner resorted to a number of official and semi-official publications with whom he was familiar from his erstwhile profession as a German civil servant, e.g. the *Reichstagshandbuch*, the *Jahrbuch der NSDAP*, the *Taschenbuch für Verwaltungsbeamte*, the *Reichsgesetzblatt*, the *Reichsanzeiger*, etc.[50] Kempner translated key sections and added them to the reports, constructing concise, informative dossiers which were highly appreciated inside OCCPAC. Hardly any other dossier would prove as conducive to his further career as the report on "the guilt of Hermann Göring," which Kempner compiled and which received a lot of attention by the higher echelons of the prosecution office. Kempner had produced a virtually full-scale indictment against Göring, which considered all his political functions and his responsibilities in the Third Reich and proved them by quoting available documents or gave hints to witnesses.[51]

Kempner's work once more attracted attention from interested quarters. Following the appointment of Robert H. Jackson as US Chief Prosecutor in an upcoming international trial of Nazi war criminals, several members of Jackson's recently established Office of Chief of Counsel, which by now had moved to London, suggested integrating Kempner into the staff.[52] Murray C. Bernays, a member of Jackson's inner circle and the conceptual father of the IMT's triad of conspiracy, aggressive war, and criminal organizations, sent his superior a letter, emphasizing that it would be "definitely useful" to have Kempner in London. Bernays particularly mentioned the study on Göring besides all the experience Kempner had to offer from his judicial dealings with National Socialists.[53] Considering that Jackson's right hand, Thomas Dodd, as well as other protagonists in the OCCPAC had already worked together with Kempner, Bernays's proposal was likely to meet with broad approval. On July 19, 1945, Kempner was thus officially offered a post by Jackson: "Dr. Kempner's services are urgently needed by the Office of the US Chief of Counsel."[54]

### Nuremberg I: Kempner in Jackson's Staff

Kempner was now filled with enthusiasm for being able to participate in this great trial, not least of all because he conceived of this opportunity as a vindication of his professional efforts and a compensation for his personal trials and tribulations in the past decade: "Of course, I would like to participate in the finale of a prosecution which I initiated in 1930, unfortunately without success. I am sure it will be much more interesting than the Viereck, Molzahn, Auhagen, Transocean sedition and other cases I was connected with."[55] A few days later, on August 2, Kempner boarded a ship to London. With his intimate knowledge of German law and bureaucracy, he soon became Jackson's right-hand man and special advisor in European law and administration, especially concerning German government administration.[56]

But Kempner was more than just a consultant to Jackson; in various functions he participated in the planning and conduction of the IMT. During the preparatory stages, he organized the analysis of the captured files, most importantly those of the economic section of the German General Staff. In mid-October 1945, he became chief of Section Seven which had been set up to anticipate the defense.[57] At the same time he dealt with the problematic issue of having far too few available defense attorneys for the defendants—a problem that jeopardized the start of the IMT. This problem had resulted from the original idea of the OCCPAC to suggest anti-Nazi lawyers as advocates, many of whom had even been incarcerated in concentration camps. These lawyers, rather predictably, were often unwilling to serve as defense counsels. Similarly, the defendants were also often not inclined to accept them. In the end, Kempner tried to find some alternative lawyers who were ready to participate in the IMT, and he indeed recruited several of the later defense counsel including Franz Exner (Jodl) and Walter Siemers (Raeder). Finally, Kempner found himself in charge of liaison with the defense counsel, i.e. he had to introduce them to the rules, procedures, and conventions of Nuremberg, and he also served as their direct contact person.[58]

After the opening of the trial, Kempner was appointed as chief of the division which prepared the trial briefs and the presentation of the cases against the individual defendants and the dossiers of the prosecution and defense witnesses. Consequently, he directed and supervised a staff of fifteen attorneys, sixteen research analysts and investigators, and an additional group of translating and clerical staff.[59] In the courtroom he presented the case against Wilhelm Frick, previously Reich Minister of the Interior.[60] As a former high official in the police department of the Prussian Ministry of the Interior, Kempner seemed to be particularly qualified for this part of the indictment.[61] In addition to these tasks, he regularly cross-examined high-ranking officials of the Third Reich before the Commissioners of the tribunal, besides interrogating the main defendants as he did, for example, with Göring or Ribbentrop. Accordingly, Kempner's "intelligent, diligent and faithful work" was appreciated as a great asset to the prosecution by Justice Jackson.[62]

The renown Kempner earned for his work at the IMT is best illustrated in a brief anecdote. When he returned to the United States after the IMT had ended in October 1946, he was not sure whether or not he would go back to Germany for the follow-up trials. Kempner was rather skeptical about a further stay at that time and preferred resuming his original work in the War Crimes branch and recruiting new personnel back in Washington over serving a second term himself.[63] However, things did not go as planned and Kempner soon found himself under considerable pressure to return to Nuremberg, although not so much from the side of the OCCPAC's successor, the Office of Chief of Counsel for War Crimes (OCCWC) under the lead of Jackson's deputy Telford Taylor. Instead, the initiative came from the tribunal's benches which was all the more unusual as—despite the judicial doubts such a procedure necessarily invoked—it was up to the prosecution to draft judges rather than the other way round.[64] But shortly after the first team of judges who were to constitute Military Tribunal I had arrived in Nuremberg, Presiding Judge Walter B. Beals sent a strong letter to Colonel Dameon Gunn from JAG, asking him urgently to convince Kempner to accept a new assignment. Beals had met Kempner at a preparatory course for Nuremberg—organized at the Pentagon by Kempner—and firmly believed in the necessity of his presence at Nuremberg.[65] Taylor was completely in accord with Beals's assessment, all the more as he faced enormous problems in recruiting qualified personnel for the prosecution office. Whatever important work was waiting for Kempner in Washington DC, Taylor could hardly afford not to make use of his talents.[66]

Kempner's decision to go back to Nuremberg and to take over the Ministries Division was made in late January or early February 1947. He was not exactly happy about the assignment, but as an attempt to shift to a new job at the State Department had failed, his decision for Nuremberg seemed the best alternative at that moment.

### Nuremberg II—Prosecutor in the "Subsequent Proceedings"

Back in Nuremberg, Kempner as an IMT veteran enjoyed an outstanding position from the beginning. Already in February he was appointed director of the Ministries Division and therefore responsible for the investigation of the Third Reich's ministerial elite in order to compile bills of indictment.[67] At first, though, Kempner was not completely convinced by the concept of the "Subsequent Proceedings" to combine trials of different professional groups of the Nazi elite, especially from separate ministerial cases. By April 1947, however, he preferred

> a combined trial of the evil managerial geniuses of the Third Reich patterned after the trial of the top policy makers we had before the International Military Tribunal. This would mean a trial which starts with Lammers in the place of Goering, Keppler in the place of Hess, State Secretary von Steengracht in the place of Ribbentrop, Ambassador Karl Ritter, Foreign Office liaison man for the army, in place of Keitel, etc. In other words, the top policy makers, already in hell, would be replaced by the executive managers of the criminal expedition.[68]

Ironically, in the end Kempner's mission to bring the Ministries case to fruition offered him such a joint, big trial, although this was not the result of a well thought-out plan but rather due to the change of American political priorities in light of the looming Cold War. Because the

American government was not willing to support the original trial program—and to pay for another five trials, including the High Command case[69]—Taylor and his staff decided to fuse the last four trials into one. As a consequence, heterogeneity characterized the choice of defendants who were of widely different political and professional provenance and rank, prompting the German press to dub Case 11 sarcastically the "omnibus trial."[70]

Anyhow, the twenty-one defendants included four former Reich ministers: Richard Walter Darrè (Food and Agriculture), Hans Heinrich Lammers (Reich Chancellery), Otto Meissner (Presidential Chancellery), and Lutz Schwerin von Krosigk (Treasury). Moreover, there were five senior and junior undersecretaries from the Foreign Office in the dock, including the main defendant Ernst von Weizsäcker (undersecretary from 1938 to 1943) and his successor Gustav Adolf Steengracht von Moyland and the two undersecretaries Wilhelm Stuckart from the Ministry of the Interior and Otto Dietrich of the Propaganda Ministry. The set of Emil Puhl, Karl Rasche, Paul Körner, Hans Kehrl, and Paul Pleiger added a sizeable faction of representatives of the private and state banking, economic offices, and heavy industry. Finally, the integration of Gottlob Berger and Walter Schellenberg meant that two high representatives and career officers of the SS rounded off the picture.[71]

In his function as chief of OCCWC's Ministries Division, Kempner was effectively responsible for the planning and conducting of the whole trial, although the economic and SS sections were partly organized by staff from the Industrialists and SS Divisions.[72] The final word and overall responsibility, though, rested with Taylor. In his opening statement, he tried to cover up the problem of heterogeneity by pointing out that, in contrast to the previous cases, this trial did not deal with a special professional group but with the political and administrative heart of the Third Reich's administration. This perspective was neatly indicated by the geographical focus on Berlin's "Wilhelmstraße," where almost all offices of the defendants had once been found.[73] The main hypothesis pursued by the prosecution was that the major part of the old bureaucratic elite was as responsible for the crimes as the National Socialist policy makers since the regime had been absolutely dependent on their know-how and their cooperation to realize their criminal plans.[74]

The indictment with its eight counts, above all crimes against peace, war crimes, and crimes against humanity, was submitted to the court on November 4, 1947. Not all defendants were accused on all counts. Kempner concentrated on the involvement of the political ministries and especially of the defendants of the Foreign Office in the Holocaust. Weizsäcker's defense strategy, however, tended to deny his knowledge about the extermination of the Jews in a first step. Then, in the further course of the trial, the lead defendant tried to cast himself as a part of the German resistance movement who had rested on his post in order to "prevent something worse." In constructing this image, he was sup-

ported by his old colleagues from the Foreign Office, most notably by
the brothers Erich and Theo Kordt, who undertook tremendous work
for his defense.[75]

Kempner and his staff tried to deconstruct this self-styled image as
a myth by presenting a vast number of documents. In the end, it was
one document that would prove particularly successful: Weizsäcker
had noted on a communiqué by the SS that the Foreign Office did not
have any objections to deport 6,000 French Jews to Auschwitz. It was
mostly on this ground that he would be sentenced to seven years in
prison because of crimes against humanity and crimes against peace.
The highest sentences, meanwhile, were handed out to  Berger (25
years), Veesenmayer and Lammers (20 years each) and Körner, Pleiger,
and Kehrl (15 years each). Furthermore and in a singular move, the
judges explicitly called for a review of the convictions, mostly because
the verdict was passed with a strong dissenting vote: Judge Powers put
on record a dissenting opinion and demanded lower sentences for all
defendants. In contrast, Kempner and Taylor found the punishment
meted out by the tribunal far too mild with regard to the responsibility
these men had for the crimes of the Third Reich.[76]

While Kempner was certainly one of the most important associates of
Taylor's who always appreciated his colleague's work and judgments,[77]
not all staff members shared this view. There were several conflicts with
some of his comrades-in-arms, particularly with Charles LaFollette,
chief prosecutor in the Justice case, who complained repeatedly about
Kempner's lack of cooperativeness and his working methods. Two epi-
sodes in particular became quite famous, or rather notorious, in this
context: in the summer of 1947, LaFollette blamed Kempner for not
having shared a document which was also very important for the Justice case; in fact, the document LaFollette demanded was nothing less
than the notorious Wannsee Protocol. After having seen the document,
LaFollette went to Taylor demanding Kempner's dismissal which Taylor, however, refused to consent to.[78] The second episode took place in
May 1948 when Weizsäcker's defense counsel blamed Kempner for having put his key witness Friedrich Gaus under pressure by threatening to
hand him over to the Soviet Union. As proof of this allegation, Weizsäcker's lawyers quoted extensively from the transcript of an interrogation
by Kempner that had allegedly fallen into their hands "by chance." The
transcript caused an instant sensation and provoked strong reactions
not only in the courtroom but also in the German public, notably in
leading circles of the protestant church, damaging the reputation of the
Nuremberg trials deeply. Officially the American administration backed
Kempner, but internally LaFollette criticized him vehemently. In a letter to Lucius D. Clay he professed his profound anger: Kempner's

> foolish, un-lawyer-like method of interrogation was common knowledge in
> Nuernberg all the time I was there and protested by those of us who antici-

pated the arising of a day, just such as we now have, when the Germans would attempt to make martyrs out of the common criminals on trial in Nuernberg.[79]

Clearly, Kempner was not universally liked among the OCCWC staff. However, due to his performance in the Ministries trial, he would become much less popular with the German public than he could have ever been among his colleagues, eventually turning into one of the most controversial figures in postwar Germany.

## Kempner as a Negative Symbol of the Nuremberg Trials

In the course of the Nuremberg trials and in the eyes of a German audience, Kempner became more and more the personification of the whole war crimes program, although with widely changing connotations. During the IMT, German spectators had gained the impression that Kempner was "our man in Nuremberg." They even seemed to be proud that at least one German took part in these proceedings on the prosecuting side. Moreover, many people wanted to profit from his high position and his influence: Kempner received a large number of petitions or requests for help, and indeed he often tried to improve things and provide help.[80] This viewpoint, however, performed a volte-face in the course of the Ministries case. In German society—especially in its upper strata and in the protestant church—the indictment was vehemently criticized as the accused civil servants did not conceive of themselves as supporters of the National Socialist Party—nor did their supporters—but as members of a functional elite which had remained at arm's length from the regime and thus bore no responsibility for its crimes. Hence, an entire and still influential stratum of German society felt its reputation was blackened by the Ministries case's indictment and found its historical role misinterpreted. Consequently, the trial was—from its early stages on—not just an investigation of personal juridical guilt but also an issue for public debate on the political and moral responsibility of the German elites for the crimes of the Third Reich. In the eyes of the defendants, their counsel, and their public supporters, this was much more than an academic question of honor—it was a politically highly charged question of their future role in the new German state.

As concretization and personification are rather effective means for communicating complex questions to the public, the debate focused more and more on the main defendant, the former Secretary of State Ernst von Weizsäcker, on the one hand, and on the chief prosecutor Kempner on the other. Weizsäcker turned into the figurehead of the old elite, although much less on his own account than due to the deliberate stylization by the German lawyers and public commentators. Therefore, it was his case which epitomized the historical dimension of trial discourse:

if Weizsäcker was acquitted, so would a whole class be. As a result, it became a primary objective of the defense to avoid his conviction at any price. In doing so, the defense strategy attempted to contest the American point of view that the old Wilhelmine elite had participated in the crimes of the Third Reich for opportunistic reasons, in favor of a historical interpretation that these men—for they were predominantly male—had played a heroic role in continuing to do their duty, or in short: to hold out in their positions. The contemporary trope to describe this interpretation—which was at the same time Weizsäcker's main argument—was the concept of partaking in bad deeds, "*um Schlimmeres zu verhüten*," i.e., the necessity to remain in one's position "in order to prevent something much worse." The other side of this apologetic interpretation was an increasing defamation of the whole war crimes trials program as "collective punishment," unjustly hurting even those who had done their best to serve an alleged "other Germany" ("*das andere Deutschland*"). And for the critics, Robert Kempner turned increasingly into the symbolic figure not only of Case 11 (Figure 1.1) but of the program as such on whom all anger could conveniently be focused.[81]

This personalization of the Ministries case was possible as both main characters represented "ideal types" of the two different political attitudes towards the Republic of Weimar and the Third Reich: Weizsäcker came from an ancient, academic, protestant, and conservative family.

**1.1** The prosecutor as editor: Robert M.W. Kempner presenting his volume on the Ministries Case to the public

*United States Holocaust Memorial Museum, Washington, D.C., Photo Archives, #66036*

His career, first in the Navy, then in the Foreign Office, was typical for the "old elite." Kempner, on the other hand, had been born into a partly Jewish family with strong ties to the natural sciences and whose political thinking could be characterized as left-liberal. Like most of the old elite, Weizsäcker had not been partisan of the Weimar democratic system but had always objected to the results of the Versailles Treaty. Even if Weizsäcker with his upper class habits had never admired the ruddy National Socialist Party, he had yet agreed with several of its ideas and tenets. Accordingly, his administrative career had not come to a sudden halt in 1933 but, in contrast, had swept him into the position of a state secretary in the Foreign Office in 1938.[82] Again in contrast, Kempner had been a strict supporter of the Republic and had participated in the movement towards further democratization of the political and juridical system. As a consequence of his involvement in 1933, he had lost his job in the Prussian Ministry of Interior according to the Law for the Restoration of the Professional Civil Service (*Gesetz zur Wiederherstellung des Berufsbeamtentums*) and had been forced into emigration in 1935. Meanwhile, Weizsäcker's resignation in 1942 and his transfer to an ambassadorship in the Vatican could hardly be interpreted as a degradation as this transfer had been at his own request.[83]

Against this background the German public perceived Kempner as a resentful retaliator who had come back to Germany only to take revenge on his former colleagues, although—as an emigrant—he could not know anything about life and times in Nazi Germany. On the other side, Weizsäcker was regarded as an almost impeccable and patriotic character who was about to fall victim to victor's justice.[84] In the face of the unprecedented and increasingly personal attacks on a single prosecutor, Hans Habe—a fellow emigrant and the editor-in-chief of the American newspaper *Neue Zeitung*—retrospectively concluded that it had been a mistake to entrust this task to Kempner. In Habe's view, this was not because Kempner had done a bad job. On the contrary, it was because he had done as thorough a job as possible under the eyes of an inimical public. From the beginning of the trial, the majority at least of vocal Germans had suspected him to be prejudiced, and—one might add—his self-confident, at times outright arrogant demeanor had hardly helped to improve things. This made Kempner an easy target and his name became a catalyst "for anti-Americanism and anti-Semitic" resentments.[85]

## Nuremberg and the Man

Although Kempner had already been a well-connected person in the Republic of Weimar, it was his part in Nuremberg, particularly his leading role in the Ministries case, which made him truly prominent. He was rather aware of this fact as he later 'legitimized' all his political and juridical statements by signing them with the supplement: "Former

Deputy Chief of Counsel for War Crimes." The vignette amply highlights that he saw all his further activities as some kind of legacy of the Nuremberg trials: as a publicist he wanted to enlighten the Germans about the Nuremberg trials and the National Socialist regime in order to prepare the ground for a serious accounting of the past.[86] He actively took part as a lawyer in the preparation and conduct of innumerable trials against Nazi criminals in the Federal Republic of Germany.[87] And finally he represented a large number of clients in restitution proceedings.

In this light it would be tempting to conclude that "Nuremberg made the man," i.e. the public person Robert Kempner. But the image generated at and shaped by Nuremberg was far from coherent. First, for most Germans Kempner was a negative symbol for the whole American war crimes trials program, while later his public persona almost became a kind of "cultural code" which stood for a specific, critical, and poignant way of dealing with the German past. For those who pleaded in favor of a critical, judicial reckoning with the National Socialist past, Kempner became an exemplary protagonist and a moral authority;[88] for the others, who denied the legitimacy of the Nuremberg trials as such, he continued to be viewed as the revenge-seeking emigrant.[89] Thus he would remain a controversial character throughout his lifetime. In the end, though, it has to be emphasized that Kempner, who profited by the Nuremberg trials, did not do so one-sidedly. With his experience, his knowledge, and his strong will to fight against all National Socialist tendencies, he also had a remarkable, active part in 'making Nuremberg'—both in its achievements and in its deficiencies.

# Notes

1. Teleconference, October 29, 1947, in NARA, RG 238, Entry 159, Box 1, Folder 1.
2. Dirk Pöppmann, "Robert Kempner und Ernst von Weizsäcker im Wilhelmstraßenprozess. Zur Diskussion über die Beteiligung der deutschen Funktionselite an den NS-Verbrechen," in *Im Labyrinth der Schuld. Täter—Opfer—Ankläger. Jahrbuch 2003 zur Geschichte und Wirkung des Holocaust*, ed. Fritz Bauer Institut (Frankfurt a.M., 2003), 163ff.
3. For the OSS, see Petra Marquardt-Bigman, *Amerikanische Geheimdienstanalysen über Deutschland 1942–1949* (Munich, 1995); Barry M. Kätz, *Foreign Intelligence: Research and Analysis in the Office of Strategic Services 1942–1945* (Cambridge, MA, 1989); Bradley F. Smith, *The Shadow Warriors. O.S.S. and the Origins of the C.I.A.* (New York, 1983).
4. Alexander Stephan, *Im Visier der FBI. Deutsche Exilschriftsteller in den Akten amerikanischer Geheimdienste* (Stuttgart, 1995), 1ff.
5. For example there was Hans Kelsen, one of the most famous experts on international law of that time. Indeed Kelsen—professor rather than practitioner—cooperated with the US authorities, too, but did not advance to more than advisory posts. Cf. Ernst C. Stiefel and Frank Mecklenburg, *Deutsche Juristen im amerikanischen Exil (1933–1950)* (Tübingen, 1991), 19, 49.
6. Cf. e.g. *Das Tagebuch der Hertha Nathorff. Berlin—New York. Aufzeichnungen 1933–1945*, 2nd edn, ed. W. Benz (Frankfurt a.M., 2010), 170ff.; Lothar Mertens,

*Unermüdlicher Kämpfer für Frieden und Menschenrechte. Leben und Wirken von Kurt R. Grossmann* (Berlin, 1997), 147ff.

7. It was his old colleague Peiser who convinced Kempner to immigrate to Italy and who offered him a job in his school, founded two years earlier. For the history of the school, see Klaus Voigt, *Zuflucht auf Widerruf. Exil in Italien 1933–1945, Vol. 1* (Stuttgart, 1989); Robert Kempner, *Ankläger einer Epoche. Lebenserinnerungen* (Frankfurt a.M., 1986), 137f.; Bericht für Herrn Kurt Grossmann zur persönlichen Information. Streng vertraulich!, Leo Baeck Institut, Kurt Grossmann Papers, Reel 6, Box 10.

8. Refoulement from April 19, 1939, in USHMM, Kempner Papers, Box 26, Folder 3.

9. Katharina Graffmann-Weschke, *Lydia Rabinowitsch-Kempner (1871–1935). Leben und Werk einer der führenden Persönlichkeiten der Tuberkuloseforschung am Anfang des 20. Jahrhunderts* (Herdecke, 1999), 33ff.

10. For Simons' career in exile, see the article "Simons, Hans," in *Biographisches Handbuch der deutschsprachigen Emigration nach 1933. Vol. 1, Politik, Wirtschaft, öffentliches Leben*, ed. Institut für Zeitgeschichte München (Munich, 1980), 703; Claus-Dieter Krohn, *Wissenschaft im Exil. Deutsche Sozial- und Wirtschaftswissenschaftler in den USA und die New School for Social Research* (Frankfurt a.M., 1987).

11. Dr. Sweeny's letter to R. Kempner from June 13, 1939, in USHMM, Kempner Papers, Folder: Correspondence 1924ff.

12. Herbert A. Strauss, *Jewish Immigrants of the Nazi Period in the U.S.A.* (New York, 1987), 288ff.

13. Kempner, *Ankläger*, 147f.

14. Dr. Sweeny's letter to Kempner from June 13, 1939, in USHMM, Kempner Papers, Folder: Correspondence 1924ff.

15. R. Kempner's letter to Dr. Wilbur Thomas from June 1941, in USHMM, Kempner Papers, Box 26, Folder 3.

16. Kempner's letter to Dr. Paul Schwarz from November 6, 1940, in USHMM, Kempner Papers, Box 26, Folder 3.

17. Edward W. Carter's letter to Robert Kempner from February 27, 1941, in USHMM, Kempner Papers, Box 26, Folder 3.

18. Kempner's letter to Hoover from December 21, 1938, in USHMM, Kempner Papers, Folder: FBI 1942–1946.

19. Cf. Cornelia Wilhelm, *Bewegung oder Verein? Nationalsozialistische Volkstumspolitik in den USA* (Stuttgart, 1998), 10ff.; Eva Schweitzer, *Amerika und der Holocaust. Die verschwiegene Geschichte* (Munich, 2004), 13ff.; *Questions and answers on regulations concerning aliens of enemy nationalities*, ed. US Department of Justice (Washington, DC, 1942).

20. Strauss, *Jewish Immigrants*, 273; Wilhelm, *Bewegung oder Verein*, 14 ; Tim Weiner, *FBI. Die wahre Geschichte einer legendären Organisation* (Frankfurt a.M.), 111ff.

21. Hoover's letter to Kempner from January 16, 1939, in USHMM, Kempner Papers, Folder: FBI 1942–1946.

22. Correspondence Kempner–Hoover from July and September 1939, in USHMM, Kempner Papers, Folder: FBI 1942–1946.

23. Part of this was the fear of subversion of the American economy by means of foreign, German-dominated cartels; see the contribution by Kim Priemel in this volume.

24. Schweitzer, *Amerika und der Holocaust*, 68ff.; Strauss, *Jewish Immigrants*, 274ff.; Gert Raeithel, *Geschichte der nordamerikanischen Kultur*, vol. 3 (Frankfurt a.M., 1995), 33ff., 136ff.; Christof Mauch, *Schattenkrieg gegen Hitler. Das Dritte Reich im Visier der amerikanischen Geheimdienste 1941–1945* (Stuttgart, 1999), 33ff.

25. The Auhagen case (1942ff.), in NARA, RG 60, File No. 146-13-2-51-236.

26. Kempner's papers on the Auhagen case, in USHMM, Kempner Papers, File: Auhagen Prosecution 1941.

27. Maximilian Saint-George and Dennis Lawrence, *A Trial on Trial. The Great Sedition Trial of 1944* (Washington, DC, 1946).

28. Kempner's letter to Dr. Sweeny, September 26, 1942, in USHMM, Kempner Papers, Folder: Correspondence 1924ff.

29. Another of the German émigré experts employed by the Justice Department was Heinrich Kronstein, an ex-official from the German Economic Ministry who was hired first by the Claims Division, then by the Anti-trust Office; Stiefel and Mecklenburg, *Juristen*, 60f., 136f.; cf. Marquardt-Bigman, *Geheimdienstanalysen*, 196.

30. Kempner's letter to SAC Sears (Philadelphia) from December 14, 1941, USHMM, Kempner Papers, Folder: FBI 1942–1946.

31. SAC Sears (Philadelphia) to R. Kempner from December 29, 1941, USHMM, Kempner Papers, Folder: FBI 1942–1946.

32. Kempner's letter to the FBI Philadelphia from January 3, 1942, USHMM, Kempner Papers, Folder: FBI 1942–1946.

33. Correspondence Hoover–Kempner about this case from October/November 1942, in USHMM, Kempner Papers, Folder: Personnel Files FBI. For the Bergsträsser case, see Claus-Dieter Krohn, "Der Fall Bergstraesser in Amerika," in *Exilforschung. Ein internationales Jahrbuch* 4 (1986): 254–75.

34. A great number of these reports can be found in USHMM, Kempner Papers, Folder: Personnel Files FBI.

35. Kempner's Memorandum from May 29, 1944 to SAC Philadelphia, USHMM, Kempner Papers, Folder: Personnel Files Kempner; Memorandum SAC Philadelphia to R Kempner from April 3, 1944, in USHMM, Kempner Papers, Folder: Personnel Files Kempner.

36. Ibid.

37. Kempner's letter to Hoover from September 2, 1943, in USHMM, Kempner Papers, Folder: Personnel File Kempner.

38. Among them had been job offers by the Investigative Section of the Alien Property Custodian and by the Research Division of the War Department, and even by the War Crime Office of JAG.

39. Dirk Pöppmann, "Der Wilhelmstraßenprozess als vergangenheitspolitischer Diskurs," in *Leipzig—Nürnberg—Den Haag. Neue Fragestellung und Forschungen zum Verhältnis von Menschenrechtsverbrechen, justizieller Säuberung und Völkerstrafrecht*, ed. Helia-Verena Daubach (Düsseldorf, 2008), 115f.

40. Douglas M. Charles, *J. Edgar Hoover and the Anti-interventionists. FBI Political Surveillance and the Rise of the Domestic Security State, 1939–1945* (Columbus, OH, 2007); Stephan, *Im Visier des FBI*.

41. Weichmann's letter to Kempner from January 10, 1942, in USHMM, Kempner Papers, Folder: FBI 1942–1946.

42. Kempner's letter to Weichmann from January 14, 1942, in USHMM, Kempner Papers, Folder: FBI 1942–1946.

43. General Ulio's letter to Robert Kempner from April 23, 1945, in USHMM, Kempner Papers, Folder: FBI 1942–1946.

44. Cf. Katz, *Foreign Intelligence*; Smith, *Shadow Warriors*; Mauch, *Schattenkrieger*; Marquardt-Bigman, *Geheimdienstanalysen*. Kempner and his wife were contributing to the M[igrations]-project of the OSS.

45. Army Service Forces, Office of the Judge Advocate General: A History of The War Crimes Office from 25 Sept 1945 to 30 Jun 1945, NARA, RG 153, Entry 135, Box 57.

46. Kempner's Memorandum for the SAC Philadelphia from May 1, 1945, USHMM, Kempner Papers, Folder: Personnel File Kempner, 1943–45.

47. William H. Beck, JR, Colonel, JAG, Chief, Administrative Division, Memorandum for the Director Civilian Personnel Division, AGO from May 3, 1945, National Personnel Records Center (NPRC), Civilian Personnel Records, Subject: Kempner, Robert, M., DOB: 10-17-1899.

48. Memorandum Ruth S. Bentiey, Acting Chief, Classification Section, Civ. Pers. Div. to the Director, Civilian Personal Division, Adjutant General's Office from May 5, 1945, NPRC, Civilian Personal Records, Subject: Kempner, Robert, M., DOB: 10-17-1899.

49. Ibid.
50. Cf. NARA, RG 238, Entry 53 E, Box 8.
51. Goering's Guilt from June 1945, NARA, RG 238, Entry 53 E, Box 18.
52. For the establishment of Jackson's office and the ensuing debates, see the extensive, detailed account by Bradley Smith, *The Road to Nuremberg* (New York, 1981).
53. Bernays's Memorandum to Justice Jackson from July 17, 1945, NARA, RG 238, Entry 53 E, Box 11.
54. Memorandum for the Adjutant General, from July 28, 1945 by Anthony Kane, Colonel, JAGD, NPRC, Civilian Personal Records, Subject: Kempner, Robert, M., DOB: 10-17-1899.
55. Kempner's letter to the JAGD from July 9, 1945, USHMM, Kempner Papers, Folder: FBI 1942–1946.
56. Cf. Jackson's Concept to an evaluation of Robert Kempner, December 1946, Library of Congress (LoC), Jackson Papers, Box 106, Folder: Personnel OCC-Staff.
57. Ibid.
58. Cf. Kempner's letter to Jackson from October 24, 1945, LoC, Jackson Papers, Box 101, Folder: Selection of Defence Counsel; Kempner's memorandum to Board of Review from October 31, 1945, in LoC, Jackson Papers, Box 101, Folder: Selection of Defence Counsel; Kempner, *Ankläger*, 237f.
59. Cf. Jackson's Concept to an evaluation of Robert Kempner, December 1946, LoC, Jackson Papers, Box 106, Folder: Personnel OCC-Staff.
60. Cf. *Trial of the Major War Criminals* (Nuremberg, 1947–49), V, 352ff. and XX, 269ff.
61. Telford Taylor, *Die Nürnberger Prozesse. Hintergründen, Analysen und Erkenntnisse aus heutiger Sicht* (Munich, 1994), 317.
62. Jackson's letter to Robert Kempner from December 11, 1946, LoC, Jackson Papers, Box 106, Folder: Personnel OCC-Staff.
63. Kempner's letter to Telford Taylor from October 22, 1946, USHMM, Kempner Papers, Box 26, Folder: F4.
64. Executive Session of the Military Tribunal I, November 12, 1946, NARA, RG 238, Entry 149, Box 2; Official Record, US Military Tribunals Nuremberg. Tribunal Records, Vol. 5, fol. 13; Teleconference, October 29, 1947, NARA, RG 238, Entry 159, Box 1, Folder 1.
65. Walter Beals's letter to Colonel Dameon Gunn from November 4, 1946, NARA, RG 153, Entry 132, Box 10.
66. For Taylor's problems to find new staff to replace the IMT prosecution, see his final report: Taylor, *Final Report*, 6, 11f., 14; cf. Taylor, *Anatomy*, 288–91. In the end, Kempner was one of only four prosecutors from Jackson's staff who also presented cases in the NMT.
67. See Telford Taylor's General Order from February 25, 1947, Bundesarchiv (BArch), OMGUS 7/60-3/8.
68. See Letter of Robert Kempner to Robert Jackson from April 3, 1947, LoC, Jackson Papers, Box 14, folder: "K" miscellaneous.
69. See the chapter by Valerie Hébert in this volume.
70. Pöppmann, "Wilhelmstraßenprozess," 104f.
71. Ibid.
72. Ibid., 103; Taylor, *Final Report*, 212f.
73. Case 11, Opening Statement of the Prosecution from January 6, 1948, *Trials of War Criminals before the Nuremberg Military Tribunals under Control Council Law No. 10* [TWC] (Washington, DC, 1952), XII, 138.
74. Ibid.
75. Pöppmann, "Wilhelmstraßenprozess," 106f.
76. Ibid., 108f. On Powers' dissenting opinion, see also the chapter by Stiller in this volume.
77. Cf. Kempner's Reports of Efficiency Rating by Taylor, NPRC, Civilian Personnel Records, Subject: Kempner, Robert M., DOB: 10-17-1899.

78. See Benjamin B. Ferencz's letter to Kempner from December 15, 1989, Columbia Law School, Telford Taylor Papers, Subseries I, Box 3, folder 34. I have to thank Jonathan Bush for ceding this document to me.
79. See Norbert Frei, *Vergangenheitspolitik. Die Anfänge der Bundesrepublik und die NS-Vergangenheit*, 2nd edn (Munich, 1997), 150.
80. Pöppmann, "Wilhelmstraßenprozess," 102.
81. Pöppmann, "Weizsäcker und Kempner," 183ff.
82. Ibid., 167ff.
83. Ibid., 170.
84. Ibid., 183ff.
85. Hans Habe, *Our Love Affaire with Germany* (New York, 1953).
86. In addition to the vast number of newspaper articles, especially Kempner's in several editions of published books, see also *Eichmann und Komplizen* (Munich, 1961); *SS im Kreuzverhör. Die Elite, die Europa in Scherben schlug* (Munich, 1964); *Das Dritte Reich im Kreuzverhör. Aus den unveröffentlichten Vernehmungsprotokollen des Anklägers Robert M.W. Kempner* (Munich, 1969).
87. See, for one minor trial, Dirk Pöppmann, "Rechtsstaat und Gerechtigkeit. Der Mord an Felix Fechenbach im Spiegel seiner juristischen Aufarbeitung vor dem Schwurgericht Paderborn," *Westfälische Zeitschrift* 157 (2007): 287–309.
88. See, e.g., *Gegen Barbarei. Essays Robert Kempner zu Ehren*, eds. Rainer Eisfeld and Ingo Müller (Frankfurt a.M., 1989); Tilman Westphalen, *Ein Advokat für die Humanität. Verleihung der Ehrendoktorwürde an Robert M.W. Kempner* (Osnabrück, 1986).
89. See, e.g., Helmut Quaritsch, *Carl Schmitt. Antworten in Nürnberg* (Berlin, 2000).

## CHAPTER 2

# A JUDGE, A PROSECUTOR, AND A MASS MURDERER

## COURTROOM DYNAMICS IN THE SS-EINSATZGRUPPEN TRIAL

*Hilary Earl*

$\mathcal{O}\!\mathit{sfs}$

**A**ll history is human history. Never was an aphorism more apt than for the SS-*Einsatzgruppen* trial in which three individuals stand out among the hundreds who participated in this, the ninth of twelve trials held at the Palace of Justice at Nuremberg between 1946 and 1949. At the centre of this trial was Otto Ohlendorf, a young and handsome family man, who was extremely well educated, "poised and polite."[1] Described as "one of the most remarkable persons ever to go on trial in any country in any age,"[2] Ohlendorf was also a notorious murderer. As leader of *Einsatzgruppe D*, one of the four mobile security and killing units to operate behind enemy lines in the Soviet Union beginning in June 1941, his unit murdered 90,000 Soviet civilians in one twelve-month period, and for this and other war crimes, he was indicted and prosecuted as the lead defendant in a case against twenty-four leaders of the *Einsatzgruppen* beginning on September 15, 1947 and ending with the judgment on April 10, 1948.

Ohlendorf's nemesis at trial was the larger-than-life presiding judge, Michael A. Musmanno. Known for his unorthodox and sometimes outrageous behavior in and outside the courtroom—for example, he once sentenced himself to a prison term to see what it was like—Musmanno began his career as a defense attorney and ended it as a judge in the state courts of Pennsylvania where his judgments are still notable.[3] His most famous clients were the legendary Italian-American anarchists Sacco and Vanzetti, whose convictions and subsequent executions prompted him to crusade against the death penalty. Musmanno was also a novelist and an actor. He earned seven university degrees, published sixteen books, and acted in dozens of plays.[4] He served as a reserve naval Captain in World War II and was the Aide to General Mark Clark, who commanded the American Fifth Army; at the end of the war he was made Military Governor of the Sorrentine Peninsula in southern Italy, although how this transpired is not at all clear.[5] In spite of all of his varied talents, Musmanno was most comfortable in the courtroom, where the ready-made audience fed his insatiable ego. So happy was he performing that if he were alive today he might be like Judge Judy or Judge Joe Brown and star in his own courtroom reality show.[6] Musmanno was a colorful and controversial personality, a real renaissance man. At Nuremberg he not only stood out as the lead jurist of Tribunal II, making all announcements and rulings, he also frequently dominated the proceedings, winning him lots of press and the respect of the German defense attorneys, whereas this behavior earned him few friends among the American prosecution team who sometimes felt he hijacked the trial.[7]

Last, but certainly not least of the triumvirate is chief prosecutor Benjamin Ferencz, a Harvard trained lawyer who prior to Nuremberg had never litigated a case in his life, and who served the final year of the war with the army yet who despised everything military.[8] At twenty-seven, Ferencz was arguably the youngest and least experienced trial attorney at Nuremberg, but he was also the chief prosecutor of the "the biggest murder trial in history"—the case against two dozen *Einsatzgruppen* leaders who were charged with the murder of one million civilians. Described as youthful and "cherubic" by Musmanno, what Ferencz lacked in experience he made up for with *chutzpah* and passion, as well as tenacity and intelligence.[9] These three men, an arrogant and intelligent mass murderer, a narcissistic and activist judge, and a very young, confident, and enthusiastic trial lawyer dominated and shaped not only the proceedings of the *Einsatzgruppen* trial, but also the historiography that came after it. None of these individuals were typical participants of Nuremberg, but rather each had a unique and dominant personality and it is the interaction between them that makes the *Einsatzgruppen* trial so memorable.

The aim of this essay is to shed light on the complex social setting of the *Einsatzgruppen* trial by examining three of its most important protagonists: the lead defendant, the chief prosecutor, and the principal judge (see Figure 2.1). While biography can be problematic methodologically, especially when it decontextualizes the individual and elevates him or her to the status of hero, for understanding this particular his-

**2.1** Protagonists on the Nuremberg stage: lead defendant Otto Ohlendorf (left), chief prosecutor Benjamin Ferencz (centre), presiding judge Michael A. Musmanno (right)

*United States Holocaust Memorial Museum, Washington, D.C., Photo Archives, #43038;*
*United States Holocaust Memorial Museum, Washington, D.C., Photo Archives, #09917;*
*Bildarchiv Preußischer Kulturbesitz/Bayerische Staatsbibliothek/Archiv Heinrich*
*Hoffmann , #50088661*

torical event it has proved to be an illuminating approach. All three participants were unusually voluble during the trial, and thus their voices stand out in the documented history of the trial. Afterwards, Musmanno and Ferencz in particular built legal reputations through the dissemination of their experiences at Nuremberg and their respective readings of the trial and, as a result, their personal experiences have helped to shape the narrative of the event. Posthumously, this may even be true for Ohlendorf who was executed on June 7, 1951, but whose other offices (such as his role as Undersecretary in the Economics Ministry) have been written about but which pale in comparison with his "fame" as a cold-blooded mass murderer. It is the complicated and complex story of three important figures at Nuremberg that this essay relates.

## The Mass Murderer

Who was Otto Ohlendorf and how did he come to be the most important defendant in the *Einsatzgruppen* trial? Ohlendorf was still a young man when British forces arrested him in Flensburg, Schleswig-Holstein in the spring of 1945.[10] He was born in 1907 in Hoheneggelsen, a small hamlet near Hannover, making him less than 40 years old when he first appeared in a Nuremberg courtroom.[11] Ohlendorf had a very long relationship with the Nazi Party. He was one of its first joiners on May 28, 1925 (membership number 6,531), and thus was considered an "old fighter" or *Alter Kämpfer*, for which he was bestowed with the highest honor—the Gold Party badge (*Goldenes Ehrenzeichen der Partei*).[12] He was politically active his entire life, working for the Party at the local level when he was still a teenager and, like many young men of his generation who joined nationalist political organizations in their youth, he found a meaningful career in the new agencies of the Party after the Nazis came to power. He earned university degrees in law and economics and he also began a PhD, which he never completed because he went to work for the Party instead.[13] There is no question that Ohlendorf was very ambitious.[14] When offered an opportunity to work in his chosen field of economics in a new Party organization called the Security Service (*Sicherheitsdienst* or SD), he jumped at the chance to make his mark. Indeed, in the offices of the SD he worked very hard gaining a reputation as a humorless Prussian who did not bow to anyone; a risky stance to adopt in an authoritarian government, but a characteristic that embodied his temperament as well as defining his career.[15] In the process of building the security, information, and intelligence offices of the Reich, Heydrich and Himmler sought out loyal and well-educated men like Ohlendorf who were ideologically committed Nazis yet who were also willing to take contrary perspectives. Ohlendorf's ideological world view, Party loyalty, and ambition ensured career success and, as a result, when Heydrich reorganized the SD in 1937–38, Ohlendorf was promoted to head up one of the central offices of the newly formed Reich Security Main Office (RSHA) Division III— SD Inland or Domestic Intelligence.[16] As head of Domestic Intelligence, Ohlendorf was in charge of compiling data on German attitudes toward Nazi policy, and it was this job that he held till his arrest in 1945. His career in the SD altered his life permanently because it was from this office that he was recruited by Himmler to lead one of the four units of *Einsatzgruppen* mobilized in the summer of 1941 to physically destroy the political and racial enemies of the Reich.[17] Ohlendorf's youth and career trajectory make him a member of Michael Wildt's "Uncompromising Generation" or *Generation des Unbedingten*.[18]

Ohlendorf was not unique. The majority of his co-defendants pursued similar career paths. With the exception of three defendants, all belonged to a cohort of men born between 1900 and 1912, a generation whose lives had been defined by the disillusionment of their youth brought on by the loss of World War I,[19] what Ulrich Herbert refers to as the *Kriegsjugendgeneration*.[20] This group was so traumatized by the unexpected defeat that they broke with the traditions and values of the past and became what Wildt describes as unleashed or unbound actors and initiators of their own futures—a classic characteristic of the interwar European fascists.[21] As students in Germany's leading universities in the interwar period, they joined radical nationalist and ultra-nationalist student political organizations and as adults they formed the leadership corps of Heydrich's RSHA.[22] They were the new German elites who embraced a worldview that was characterized by action and not fixed ideologies; they understood politics as a revolutionary impulse, not a theoretical concept to be debated or written about. They were not men of words, but of deeds; unfettered by the constraints of bourgeois

Europe, they were free to promote the German nation and advance their new political ideology of action.[23] They were a generation of young fascists whose worldview helped to shape the Third Reich and realize its murderous policies and Otto Ohlendorf, as it turns out, was emblematic of this ready-to-act and "uncompromising generation."[24] It was precisely this disposition and willingness to act that ensured that Ohlendorf would be drafted into a leadership position with the *Einsatzgruppen* when the time came, and indeed he was recruited in May 1941 to head up *Einsatzgruppe* D which operated alongside the 11th Army in the Russian Crimea.[25] As it turns out, Ohlendorf was just as committed to his fieldwork as he was to his desk job, spending a year in the Soviet Union as head of a mobile killing unit.[26] When the British arrested him on May 23, 1945, his uncompromising disposition and colossal arrogance got the better of him and he was voluble to his own detriment.[27]

What did Ohlendorf tell his captors, or more appropriately, what didn't he tell them?[28] In exchange for his freedom and with the expectation that he could be of value to the British occupation authorities, initially Ohlendorf was prepared to offer them his services and expertise in intelligence gathering in the occupation and governance of Germany. His arrest record and the intelligence reports of the British suggest he had thought this idea through as he carried with him to his arrest a brief case which contained his "plan" for "an underground intelligence organization" he intended to establish for the Allied Control Commission.[29] Clearly he had an overly optimistic view of his future in occupied Germany but he was a smart man and realized quite quickly that the British were less than enthusiastic about his idea. After they sent him to prison with the other captured war criminals, he soon changed his strategy, offering the British as much information about the crimes of his superiors as he possibly could, undoubtedly in the hope of winning them over, much the same tactic as Albert Speer employed during his imprisonment. During the very early phase of his captivity with the British, Ohlendorf was understandably reticent to talk about his work with the *Einsatzgruppen*. His silence about that work ended though some time in August 1945 when the intelligence records show that he began to talk about his deeds on the eastern front. While not as forthcoming as he later would be with the Americans, Ohlendorf did confess to numerous crimes including supervising the murder of 90,000 civilians while head of *Einsatzgruppe D*.

Ohlendorf's descriptions of his activities in the *Einsatzgruppen* prompted the British to transfer him to their American allies for questioning, as the Americans were in the process of gathering evidence against Ernst Kaltenbrunner, Heydrich's replacement as head of the RSHA and an intimate of Ohlendorf's. While in American custody, Ohlendorf became even more talkative, perhaps even effusive, making him the perfect prosecution witness for the upcoming trial at Nuremberg. There is no paper trail to explain the process by which Ohlendorf became a prosecution witness at the IMT trial, but it appears as if he had no demonstrable objections to it. What we do know with certainty is that it was Lieutenant Colonel Smith W. Brookhart, the "rock-jawed son of a famous midwestern [Iowan] senator," who prepared him as a witness for trial.[30] The two men spent hours together, talking over the details of the crimes of the Third Reich and Ohlendorf's personal knowledge of those who committed them.[31] Like with the British earlier, Ohlendorf described in shocking detail the various types of killing methods employed by the *Einsatzgruppen*. He also explained how they identified their victims, rounded them up, robbed, and killed them. He talked about the psychology of his men and how the victims seemed to respond to them. And, most surprisingly of all, he told his captors exactly how many civilians—mostly Jews—his unit had killed in the 12 months he was in charge of it. He held nothing back. There seemed to be no limits to what Ohlendorf was willing to discuss with Brookhart. For instance, he told the Lieutenant Colonel about the secret agreement between the German High Command and the RSHA that enabled Hitler's plan for a war of extermination to be carried out in the east. He also told Brookhart about the special relationship between the *Einsatzgruppen* and the army, but mostly their time was spent talking about the decision-making process and the day-to-day activities of his unit.[32] He was so forthcoming during these sessions that anyone who reads the transcripts might leave with the impression that Ohlendorf was not a prisoner of American authorities at all, but rather a confidant or perhaps even a friend of Lieutenant Colonel Brookhart.

Ohlendorf's recall, volubility, and comportment made him a perfect prosecution witness. On January 3, 1946, the day after the court heard Hermann Gräbe's affidavit describing the gruesome details of an *Einsatzkommando* execution he had witnessed, Ohlendorf was called to the stand as a prosecution witness against Kaltenbrunner.[33] Young and refined, the apparent "antithesis" of Nazi barbarity, Ohlendorf so captivated the court that what he said has had a lasting impact on those who heard it and arguably on posterity as well, especially since our early knowledge of the *Einsatzgruppen* and their activities comes largely from the Nuremberg trials and evidence such as Ohlendorf produced.[34] Unlike other defendants and witnesses at Nuremberg, Ohlendorf was not easily rattled, one reporter compared his comportment to that of Herman Göring who is remembered for humiliating the American Chief Prosecutor, Robert H. Jackson during his cross-examination, and Henry Lea, an interpreter at the trial described him as the epitome of composure.[35] What shocked people most about Ohlendorf though, was the perceived disconnect between the intelligent and seemingly normal man in front of them and the barbaric crimes he described to the court. It was the dual nature of Ohlendorf that later prompted Judge Michael Musmanno to refer to him as "Dr. Jekyll and Mr. Hyde."[36] As the court quickly learned, well-dressed and educated men can and do commit atrocious deeds. As Ohlendorf freely admitted, *Einsatzgruppe D*, the mobile security unit he commanded between May 1941 and June 1942, killed approximately 90,000 men, women, and children. After robbing victims of their possessions, the victims were shot, and beginning in December 1942 the women and children were asphyxiated by carbon monoxide in the so-called gas vans.[37] Ohlendorf's testimony forced those present in the courtroom to confront head-on "the inescapable reality ... of [what] mass murder,"[38] meant in the Third Reich; and as Hans Frank aptly predicted, knowing this reality sealed Ohlendorf's fate.[39]

Beginning with Ohlendorf's confessions to the British in the spring of 1945, the Office of Chief of Counsel for War Crimes (OCCWC) had a growing body of evidence against Ohlendorf, yet American investigators were uncertain about whether or not to prosecute him. Some believed the USSR would want to have him extradited because his crimes were committed on Soviet soil and, under article 4(c) of the Nuremberg Charter, the USSR had the right to try him and anyone else for that matter who committed crimes against humanity or war crimes on their territory.[40] As it turned out, the Soviets were interested in prosecuting him but they never followed through with an extradition order and thus the Americans were free to prosecute him as they saw fit. As Hans Frank noted earlier, it was clear that at some point Ohlendorf was going to have to answer for his crimes. That time came when the American research team in Berlin, led by the young and enthusiastic Benjamin Ferencz, accidentally discovered (and read) the *Einsatzgruppen* reports in the Gestapo headquarters some time in late 1946 or early 1947.[41]

## The Prosecutor

Like Ohlendorf, Ferencz is central to this story. Not only did his research team locate some of the most damning evidence against Ohlendorf and the other leaders of the *Einsatzgruppen*, he also convinced Telford Taylor, the Chief of Counsel for War Crimes and the man ultimately responsible for all indictments, to hold the leaders of the *Einsatzgruppen* to account for their part in the genocide on the eastern front.[42] In other words, without Ferencz there might not have been a coordinated trial against the *Einsatzgruppen* leaders. Ferencz unquestionably played an important role in this trial, yet he also serves as a good example of the rhetorical and narrative dominance of the NMT protagonists, who, through lectures, speeches, and interviews they gave and articles and books they published, gained prominence of place in the history and historiography of these trials. A case in point is Ferencz who has consistently portrayed himself as *the* central figure in the *Einsatzgruppen* trial.[43] This is not pure ego. He did play a central role in the trial, just not *the only* role. Why he has figured so prominently in the history and historiography has a lot to do with his animated personality. Combine strong personality traits with his adroit speaking skills and gift for storytelling and it is not difficult to see why authors writing on this subject turn to him to add color to their own bland narratives (recall Rebecca West's criticism that the Nuremberg trials were colossally boring). Nor was Ferencz one to shy away from an interview; in fact more than 60 years later, he is still willing and able to offer his interpretation of what transpired at Nuremberg. His willing participation has ensured that virtually every account of the NMT features an interview with him—the present author's included. He has also attended every major conference on the subject of Nuremberg, most often as an invited and honored guest, and for these reasons it is his perspective that dominates the historiography of the *Einsatzgruppen* and other Nuremberg trials more generally.[44]

Not only is Ferencz willing to talk about his first-hand experiences, he has had more opportunity to do so as he has also outlived most of his contemporaries and often he is the only person still alive who has a first-hand perspective of the event. Longevity is not the only reason he has been so influential though. Ferencz stayed involved with international judicial issues throughout his career; in fact it has been his life's work.[45] He was one of the few American attorneys who did not leave Europe immediately after the conclusion of the trials as did most of his contemporaries; rather, he stayed in Germany until 1956 as Director of the Jewish Restitution Successor Organization (JRSO) to help indigent Jewish survivors gain compensation for the loss of their property during the war and for the ordeals they experienced under Nazi domination.[46] After that work was completed in 1956, he went back to the United States and practiced law for a time, and in 1970 he became an active and vocal lobbyist for world peace and the establishment of a permanent international criminal court; to this end he has published many books on the topic, he has spoken to the UN and countless other legal and humanitarian organizations, and when the International Criminal Court (ICC) became permanent, he was an honored guest at the opening ceremonies.[47] He is, simply put, a tireless and devoted activist for international peace and justice. Most importantly for this story, though, is that Ferencz has an enormous personality, a man of lesser passion and charisma might not have been so memorable or so tenacious.[48] The question here then is, who is Ferencz, how did he get to Nuremberg, and what did he do once there?

Ferencz was born in Soncutta-Mare, Romania to Joseph and Sarah Ferencz on March 11, 1920. His parents immigrated to the United Sates when he was still an infant, so for all intents and purposes, he spent his entire life in the United States.[49] He went to college in New York City then on to Harvard Law School, where he was the protégé of noted criminal law expert Sheldon Glueck, who helped draft the Nuremberg Charter.[50] Ferencz's road to Nuremberg is an interesting and colorful one. He tells the story of a young Harvard law student who was so patriotic that he was determined to serve his country and enlisted in the army in 1943; while he was fortunate that he never had to kill another human being, he was nonetheless disillusioned with what he describes as a "dehumanizing ordeal" in the US Army and from the time he entered boot camp he counted the days till his discharge.[51] He found some respite when, in February 1945, the army put his legal training to use and gave him a job as a war crimes field investigator with the Judge Advocate's office.[52] Ferencz's letters to his wife Gertrude describe the exciting and fast-paced work in which he engaged, and how many of the investigations he was involved in led to military trials. He is cavalier but unapologetic when he talks about the less than upstanding methods by which he gathered evidence in these and other war crimes cases he worked on. For example, in one instance Ferencz describes travelling to Frankfurt in search of evidence in the IG Farben case. Unable to find evidence of even "one little murder," Ferencz reported his disappointment.[53] In what has become known as a classic "Ferenczism," he set out to rectify the wanting evidentiary situation. Calling a meeting of the surviving board members of IG Farben, Ferencz

> ... carefully explained to these gentlemen that I was from Nuremberg, letting it roll significantly off my tongue, and was interested in certain operations of their little company. I suggested that we were concerned with the details as they pertained to 2 or 3 of the top men, for there was talk of re-organizing Farben with a new directorate, and we would have to know which of the top 2 or 3 would be affected by our denazification policy. Meanwhile my good cigarettes are going round the table. Somehow the idea [sic] became prevalent that if they played ball in the right way they might possibly be the new top men in their beloved industry [sic]. (So help me I made no promises!). The effect was most amazing. Before I could say 'Heil Hitler' these 3 characters start bringing me the most amazing reports.[54]

Getting the documents out of the Farben offices was more difficult than he anticipated, but it was not beyond his capabilities. He recounts the story:

> By an act of God it happened that 2 Frenchmen were working in the same room as Miss G.[lassman] and myself. They had a very pretty machine with which they were taking pictures of all sorts of silly papers pertaining to the Buna process. I gave them the old 'comment allez-vous', some cigarettes, 2 bars of chocolate, and the use of the command car to take home every [sic] evening, and in return—they took pictures of all my documents too. Result: I shall bring home the bacon on microfilm.[55]

This was one of the more benign stories Ferencz has related over the years.[56] In other instances his methods of evidence gathering were much more heavy-handed, particularly during investigations he did for the army. To be sure, he makes clear distinctions between the field-work he did for the army and the investigations he carried out for the OCCWC trials at Nuremberg; the two processes were, he admits, quite different. The difference may be more of degree than of kind, yet Ferencz does not consider what he did unfair or the consequences unjust. He believes himself to be deeply committed to the law—the fact that he has campaigned his entire life for the establishment of a permanent international criminal court supports this claim.[57] But, as he notes, the war and early years afterward were a different time, before rules were codified and processes entrenched. He had a job to do, and he would do it to the best of his ability; thus it is not surprising that he always got the job done. In spite of finding war crimes investigation rewarding work, he was nonetheless quite happy to leave the army at the first opportunity, which came on December 26, 1945.[58]

A shortage of qualified personnel and Ferencz's expertise as a war crimes investigator meant he was in demand and it was only a short time after his honorable discharge from the army that he was recruited by Telford Taylor's office to return to Nuremberg as head of the Berlin Branch of the OCCWC.[59] It was while in Berlin that a member of his staff accidentally found a binder full of confidential field reports of the *Einsatzgruppen*—the so-called *Ereignismeldungen*.[60] It was the contents of these reports—there were 195 in total—that led Ferencz to ask Taylor to prosecute immediately the leaders of the four groups in a trial devoted solely to the crimes they had committed on the eastern front. The reports were an evidentiary windfall. They contained all the details of the *Einsatzgruppen*'s two-year killing spree of approximately 1 million Soviet civilians, mostly Jews, including where they were killed, by which unit, and for what reason (some of the reports offered euphemistic reasons for execution, none of which bare any resemblance to Nazi racial ideology, yet which justify murder along military lines, such as the victims were partisans). Ferencz recalls that, once he realized how important the reports were, he immediately flew back to Nuremberg to show Taylor and to suggest that the OCCWC prosecute members of these groups.[61] Although he was initially hesitant, Taylor seemed easily persuaded when Ferencz volunteered to work the case. Because of a shortage of qualified personnel, Taylor appointed Ferencz as the chief prosecutor of the case and, as it turns out, the trial of 24 *Einsatzgruppen* officers for the murder of one million people would be the first and most important trial of the Harvard graduate's long career.[62]

Once it had been decided that there would be a trial of *Einsatzgruppen* personnel, Ferencz and his team spent the better part of five months (between March and July 1947) preparing for trial. They had a lot to do and little time to do it. They located defendants, tracked down evidence, and interrogated potential witnesses; they compiled lists of victims and they consulted with US allies to extradite potential defendants. Ferencz and his team, consisting of John Glancy, Peter Walton, James Heath, and Arnost Horlick-Hochwald, realized that they could not prosecute all the members of the *Einsatzgruppen*, there simply were too many. Even if they had decided to indict only the leaders of the four groups, they were still too numerous to prosecute in a single trial because there were only twenty-four seats in the courtroom and there were eighty-four such leaders. Of these, Ferencz and his team selected men who were elite members of the killing squads and who, like Ohlendorf, had come from the offices of the SS and SD. Most importantly though, the defendants had to be accessible to Ferencz's team, they already had to be in custody or they could be easily located and extradited from other occupation zones.[63] In fact, availability of defendants and the quality of evidence were the two most important factors that led to indictments. Ferencz and his team had a lot of evidence to sift through, including sworn affidavits, SS personnel records, and of course, the *Einsatzgruppen* reports. While the *Einsatzgruppen* reports were vital to their case, they did not clearly establish individual guilt, thus they had to use good old-fashioned deductive reasoning to determine who was and who was not in charge of a unit, and by mid-June 1947, they had their roster of indictees. Not surprisingly Otto Ohlendorf was the lead defendant.[64] Twenty-three others were also indicted.[65]

Apart from discovering the *Einsatzgruppen* reports, Ferencz makes little or no mention of pre-trial issues, nor does he talk much about the trial itself in any of his interviews. He tells an anecdote about coming face-to-face with Ohlendorf in the death house at the conclusion of the trial, but most of Ferencz's Nuremberg stories are limited to observations about some of the more memorable defendants and of course his opening and closing statements to the court, which he remembers verbatim. A close look at the transcript offers an explanation for this. Outside of making the opening and closing statements at the trial and presenting the evidence against *Einsatzgruppe B*, Ferencz does not play the major role in the day-to-day happenings of the trial.[66] One reason for this is because he opted to prosecute the defendants by document alone. Although he claimed there were plenty of witnesses he could have called (presumably he is referring to individuals who either survived the executions or who witnessed them first hand), his case did not require them, or experts, or testimony of any kind because "I knew the circumstances under which the victims had been murdered ... it was bedlam ... [calling witnesses] was too risky ... I was going to hang these guys on their own documents. I was going to nail them as members of the extermination squads by presenting their documents."[67] Ferencz's decision to try the case by document alone meant that it was presented in less than two days, record time at Nuremberg where prosecution cases often dragged on for weeks and sometimes even months. Even the case against Field Marshal Erhard Milch—a sole defendant in a single trial— took longer to present than the case against the entire group of twenty-four *Einsatzgruppen* officers.[68] In spite of such a speedy presentation of the evidence, the trial lasted nearly eight months, largely because every single defendant opted to testify, and in doing so, they opened themselves up to cross-examination by the prosecution. Thus, one by one each defendant took the stand and one by one their testimony was challenged, not by the prosecution team as one might anticipate though, but rather by the presiding judge, Michael Musmanno, who was one of the most active and participatory judges at Nuremberg and whose questions set the tone of the trial, and whose larger-than-life personality also made it legally and historically memorable.[69]

## The Judge

Born in McKees's Rock, Stowe Township, Pennsylvania on April 7, 1897, Musmanno, came from a large Italian family and, like many children of immigrants, his parents strongly encouraged him to get an education. Musmanno did not disappoint.[70] He demonstrated a life-long passion for learning, earning an almost ridiculous number of university degrees— seven in total, including a Doctorate in Juristic Science from American University and a Doctor of Jurisprudence from the University of Rome. He also took courses at Oxford, Harvard and the University of Notre Dame and was a Fellow at the International Academy of Law and Science.[71] With all that education, one wonders how Musmanno found time for anything else. As it turns out, he didn't. He devoted all of his energy to his professional self, never marrying and eventually earning a reputation as a workaholic, a practice he maintained throughout his career and perhaps contributing to an early death in 1968.[72] Sacrificing his personal life for his professional one, his hard work paid off in 1923 when he became a lawyer after writing the Pennsylvania bar examination. Despite passing with flying colors, he had difficulty finding a permanent position. It was during this time that he published his first significant piece of writing in the *New York Times*, which he later turned into a monograph titled *Proposed Amendments to the Constitution.*[73] Musmanno received accolades for his efforts, which fed his burgeoning ego and encouraged a life-long passion for writing. It is a good thing he did not abandon his legal career though, as the other 15 books he wrote were not exactly literary achievements and some were simply awful and unreadable—verbose, melodramatic, some were even fabricated.[74] One reader observed his tendency to write "impressionistically,"[75] while another was not nearly so kind, caustically noting the biography of his mother and father was "unquestionably the worst book I have ever attempted to read."[76] Even the books that purported to be historical suffered from his fondness for melodrama and over-the-top prose. He often sacrificed fact for fiction, as was the case with his memoir of the *Einsatzgruppen* trial inaptly titled *The Eichmann Kommandos.* Published in 1961, the book is not entirely reliable. It opens with a scene from the trial of Adolf Eichmann in Jerusalem in which Musmanno had testified as an expert witness for the prosecution.[77] As Musmanno told the court in Jerusalem and then later wrote in his book, the *Einsatzgruppen* were the brainchild of Eichmann and the defendants all answered to him. He also claimed that,

[i]n all Jewish operations, the RSHA chain of command linked from Hitler to Himmler, Himmler to Heydrich, Heydrich to Mueller, and Mueller to Eichmann. However, since the "final solution to the Jewish question" lay close to Hitler's heart—if one can use the term in ghastly an association—Hitler occasionally snapped the intervening links and dealt directly with Eichmann … [t]hus it was that Himmler made Eichmann the chief engineer of the most extensive murder apparatus in the history of the human race. … [S]pecifically, Eichmann recommended the formation of a mobile force which, moving in fast trucks and motor cars, could keep pace with the army and shoot the Jews on location, as had been done in the successful Polish campaign.[78]

This plainly was not true since Eichmann had had little or nothing to do with the creation of the *Einsatzgruppen* in 1941. As was Musmanno's style though, he wrote as if everything were established fact, yet he did not produce a single footnote or a reference to substantiate his claims. What is so fascinating about this is not that Musmanno got the history of the *Einsatzgruppen* wrong—admittedly it is a confusing and complicated story—but rather that he seemed to do so deliberately. He so wanted to take part in the historic Eichmann trial *and* to publish his book on the *Einsatzgruppen* trial that he was willing to sacrifice truth and fact for public exposure and drama, something he was plainly unapologetic about.[79] More importantly for the way that the *Einsatzgruppen* trial played out, was that Musmanno's early career as a lawyer shaped his later behavior as a judge.

Musmanno began his legal career as a defense attorney in 1923, when he went to work for a Philadelphia law firm. He was an exceptionally successful litigator, winning over juries with his dramatic performances and his persuasive arguments meant he seldom lost a case. When he did, he was utterly devastated and like a petulant child, contemplated quitting the profession for good. After one such incident, he took a leave of absence from his job, and in 1924 went to Italy for a year. Upon his return to the United States he gained almost instant fame when he defended a Pennsylvania coal miner who had been unjustly arrested. This David and Goliath story led to a film, *Black Fury*, which he later turned into a book, about the injustices of the Pennsylvanian iron and coal industries.[80] Thus began Musmanno's life-long drive to help those he perceived as underdogs and most in need of his help.

The defining moment of Musmanno's career came in 1927, when he went to the aid of the now-famous Italian-American anarchists, Nicola Sacco and Bartolomeo Vanzetti, whose case he had been following with great interest. Seven years after the pair originally had been found guilty of robbery and murder in Braintree, Massachusetts, and while awaiting their execution, Musmanno took a hiatus from the law firm he worked for to go to Massachusetts to appeal the case *pro bono*. Undoubtedly he was moved to act by what he perceived to be the injustice of the case and he genuinely seemed to believe that Sacco and Vanzetti were innocent, the victims of a class war against Italian immigrants by corrupt and wealthy political figures. Even at this early stage in his career, Musmanno suffered from hubris, naively believing that he would be the one lawyer capable of righting this wrong. Needless to say, he was not successful and Sacco and Vanzetti were electrocuted on August 10, 1927. Their execution transformed Musmanno forever.[81] From his work against the coal and steel magnates, he understood the power of big business; now he came to see that the judicial system he so believed in was also flawed and as a result he became an advocate for the abolition of the death penalty in the United States.[82] Musmanno remained a strong and vocal opponent of the death penalty throughout his life, which on the surface seems to contradict his later behavior at Nuremberg, where he sentenced fourteen defendants in the *Einsatzgruppen* trial to death. Yet his actions at Nuremberg were not a rejection of his convictions, despite the seeming divergence from his previous position. Musmanno's opposition to the death penalty rested neither on principle nor on the moral belief in the sanctity of life. What bothered him so much was the possibility of the miscarriage of justice.[83] He found it intolerable that innocent people were executed because of a fallible legal system that often privileged political power over justice and that did not always acquit the innocent.[84] Of course, this position could be interpreted quite ironically, especially in light of his own questionable legal ethics as demonstrated in his near-perjured testimony at the Eichmann trial in 1961, and there was also his relentless red-baiting during the McCarthy era that some would argue compromised his legal integrity altogether.[85] The child was indeed father to the man. To understand the man he had become and his role in the *Einsatzgruppen* trial, we must understand his unquenchable desire to be the centre of attention and to create drama (and write a book) about every event he participated in. Much to the chagrin of many, that is exactly what Musmanno did at Nuremberg.

It was no accident that Musmanno found his way into the Nuremberg courtroom. During the years that preceded World War II, he had been working as a judge of the Allegheny County Court of Common Pleas in Pennsylvania. No one could accuse Musmanno of a lack of patriotism. He had been an infantryman in the last year of World War I, and when war broke out in Europe in 1939, he enlisted as a reservist in the Navy. Less than one month after the bombing of Pearl Harbor, Musmanno was called to active duty, and he was mobilized for the Allied campaign in Italy in 1943.[86] He was wounded several times but not demobilized, and when the Allies liberated the southern Italian city of Sorrento, Musmanno was made Military Governor of the Sorrentine Peninsula. The military soon regretted their decision when they discovered just what a rogue Musmanno could be, and his outrageous behavior (for example, he illegally sequestered a ship to bring olive oil to the people of the Sorrentine and on another occasion he personally defended the honor and property of Benedetto Croce by blocking the entrance to his house) prompted them to transfer him to Austria to work with General Clark who was named American High Commissioner.[87] In Vienna, Musmanno worked as a judge hearing cases of those individuals who the Soviets wanted to forcibly repatriate.[88] While in Austria, Musmanno followed the Nuremberg trial closely, especially the case against the German naval commanders Karl Dönitz and Erich Raeder, and was delighted when the Navy transferred him to Nuremberg to work with Admiral William Glassford to help review the cases against the German admirals.[89]

Musmanno's timing was perfect. His arrival in Nuremberg coincided with the beginning of the NMT, a time when Taylor was desperately seeking "high caliber judges" to man the tribunals.[90] Musmanno came to Taylor's attention as soon as he arrived because Musmanno had decided to write a book about the last days of the war and to do so he needed to interview former Nazis, most of who were in US custody. To gain access to them he had to be introduced to Taylor. Between September 1946 and May 1948, Musmanno interviewed more than 200 witnesses to Hitler's last days—including his young secretary Traudl Junge—that culminated in his 1951 book *Ten Days to Die*.[91] There was some concern about the "appropriateness of [a] naval officer with the rank of commander sitting on [a] tribunal which may be called upon to try field marshals and high ranking generals," but because the OCCWC had a terrible time finding qualified judges and Musmanno was enthusiastic to serve on the bench, they made him an alternate.[92] Not long thereafter, on December 14, 1946, the Deputy Military Governor, Lucius Clay elevated him to the position of full-time member of Tribunal II which was convened to hear the case against Field Marshall Erhard Milch.[93]

The Milch case (January 2, 1947–April 17, 1947) was Musmanno's initiation into the Nuremberg trial system. It was the first case he heard and, as was to become the pattern, he completely engrossed himself in the trial paying close attention to all of its details. The Milch trial was unusual in so far as it was the only NMT to have one single defendant in one single trial. Milch was a German Field Marshal and second to Goering in the Air Force who was indicted by the Americans for war crimes and crimes against humanity largely for his role in the slave labor program.[94] The tribunal, under the leadership of Robert M. Toms, found Milch guilty on all counts. Given the unanimity of the tribunal's decision, it is strange that Musmanno decided to write a concurring opinion, certainly nothing in the Nuremberg guidelines said he had to do this. Judge Fitzroy D. Phillips also wrote a concurring opinion, yet his was but a fraction of the length of Musmanno's.[95] Compared to his fiction writing, Musmanno's judgment in the Milch case is well written and insightful, illustrating his deep interest in the trial. Following the Milch case, Musmanno was appointed to serve as a judge in the case against Oswald Pohl who was the head of the SS Economic and Administration Main Office, more commonly known as the WVHA. Again Musmanno wrote a very long, but astute concurring opinion which offers a fairly cohesive view of the Nazi extermination process.[96] While still working on the Pohl case, Taylor asked Musmanno to preside over the *Einsatzgruppen* trial. Not one to put his personal life before his professional one, he jumped at the chance to make history and he was appointed presiding judge for Tribunal IIA.[97]

Musmanno was in his element at Nuremberg. He worked very hard. From opening statements through sentencing, he presided over the *Einsatzgruppen* trial as if he had a personal stake in it. He had no trouble whatsoever establishing his total authority in the courtroom, a sign that he was both comfortable in his role as presiding judge as well as being intensely interested in the course of the trial. Unlike his two colleagues on the bench (John Speight and Richard Dixon) who, according to Ferencz, slept through the trial,[98] Musmanno seemed enlivened by the day-to-day business of the court, listening intently to every word and actively engaging in all elements of the proceedings.[99] In part because of his legal training as a defense attorney and in part because of the perceived miscarriage of justice against Sacco and Vanzetti, Musmanno afforded the defense a tremendous amount of leeway by flouting the rules of evidence and allowing them to submit any and all evidence that might prove the innocence of their clients, including the sex life of the Antarctic penguin.[100] As Ferencz described the practice, "every defendant would present bushels of affidavits from distinguished Germans lying through their teeth ... and Musmanno would say they were 'admissible'" regardless of the circumstances.[101] Exercising his discretion and bending the rules of procedure was typical behavior for Musmanno, prompting the defense attorneys to commission a one and a half foot brass penguin which they presented to Musmanno at the conclusion of the trial in appreciation of his now famous "Penguin Rule."[102]

Where Musmanno really left his mark, though, was in his role as cross-examiner. It was his proclivity to showmanship coupled with a genuine interest in the trial that prompted him to become involved in the case on a daily basis.[103] Cross-examination is normally the job of the prosecution, and while they often started the process, they rarely were able to finish because the presiding judge would step in and take over. As the conservative German weekly *Die Zeit* reported, "Musmanno is master in cross-examination, of an incorruptible sense of justice and the only judge in Nuremberg to whom the defendants prior to the judgment expressed their thanks for the manner in which he conducted the trial"; no small tribute from a German press known more for their harsh criticism of Nuremberg than their praise.[104] The record shows from the beginning Musmanno had been an exceptionally active participant in all proceedings, and questioned witnesses regularly. Ferencz did not seem to mind that the judge stepped in to question witnesses—after all the judges at Nuremberg were afforded the right to do so—what annoyed him so much was the manner in which he did it. Whereas Ferencz was trying to "convey a somber atmosphere" in the court, Musmanno would "jump in with some joke [or] break into spontaneous Italian, and his rulings always favored the defense."[105] What is undeniable though, is that Musmanno was often more able to cut to the chase of defendant testimony to illustrate the weaknesses in their defense.

The first and most confident defendant to take the stand was Ohlendorf. Ferencz did not want to question Ohlendorf himself, so he gave the task to James Heath, who Ferencz and Musmanno both describe as a "tall and handsome ... Southern gentleman."[106] Ohlendorf proved more than Heath could handle though. Apparently Heath was not at the top of his game, and was on the verge of being fired as a prosecuting attorney because of a personal problem that compromised his ability to do his job effectively.[107] No one else was prepared to step in either. The chief of the prosecution team, Ferencz, had graduated from Harvard Law School, but at age twenty-seven he had never had the opportunity to try a single criminal case, let alone prosecute a case against major war criminals.[108] Even the more experienced members of Ferencz's team were unprepared to deal with the likes of Ohlendorf. Peter Walton and John Glancy, were "cast-offs," unwanted by the prosecution teams in other trials and were picked up by Ferencz when, at the eleventh hour, the leaders of the mobile killing units were indicted, but Ferencz remembers them as lazy.[109] Why Arnost Horlick-Hochwald was not given the task is anyone's guess. He was the most experienced trial lawyer on the team and according to Ferencz, really the "only good" lawyer assigned to the case, but he was also Jewish so this may have influenced Ferencz's decision.[110] In any case, the purpose of cross-examination is to challenge the credibility of witness testimony; a good cross-examiner can detect inconsistencies, weaknesses, exaggeration and lies and make them apparent to the court. No one on Ferencz's team seemed up to this challenge, which opened the door for an activist judge like Musmanno to step in. This is exactly what happened.

More often than not, Musmanno was totally unsatisfied with the answers of the defendants and his questioning led to some memorable moments at trial. For instance, when Heath asked Ohlendorf about the morality of the Führer-order to kill all Jews, Ohlendorf responded that orders are orders; he never considered the matter one way or the other, he simply carried out the order because it was his duty.[111] Completely unsatisfied with this answer, Musmanno stepped in to test the veracity of Ohlendorf's defense. In what was to become a pattern of questioning, he posed a hypothetical question to the defendant: he asked Ohlendorf if he had been given the order to kill his sister, would he not have considered "whether it was right or wrong—morally—not politically or militarily, but as a matter of humanity, conscience, and justice between man and man?"[112] In classic Ohlendorf double-speak, he told the judge that his question was like comparing apples and oranges, "it brings a completely private matter into a military one; that is, it deals with two events which have nothing to do with one another."[113] Musmanno grew visibly angry, but Ohlendorf refused to budge, his defense rested on the issue of superior orders, so yes, if he were ordered to, he *would* kill his sister.[114]

Ohlendorf was not like other defendants. He did not seem easily rattled and he genuinely seemed able to divorce himself from his immoral actions. Many people came to court just to see him, a mass murderer whose story had been widely reported in newspapers. Musmanno recalled that he had a certain appeal and some women even "sought to pass him notes offering encouragement and endearment."[115] Most notable, though, was Ohlendorf's gift of speech. As Musmanno recalled, Ohlendorf had the narrative talents of a professional storyteller, his testimony was "erudite and profound," and resembled a philosophy professor more than a man pleading for mercy.[116] Ohlendorf was not an easy defendant to contend with, he appeared very confident on the stand which gave him an air of credibility, and as hard as the prosecution tried, they could not get him to admit he had done anything wrong let alone break his defense of superior orders. Not all defendants were as strong or convincing as Ohlendorf, and when Musmanno got hold of them, many crumpled under his persistent and sometimes angry questioning. One of the most dramatic examples came during Musmanno's cross-examination of Paul Blobel.[117]

Blobel was one of the most notorious of all the *Einsatzgruppen* leaders. As head of *Sonderkommando 4A*, he had supervised the largest killing spree on the eastern front, the Babi Yar massacre of September 29–30, 1941 in which 33,771 Jews were murdered in a ravine just outside the Ukrainian city of Kiev. In an attempt to justify his role in reprisal killings in the Soviet Union, and to illustrate they were a natural part of war, Blobel defiantly pointed out that it was a "well known fact" that General Dwight Eisenhower had ordered reprisal killings at a ratio of 200 Germans for every one American killed. A fierce nationalist, Musmanno was outraged by Blobel's claim and demanded to know exactly where Blobel got this figure. Blobel stated matter-of-factly that "all of Germany knew it." Musmanno demanded proof. Blobel could not provide any first-hand evidence, nor could any of his co-accused when asked. Even Blobel's attorney denied knowledge of such an order. One by one, Musmanno went around the courtroom and questioned all of the German attorneys and sure enough, not one of them admitted knowledge about Eisenhower's reprisal order. Looking for contrition, and perhaps a little blood, Musmanno obliterated Blobel's testimony when he asked him one last time if he could name a single person who had seen such an announcement. Utterly deflated, Blobel stated he could not and begged for Musmanno's "pardon."[118] Described as "one of the most able examinations in courtroom history," Musmanno's cross-examination of Paul Blobel firmly established his domination in the courtroom.

Musmanno's natural inclination toward showmanship, and his years of experience as a defense attorney not to mention his acting career, served him well on the bench at Nuremberg. But memories of the Sacco-Vanzetti execution still haunted him and when the time came to pass judgment, he was forced to seek spiritual council to come to terms with the horrible "realization" that he would be "required to impose the death sentence on some of the defendants."[119] According to his memoirs, it was almost more than Musmanno could bear; in the solitude of the monastery where he stayed though, he was able to make peace with his decision.[120] He decided that he would only sentence to death those he was certain were guilty of murder and that meant they had had to admit to their crimes on the stand. If a defendant did not admit to wrongfully killing at least one person, he would not pass a sentence of death. Shocking as this might seem given he had accepted the job knowing full-well that he might be required to impose sentences of death, his decision was in keeping with his long-standing view of the possible mistakes of the American judicial system. Musmanno's decision of course meant that Ohlendorf would receive the death penalty as he had admitted to supervising the murder of 90,000 civilians while he was head of *Einsatzgruppe D*. That he was willing to place his own sentencing standards above those of the law he had sworn to uphold may be one of the reasons he was later singled out for "sloppy" verdicts and legal decisions.[121] At the time though, he was praised for his legal opinion. In the end, along with Ohlendorf he sentenced thirteen others to death, he handed out two life sentences, released one defendant with time-served, and the remaining defendants were given varying degrees of incarceration. Under the circumstances, this was as fair a sentencing as the defendants had any right to expect—and, one might add, a degree of conscientious action none of them had shown to their victims.

## Historical Narratives and the *Einsatzgruppen* Trial

Unlike any of the other Nuremberg trials, the *Einsatzgruppen* trial was the first and arguably only war crimes trial to deal exclusively with individuals whose sole job was their participation in the genocidal murder of the Jews, making it significant in the history of the Third Reich and the Holocaust. To be sure, the other eleven trials dealt with crimes against the Jews, but only the *Einsatzgruppen* trial focused almost exclusively on the "Final Solution to the Jewish Question".[122] From opening statement to closing, the trial was devoted to constructing a narrative of Nazi genocide and the *Einsatzgruppen*'s role in it; the prosecution's interpretation combined with Ohlendorf's testimony was central to producing this narrative. It was a simple and powerful story in which Hitler's hatred of the Jews and his orders to the SS—the so-called *Führerbefehl*—led directly to their murder and, unlike in the other NMT that focused on other agencies of murder, the villains in this story were hybrids; men who gave orders to kill and who also ensured the orders were carried out in the field. Our historical understanding of the "Final Solution" and the *Einsatzgruppen*'s role in it was shaped by the trial and its participants; the prosecutors and the way they conceived of the role of the *Einsatzgruppen* in the murder of the Jews contributed to subsequent historical interpretations, most especially though, our understanding of the genesis of the Final Solution was articulated by Ohlendorf, whose narrative of the events still has currency today.

The genesis of orders to the *Einsatzgruppen* is a source of some debate among historians of the Final Solution, largely because we have no documentary record of the decision-making process.[123] In 1945 though, Ohlendorf left no doubt that the decision to "exterminate all Jews" was made before June 1941 and "by Hitler directly" and that Himmler repeated Hitler's orders orally on two occasions, once in May 1941 (four weeks before the *Einsatzgruppen* were deployed), and then again in September when he visited the front.[124] Ohlendorf made it perfectly clear who was in charge of killing operations. The *Einsatzgruppen*, he explained repeatedly, were controlled by higher authorities; Hitler, Himmler, and Heydrich were their bosses.[125] Ohlendorf remained faithful to this story during his entire incarceration, never once deviating from it. Because of a lack of documented facts available to the prosecution and the tribunal, when he told about the order by Hitler, the so-called *Führerbefehl* to murder all Soviet Jews, men, women, and children, no one doubted him and besides, it also reinforced their own pre-existing ideas about the hierarchy of the Third Reich. It especially reinforced their assumption that all decisions pertaining to racial policy and the Jews came directly from Hitler.[126] In other words, the judges and the prosecutors believed Ohlendorf's claim that the *Führerbefehl* was *the* directive, given by Hitler, to kill all Soviet Jews because murder on such a grand scale could not be accidental, but rather it had to be premeditated.[127]

In the absence of documentary evidence, Ohlendorf's testimony established a version of the Final Solution that was clearly hierarchical and premeditated—what in the historiography is referred to as "intentionalist".[128] According to Ohlendorf, Hitler, Himmler, and Heydrich were at the center of the decision-making process and the members of the killing units had little or no agency—rather they were as Ohlendorf told his captors, simply following orders. His co-defendants reinforced the 'obedience to superior orders' defense as one by one, they took the stand and told the court that even though they deeply respected Hitler, they had no power to alter his decisions; rather they were, as one defendant significantly noted, "small wheel[s] in a large machinery," with no choice but to obey.[129] The idea that the murder of the Jews was a large and complex bureaucratic process carried out by the SS and SD on the orders of Hitler was persuasive and influenced some of the most prominent postwar scholars such as Helmut Krausnick, Martin Broszat, Lucy Dawidowicz, and Leon Poliakov.[130] The trial especially influenced the work of Raul Hilberg who used its records to explain the machine-like nature of the destruction process.[131]

In the history of the historiography of the Holocaust, there is no question that the *Einsatzgruppen* trial occupies an important place. The trial provides a relatively in-depth and descriptive narrative of the crimes perpetrated in the USSR and the Baltic states during World War II that came directly from the perpetrators themselves. The legal and procedural norms that governed the *Einsatzgruppen* trial may have distorted our historical understanding of certain elements of the Final Solution, but the law did not get everything wrong. Broadly speaking, it recognized that the racial crimes of the Third Reich were not solely the responsibility of one man; rather it highlighted just how many people and agencies were required to carry out Hitler's vision. Along with distinct and sometimes contradictory narratives, the Nuremberg trials also produced courtroom personalities. Ohlendorf, Ferencz, and Musmanno all contributed their own unique characteristics to this historically important trial. Ohlendorf is remembered for his guile, Ferencz for his tenacity, and Musmanno for his showmanship. In the end though, it was Ohlendorf's contribution that proved most noteworthy. For better or for worse, he was the dominant figure in the trial, and it is his description of events that has had the most significant impact on the historiography of the Final Solution.

# Notes

1. Michael Musmanno, *The Eichmann Kommandos* (London, 1962), 93. *Der Spiegel* reported that Ohlendorf, together with Hjalmar Schacht, scored the highest marks on the IQ tests administered to the Nuremberg prisoners. See "Absolut Notwendig," *Der Spiegel*, February 7, 1948, Navy File 2140, Personal Papers of Michael Angelo Musmanno, Gumberg Library, Duquesne University, Pittsburgh (henceforth MMP).
2. Musmanno, *Eichmann Kommandos*, 93.
3. For example, see letter from J. Edgar Hoover to Musmanno, July 25, 1957 in MMP, Anti Communist File 1288.
4. His books include: *Black Fury, Proposed Amendments to the Constitution, After Twelve Years, Listen to the River, Ten Days to Die, The Soldier and the Man, Across the Street from the Courthouse, The Eichmann Kommandos, Justice Musmanno Dissents, Verdict!, The Story of the Italians in America, World War II in Italy, An American Replies, Columbus was First, That's my Opinion,* and *The Glory and the Dream.*
5. Memorandum, Musmanno to Naval Staff Personnel Officer, December 12, 1946, MMP, Navy file 2340.
6. Alluding to the theatrical nature of the courtroom, Musmanno said, "All the world's a court and its men and women merely judges and defendants," undated letter, MMP, Nuremberg Correspondence file 1445.
7. Interview with Benjamin Ferencz, April 24, 1997.
8. Ibid.
9. Musmanno, *Eichmann Kommandos*, 60.
10 Case Record of Otto Ohlendorf, April 27, 1948 in NARA RG 338, Judge Advocate Division (JAD), WCB, Records of Executed Prisoners, 1946–1951, Box 9, Folder Ohlendorf. On the arrest of the personnel of the RSHA Office III SD Domestic, see Michael Wildt, *Generation des Unbedingten: Das Führungskorps des Reichssicherheitshauptamtes* (Hamburg, 2003), 731–45.
11. Lebenslauf des Otto Ohlendorf, in Personalbericht, in NARA RG 242, Berlin Document Center (BDC), A3342 SSO-356A, frame 862, 866. Ohlendorf was a witness for

the prosecution of Ernst Kaltenbrunner and testified for the first time at Nuremberg in January 1946.

12. Ibid., 866; Letter from Heydrich to Himmler, October 2, 1941, ibid., frame 892.

13. Letter from Ohlendorf, May 18, 1936, Personalbericht, ibid., frames 943–45.

14. Interrogation, Ohlendorf, November 9, 1945, NARA, M-1270, Interrogation Records, Roll 13.

15. Intelligence Report (Ohlendorf), CSDIC UK, September 30, 1945, NARA, RG 319, Records of the Army Staff, Records of the Office of the Assistant Chief of Staff, G-2, Security Classified Intelligence and Investigative dossiers, Box 165a, Folder Ohlendorf; Heinz Höhne, *The Order of the Death's Head: the Story of Hitler's SS* (New York, 1972), 356–57.

16. Hanno Sowade, "Otto Ohlendorf: Non-Conformist, SS leader, and Economic Functionary," in *The Nazi Elite*, eds. Ronald Smelser and Rainer Zitelmann (New York, 1993), 157. On the organizational history of the SD and RSHA, see Wildt, *Generation des Unbedingten*, 283–415.

17. Testimony, Ohlendorf, October 8, 1947, NARA, M-895, The United States of America v. Otto Ohlendorf et al. [Einsatzgruppen Trial Transcript], Roll 2, 489.

18. Wildt, *Generation des Unbedingten*, 11–12. For a complete history of Einsatzgruppe D and Ohlendorf's role in it, see especially Andrej Angrick, *Besatzungspolitik und Massenmord: Die Einsatzgruppe D in der südlichen Sowjetunion 1941–1943* (Hamburg, 2003); id., "Otto Ohlendorf und die SD-Tätigkeit der Einsatzgruppe D," in *Nachrichtendienst, politische Elite, Mordeinheit. Der Sicherheitsdienst des Reichsführers SS*, ed. Michael Wildt (Hamburg, 2003), 267–302.

19. See Hilary Earl, *The Nuremberg SS-Einsatzgruppen Trial, 1945–1958: Atrocity, Law, and History* (New York, 2009), 96–134 for a discussion of the social characteristics of the defendants in the trial.

20. Ulrich Herbert applied the term to Werner Best and his generation. See Ulrich Herbert, *Best. Biographische Studien über Weltanschauung, Radikalismus und Vernunft 1903–1989* (Bonn, 1996).

21. Wildt, *Generation des Unbedingten*, 24–25, 41–52.

22. Ibid., 72–80, 23–29.

23. Ibid., 11–14, 23–29; Wildt, "The Spirit of the Reich Security Main Office (RSHA)," *Totalitarian Movements and Political Religions* 6, 3 (2005), 339–40.

24. Wildt's *Generation des Unbedingten* was recently translated into English as *An Uncompromising Generation: The Nazi Leadership of the Reich Security Main Office*, trans. Tom Lampert (Madison, 2009).

25. "Chronological Record of Full Time Employment and Military Service," Ohlendorf Questionnaire, October 20, 1945, NARA, M-1270, Interrogation Records of War Crimes Proceedings at Nuremberg 1945–1947, Roll 13.

26. Ibid.; Interrogation Summary, October 24, 1945, NARA, M-1270, Roll 13; Angrick, *Besatzungspolitik und Massenmord*; id., "Otto Ohlendorf."

27. Case Record of Otto Ohlendorf, NARA, RG 338, JAD, WCB, Records of Executed Prisoners 1946–1951, Box 9, Folder Ohlendorf.

28. For detailed descriptions of Ohlendorf's confessions, see Earl, *The Nuremberg SS-Einsatzgruppen Trial*, 46–75; id., "Confessions of Wrong-doing or How to Save Yourself from the Hangman? An Analysis of British and American Intelligence Reports of the Activities of Otto Ohlendorf, May–December 1945," in *Secret Intelligence and the Holocaust*, ed. David Bankier (New York and Jerusalem, 2006), 301–26.

29. "Notes on Corruption and Corrupted Personalities in Germany," CSDIC (UK), August 11, 1945, PW Paper 133, SS-Gruppenführer Otto Ohlendorf, NARA, RG 319, Records of the Army Staff, Security Classified Intelligence and Investigative Dossiers, Box 165A, Folder Ohlendorf.

30. Wildman Smith Brookhart was Brookhart's father. Robert Conot, *Justice at Nuremberg* (New York, 1983), 233.

31. Ohlendorf was interrogated dozens of times.

32. For example, see the interrogations of Ohlendorf from October 24, 25, 26, 29, and 30; November 26, 1945, NARA, M-1270, Roll 13.

33. Conot, *Justice at Nuremberg*, 231–32; Testimony of Otto Ohlendorf, January 3, 1946, *Trial of The Major War Criminals before the International Military Tribunal, Nuremberg, 14 November 1945–1 October 1946 [IMT]*, IV (Nuremberg, 1947), 309–55.

34. Conot, *Justice at Nuremberg*, 233–35. For example, Raul Hilberg's *Destruction of the European Jews* relied heavily on the Nuremberg transcripts and documents.

35. Telford Taylor, *The Anatomy of the Nuremberg Trials: A Personal Memoir* (New York, 1992), 248–49. On the Göring–Jackson exchange, see Michael R. Marrus, *The Nuremberg War Crimes Trial 1945–1946: A Documentary History* (New York, 1997), 107–13.

36. Judgment, April 8, 1948, NARA, M-895, Einsatzgruppen Trial Transcript, Roll 7, 132.

37. Testimony of Ohlendorf, January 3, 1946, *TWC*, IV, 319–23.

38. Gustave M. Gilbert, *Nuremberg Diary* (New York, 1995), 101.

39. Hans Frank quoted in Taylor, *Anatomy of the Nuremberg Trials*, 248.

40. M. Cherif Bassiouni, "The History of Universal Jurisdiction and its Place in International Law," in *Universal Jurisdiction. National Courts and the Prosecution of Serious Crimes under International Law*, ed. Stephen Macedo (Philadelphia, 2004), 52.

41. For a discussion of their discovery, see Ronald Headland, *Messages of Murder: A Study of the Reports of the Einsatzgruppen of the Security Police and the Security Service, 1941–1943* (London, 1992), 11–15.

42. Letter Ferencz to Hilary Earl, February 27, 1997.

43. Ferencz has a website. See http://www.benferencz.org/index.php?id=1.

44. Ferencz is a well-known story-teller and his website contains podcasts of several of his favorites. See http://www.benferencz.org/index.php?id=8&section=1. Ferencz also gave a long oral history to the USHMM, RG 50.030*269, Interview with Benjamin B. Ferencz, August 26, 1994. I interviewed Ferencz twice, on April 24 and May 24, 1997.

45. Ferencz is the author of nine books, most of which concern international law, peace, and the establishment of a permanent international criminal court. See his website for a description of the books: http://www.benferencz.org/index.php?id=6&book=16

46. Robert Kempner also stayed in Nuremberg after the conclusion of the trials. See Dirk Pöppmann's chapter on Kempner in this volume. Ferencz tells the story of how he became involved in this organization on his web page: http://www.benferencz.org/index.php?id=8&story=37

47. For example, Ferencz, *An International Criminal Court: A Step Toward World Peace* (Oceana, 1975).

48. For example, listen to the interview with Ferencz by Joan Ringelheim at the USHMM in 1996: http://www.benferencz.org/index.php?id=5&media=8.

49. Biographical Data, Nuremberg Subsequent Proceedings, undated, NARA, RG 153, Judge Advocate General Army, War Crimes Branch, Nuremberg Administration files 1944–1949, Box 3, Book 5, 85-2.

50. Letter, Ferencz to Eugene Kaufman, Executive Director Hias, Baltimore, January 8, 1958, USHMM, RG 12.000, Benjamin B. Ferencz Collection (BBF), Drawer 11, Biographical Material, Folder A, Personal Correspondence. Glueck wrote, *The Nuremberg Trial and Aggressive War* (New York, 1946).

51. Interview with Ferencz, April 24, 1997 and Ferencz Oral History, USHMM, RG 50.030*269, Tape 1/3, August 26, 1994.

52. Letter, Ferencz to his wife Gertrude, February 20, 1945; Letter, May 15, 1945, USHMM, RG 12.000, BBF, Drawer 31 Einsatzgruppen Trial, Box 1, Folder J, Letters from Benjamin Ferencz to Gertrude 1945–1946.

53. Ferencz to James Heath and/or Drexel Sprecher, June 15, 1946, NARA, RG 238, Entry 192, Box 1, Folder 4. I want to thank Kim C. Priemel for kindly sharing this document with me.

54. Ibid.

55. Ibid.

56. For example, Ferenz told me about how he extracted information out of local Germans who had killed downed American fliers and it was very different. Interview with Ferencz, April 24, 1997.

57. Ibid.

58. Biographical Information and Material regarding Gertrude Ferencz, USHMM, RG 12.000, BBF, Drawer 11, Biographical Material, Box 1, Folder A, Gertrude Ferencz Biographical Material.

59. Ferencz was made the head of the Berlin Branch of OCCWC on August 16, 1946. Memorandum OCCWC Military Detachment to Ferencz, August 16, 1946, USHMM, RG 12.000, BBF, Drawer 11, Biographical Material, File C, Job related biographical material; Memorandum OCCWC to Ferencz, APO 124A US Army, August 26, 1946, NARA, RG 238, Entry 159, Box 4, Folder Mr. Ferencz.

60. "The Nuremberg Lawyers," *The National Law Journal* 17, 2 (1980), USHMM, RG 12.000, BBF, Drawer 11, Biographical Material, Box 2, Folder J, 2/2 News Clippings.

61. Interview with Ferencz, April 24, 1997.

62. Ferencz describes locating these documents and how the trial came to be in an interview he had with Joan Ringelheim of the US Holocaust Memorial Museum on October 5, 2004: http://www.benferencz.org/index.php?id=5&media=8

63. On how the trial was prepared, see Earl, *Nuremberg SS-Einsatzgruppen Trial*, 79–95.

64. Benjamin Ferencz, *Less than Slaves: Jewish Forced Labor and the Quest for Compensation* (Cambridge, MA, 1979), xv.

65. The list of defendants comprised:

| | |
|---|---|
| Jost, Heinz | Einsatzgruppe A |
| Naumann, Erich | Einsatzgruppe B |
| Rasch, Otto | Einsatzgruppe C |
| Ohlendorf, Otto | Einsatzgruppe D |
| Biberstein, Ernst | Einsatzkommando 6 |
| Blobel, Paul | Sonderkommando 4a |
| Braune, Werner | Einsatzkommando 11b |
| Blume, Walter | Sonderkommando 7a |
| Fendler, Lothar | Deputy Chief SKo 4b |
| Haensch, Walter | Sonderkommando 4b |
| Graf, Matthias | Officer Einsatzkommando 6 |
| Hausmann, Emil | Einsatzkommando 12 |
| Klingelhöfer, Waldemar | Vorkommando Moscow |
| Nosske, Gustav | Einsatzkommando 12 |
| Ott, Adolf | Einsatzkommando 7b |
| Radetzky, Waldemar von | Deputy Chief SKo 4a |
| Rühl, Felix | Officer Sonderkommando 10b |
| Sandberger, Martin | Sonderkommando 1a |
| Schulz, Erwin | Einsatzkommando 5 |
| Seibert, Willy | Deputy Chief Einsatzgruppe D |
| Six, Franz | Vorkommando Moscow |
| Steimle, Eugen | Sonderkommando 7a & 4a |
| Strauch, Eduard | Einsatzkommando 2 |
| Schubert, Heinz | Officer Einsatzgruppe D |

66. According to Musmanno, *Eichmann Kommandos*, 60, "Ferencz divided the prosecution trial work among four lawyers. He himself undertakes the responsibility of presenting the evidence against the defendants who belonged to Einsatzgruppe B,

and Walton is to handle Einsatzgruppe D. John E. Glancy [sic] will prosecute the members of Einsatzgruppe A and Arnost Horlick-Hochwald Einsatzgruppe C."

67. Interview with Ferencz, April 24, 1997.

68. The prosecution of Milch took eight full days. See Milch case, "Introduction," *TWC*, II, 355.

69. For an in-depth discussion of Musmanno's career, see Earl, *Nuremberg SS-Einsatzgruppen Trial*, 217–64.

70. Musmanno and the Modification of the 1794 Sunday Laws of Pennsylvania, MMP, loose documents.

71. Biographical Outline, Pennsylvania Supreme Court, Justice Michael A. Musmanno, MMP, Biographical January–June 1968, file 940.

72. Michael Musmanno, *Verdict! The Adventures of the Young Lawyer in the Brown Suit* (New York, 1963), 28–29; Julia Edwards, "Sailor on the Bench," *Weekend Gazette*, April 24, 1948, MMP, Nuremberg Clippings file 2150.

73. Musmanno, *Proposed Amendments to the Constitution* (Washington, DC, 1929).

74. With the exception of *The Eichmann Kommandos*, Musmanno's books are not readily available at most libraries. The Library of Congress has a complete set of his books as does the Duquesne University archive that houses Musmanno's papers.

75. Letter from Henry Lea to Benjamin Ferencz, December 10, 1989, USHMM, BBF, 12.000.

76. Letter, Robert (last name illegible) to Alvin Rockwell, OMGUS, July 21, 1948, Harry S. Truman Library (HST), Alvin Rockwell Papers.

77. Musmanno, *Eichmann Kommandos*, 11–24.

78. Ibid., 38–40.

79. "US Judge Stirs Eichmann Trial," *The New York Times*, May 16, 1961, MMP, Loose Documents.

80. *Black Fury* was a film produced by Warner Brothers in 1935 and in 1966 Musmanno turned the story into a book.

81. Musmanno, *Verdict!*, 239–93.

82. Musmanno had been a member of the American League to Abolish Capital Punishment since 1925, but became more active after the execution of Sacco and Vanzetti in 1927. See Musmanno, "Is it Possible to Execute Innocent Men?" Address to the annual conference of the American League to Abolish Capital Punishment, New York, April 26, 1940, MMP, Capital Punishment file 1477.

83. For example, see Musmanno's letter to Benjamin Ferencz, April 13, 1948, USHMM, 12.000, BBF, Drawer 11 Biographical Material, Box 1, Folder c, in which he writes, "Your letter brought tears to my eyes. That one who represented the Prosecution so ably and vigorously should understand and appreciate the intolerable burden of the judge in imposing the sentence of ultimate penalty, is something that moves me deeply."

84. Musmanno, "Death Penalty does not Prevent Crime," Letter to the Editor, in *New York Herald Tribune*, May 1963, MMP, Capital Punishment file 1477.

85. For example, see exchange of letters between Musmanno and J. Edgar Hoover 1959–1960, MMP, Anti Communist file 1288.

86. Memorandum, Musmanno to Naval Staff Personnel Officer, December 12, 1946, MMP, Navy file 2340.

87. Musmanno, notes to himself, undated, MMP, Soviet Board file 1101.

88. "Musmanno Transferred from Italy to Austria," *Pittsburgh Gazette*, July 28, 1945, MMP, Scrapbook 1946–1949, Loose Documents.

89. Memorandum from Commander Talbot to unidentified person, May 12, 1946, MMP, Navy file 2340.

90. Memorandum Nr. 4038 from Taylor to Jackson, September 2, 1946, in Library of Congress, Robert H. Jackson Papers (RHJ), Box 110, Nuremberg War Crimes Trial, Office file, US Chief of Counsel, Folder 2 Subsequent Trials.

91. Copies of these interviews are available in Musmanno's archive at Duquesne University.
92. Memorandum, secret, from Taylor to War Department, November 21, 1946 and cable to AGWAR from OMGUS, November 20, 1946, NARA, RG 466, Box 10, War Crimes Trials, Folder Correspondence 1946–1947, HICOG, Prisons Division, Security Segregated Records 1945–1947.
93. Memorandum from Lucius D. Clay to Musmanno, December 14, 1946, MMP, Navy file 2340.
94. Milch case, Indictment, *TWC*, II, 360.
95. Milch case, Concurring Opinion of Judge Michael A. Musmanno, ibid., 797–859.
96. Pohl case, Concurring Opinion of Judge Michael A. Musmanno, *TWC*, V, 1064–1167. See Jan Erik Schulte's and Alexa Stiller's chapters in this book for further discussion.
97. Memorandum from Clay to Musmanno, September 10, 1947, MMP, Navy file 2340.
98. This may or may not be accurate, but what is certain is these two have minimal presence in the transcript of the trial.
99. Interview with Ferencz, April 24, 1997.
100. Musmanno, *Eichmann Kommandos*, 246–47.
101. Interview with Ferencz, April 24, 1997.
102. The brass penguin can be found in Musmanno's archive at Duquesne University. Musmanno, *Eichmann Kommandos*, 243–44.
103. Musmanno, *Eichmann Kommandos*, 82–83.
104. Untitled newspaper clipping, *Die Zeit*, April 1, 1948, MMP, General Lucius D. Clay file 1138.
105. Interview with Ferencz, April 24, 1997.
106. Ibid.; Musmanno, *Eichmann Kommandos*, 60.
107. Interview with Ferencz, April 24, 1997.
108. Despite the fact that the *Einsatzgruppen* trial was Ferencz's first case, he told the present author that he was not nervous, but incredibly confident of his abilities. See Interview with Ferencz, April 24, 1997.
109. Ferencz states that Heath was a good lawyer, but was unable to "get down to the task" because of a drinking problem. Ferencz also recalled that, while Glancy and Walton were decent people, they "were not competent lawyers." When the transcript of the trial was published in 1951, Heath was not listed as part of the prosecution team in the *Einsatzgruppen* case, but was instead referred to as "consultant." See Prosecution Counsel, *TWC*, IV, 11.
110. Letter from Benjamin B. Ferencz, February 27, 1997, 1 and interview with Ferencz, April 24, 1997.
111. Testimony, Ohlendorf, October 9, 1947, NARA, M-895, Einsatzgruppen Trial Transcript, Roll 2, 631–633.
112. Cross-examination of Ohlendorf by Musmanno, October 15, 1947, ibid., Roll 2, 750.
113. Testimony, Ohlendorf, October 15, 1947, ibid., Roll 2, 752.
114. Ibid., my emphasis.
115. Musmanno, *Eichmann Kommandos*, 106–7.
116. Ibid., 248.
117. Letter from Noah Jacobs, Office Chief of Counsel War Crimes to Charles Denvers, in *The Pittsburgh Post-Gazette*, December 29, 1947, MMP, Nuremberg Correspondence file 1445.
118. Cross-examination of Blobel by Musmanno, October 30, 1947, NARA, M-895, Einsatzgruppen Trial Transcript, Roll 3, 1728–1732.
119. Musmanno, *Eichmann Kommandos*, 253.
120. Ibid., 254–55.
121. Judge Peck quoted in Thomas Alan Schwartz, "Die Begnadigung deutscher Kriegsverbrecher: John J. McCloy und die Häftlinge von Landsberg," *Vierteljahrshefte für Zeitgeschichte* 38, (1990), 394, note 60.

122. For example, Case 1, the doctor's trial dealt with crimes committed against civilians in the form of medical experiments and the euthanasia program and the RuSHA trial—Case 8, dealt with crimes against a wide variety of groups, including Poles and Jews. Cf. Paul Weindling's and Alexa Stiller's chapters in this book.

123. For example, Jürgen Matthäus, "A Case of Myth-Making: The 'Führer-Order' during the Einsatzgruppen Trial, 1947–1948," unpublished article, the United States Holocaust Memorial Museum, 1–20 is skeptical about when the decision was made and believes that the genesis of the idea of a "Führerbefehl" comes from Ohlendorf. He is not alone. Many historians believe that the decision to murder all Soviet Jews did not happen until at least August 1941. See Klaus-Michael Mallmann, "Die Türöffner der 'Endlösung,'" in *Die Gestapo in Zweiten Weltkrieg: 'Heimfront' und besetztes Europa*, eds. Gerhard Paul and Klaus-Michael Mallmann (Darmstadt, 2000), 437–38.

124. Summary of morning interrogation of Otto Ohlendorf, October, 1945, Nuremberg, NARA, M-1270, Roll 13, 3; Evening interrogation of Ohlendorf, October 24, 1945, 7–8; 14–15, ibid. See also Letter to Colonel Amen from Lt. Col. S.W. Brookhart, October 24, 1945, ibid., 1.

125. Ibid.; Summary of morning interrogation, Otto Ohlendorf, October 25, 1945, Nuremberg, NARA, M-1270, Roll 13, 1–2.

126. As the prosecution noted in their opening statement, "They put their faith in Hitler and their hope in his regime." Opening Statement of the Prosecution, *TWC*, IV, 31.

127. Ibid.

128. I have also seen it referred to as the Nuremberg interpretation and Nuremberg historiography.

129. Testimony, Werner Braune, November 25, 1947, NARA, M-895, Einsatzgruppen Trial Transcript, Roll 4, 3035 and 3047–48.

130. Leon Poliakov used the Nuremberg documents for his study, *Harvest of Hate*, published in 1954. Helmut Krausnick and Martin Broszat in their early study of the regime, *Anatomy of the SS State*, translated by Dorothy Long and Marian Jackson (Frogmore, 1973) originally published in 1965 as *Anatomie des SS-Staates*, used the Nuremberg documents as did Lucy S. Dawidowicz, *The War against the Jews, 1933–1945* (New York, 1975).

131. Raul Hilberg used "nearly forty thousand prosecution documents" including documents from the Einsatzgruppen trial to write his masterful, *The Destruction of the European Jews* (1961). See Hilberg, *The Politics of Memory: The Journey of a Holocaust Historian* (Chicago, 1996), 70. Hilberg's revised and definitive edition was published in 1985 as 3 volumes and is slightly different than the original. This essay uses the 1961 version.

CHAPTER 3

# VICTIMS, WITNESSES, AND THE ETHICAL LEGACY OF THE NUREMBERG MEDICAL TRIAL

*Paul Weindling*

❦

## The "Nameless Dead"

The victims of these crimes are numbered in the hundreds of thousands. A handful only are still alive; a few of the survivors will appear in this courtroom. But most of these miserable victims were slaughtered outright or died in the course of the tortures to which they were subjected. For the most part they are nameless dead. To their murderers, these wretched people were not individuals at all. They came in wholesale lots and were treated worse than animals. They were 200 Jews in good physical condition, 50 gypsies, 500 tubercular Poles, or 1,000 Russians. The victims of these crimes are numbered among the anonymous millions who met death at the hands of the Nazis and whose fate is a hideous blot on the page of modern history.[1]

Telford Taylor (Chief of Counsel for the US Nuremberg trials) delivered the above passage as part of an eloquent opening address for the "Medical case" on December 6, 1946. His evidence of the killings raised the problem of victims' testimony about harrowing experiments, often with a murderous and genocidal intention. Taylor accused defendants of a conspiracy to undertake scientized murder. He vividly delineated the racial mindset of the Nazi human vivisectors, as supplying new techniques of scientific "genocide," as part of the endeavor to engineer a new racial order.[2] His usage of the novel term of "genocide" conveyed the prosecution's view that racial aims underpinned the experiments, some taking a victim to the point of death, as part of the Nazi medically administered and sanctioned extermination policies. The Medical trial was intended to prosecute a key element of Nazi racial policy and mass murder.

Why the Medical trial was the first of the successor trials to the IMT at Nuremberg requires explanation. Here one has to take account of a remarkable set of circumstances at the level of high politics connected to the origins of the Cold War, as well as how war crimes investigators and scientific intelligence officers became shocked by Nazi atrocities in their encounters with survivors. Taken aback by the evidence of Nazi atrocities, Taylor was committed to ideas of justice for the victims of Nazi crimes. His role amounted to that of manager of a factory-scale legal organization at Nuremberg to produce justice. Although primarily interested in trials of German industrialists and the military high command, he needed a successful (but politically less contentious) trial to open the series, and the Medical trial with its incidents of experiments as hands-on murder and torture provided such an opening.[3]

Any analysis of the origins of the Medical trial has to weigh political expediency against the Allied commitment to human rights. War crimes investigators and those involved in the administering of justice had a mindset committed to humane values, which were formulated in response to the Nazi atrocities. The inhumanity of Nazi medicine gave the Allied investigators crucial insight into broader issues of power and policy in Nazi Germany. Former prosecuting lawyers such as John H.E. Fried (an expert on slave labor) argued that the Nuremberg trials presented fundamental evidence of the Holocaust.[4] Certainly, the International Military Tribunal (IMT) provided the definitive basis for the statistics of genocide.[5] The Allied effort to bring to justice the perpetrators of what the scientific intelligence officer, John Thompson, first called "medical war crimes" in November 1945 showed how agendas of biological and racial purification resulted in hands-on violence, torture, and acts of medically condoned destruction. Thompson's achievement was to focus attention of Allied scientific intelligence officers, and war crimes investigators on medical war crimes. By the summer of 1946, he and his collaborators in British, French and US war crimes investigation units had assembled enough evidence for the mounting of a trial of medical atrocities.[6]

The histories of the Nuremberg trials and other trials of Nazi atrocities are very often presented as a matter of decisions reached at a high political level, and of politicians interacting with senior military and judicial figures. The context appears one of political expediency, and analysis is restricted to courtroom proceedings. The Medical trial, however, requires a more ground up approach, as well as engaging with events and evidence outside the courtroom. Medical intelligence and war crimes officers interacted with survivors and witnesses of Nazi medical atrocities, and then lobbied military and political "high-ups" for arrest and prosecution of perpetrators. This broader approach means that defendants' and witness testimonies and affidavits provide insight into the implementation of the Holocaust, and the structures and exercise of power in Nazi Germany and its racial war.[7]

The mindset of key figures like prosecuting counsel and judges was shaped by events beyond the courtroom, not least by a wider discourse on the ethics of Nazi research. For those protagonists investigating evidence of criminality, the issue is more whether they received political support and resources for investigating racial atrocities. The Medical trial reveals that racial atrocities were investigated in some detail. Strong cases were made for the criminality of eugenic sterilization by X-rays, and "euthanasia" (inverted commas denote how the Nazi killings of the sick and mentally ill were coercive rather than involving any element of free choice). Indeed, plans for a second Medical trial at Nuremberg—to focus on geneticists—and the eventual prosecution of the *Einsatzgruppen* suggest that the American authorities continued to take a serious view of "genocide" (a new concept postulated by the lawyer Raphael Lemkin) and crimes against humanity.[8] While the trials may be seen as developing the laws on war and crimes against humanity, they have considerable significance as an attempt to bring to light the dynamics of Nazi power, and the motives of individual perpetrators, and the impact of atrocities on victims.

The historiography of the Medical trial falls into two camps. Holocaust historians have argued that Nuremberg was a flawed enterprise and that the US military lawyers and war crimes analysts did not bring the major culprits to trial, and that the quality of prosecution meant that major aspects of the Nazi criminality went unprosecuted. The alternative position is that the trials did indeed bring to light major aspects of Nazi criminality, and that although necessarily selective in terms of who was available for prosecution, the major contours of the Nazi racial endeavor were revealed. Here a crucial issue revolves around the witnesses, who were either the research subjects, or who were prisoners involved in carrying these out or, like the *"Arztschreiber"* (medical secretary) Eugen Kogon in Buchenwald and Hermann Langbein in Auschwitz, in documenting them.[9]

Historians have pointed out that non-Jews were the main witnesses at the IMT, as there was concern that Jewish evidence might be perceived as biased.[10] The historian Michael Marrus sees the IMT as dealing with the murder of European Jews in a sporadic and uneven manner. He is, moreover, categorical in criticizing the Medical trial as failing to tackle Nazi eugenics.[11] Such an argument is constructed from evidence at a high political level, rather than engaging with how war crimes investigators working in conjunction with victims made the Medical trial possible. For those at the grass roots of the evidence of criminality, the issue is more whether they received political support and resources for investigating racial atrocities, rather than the turning of a blind eye to the Holocaust. The evidence on genocide[12] deepens if we consult the trial documents, and expands immensely when one locates the relevant archives of the trial, as well as personal papers of expert witnesses and trial observers. Relying on the printed summary accounts in the "Green Series" published after the trials is simply insufficient. Study of the Medical trial requires consultation of the full trial proceedings as well as of a range of archives dealing with the trial, its preparation, and protagonists on the prosecution and defense side. Here one might mention the transcripts of pre-trial interrogations of defendants, the records of the Berlin Document Center team who worked closely with the prosecutors, and the papers of the French medical observer, François Bayle at the Archives de France as containing US prosecutors' correspondence, and the gathering of victims' testimonies of first-hand experiences. The documentary basis for the Medical trial shows Marrus's depiction, based on the published digest on the Medical trial, as flawed.

The notion of the denial of a specifically Jewish "voice" raises the question how far the documents approach of the US prosecution marginalized the victims. Certainly the prosecution spent time reading into the court record documents that they hoped would lead to conviction, while the German defense lawyers were able to question veracity and meaning. The so-called "Diary" of the Buchenwald bacteriologist, Erwin Ding-Schuler is an example of a contested source. The prosecutors considered that the victims could positively sway the judges through allowing victims to speak, and in the case of the gashed and wounded legs of the sulphonamide experiment victims create a positive impact on the judges. Yet the prosecutors certainly selected for strategic reasons the persons whose voice might best convince the tribunal. On the other hand, witnesses from a broad range of backgrounds, including Jewish and Roma, gave voice to their experiences. The question thus arises as to whether the victims were marginal to the mainly documents-based prosecution.

The further question arises to what extent the Medical trial was a self-contained event, one that dealt with a set of distinctive issues relating to ethical abuses of medical power? The alternative is whether the Medical trial prepared the way for prosecutions of racial policy, with other SS-related trials, namely the Race and Settlement, *Einsatzgruppen* and Pohl trials? Here, the Medical trial establishes an agenda concerned with racial atrocities, and the expectation would be of intersecting evidence and testimonies linking these trials.[13] One might also examine plans for a second Medical trial that was to deal with the racial anthropologist, Josef Mengele at Auschwitz and his links with the Kaiser Wilhelm Institutes in Berlin.

The continuing role of the Polish expatriate lawyer and genocide theorist, Raphael Lemkin, at the Nuremberg trials is telling evidence against the interpretation of the marginalizing of issues to do with genocide (as the wholesale physical and/or cultural extermination of an ethnic group) and (to use a later but more familiar term concerning Nazi racial killings of Jews, Roma, the mentally disabled, and other persecuted persons) of the Holocaust. The Chief Prosecutor at the IMT, Jackson, had appointed Lemkin as legal consultant. His appointment was continued by the US war crimes section under David "Mickey" Marcus—a pronounced sympathizer for Jewish causes. Lemkin contacted Marcus about "the participation of German Industrialists and Bankers in Genocide," citing the manufacture of Zyklon B, as well as the industrial organization of the killing installations in an effort to bridge the military-industrial paradigm with that of genocide.[14] Lemkin linked mass murder to biological and medical strategies to eradicate ethnic groups and cultures. His analysis of the biology of annihilation was especially significant for war crimes prosecutions of medical atrocities. He saw a German attempt to change "the balance of biological forces" to gain "numerical, physical and economic superiority". He condemned preventing births as a means of physically destroying any ethnic, racial, or religious group, and the forcible transfer of children to another group—both key features of Nazi racial and population policy.[15] Lemkin highlighted the racial dimensions of family and population policy, in which medical experts were massively involved.[16]

Lemkin's contacts with Jewish leaders in London in August 1945 led to inserting the charge of genocide in the Nuremberg indictment.[17] His encyclopedic concept of genocide covered "not only the destruction of the Jews and Poles but also gypsies," thereby reflecting the diversity of the ethnic background of the victims of the human experiments.[18] He saw the genocidal destruction of the Jews included human experiments, and this occurred within a broader historical and sociological framework. On September 28, 1945, Lemkin addressed a memo to Telford Taylor that the defendants at the IMT were responsible for cultural and physical genocide by lowering the victim groups' birth rate, and by policies of starvation and subjugation to unhealthy conditions.[19] He criticized the concept of "crimes against humanity" as tied to proving a conspiracy to commit medical atrocities, which for legal purposes were shown to amount to hands-on murder.[20]

In the spring and summer of 1946, Lemkin was in touch with both the British scientific intelligence initiative of the Field Intelligence Agency, Technical (FIAT), and the French war crimes authorities at the time of their initiatives on "medical war crimes" (a term introduced by the FIAT officer John Thompson).[21] These informal links have to be set against the legal parameters of the trials. By the time of the Medical trial, the polarity between the officially favored concept of "crimes against humanity" and genocide was apparent.[22] Lemkin triumphed at the General Assembly of the nascent United Nations. He lobbied delegates to the UN Economic and Social Council to condemn genocide as a crime under international law on December 11, 1946—just two days after the Medical trial opened.[23] Lemkin was keen to point out that the Nuremberg trials were no substitute for a Genocide Declaration, in that the Declaration was agreed by nations as equals to prevent and prosecute genocide. But he remained interested in the extent that the Nuremberg trials, and specifically the Medical trial, were genocide trials.

The expert witness—and medical adviser—for the prosecution at the Medical trial, Leo Alexander was on friendly terms with Lemkin. They had met at Duke University, North Carolina in 1941.[24] He promptly consulted "old Lemkin" in Washington on November 12, 1946, when he was given a batch of "genocidal material." Lemkin had just decided to resign from the US War Department, to devote himself full time to securing the United Nations Genocide Convention.[25] Lemkin's view was that the Medical case dealt with how genocide was implemented scientifically.[26] He argued, "by attaching the stigma of genocide to the acts of the defendants we will effectively preclude them from invoking the plea that their experiments were scientific."[27] He classed the Nazi doctors as "professional genocidists," who developed methods for realizing "the most hideous genocide program the world has ever witnessed." He included human experiments, and prevention of births, especially coerced sterilization as momentous chapters added by the Nazis to the long and still unfolding history of genocide. Medicine provided psychological conditioning for the killers "who regard their odious task as they would fighting a plague."[28]

Lemkin was pleased that Taylor used the term "genocide" in his opening address, and felt that the Medical trial was potentially a classic genocide case.[29] But he was disappointed that Taylor and the US prosecutors—following the lead Lemkin's fellow jurist Hersch Lauterpacht had given[30]—continued to use the generic accusation of crimes against humanity rather than the more specific charge of genocide as the basis for the Medical case—and indeed for ensuing cases. For this meant a missed opportunity to insert genocide into international law, and to prevent its recurrence. Taylor insisted that crimes against humanity as endorsed by Control Council Law No. 10 covered "persecutions on political, racial or religious grounds." As Taylor explained at a meeting in Paris on April 25, 1947, it was not a question of isolated acts of murder or violence but wholesale, nationwide campaigns "to make life intolerable for, to expel, to degrade, to enslave, or to exterminate large numbers of the civilian population."[31]

One limitation, which shaped the scope of what could be prosecuted but not on a consistent basis, was that cases could only involve crimes against Allied nationals. It meant that Nazi medical and racial abuses such as sterilization, whether legal or illegal, prior to the September 1939 onslaught against Poland, could not be prosecuted (unless the victims were non-German). Fortuitously, the wave of human experiments and coercive "euthanasia" coincided with the declaration of war in 1939. The court took the view that crimes had to be committed

against non-Germans; crimes against Germans being left to the jurisdiction of German courts.[32] Lemkin saw the weakness of tying crimes
against humanity closely to war crimes. However, he continued to be
esteemed as an authority on Nazi mass murder. In February 1947 Judge
Beals (the senior judge at the Medical trial) requested that the US War
Department provide him with a copy of Lemkin's book on *Axis Rule in
Occupied Europe*.[33] Lemkin was convinced that the human experiments
were designed to test mass killing techniques. This was a point on which
he and the prosecution medical expert, the neurologist Leo Alexander,
were in agreement. But when the defense case opened, the defendants
vehemently denied that the medical and poison gas experiments were
pilot exercises in mass annihilation, and the charge was seriously pursued
in the Nuremberg courts.

Lemkin wanted the utilization of Zyklon B prosecuted, and when the
trial was over the World Jewish Congress was concerned that the planners of genocide were not prosecuted.[34] Lemkin kept a critical eye on the
proceedings. On January 10, 1947, his memo on "the Importance of the
Genocide Concept for the Doctors Case" presented a devastating critique
by arguing that: "The Doctors case has nothing to do with the misuse of
human life for science." He warned that the trial should remain based on
the war crimes concept, rather than on violations of medical ethics involving the relationship between doctor and patient. An individual scientist
might stray from the canons of professional ethics—but "by attaching the
stigma of genocide to the acts of the defendants, we will preclude them
from effectively and justly from invoking the plea that their experiments
were scientific." For murder should not be camouflaged as science.[35] This
position was problematic in that by not recognizing the experiments
as part of the scientific endeavor of the Third Reich, the role of Nazi
research organizations like the German Research Foundation (*Deutsche
Forschungsgemeinschaft, DFG*) and the *Kaiser-Wilhelm-Gesellschaft*
(KWG), and associated academics would go unprosecuted. Lemkin hoped
that the prosecution would develop its case on the basis of the genocide
concept.[36] He criticized Alexander's term for the murderous nature of
the experiments as "thanatology" (the term conveying Alexander's view
of the Nazi "idolatrous (fiendish) delight in death."[37] Drawing on the
living space ideology of the geographer Karl Haushofer, Lemkin favored
a geopolitical and "genopolitical" approach (the latter concept betrayed
a biologistic strain in his analysis) to Nazi medical war crimes.[38] Lemkin considered that "geo-medicine" (a geographical approach to medicine
applying Haushofer's concept of geopolitics) had a key role in generating
murderous medical research, necessitating the need to link medicine to
plans for racial expansion.

The intentions of the trial were, first, to show how experiments were
pilot studies for Nazi mass killings, and, second, to expose the inhumanity of Nazi research ethics. Obtaining witness testimony was necessarily problematic. The prosecutors faced the challenge of overcoming

the silence of the dead, the stigma felt by violated victims, in order to make sense of medicalized murder and brutality. Yet, the prosecution was able to develop its case by means of victims at two levels. First, there were those victims who could testify that a particular defendant had abused, mishandled and grievously wounded them. Second, there was a group of concentration camp internees who had documented the procedures. In some cases these were the victims of the experiments themselves, but in others it was prisoner clerical staff like Eugen Kogon (author of the classic treatise dissecting the SS State, published in 1946[39]) or Gerrit H. Nales who compiled a list of the victims of typhus vaccine experiments at the concentration camp of Natzweiler. Although surviving victims were from experiments carried out in concentration camps, some experimental research was carried out in clinics. One medical location scrutinized was the anatomy institute in Strasbourg, with regard to the Jewish anatomical collection. This was linked to the camp of Natzweiler-Struthof where the killings were carried out. Other medical locations were mentioned in connection with concentration camp atrocities. The Robert Koch Institute was linked to the prosecution of the bacteriologist Gerhard Rose for vaccine experiments in Berlin.

We find a point of comparison between the American trials, based mainly on mining evidence from the mass of documents, with British war crimes trials, where witnesses gave crucial nuggets of evidence. The Medical trial's greater reliance on witnesses than the other Nuremberg trials can be explained by the considerable British input in terms of the preparation of the case and the defendants. British war crimes investigators, the forensic pathologist Keith Mant, and his military scientific intelligence contact John Thompson (formerly a US citizen but seconded to the British military via the Canadian Air Force) provided substantial evidence on which the trial was based. A prime example was the trial against Bruno Tesch conducted for supply of Zyklon B to Auschwitz, when Tesch was found guilty by courtroom cross-examination and witness testimony.[40] This contrasts to the IG Farben trial, when despite the massive documentation, the case failed on the crucial issue of the supply of Zyklon B to Auschwitz with intent to implement mass murder.[41] Another example is the British-administered Ravensbrück trial in Hamburg from December 5, 1946 to February 3, 1947. Among the defendants were camp doctors, nurses and prisoners accused of complicity in medical atrocities. Polish victims (Helena Dziedziecka, Helena Piasecka, Zofia Sokulska, and Maria Adamsk) gave evidence, and there was a highly vocal delegation of French camp survivors.[42]

A factor in the hybrid nature of the Medical case was that it was itself a composite of British evidence gathered against defendants for atrocities in the women's camp of Ravensbrück, an American case for the low pressure and freezing experiments which were perpetrated at Dachau concentration camp, and a French case for atrocities at Strasbourg and the camp of Natzweiler-Struthof in Alsace. In May 1946 a division of labor had been agreed between the Western Allies on the topic of "medical war crimes," itself a new concept coined by an Allied scientific intelligence officer, neurophysiologist John West Thompson in November 1945.[43] Thompson had raised the issue of the criminality of— he alleged—90% of German wartime research, and so set in motion the collecting of evidence of victims' injuries. An American with an Edin- burgh medical degree, his cosmopolitan background helped him liaise with the Western Allies, and Thompson staffed an office at the Grand Hotel Nuremberg for the duration of the Medical trial. He supplied and monitored evidence, and interrogated defendants. His colleague the military pathologist Keith Mant also assisted the US prosecutors in obtaining evidence. War crimes investigation units and scientific intelli- gence collaborated in taking of victims' testimonies.[44] The Medical case at Nuremberg was an outcome of inter-Allied collaboration. Taylor, for pragmatic reasons, took on board considerable prosecution prepared by British war crimes investigators, so as to start the series of high profile trials. While Taylor's priorities in these trials were really industrialists and the German high command, he considered the Medical trial a clear- cut case, suitable for starting the series of trials under his jurisdiction.

The prosecutors' main priority was to secure convictions of perpe- trators. The lawyers did not have a remit either to reconstruct the full extent of the experiments, to determine overall numbers of victims of medical atrocities, let alone to provide for care and compensation. Thompson, when British trial observer at Nuremberg, pointed out that the flaw in such a trial was that when a perpetrator was missing or no longer alive, their misdeeds could not be rendered legally accountable. An International Scientific Commission, instigated by Thompson and supported by the British and French, worked to gather documentation parallel to the trials with the brief of a full reconstruction of the totality of all Nazi human experiments.[45]

## The Search for Victims

Victims and prisoners had resisted and sabotaged experiments during the war. On liberation they also called for documentation and justice. The victims gathered evidence and gave accounts of their experiences to war crimes investigators. They took a significant role in the Medi- cal trial.[46] Taylor's team was energetic, when the decision was made in August 1946 to hold a Medical trial, recognizing the value of Thompson's documentation on human experiments. Taylor launched a dual strategy to sift through the documents amassed in the US-controlled Documents Centers in Berlin, Heidelberg, and Dachau, and to search for witnesses. The Americans understood that documents were authentic whereas testimony could be fabricated, especially when whole groups conspired to argue that what had gone on was innocuous. The use of documents placed the burden on the defense lawyers to disprove authenticity or to demonstrate that the prosecution was misinterpreting them. The incantation of documents into the court record dominated the proceedings. Deputy Prosecutor James McHaney reflected, "the documents were of their own making—and they came back to haunt them," by which he meant the Nazi scientists and medical bureaucrats.[47]

While documentary proof was considered to be of a higher order of reliability, the American authorities decided to collect affidavits from victims, and to field selected witnesses to develop the human side of their case. The prosecution contacted the "Victims of Fascism" organization for witnesses to the medical experiments.[48] The prosecutors made public appeals for testimonies on sterilization and castration, in particular in Czechoslovakia.[49] The Czechoslovak and Polish observers supported the Medical trial with witnesses and evidence. The Polish government facilitated the travel of the Ravensbrück women sulphonamide experiment victims—the self-styled "Rabbits"[50] whose legs were horribly wounded after the SS leader Reinhard Heydrich had been assassinated, and the orthopaedic surgeon Karl Gebhardt wanted to demonstrate that sulponamide drugs could not have saved Heydrich's life—as witnesses for the trial. The Polish observer at Nuremberg, Captain Acht, obtained evidence for the prosecution expert witness, Leo Alexander's resourceful assistant, Maryann Shelley, who was equipped with stocks of cigarette cartons to reward assistance.[51] Victims wrote spontaneously to the US prosecutors, particularly on the need to bring key perpetrators like Josef Mengele to trial.[52] However, the prosecution feared that testimony could be challenged as exaggerated.

Taylor devolved the Medical trial to the prosecutors McHaney and Alexander G. Hardy, assisted by the Czechoslovak (and incidentally Jewish) prosecutor Arnost Horlick-Hochwald for the "euthanasia" part of the case.[53] McHaney saw what happened on the ground in the concentration camps as less significant than that the experiments had high-level authorization. He later reflected, "I was not interested in that selection of who was to be cremated."[54] The Nuremberg prosecutors had their eye on the devastation inflicted by the German military, and the human experiments appeared as the significant characteristics of the Nazi "Behemoth" (the term of the political scientist Franz Neumann to denote the vast and illegal machinery of Nazi power), whereas they saw the grim slaughter in the concentration camps as essentially a matter of routine. But they did not ignore the racial master plan of resettlement and extermination. Strong cases were made for the criminality of X-ray and other forms of sterilization and "euthanasia," securing death sentences for the SS officials Karl Brandt and Viktor Brack.

The Nazi medical experiments intersected with the Holocaust in so far as Jewish victims, and especially women and children, were major targets of medical research at Auschwitz. The suffering of the Jewish victims was extensive, and experiments were often fatal, or the victims subsequently killed. Yet, prior phases of the Nazi experiments were directed against other groups of internees, so that the victims were drawn from many different nationalities, occupations, and age groups. Poles were certainly the largest group of victims. Polish and Czech Catholic priests were one important group, used for aviation and freezing experiments. At the time (and until today), there were varying estimates of numbers of victims and who they were. The SS administrator, overseeing the concentration camps, Oswald Pohl spoke of 300–400 victims in a series of only eight experiments in concentration camps, whereas the prosecutors alleged hundreds of thousands of victims.[55] Certainly, prosecutors had no way of judging how representative witnesses were of the overall numbers of victims.

## Selection of Witnesses for Court

Witnesses were carefully selected for the impact they would make on the judges. A listing of the witnesses for the prosecution is presented in Table 3.1, broken down by sex and ethnicity in Table 3.2. The neurologist Leo Alexander prepared lengthy briefing papers on witnesses for the prosecutors. The prosecution wanted witnesses to be articulate and alert, and to come across as previously healthy individuals who had been grievously injured by the experiments. Prominence was given to "the Polish girls" as star witnesses at the Medical trial. They were eloquent and good looking. Publicity shots showed Władysława Karolewska, Jadwiga Dzido, Maria Kuśmierczuk and Maria Broel-Plater, arriving, and giving evidence (see Figure 3.1). The US press campaign was a means of obtaining public support for the trials, and revulsion against the accused for having gratuitously violated priests, students, and individuals who were clearly victims of an unjust regime.

These self-styled experimental "rabbits" had a good claim to prominence, by virtue of their articulate protest against the experiments. They had courageously protested at Ravensbrück against the experiments as a violation of their human rights and as prisoners of war, and repeatedly challenged the authority of the camp commandant. The reading of documents, and contests over authenticity and validation, were punctuated by chilling testimony from witnesses. The four Ravensbrück "rabbits" were selected as intelligent young women. Alexander stressed that these Polish victims were bright and attractive young "girls" (this expression for the female victims was always used by Alexander and other prosecutors), and that they were not "sub-human." The prosecution calculated that the students of medicine (Maria Kuśmierczuk, born January 1, 1920) and pharmacy (Jadwiga Dzido, born January 26, 1918) would make a strong impact on the court.[56] "They all have intelligence and charm and let them sparkle a little," Alexander advised prosecutor McHaney.[57] The others to testify were Maria Broel-Plater (born December 18, 1913,

**Table 3.1:** Witnesses for the Prosecution in Case 1

| Name | Capacity | Nationality | Occupation | Date | Experiment |
|---|---|---|---|---|---|
| Anon. (b. 28.2.1920) | Victim | Polish | | | Sterilization: Auschwitz |
| Broel-Plater, Maria | Victim | Polish | Pharmacy student | 19–20 Dec | Leg wounds: Ravensbrück |
| Broers, Constantyn J. | Prisoner-assistant | Dutch | Medical student | 30 June | Typhus vaccines: Buchenwald |
| Dzido, Jadwiga | Victim | Polish | Pharmacy student | 20 Dec | Bone/wounds |
| Eyer, Olga | Secretary | German (Alsace) | Secretary | 15 Jan | Typhus vaccines |
| Grandjean, Henri-Jean | Prisoner | French | Officer | 6 Jan | Natzweiler experiments |
| Henripierre, Henry | Assistant | French | Institute porter | | Skeletons |
| Holl, Ferdinand | Kapo of the Revier | German | Anti-Nazi | 3 Jan | Mustard gas |
| Höllenrainer, Karl | Victim | German | Salesman | 27 Jun, 1 Jul | Seawater |
| Ivy, Alexander | Neurologist | US | Professor/ clinician | 12–16 Jun | |
| Karolewska, Władysława | Victim | Polish | Teacher | 20 Dec | Bone/wounds |
| Kirchheimer, Fritz | Prisoner-assistant | German | Salesman | 8–9 Jan | Buchenwald Typhus |
| Kogon, Eugen | Secretary | Austrian | Journalist/ economist | 6–8 Jan | Buchenwald experiments |
| Kuśmierczuk, Maria | Victim | Polish | Medical student | 20 Dec | Bone/wounds |
| Laubringer, Josef | Victim | German | Fairground operator | 27 Jun | Seawater experiments |
| Leibbrand, Werner | Psychiatrist | German | Psychiatrist | 27 Jan | Ethics |
| Levy, Robert | Prisoner doctor | French | Surgeon | 17 Dec | X-ray sterilization |
| Lutz, Wolfgang | Refused to carry out experiments | German | Stabsarzt | 12 Dec | Cold, pressure |
| Maczka, Zofia | Prisoner assistant | Polish | Radiologist | 10 Jan | Bone/wounds |
| Mennecke, Fritz | Psychiatrist | German | Psychiatrist | 16–17 Jan | Euthanasia |
| Michalowski, Father Leo | Victim | Polish | Priest | 21 Dec | Cold |

| Name | Capacity | Nationality | Occupation | Date | Experiment |
|---|---|---|---|---|---|
| Nales, Gerrit Hendrik | Nurse | Dutch | | 30 Jun | Seawater |
| Neff, Walter* | Prisoner nurse, Rascher's assistant | German | Farmer | 17–18 Dec | TB, cold, pressure |
| Römhild, Ferdinand | Secretary to Hoven | German | Sales manager | 14 Jan | Typhus, euthanasia |
| Schmidt, Edith | Technician | German | Technician | 9 Jan | Typhus vaccine |
| Schmidt, Walter | Senior physician | German | Psychiatrist | | Euthanasia |
| Stöhr, Heinrich Wilhelm | Nurse | German | SPD politician | 17 Dec | Leg wounds, seawater |
| Tschofenig, Josef | Victim | Austrian | Landtags-abgeordneter | 17 Jun | Seawater |
| Vieweg, August Heinrich | Witness | German | Printer | 13, 16 Dec | Dachau malaria |
| Vorlicek, Joseph | Prisoner nurse | Austrian | Truck driver | 17 Jun | Seawater |

*Neff was witness for the Tribunal.*

**Table 3.2:** The Prosecution Witnesses in Case 1 by Sex and Ethnicity

| Category | Number |
|---|---|
| Prosecution witnesses | 28 |
| Male | 21 |
| Female | 7 |
| Jews | 1 |
| Poles (including one Polish Jew) | 7 |
| French | 3 |
| German | 14 |
| Austrian | 2 |
| Dutch | 2 |

a bacteriological laboratory assistant), and Władysława Karolewska (born March 15, 1909, and a junior school teacher). The neurologist Alexander spent days preparing his presentation of the victims' leg wounds, taking careful medical notes and observations.[58] Here, the victim became forensic evidence, presented to the Tribunal, although the concerns were humane. Alexander testified on December 20, 1946 as expert witness for the prosecution, demonstrating the scars of the wounds to the court, and explaining that the wounds were seriously disabling and painful with the

**3.1** Telling their story: former Polish inmates of the Ravensbrück camp on their arrival in Nuremberg (from left to right): Jadwiga Dzido, Maria Broel-Plater, Maria Kuśmierczuk, Władysława Karolewska

*United States Holocaust Memorial Museum, Washington, D.C., Photo Archives, # #43033*

lack of post-operative care. Judge Sebring remembered them (incorrectly) as the only survivors of the 70 Polish Ravensbrück experimental victims.[59]

The prosecution also used witnesses who had expert knowledge of atrocities. The radiologist Zofia Maczka gave evidence about victims who had not survived the operations. She spoke about the myth that victims of operations were pardoned (this was a point that the prosecution made to reject the claim by SS doctors that victims were volunteers undergoing discomfort for ultimate release), but instead recounted how victims were X-rayed to assess the effects of the sulphonamide "treatment," and then shot. Finally, there came the commandant's order for the remaining victims to assemble, indicating that they were all earmarked for execution, but instead the victims dispersed and were hidden. Alexander prepared the questions for the prosecutor McHaney to elicit this crucial information for the court record.[60]

The prosecution drew a distinction between the educated (as in the case of the seawater experiment) and uneducated (but not unintelligent) experimental victims. While the gratuitous injuries inflicted on the educated might make a strong impact on the Tribunal, the prosecution argued that the uneducated experienced greater anguish.[61] Taking medical students

as victims showed the SS doctors as callous, and the youngest defendant
Fritz Fischer conceded this when he volunteered for the Eastern front
rather than continue experiments. The case—dealing with Himmler's
physician Karl Gebhardt, the repercussions of Heydrich's assassination,
and the medical needs of the German army in its Barbarossa campaign
against the Soviet Union—meant that the young women's testimonies
were strategically important for the prosecution in linking the experiments to the racial policies of the SS.

The court appearance of the Catholic priest Leo Michalowski on
December 21, 1946 was "deeply impressive."[62] Michalowski was a survivor of Sigmund Rascher's horrific air pressure and cold experiments.
Here, the target was both the SS and the German Luftwaffe (air force).
Survivors of the Dachau experiments made it clear that the selection had
depended on age and physique, irrespective of nationality.[63] Rascher had
wanted men who were as fit in appearance as a German airman. Hans Hornung (a German national, sent to Dachau for having had sexual relations
with a Jewish woman) was selected for freezing experiments—despite
being aged 40—for his strong physique. Hornung (who conveniently for
the prosecution still lived in Dachau working as a salesman) described his
selection by Rascher, and the series of increasingly severe experiments
carried out on him, the sensations during and after the experiments, and
Rascher's conduct towards him.

Auschwitz figured at the Medical trial as a locus for human experiments, sterilization and "euthanasia," and a source of experimental
victims elsewhere. Defendants elaborated on how they helped individual
Jews facing persecution. Himmler's masseur, the rather dubious (and
mercenary) Felix Kersten testified on behalf of Rudolf Brandt that he
"always helped" Kersten's efforts to free imprisoned victims.[64] But it
was difficult to deny virulent antisemitism. The accused Joachim Mrugowsky, chief of the Hygiene Institute of the Waffen-SS, and Herta
Oberheuser had written antisemitic tracts for those with a longstanding
track record of NSDAP and SS activism. The majority of the accused
had worked in or had at least visited concentration camps. But all vehemently denied any role in the mass murder of Jews. Karl Brandt—
Hitler's escort surgeon and later Reich Plenipotentiary for the Civil and
Military Health—was at pains to point this out.[65] Kurt Blome, the SA
doctor in charge of biological warfare, similarly sought to extricate himself from the accusation that he had contributed to genocide.[66] Blome
secured testimony that he planned to lobby party high-ups to correct
unpleasant aspects of NSDAP as represented by the rabid antisemite
Julius Streicher and restore a moral tone.[67] The prosecution, by way
of contrast, saw the trial within the parameters of genocide and racial
atrocities, while the defense continued to make strenuous efforts to
counter the charge that the experiments were a pilot for genocide.

One key problem was to identify survivors. The Austrian doctor, Wilhelm Beiglböck, who conducted the 1944 seawater drinking experiments at

Dachau, had been denounced to the Austrian police by a Roma victim. This was the one defendant brought before the court as a result of action by the civil police, and here the German police failed to act on the identification of perpetrators. Beiglböck altered names of seawater experiment victims to stop prosecutors locating witnesses, while he tried to find witnesses to testify on his behalf. Beiglböck's lawyer advertised on June 30, 1947 for experimental subjects, and obtained five testimonies of good treatment in seawater tests from four Austrian citizens and one French witness.[68]

There were then numerous categories of victims, and Catholics, Roma, and Jews all gave evidence. One of the tasks of the prosecution's expert witness was pre-trial interrogations. Alexander described how "the hectic rush of getting documents ready and getting the right witnesses selected and into Nurnberg on time is absorbing everybody. I have spent a lot of time on interrogations of the witnesses to separate the wheat from the chaff, but we really have some witnesses now."[69]

The prosecution recognized the significance of testimonies by Roma (in fact rather rare at the Nuremberg trials) and Jews. The defense was cautious in challenging stunning evidence of human butchery, and how this met protest, evasion, and resistance. Victims stated whether s/he had volunteered. The victim Ferdinand Holl (who testified about experiments at the concentration camp of Natzweiler) was asked "did you consider this a normal medical experiment," and he replied that "we were not allowed to think in the camp." From the start—it was established how none of the experimental subjects were volunteers, few received anesthetics or proper aftercare, and in the rare cases when food and cigarettes were offered as inducements, this was offset by the coercive regime of the camps.[70]

The seawater drinking experiments were conducted on 44 Roma, who were held as "asocials." Beiglböck claimed that he had been experimenting on petty criminals whose sentences would be mitigated. He still took a racial view of his experimental victims as congenital social parasites.[71] His evidence was sensationally countered by the German Roma Karl Höllenrainer, whose liver had been punctured, and who had been forced to drink putrid yellow water. He had lost his child, sister, and both of her children at Auschwitz. When Höllenrainer was asked to identify Beiglböck, he sprang into the dock and punched the defendant.[72] This was a dramatic moment when a victim had to confront his erstwhile perpetrator, and the incident shows the strain felt by victims.

The psychiatric expert Alexander reflected on the tension generating this witness's violence. Having worked on the effect of stress on aircrew on bombing missions, Alexander diagnosed that the witness suffered from "an anxiety-tension reaction of a type similar to what combat veterans who have been through severe crushing-threatening experiences in the course of their combat duty during the war [experienced]. This anxiety-tension which builds up and is again revived by memories of the experiences, creates a potential of aggressiveness, which is bound to burst out in emotional stress." Alexander pointed out that Höllenrainer had been cross-examined mercilessly and, told by the defense lawyer not to be eva-sive "as gypsies usually are," had encountered renewed expressions of racism. Höllenrainer's striking of Beiglböck earned him a sentence of 90 days for assault. The court needed to assert its impartiality and authority. Yet, he was soon released on parole.[73]

A great gulf separated the victims, who had the physical and psycho-logical scars of atrocious experiences, from the patchy evidence of the new drugs and vaccines, which the Germans were testing. It was often difficult to link the ordeals experienced by camp prisoners with the specific charges made against the accused. The prosecution bridged the gulf between witness testimony and documents with testimonies from witnesses who had observed the atrocities and at the time documented them. The witness gave the prosecution the opportunity to personify and identify the "nameless dead." Visiting the Netherlands, Alexander located a Dutch witness Constantyn J. Broers, who was a medical stu-dent and prisoner assistant to the virologist Eugen Haagen, who had experimented massively on Roma sent to him from Auschwitz. Alexan-der also found Gerrit H. Nales, who helped define the case as a murder case by giving details of Haagen's individual victims.[74]

> The fact that Mr Nales knew exactly the names, dates and places of birth in regard to most of Haagen's victims added an air of definiteness which helped the judges to find themselves on familiar ground, namely on the ground of murder cases of definite specific persons. After each name he was asked whether he saw the corpses and he said 'yes' and in most cases added spe-cific statements that he, himself, walked the corpse before sending it to the morgue from the autopsy room. The great definiteness was impressive and a sort of relief from the nameless murdered masses which we dealt with on so many other occasions.[75]

McHaney highlighted "the extent to which the patients suffered."[76] Initially prisoners volunteered for additional food and were told that experiments were harmless. As time went on, victims were increasingly coerced; at the end of the Reich they were centrally selected from other camps. The experiments met with protest, sabotage, and resistance. The prisoners tried—as far as possible—to attenuate the dangers of experiments: temperatures could be reduced in the case of the freezing experiments, and the strength of injected pathogens could be reduced. An affidavit by the philosophically perceptive prisoner-researcher, Lud-wik Fleck, who had been transferred from Auschwitz to Buchenwald, indicated the low level of scientific competence of the bacteriologist Ding-Schuler. The reflections of this critic of experimental science was telling evidence of German scientific incompetence.[77]

When preparing the Medical trial, the interrogators hunted for evi-dence of genocidal activities by the SS. The SS *Ahnenerbe* organization was a prime target, given its interest in Germanic archaeology and medical research. The interrogators delved into the links of its chief administrator, Wolfram Sievers, who had collaborated with Karl Brandt, the anatomist August Hirt, and the SS official Adolf Eichmann with respect to obtaining bodies from Auschwitz for the Reich University Strasbourg anatomical institute.[78] The prosecution looked for evidence of medical killing. Sievers had been concerned with racial anthropology—his diary noted meetings with the KWI anthropologist and SS officer Wolfgang Abel, his assistant, Bruno Beger, who had examined Soviet prisoners and measured skulls in Auschwitz, and the statistician of the Final Solution, Richard Korherr. Although Sievers was condemned for his involvement in the killing of Jews for the Strasbourg skeleton collection, and although the eugenic and anthropological concerns of the *Ahnenerbe* were marginal to the hands-on murder strategy of the trial, there was an engagement at the trial with race and eugenics.[79]

The prosecution interrogated Jewish survivors of Auschwitz for evidence on Mengele and other doctors conducting human experiments.[80] The British interest in medical war crimes led to scrutiny of the gynecologist Clauberg's gruesome fertility experiments on Jewish women, mostly from Greece, in Auschwitz. Taylor outlined the links between euthanasia and genocide, and quoted a letter from Brack to Himmler on the links between the T4 euthanasia organization, and providing personnel for the "special mission" of Globocnik, who directed the extermination camps of the Operation Reinhardt.[81] In March 1947 the German legal adviser, Robert Kempner, preparing for the Ministries trial, discovered the Wannsee Protocol—Taylor was aghast at the calculated murder.[82] Nazi race experts defined not only Jews, but also "gypsies" as meriting total eradication. Other "races" like Slavs were defined as inferior and earmarked for exterminatory measures. Medical expertise was essential to maintain the fitness of higher races by eliminating the mentally ill and the severely disabled, and preventing reproduction of carriers of inherited diseases. In the press the trial was presented as a genocide trial, while court proceedings dealt with mass murder.[83]

## Sterilization

The prosecution collected evidence from victims of sterilization. They presented X-ray sterilization and "euthanasia" selections from the camps for killing in the gas chambers in psychiatric hospitals as a link between the medical experiments and genocide. Many victims and witnesses spontaneously contacted the Nuremberg prosecutors. French associations of survivors pressed their government to forward evidence, and insisted on the case as one of genocide affecting all who lost their lives in the camps.[84]

The prosecution made efforts to locate victims of sterilization. A former Spanish Republican officer came forward to testify that his sterilization in

April 1942 while a prisoner in Dachau was punitive. Alexander was able to provide reassurance that the operation was not as damaging as feared.[85] The interrogator Fred Rodell recollected the agony and sickness of a Jewish survivor of the sterilizations in Auschwitz: "He could only stand for ten minutes and then could only sit for 20 minutes and would have to lie down. I was there when the doctors examined him. He was jet black from the waist to the thighs and his insides were burned."[86] Alexander took up the case in November 1946, providing the prosecution with a deposition and photos of the injuries:

> Emotionally this man was deeply hurt and humiliated by his mutilation. He has not yet been able to tell even his own sisters about it. Although all this happened through no fault of his own, he feels deeply ashamed about his castration. He is afraid that his increasing gain of weight and loss of male characteristics are bound to ultimately give him away for the wreck which he has become. He feels that he has no future and has nothing to live for and has had no real life so far, and nothing to really live for ahead of him. At times his thought and emotions overcome him and he begins to cry when talking about what has happened to him. When he heard over the radio that the people responsible for the German medical atrocities are going to be tried, he decided that it was his duty to come here and to testify although he is afraid that, especially if his name is printed in newspapers, his sisters might find out about his condition that way. However, he feels that it is his duty to be helpful in bringing those responsible for the atrocities, to which he and others have been subjected, to justice. It appears that he is one of 100 young Jewish boys who were castrated for no reason other than to confirm the fact that they had been sterilized by sufficient X-ray radiation as if X-ray burns which resulted from a fifteen minute exposure were not enough to prove that point. A great many of his fellow sufferers have in the meantime developed cancer of the irradiated skin. While his skin is severely indurated no evidence of cancer is yet discernible.[87]

This was the one Jewish victim who testified in court. Other experiments were presented to the court and public as providing "the techniques for genocide."[88] Given that none of the defendants had worked in Auschwitz, there was less scope for Jewish victims at the Medical trial. Nuremberg became a public focus for victims willing to testify: in one case a sterilization victim wrote "my sister has just informed me that the wireless stations have requested to report all who were compulsorily castrated during the Nazi regime. I am one of these victims. The marks of the operation shall to be seen and will prove this."[89] Their evidence was important to understand the conduct of the experiments, to ascertain the identity and numbers of the victims, how they were treated, and to ascertain who was involved. The victims countered a general pattern of denial of visits to concentration camps. Importantly, the court was sensitive to the injuries of this victim—the court agreed that the victim's identity should be protected, and his name deleted from the court record.[90]

Given that the Nazis flagrantly flouted the provisions of the sterilization legislation of July 1933, it laid them open to charges of illegal sterilization. The prisoner doctor, Robert Levy,[91] gave evidence about experimental operations in Auschwitz. He was a French citizen but had served with the German army in World War I for two years and in the French army in 1939–41. He was arrested in May 1943 by the Gestapo in Limoges for anti-German political propaganda. He worked in the central hospital in Auschwitz, and then in Mauthausen concentration camp. As chief surgeon in the Auschwitz *Revier* (i.e., camp hospital), he found patients had been used for sterilization experiments, their testicles were extracted, or they were exposed to X-rays. These patients had ulcers, were psychologically disturbed, and showed effeminate traits: "Dr Levy is very certain that few of the patients so treated can be alive … most of the patients were very unhappy and psychologically broken by the sterilization … more serious cases developed into X-ray cancer."[92]

The French collected testimony about medical atrocities in the camp of Struthof-Natzweiler. A deposition of May 25, 1945, to the French War Crimes authorities described the preparations of human testicles by the SS anatomist Hirt at Strasbourg, and 54 slides of arrested spermatogenesis (the specialism of Hirt's assistant Anton Kiesselbach) derived from experiments at Struthof:

> As a result of this report the Academy of Medicine appointed a Commission for the purpose of dealing with the activity of German physicians as regards prisoners and deportees. This Committee has not yet met, but Prof Vincent of 'Val de Grace', confirmed that he had heard of similar incidents and so had Prof Richet. I also report another story well known. During the occupation and published in a small resistance paper, concerning the experiments conducted by a Prof of Histology from Berlin, whose reputation, by the way, seems exaggerated to me. A Dr Stive [actually Stieve] had the nerve to publish in a German magazine of 1944 observations made of haemorrhages produced in women by bad menstruation. These experiments were conducted on normally menstruating female prisoners who were told that they were about to be shot, thus producing an internal haemorrhage which was studied by Dr Stieve.[93]

Stieve and Kiesselbach enjoyed successful postwar careers, the former as professor of anatomy in Berlin and the latter at Düsseldorf.[94] Again, this represents the difficulty of focusing on just twenty medical defendants rather than a comprehensive documentation.

## Connecting the Trials

The human experiments continued to have a place at the Nuremberg trials. The trials were linked by drawing on a common bank of documents, by prosecutors (notably Taylor and McHaney as chief of the SS division), by defense lawyers, certain judges who served for a number of cases, and by witnesses. We see this in the cases against Air Marshall Erhard Milch, the Flick case (when slave labor witnesses testified to how drugs suppressed menstruation[95]), and the case against IG Farben, when leading managers of pharmaceutical concerns were accused. The indictment of Milch accused him of responsibility for having the authority over the low pressure and freezing experiments.[96] Milch attended a showing at the Air Ministry of a film of the pressure experiments (only stills survive from the film).[97] The defense shifted responsibility onto the absent Rascher. Evidence from the SS *Ahnenerbe* head Sievers and the prisoner assistant Walter Neff indicated that Rascher as Luftwaffe officer had had support from Milch. An example of this was provision of a Luftwaffe pressure chamber to the Dachau camp. The case of Sievers shows how the accused in one trial could be a witness in another. Milch's lawyers made strenuous efforts to locate his deputy Erich Hippke, who alleged a—rather dubious—distinction between air force experiments on volunteers, and the SS experiments on concentration camp prisoners. The acquittal of Milch on the count of having responsibility for the low pressure and freezing experiments made prosecutors wary of the chain of command approach that linked a set of research atrocities to the Nazi elite and their genocidal master plan. This judgment on April 16, 1947, while the Medical case was still proceeding, undermined the prosecution case for the pressure experiments.[98]

The trial against the SS administrator Oswald Pohl and others of the Economic and Administration Main Office, or Case 4, opened in April 1947 while the Medical case was still in progress. The Prosecutors transferred evidence from the Medical trial to Pohl and associates. Count 2 (section 18) of the charge accused Pohl of facilitating: "medical, surgical, and biological experimentation on involuntary human subjects; criminal sterilization and castration of involuntary human subjects." Section 22 of the charge stated: "The defendants assisted in planning and carrying out medical, surgical, and biological experiments upon hundreds of involuntary human subjects without regard to the lives of such subjects, resulting in the murder, torture, and ill-treatment of hundreds of persons."[99] The experiments were linked to other methods of extermination including castration, sterilization, and "euthanasia."[100]

The prosecutor James McHaney, who had taken a key role in the Medical trial, now directed the case against Pohl, who was represented by Alfred Seidl, a seasoned defense lawyer who had already defended Hans Frank and Rudolf Heß. McHaney accused Pohl of making the constant supply of "human guinea pigs" available. The human experiments highlighted the criminality of the concentration camp system. As the US counsels could link most defendants to the concentration camps, they in turn tried to locate most crimes in the camps as well. Pohl, as the head of the SS Economic and Administration Main Office (*Wirtschafts-Verwaltungshauptamt*, WVHA) provided the resources that allowed the medical crimes to occur. Sommer, the deputy head of office D II (labor allocation) was found guilty for having been involved in all aspects of D II which included human experiments. A witness, Rev Stanisław Wolok, stated: "Of the twenty of us who were taken for experimental purposes, seven died a horrible death. Others remained crippled for the rest of their lives. These were the methods utilized by barbaric Hitlerites in their attempt to make medical progress."[101]

One victim, who was sterilized, and having been a witness at the Medical trial was again a witness for the prosecution: "In Court he broke down and wept as he related his harrowing experience and, in a state of shame and mortification, asked the Tribunal not to divulge his name so that his only surviving relative, a sister, might not know what had happened to him."[102] The defense attempted to show a lack of knowledge on behalf of certain defendants, but Pohl admitted his role in supplying victims, although he understated numbers.[103] Josef Ackermann as witness related a range of medical atrocities at Buchenwald as evidence against the accused. What was important is that the experiments on Jewish children were directly linked to genocide: "Only a Shakespeare could find the appropriate level of literary ignominy to which to consign the SS general who ordered the execution of 20 children because they had been experimented on, and then sent to the gas chambers, [and of] the four nurses who had witnessed the experiments."[104] At Auschwitz, one SS doctor, Mengele, conducted a series of experiments on twin children. During the experiment he accorded them the best of care, provided excellent lodging, and abundant food. The children were valuable for his studies ordered by the *Rassenforschungsinstitut* (Institute for Racial Research) in Berlin. Once the experiment was completed, he "took the children to the gas chamber where he himself shot them down with the pistol."[105]

The fact that victims did not volunteer or consent was part of the prosecution case in the successor trials. The issue was raised in the trial against twenty-three officials of the IG Farben chemical corporation, when the extensive typhus (*Fleckfieber*) experiments at Buchenwald were part of the prosecution case. The defense countered that conscientious tests with animals were carried out to ensure the safety of the drugs.[106] Moreover, the defense alleged that the criteria for criminality of experiments established at the Medical trial were not met. The defense argued, using evidence from the Buchenwald camp doctor, Vetter (a former scientist at Elberfeld), that rather than (criminal) experiments, there had been allegedly legitimate "clinical tests" or "practical tests."[107] "Medical Experiments" figured as part of Count 3 (slave labor) in the charges against the defendants. Here the charge was of: "Experiments on human beings (including concentration camp inmates), without their consent, were conducted by Farben to determine the effects of deadly gases, vaccines, and related products."[108] The sterilization experiments at Auschwitz were considered to have used pharmaceutical products manufactured by IG Farben.[109] The Farben conglomerate was accused of funding a circle of friends of Himmler involving IG officials (notably the chemist Heinrich Bütefisch, prosecuted at Nuremberg for his period directing the Auschwitz-Monowitz plant and abusing slave labor) and the convicted *Ahnenerbe* official, Sievers.[110] Heinrich Hörlein (who discovered luminal and helped develop sulpha drugs), Carl Lautenschläger, Albert Demnitz, and other IG managers were accused of supporting the lethal typhus experiments of Vetter and Ding-Schuler at Buchenwald.[111] This accusation linked the accused to medical officials of the SS, such as the deceased Conti and the convicted Mrugowsky of the Hygiene Institute of the Waffen-SS; a link was also established to the convicted military medical officer Handloser. The Farben products Acridin and Rutenol were supplied for experiments that resulted in deaths. The prosecutors pointed out that these officials received reports on the fatal experiments, one showing that twenty-one out of thirty-nine victims died. Hörlein could summon extenuating witness testimonies by fellow scientists that the judges found persuasive. Hörlein, Otto Ambros and Fritz ter Meer were in the event acquitted.

The other element of the charge against such officials as Krauch was involvement in mustard gas experiments and development of other chemical—and indeed atomic—warfare agents.[112] Indeed, the defense took the position of a collective denial of responsibility and knowledge of the criminal experiments at Auschwitz.[113] On the other hand, as individuals they pleaded that they were conscientious professionals. The judges accepted the distinction between an experiment (*Versuch*) and a clinical test or trial:

> Without going into detail to justify a negative factual conclusion, we may say that the evidence falls short of establishing the guilt of said defendants on this issue beyond a reasonable doubt. The inference that the defendants connived with SS doctors in their criminal practices is dispelled by the fact that Farben discontinued forwarding drugs to these physicians as soon as their improper conduct was suspected. We find nothing culpable in the circumstances under which quantities of vaccines were shipped by Farben to concentration camps, since it was reasonable to suppose that there was a legitimate need for such drugs in these institutions. The question as to whether the reports submitted to Farben by its testing physicians disclosed that illegal uses were being made of such drugs revolves around a controversy as to the proper translation of the German word "Versuch" found in such reports and in the documents pertaining thereto. The prosecution says that "Versuch" means "experiment" and that the use of this word in said reports was notice to the defendants that testing physicians were indulging in unlawful practices with such drugs. The defendants contend, however, that "Versuch," as used in the context, mean "test" and that the testing of new drugs on sick persons under the reasonable precautions that Farben exercised was not only permissible but proper. Applying the rule that where from credible evidence two reasonable inferences may be drawn, one of guilt and the other of innocence, the latter must prevail, we must conclude that the prosecution has failed to establish that part of the charge here under consideration.[114]

This verdict of the judges at the IG Farben trial, that "tests" were permissible, effectively reversed the verdict and guidelines pronounced by the judges at the close of the Medical trial. The distinction between a therapeutic "test" and an experiment relied on some skilful conjuring with terminology by the defendants and defense lawyers.

## Aftermath

The agenda of documenting the human experiments was attempted by the International Scientific Commission established by Thompson, which gathered vast quantities of documents on Nazi research atrocities. Thompson pointed out that trials could only ever prosecute a handful of the perpetrators. A further notable legacy was the "Nuremberg Code" (the term Code was only used from 1963) for an enlightened or informed consent in experimental research. That has been a major concern for a bioethics agenda scrutinizing the Medical trial. The judges included the experimental subject's right to depart from any experiment at any time.[115] The principles of a voluntary or enlightened consent became transformed into the idea of an informed consent, as a requirement for all clinical research and therapy. The principle has been extended into other spheres of academic research, and indeed into all aspects of human relations.

The trials could only allow a voice to a very few victims. Their testimonies were important for securing convictions, but what is still missing is any study of who the victims were, and how they coped with their injuries and traumas. In effect such a study would fulfill the agenda of Thompson's International Scientific Commission. Physicians involved at the Medical trial were compassionate: Alexander supported medical care for the Polish "Rabbits," helping to bring over thirty of them to Boston in 1958-59. Women's organizations took up the case of the need for compensation for female victims of the experiments, particularly of the victims of Ravensbrück sulphonamide experiments. The UN's section on women kept a watchful eye on the issue.[116] The French survivors' organization ADIR *(Association nationale des anciennes déportées et internées de la Résistance)* had a number of women activists on this issue, not least the Ravensbrück survivors, Geneviève de Gaulle-Anthonioz (niece of General de Gaulle) and the anthropologist Germaine Tillion. The Polish "Rabbit" Janina Iwa ska was active in pressing for compensation, and the American publicist, Caroline Ferriday, lobbied in the United States. Victims were widely dispersed after the war and many nationalities were involved.

The Nuremberg proceedings had a profound impact on the lawyers and doctors involved. The lawyers Benjamin B. Ferencz, John H.E. Fried (formerly special legal consultant to the tribunals), Oscar Schachter, and especially Egon Schwelb took up the cause of victims, and worked through the UN Human Rights Commission and other agencies to secure surviving victims' need for compensation and—although never resolved—the costs of medical care. The UN Commission on the Status of Women adopted at its 4th session in 1950 a resolution calling attention to the plight of women survivors of concentration camps who were subjected to medical experiments. At the Economic and Social Council, the report from the Commission was examined, the view being expressed that the United Nations lend its support to negotiations between the Allied High Commission and the Federal German Government for compensation legislation in Germany for these victims. To this end, the Council adopted resolution 305 (XI) on July 14, 1950. The UN Secretary-General was requested to consider with the competent authorities and institutions the means for alleviating the plight of survivors of concentration camps who were the victims of the so-called "scientific experiments." On July 26, 1951 the Federal Republic's observer informed the UN that it would compensate all victims.[117]

One issue was the numbers of victims. The UN initially considered that very few survived the experiments, basically seeing the Ravensbrück "Rabbits" as the main group of about 70 survivors: overall there were considered to be, "[p]ossibly less than one hundred or only a couple of hundred." But the more the UN engaged with the issue, the more estimates rose. By December 5, 1950, the UN thought there might be perhaps one hundred or two hundred persons. By the close of 1951, the Germans estimated 2,800 victims, but that only a small number could have survived. By 1952 the UN had details of about 600 survivors, although actual numbers of survivors are far higher.

The compensation legislation turned out to have been poorly constructed as the German government turned down many applications for political or racially motivated reasons. Thompson was among those in the 1960s protesting against the Federal Republic's compensation for the experiment victims that was often paltry and traumatizing in the medical certification by physicians who showed no acceptance of the idea of "survivors' trauma."[118] The slave labor compensation between 1998 and 2004 awarded fractional amounts under a cryptic rubric of *"sonstige Personenschäden"* (i.e., other injuries) that victims have found wholly inadequate. The costs of ongoing medical care have remained problematic.

The doctors, Alexander and Thompson, moved away from neurology and neurophysiology, and supported a deeply humane patient care. Alexander assisted with care for Polish victims of the Ravensbrück leg wounding experiments.[119] Thompson not only joined protests on compensation procedures and lack of recognition of survivors' trauma, but he worked with UNESCO to provide therapy for Germany as a sick people, by supporting an integrated youth, education, and social science program.

Overall, the victims of human experiments have never received full recognition in terms of a full history of the experiments, and the very large numbers affected. The issues of compensation and medical care for the victims have also never been adequately resolved. On the one hand, clusters of victims have been identified, but on the other hand, Holocaust history saw eugenics and "euthanasia" as key lead-up stages to the Final Solution. With the interpretative shift arising from the paradigm of the "racial state," the state—itself a malignant historical force—is presumed to be the primary culprit rather than the research-hungry defendants. Further questions thus have remained, not least, the full extent of the research atrocities, care for surviving victims, and compensation for survivors.[120]

Yet the chill still evoked by Taylor's resonating words about the nameless dead raises questions as to how the victims of the Nazi medical atrocities have been and can properly be commemorated. The courtroom witnesses represented a handful of the thousands of victims, although their testimonies had a strong impact on the proceedings. The Nuremberg trials represent a vortex bringing together documents and witnesses. Their legacy for understanding Nazi Germany has been immense, and their postwar experiences provide revealing insight into a range of issues concerning justice and compensation. Historians are only just beginning to adequately confront these problematic issues.

## Notes

1. Telford Taylor, Opening Statement, 9.12.1946, *Trials of War Criminals before the Nuernberg Military Tribunals under Control Council Law No. 10 [TWC]*, 15 vols (Washington, DC, 1949–53), I, 27.
2. Ibid., 37–38, 48.
3. Paul Weindling, "From International to Zonal Trials. The Origins of the Nuremberg Medical Trial," *Holocaust and Genocide Studies* 14 (2000): 367–89.
4. John H.E. Fried, "Nuremberg and the Holocaust," in *Toward a Right to Peace: Selected Papers of John H.E. Fried* (Northampton, MA, 1994), 15–32.
5. William Seltzer, "Population Statistics, the Holocaust, and the Nuremberg Trials," *Population and Development Review* 24 (1998): 511–52.
6. Paul Weindling, *John W. Thompson, Psychiatrist in the Shadow of the Holocaust* (Rochester, NY, 2010).
7. Michael Marrus, "The Nuremberg Doctors' Trial in Historical Context," *Bulletin of the History of Medicine* 73 (1999): 106–23.
8. On the second Medical trial, see: Paul Weindling, "'Tales from Nuremberg': the Kaiser Wilhelm Institute for Anthropology and Allied Medical War Crimes Policy," in *Geschichte der Kaiser-Wilhelm-Gesellschaft im Nationalsozialismus. Bestandsaufnahme und Perspektiven der Forschung*, 2 vols, ed. Doris Kaufmann (Göttingen, 2000), 621–38.
9. Eugen Kogon, *Der SS-Staat. Das System der deutschen Konzentrationslager* (Munich, 1946); Hermann Langbein, *Menschen in Auschwitz* (Vienna, 1972).
10. Michael Marrus, *The Nuremberg War Crimes Trial, 1945–46. A Documentary History* (Boston, 1997), 191–93; Donald Bloxham, *Genocide on Trial: War Crimes Trials and the Formation of Holocaust History and Memory* (Oxford, 2001), 64.
11. Marrus, "Nuremberg Doctors' Trial."
12. On Lemkin's commentary on the Medical Trial, see Paul Weindling, *Nazi Medicine and the Nuremberg Trials. From Medical War Crimes to Informed Consent* (Basingstoke, 2004), 102–3, 231, 235–36.
13. See the preliminary page, "Arrangement of Subject Units by Publication," in all TWC volumes.
14. Lemkin to Marcus, January 13, 1947, NARA, RG 153, 86-2-2, Box 9, Book 2.

15. Raphael Lemkin, *Axis Rule in Occupied Europe. Laws of Occupation, Analysis of Government, Proposals for Redress* (Washington, DC, 1944), xi–xii.
16. Lemkin to Marcus, January 10, 1947, "The Importance of the Genocide Concept for the Doctor's Case," NARA, RG 153, 86-3-1, Box 10, Book 1; Gunn to McHaney, January 29, 1947, Memo by Lemkin (January 21, 1947), "Planning of a special Trial on Abduction of Women into Prostitution," NARA, RG 153, 86-3-1, Box 10, Book 1.
17. Autobiography, NYPL, Lemkin Papers, Reel 2, 4.
18. Lemkin to Gypsy Lore Society, August 2, 1949, NYPL, Lemkin Papers, Reel 1.
19. Lemkin to Telford Taylor, September 28, 1945, NYPL, Lemkin Papers, Reel 4.
20. Lemkin to Marcus, January 10, 1947, "The Importance of the Genocide Concept for the Doctors Case," NARA, RG 153, 86-3-1, Box 10, Book 1.
21. Meeting of Touffait, Lemkin, and Gunn, May 28, 1946, Archives de France [AdeF], BB/30/1786; Minutes of 108th meeting held on June 19, 1946, present Dr Lemkin with Lt Kintner, United Nations Archives, Geneva, [UNA], UNWCC, M 108; H.H. Wade to Smith, July 24 and August 2 and 12, 1946, Royal College of Physicians Edinburgh [RCPE], Smith Papers, Box 9, Folder 94, War Crimes.
22. "The Crimes of Genocide," December 10, 1946, NARA, RG 153, 85-2, Administrative files, Book 1; December 18, 1946, UNA, UNWCC, M 129.
23. UN Economic and Social Council, "Prevention and Punishment of Genocide." Historical Summary, November 2, 1946–January 20, 1947, E/621 (26 Jan 1948); Lawrence J. LeBlanc, *The United States and the Genocide Convention* (Durham, NC, 1991), 19–23. The Convention was adopted by the United Nations General Assembly in Paris on December 9, 1948. The United States ratified the Convention in 1988; see *The United Nations and Human Rights 1945–1995* (New York, 1995), 18–22.
24. Lemkin was at Duke University from 1941 to 1942.
25. Summary of the activities of Raphael Lemkin, NYPL, Lemkin Papers, Reel 2, 6.
26. Alexander Logbook, November 13, 1946, Alexander Papers Durham, North Carolina [APD], 4/33.
27. Cf. *New York Times*, November 21, 1946.
28. History of the Genocide Convention, NYPL, Lemkin Papers, Reel 3, 3–5.
29. Raphael Lemkin, "Genocide as a Crime under International Law," *The American Journal of International Law* 41 (1947): 146–51, footnote 6.
30. Cf. Ana Filipa Vrdoljak, "Human Rights and Genocide: The Work of Lauterpacht and Lemkin in Modern International Law," *European Journal of International Law* 20 (2010): 1184–86.
31. Telford Taylor, "The Meaning of the Nuremberg Trials," an address at the Palais de Justice, Paris, April 25, 1947, NARA, RG 153, 89-2, Box 16, Folder 4, Book 1.
32. Ibid.
33. Beals to Gunn, February 27, 1947, University of Washington Archives [UWA], Beals Papers, Box 1, Folder 32; Gunn to Beals, March 7, 1946, ibid., Folder 6; Carnegie Endowment for International Peace to Beals, March 10, 1947, ibid., Folder 16.
34. Lemkin memo to Taylor, October 30, 1946, NARA, RG 153, 84-1, Box 1; WJC to Secretary of the Army, Kenneth Royall, November 21, 1947, ibid.
35. Lemkin, "The Importance of the War Crimes Concept for the Doctors Case," Memorandum for Col David Marcus, January 10, 1947, NARA, RG 153, 86-3-1, Box 10, Book 1; *The Nuremberg Medical Trial 1946/47. Transcripts, Material of the Prosecution and Defense. Related Documents*, eds. Klaus Dörner, Angelika Ebbinghaus and Karsten Linne, in cooperation with Karlheinz Roth and Paul Weindling. Microfiche Edition [hereafter MT] (Munich, 1999), 8/1802–4.
36. NARA, RG 153, 86-3-1, Box 10, Book 1.
37. Alexander Logbook, thanatology, see entries for November 21, 24, and 28, 1946; on "thanatolotry", see March 1, 10, and 11, 1947, APD, 4/35.
38. Gunn to Beals, January 3, 1947 [actually dated December 3, 1946 but in reply to a letter of December 21, 1946], UWA, Beals Papers, Box 1, Folder 6.
39. For Kogon, see Jan Erik Schulte's contribution in this volume.

40. National Archives, Kew [TNA (PRO)], WO 235/83; *Law Reports of Trials of War Criminals*, 15 vols (London, 1947–49), I, 93–103; Angelika Ebbinghaus, "Der Prozess gegen Tesch und Stabenow. Von der Schädlingsbekämpfung zum Holocaust," *1999 – Zeitschrift für Sozialgeschichte des 19. und 20. Jahrhunderts* 13 (1998): 16–71.

41. Eugen Kogon, Hermann Langbein, Adalbert Rückerl, et al. (eds.), *Nationalsozialistische Massentötungen durch Giftgas* (Frankfurt a.M., 1986).

42. Procès de Ravensbrück, Archives de l'occupation française en Allemagne, Colmar [AOF], AJ 3633, p. 132, d 6087; Ravensbrück trials, TNA (PRO), WO 309/1655–63.

43. Weindling, *Thompson*.

44. Ibid.

45. Paul Weindling, "Die Internationale Wissenschaftskommission zur Erforschung medizinischer Kriegsverbrechen," in *Vernichten und Heilen. Der Nürnberger Ärzteprozess und seine Folgen*, eds. Angelika Ebbinghaus and Klaus Dörner (Berlin, 2001), 439–51.

46. Weindling, *Nazi Medicine*; Weindling, "Akteure in eigener Sache: Die Aussagen der Überlebenden und die Verfolgung der medizinischen Kriegsverbrechen nach 1945," in *Die Verbindung nach Auschwitz. Biowissenschaften und Menschenversuche an Kaiser-Wilhelm-Instituten*, ed. Carola Sachse (Göttingen, 2004), 255–82.

47. Telephone conversation [between Lifton and] James McHaney, June 8, 1977, NYPL, Lifton Papers, M9, 9.

48. [Memo by] Olga Lang, November 5, 1946, NARA, RG 153, 100-621, Box 59. "Opfer des Faschismus" Ausschüsse were precursors of the Vereinigung der Verfolgten des Naziregimes (VVN) = Society of People Persecuted by the Nazi Regime (founded from October 1946).

49. Letters [from victims] to trial authorities, AdeF, BB/35/260; Radiogram of court by US requesting evidence, October 31, 1946, Czech State Archives [CSA].

50. Dunja Martin, "'Versuchskaninchen'—Opfer medizinischer Experimente," in *Frauen in Konzentrationslagern: Bergen-Belsen, Ravensbrück*, eds. Claus Füllberg-Stolberg et al. (Bremen, 1994), 113–22.

51. Maryann Shelley statement, APD, 4/35.

52. Gizella Perl to Office of US Chief of Counsel, January 11, 1947, and Perl to Damon Gunn, October 7, 1947, re Mengele, NARA, RG 153, 100-1184, Box 93.

53. Arnost Horlick-Hochwald (original name Ernst Hochwald) had been part of the Czechoslovak legal team under Boghuslav Ečr supporting the prosecution at the IMT. Horlick-Hochwald's subsequent biography is unclear.

54. Notes on McHaney, March 29, 1978, NYPL, Lifton Papers, M9, 7.

55. Pohl affidavit, March 26, 1947, NARA, M-1019, 54; Taylor, Opening Statement, *TWC*, I, 27–74; Weindling, *Nazi Medicine*, 187.

56. Alexander to McHaney, "General Nature of the Evidence," December 18, 1946, NARA, RG 238, Entry 188, Box 2; Alexander on Dzido, December 18, 1946, ibid. For clinical examination, see: Alexander, memo on Jadwiga Dzido to McHaney and Hardy, December 17, 1946, ibid.; also Memo on Kusmierczuk to McHaney and Hardy, Clinical Notes, December 17, 1946, ibid.; Broel-Plater, clinical examination by Alexander, December 17, 1946, ibid.

57. Alexander to J.M. McHaney "General Nature of the Evidence to be brought out by Maria Broel-Plater, Wladyslawa," December 18, 1946, APD, 4/38.

58. Alexander, Case history of the Polish witnesses: Broel-Plater, Karolewska, Dzido and Kuśmierczuk by Dr. Leo Alexander, December 17, 1946, APD, 4/35.

59. "The Medical Case," Sebring Papers, Stetson College of Law, St Petersburg, Florida, 9–10.

60. "Testimony of Dr. Zofia Maczka," Alexander to McHaney, January 9, 1947, APD, 4/35.

61. Alexander to McHaney, "Suggestions for Questions of Dr WCS Ladell," February 25, 1947, APD, 4/35.

62. Leo Alexander, Diary, December 21, 1946, Court transcript, 871–886, APD, 4/33.

63. Hornung interrogation by Meyer, December 20, 1946, APD, 4/34; Alexander memorandum to McHaney, December 20, 1946, ibid.
64. Kersten, October 29, 1947, Staatsarchiv Nürnberg (StAN), Rep 502A, KV-Verteidigung, Handakten Hofmann, No. 6.
65. Clemency plea, April 7, 1948, MT 5/2604.
66. Blome note, January 13, 1947, StAN, Rep 502A, KV-Verteidigung, Handakten Sauter, No. 7.
67. Blome note, January 13, 1947, StAN, Rep 502A, KV-Verteidigung, Handakten Sauter, No. 7.
68. Gustav Steinbauer appeal, August 10, 1948, with testimonies of Raimund Papai, Georg Papai, Xaver Reinhart, NARA, RG 153, 84–8, Box 1; Rudolf Aschenauer, *Landsberg. Ein dokumentarischer Bericht von deutscher Seite* (Munich, 1951), 64–68.
69. Leo Alexander to Phyllis Alexander, December 10, 1946, Alexander Family Papers, Boston [AFP].
70. Neff on December 18, 1946, MT 2/719; Holl on January 3, 1947, MT 2/1128.
71. June 10, 1947, MT 2/9017.
72. MT 2/10229–10234.
73. Alexander to McHaney, Neuro-psychiatric examination of the witness, Karl Höllenrainer, June 28, 1947, APD, 4/33; Court order of June 28, 1947, MT 6/1612; Court order of July 21, 1947, NMT 6/1622–3.
74. Leo to Phyllis Alexander, July 1, 1947, AFP; Alexander to McHaney, "Two Important Witnesses against Dr. Haagen," May 28, 1947, APD, 4/35.
75. Leo to Phyllis Alexander, July 1, 1947, AFP.
76. On Ding's Acridin experiments, MT, 2/1183–7, 1224.
77. Paul Weindling, *Epidemics and Genocide in Eastern Europe* (Oxford, 2000), 363–65, 427; id., "The Fractured Crucible: Images of the Scientific Survival. The Defence of Ludwik Fleck," in *Penser avec Ludwik Fleck—Investigating a Life Studying Life Sciences*, eds. Johannes Fehr, Nathalie Jas and Ilana Löwy (Zurich, 2009), 47–62; Olga Amsterdamska, Christian Bonah, Cornelius Borck et al., "Medical Science in the Light of a Flawed Study of the Holocaust: A Comment on Eva Hedfors Paper on Ludwik Fleck," *Social Studies of Science* 38 (2008): 937–44.
78. Sievers interrogation, August 20, 1946, NARA, M-1019, 68, 7.
79. Sievers diary, MT 3/410–442. Cf. Michael Kater, *Das "Ahnenerbe" der SS. 1935–1945. Ein Beitrag zur Kulturpolitik des Dritten Reiches* (Stuttgart, 1974), 261–64.
80. Jan Ochocki interrogation, January 13, 1947, NARA, M-1019, 50.
81. MT 2/110; Brack interrogation citing Globocnik, MT 2/587.
82. Robert M.W. Kempner, *Ankläger einer Epoche. Lebenserinnerungen* (Frankfurt a.M., 1983).
83. J.M. Inbona, "Le procès des médecins allemands. Leur responsabilité dans la Technique du Génocide," *La Presse Médicale* 21 (1947): 251–52.
84. Inbona, "Le procès des médecins allemands," 251–52; AOF, AJ, c. 3645, p. 287, no. 8949; "Pouvez-vous aider la justice française?," *Bulletin de liaison de l'amicale de Dachau, Comité de l'île de France* 6 (Fédération Nationale des Déportés et Internés Résistants et Patriotes, 1946).
85. Interrogation of Herbert Alfred Schwind by Meyer and Alexander, December 12, 1946, NARA, M-1019, 68, 4.
86. Rodell interview, Fortunoff Video Collection, Yale University.
87. Sterilisation, Rapports et documents Leo Alexander, November 22, 1946, AdeF, BB/35/274.
88. Wolfe Frank radio interview with Alexander, APD, 4/40.
89. Geo Doering, Schleswig, to US Mil. Gov., January 23, 1947, AdeF, BB/35/260, 4a Procès I: instruction (correspondance), 133890.
90. Sterilization, Rapports et documents Leo Alexander, November 22, 1946, AdeF, BB/35/274; MT 2/600, 3/543ff.
91. Born May 20, 1894 in Dettweiler in Alsace (Bas-Rhin).

92. MT 2/605–8, 4/5957–8.
93. Declaration at School of Medicine by Christian Champy, Professor of Medicine, Paris (NO-521), AdeF, BB/35/274; Hermann Stieve, "Paracyclische Ovulationen," *Zentralblatt für Gynäkologie* 7 (1944): 260; Ernst Klee, *Auschwitz, die NS-Medizin und ihre Opfer* (Frankfurt a.M., 1997), 97–111.
94. See Ernst Klee, *Das Personenlexikon zum Dritten Reich. Wer war was vor und nach 1945* (Frankfurt a.M., 2003), 307f., 603.
95. Evelokia Voytovitch and Sonia Cheyko on May 1 and 2, 1947, APD, 4/34; Leo Alexander to Hardy, "Preparation of the Pokorny Case," May 29, 1947, ibid.
96. Ulrich-Dieter Oppitz, *Medizinverbrechen vor Gericht. Das Urteil im Nürnberger Ärzteprozeß gegen Karl Brandt und andere sowie aus dem Prozeß gegen Generalfeldmarschall Milch* (Erlangen, 1999).
97. See the proceedings on January 14, 1947 for medical experiments, trial transcript [Milch case] 369–487.
98. Case II, Judgment, *TWC*, II, 773–79. For a different view, see Concurring Opinion by Judge Michael A. Musmanno, *TWC*, II, 836–48.
99. Case IV, Opening Statement, *TWC*, V, 225.
100. Under count 1, the indictment mentioned three medical crimes: medical experiments, sterilization and castration, and euthanasia. Count 2, section 18 dealt with human experiments, sterilization and castration, section 21 with euthanasia and sterilization, and section 22 with human experiments. In his opening statement, McHaney extensively mentioned human experiments, sterilization and euthanasia (especially 14 f 13).
101. Case IV, *TWC*, V, 124, PS-1943.
102. Case IV, *TWC*, V, 850–51, 971; trial transcript, 633.
103. Pohl affidavit, dated June 23, 1946 (NO-065, Pros. Ex. 183).
104. Pohl Case, Concurring Opinion by Judge Michael A. Musmanno, *TWC*, V, 1075.
105. Ibid.
106. IG Farben Case, *TWC*, VII, 250.
107. Ibid., 253, 328.
108. Indictment, *TWC*, vol. VII, 54, 55.
109. Ibid., 55.
110. Ibid., 56.
111. Case VI, *TWC*, VII, 203–4.
112. Ibid., 1035–37.
113. Case VI, Closing Statement for all defendants, *TWC*, VIII, 972.
114. Case VI, Decision and Judgment, *TWC*, VIII, 1172.
115. Weindling, Nazi Medicine, 340–41; George Annas and Michael Grodin, *The Nazi Doctors and the Nuremberg Code* (Oxford, 1992).
116. A Compensation for Injuries, June 1, 1950, Shamsee to Weis re Iwanska, UNA, SOA 417/3/01; George Brand (UK) to E. Garcia-Sayan August 10, 1950, Possible Program of Aid to Victims of Medical Atrocities cc to Mary Tennison-Woods, head of section on women, NY, ibid.
117. Baumann, *Menschenversuche*, 57–61.
118. Weindling, *Thompson*, 309–10; Constantin Goschler, *Wiedergutmachung. Westdeutschland und die Verfolgten des Nationalsozialismus 1945–1954* (Munich, 1992).
119. Weindling, *Nazi Medicine and the Nuremberg Trials*, 329, 337.
120. Stefanie Michaela Baumann, *Menschenversuche und Wiedergutmachtung. Der lange Streit um Entschädigung und Anerkennung der Opfer nationalsozialistischer Humanexperimente* (Munich, 2009); Stefanie Michaela Baumann, "Opfer von Menschenversuchen als Sonderfall der Wiedergutmachung," in *Grenzen der Wiedergutmachung. Die Entschädigung für NS-Verfolgte in West- und Osteuropa, 1945–2000*, eds. Günther Hockerts et al. (Göttingen, 2006), 147–96.

## CHAPTER 4

# SEMANTICS OF EXTERMINATION

## THE USE OF THE NEW TERM OF GENOCIDE IN THE NUREMBERG TRIALS AND THE GENESIS OF A MASTER NARRATIVE

*Alexa Stiller*

☙§§☙

This chapter could also be entitled: "Genocide: from a broad analytical concept of oppression, persecution, and extermination, to a crime of mass murder," as this is exactly what happened to the new term between 1944 and 1949. Some scholars have already shown that Lemkin's original concept of genocide, which he published in 1944,[1] had been more comprehensive than that adopted by the United Nations Convention on the Prevention and Punishment of the Crime of Genocide.[2] The same can be observed in the Nuremberg trials in which the crime of genocide was not consistently seen as congruent with the Holocaust, i.e., the mass murder of the European Jews. Instead, the prosecutors and some judges defined genocide much more broadly and conceived Nazi occupation policies during World War II as genocide against people. Raphael Lemkin's book, *Axis Rule in Occupied Europe*, had a bearing on the usage of the term in the Nuremberg trials.

Significantly, Lemkin's concept of genocide was most prominent in a trial on the Nazi population, settlement, and Germanization policy in occupied territories, mainly Poland. The Race and Settlement case of the United States against Ulrich Greifelt et al., known also as "RuSHA case" or *Volkstumsprozess*, was explicitly conceptualized as a "genocide trial." Consequently, the Race and Settlement case stands in the center of the present analysis on the usage of the word genocide and its definition within the Nuremberg trials.

The trial's framing was immediately apparent from the *New York Times* headline "Fourteen Germans Listed in Genocide Case" on the first day.[3] And on March 11, 1948, another article on the same case concluded that eight defendants were found "guilty of directing the mass extermination of people in twelve 'inferior' nations." The main defendant, Greifelt, was described as, "the driving force of the genocide program."[4] Furthermore, the United Nations War Crimes Commission (UNWCC) stated in 1949 that this trial has been of "fundamental importance, examining with particular reference to Poland ... the crime of genocide."[5] And when the American series on the *Trials of War Criminals before the Nuremberg Military Tribunals* was published in 1953, a short description of the trials claimed that a "systematic program of genocide" had been charged in the Race and Settlement case.[6] Genocide, then, was the term used to name the extermination of nations.

But neither of the two important document series on the war crimes trials employed this phrase for any other Nuremberg trial. This implies that neither the *Einsatzgruppen* case, in which former SS officers were charged with mass shootings mainly of Jews but also of other people in the occupied Eastern territories, nor the Ministries case, in which the Wannsee conference played a decisive role and therefore defendants were charged with knowledge of and contribution to the mass murder of the European Jews, were explicitly considered as "genocide trials." The *New York Times* did not label the *Einsatzgruppen* case a genocide trial. Instead its blunt headline of 1947 stated that "SS Officers are indicted in the Murder of Million Persons."[7] The *Einsatzgruppen* case was universally regarded as "the biggest murder trial in history."[8]

Obviously, in the years between 1945 and the 1960s, genocide was conceptualized differently from that on which most contemporary Holocaust and genocide scholars would agree, that is the definition of the Genocide Convention. The Nazi extermination of the European Jews is often considered as a synonym of genocide, as the prototype or "ideal type" of genocide, while some scholars insist that the Holocaust is a unique phenomenon, other cases of destruction and extermination of peoples are still strongly controversial.[9] In a contrasting trend, research in genocide studies places mass violence in a broader historical and sociological framework.[10] The mass murder of the European Jews, it will be argued, should therefore be seen and can only be fully analyzed in the context of the entire Nazi persecution and extermination policy.[11]

It is less important to list how many times the protagonists in the Nuremberg trials used the word genocide than to examine how the prosecution and the judges interpreted the aims and conduct of the Nazi persecution and extermination policy in general. William A. Schabas and Frank Selbmann have examined the Nuremberg trials' usage of the charge of

genocide but, perhaps due to their legal perspective, they have erroneously identified the contemporary use of the term genocide with the later
definition of the Genocide Convention.[12] As Lemkin's original concept was
not limited to the mass murder of Jews, this analysis is neither a study of
Lemkin's thoughts about the Holocaust[13] nor of the definition and documentation of the Holocaust within the Nuremberg trials.[14] This chapter
will show that the new term genocide was not applied exclusively to Nazi
crimes against the Jews in the trial against major war criminals before
the International Military Tribunal (IMT) and in several of the twelve
subsequent proceedings before the Nuernberg Military Tribunals (NMT).

This chapter will proceed by tracing the theoretical unfolding of the
new term from its first appearance in Lemkin's book to the Genocide
Convention in 1948 and, at the same time, by showing the practical
application of the new term and the transformation of the meanings of
genocide from the IMT to the NMT trials. Particular attention will be
paid to the Race and Settlement case and a brief excursion will tackle
the early Polish trials against war criminals.

## Lemkin's Original Concept

Raphael Lemkin coined the new term genocide on the basis of a comprehensive analysis of Nazi occupation policy in the World War II. Explaining the need for "new conceptions for destructions of nations," he did not
claim that the crime as such was new, but simply that it required "new
terms."[15] Lemkin regarded genocide (the German translation of the word
means *Völkermord*[16]) not exclusively as a crime of mass murder of entire
national, racial, or religious groups. His initial concept was based on the
assumption of Nazis' having waged a "war against people."[17]

The simultaneity of denationalization, destruction of the local population and their institutions in the occupied territories by political, economic, social, cultural, and moral methods was at the heart of Lemkin's
notion of genocide. In considering a term for these policies, Lemkin
rejected the older term of denationalization because it did not include
biological and physical methods of exterminating certain peoples. Nor
did it include the aims of the oppressors which Lemkin saw as imposing
their own "national pattern"—in the Nazi case this was the biologically
motivated policy of Germanization and settlement.[18]

Lemkin's thoughts clearly arose out of the idea of the protection
of minorities which had been at the core of legal discussions in interwar Europe.[19] Sharing the contemporary view that ethnic groups, as
well as nations, were primordial, it was obvious to him that minorities
required special protection.[20] The forced assimilation and forced migration of specific groups led to the destruction of culture which appeared
as extermination of a minority group per se. Like Lemkin, Josef L.
Kunz, an Austrian-American legal scholar and expert in the field of

minority rights, put the Nazi persecution and extermination policy in the context of minority politics. Kunz identified four different methods that the Nazis, as well as other nation-states in the interwar period, had used in order to destroy ethnic minorities: first, forced denationalization (resp. assimilation), secondly, annexations of territories (irredentism), thirdly, a "voluntary" or compulsory exchange of population and other forms of forced migrations; and, fourthly, the physical extermination of national or ethnic minorities.[21]

Lemkin's new concept of genocide incorporated a whole set of different "techniques": denationalization and Germanization as methods of forced cultural assimilation *and* biological extermination; destruction of political and social institutions as methods of oppression but closely connected with plundering and compulsory labor as economic *and* biological methods of enslavement *and* extermination; forced emigrations, deportations, and replacements as physical methods for achieving an economic, cultural, *and* biological usurpation of the soil; decrease of nutrition and health service—as well as mass killings—as economically *and* biologically motivated methods for achieving the extermination of certain peoples while simultaneously strengthening the own people and other specific groups selected for assimilation.[22]

It is crucially important to keep in mind that the main aim of Lemkin's study was the documentation of the legal basis of the crimes committed under Axis rule,[23] and he created the new term genocide from this empirical analysis of Nazi occupation policy. He did not mean that the Nazis committed one, two, or many genocides—the entire occupation policy was a program of genocide with two phases: "one, destruction of the national pattern of the oppressed group; the other, the imposition of the national pattern of the oppressor."[24] Both sides of this Nazi genocide policy—also known as racial population policy—were inextricably intertwined with one another.[25] And by seeing this nexus of the Nazis' persecution and extermination policy on the one hand, and Germanization and settlement policy on the other, Lemkin was able to extract the motivation and objectives of the Nazis—territorial expansion, Germanization of the conquered countries, and economic exploitation intertwined with an extermination of all "undesired" groups of populations.[26]

## Genocide in the Inter-Allied Trial before the IMT

Lemkin's ideas had a tangible presence at Nuremberg, both through his work and his person. As a member of the US delegation and, later on, one of the legal advisors to the US chief prosecutor Jackson, Lemkin played a part in the formulation of the IMT indictment. He also corresponded with some of the prosecutors on genocide, and his book *Axis Rule* was widely read and discussed by the members of the different delegations.[27] Under count 3, war crimes, the indictment argued that the defendants had "conducted deliberate and systematic genocide, viz., the extermination of racial and national groups, against the civilian populations of certain occupied territories in order to destroy particular races and classes of people and national, racial, or religious groups, particularly Jews, Poles, and Gypsies and others."[28] For the first time the concept of genocide was applied in a court case. Furthermore, the indictment mentioned the extermination of "persons whose political belief or spiritual aspirations were deemed to be in conflict with the aims of the Nazis."[29] Genocide was defined as the annihilation and destruction of national, racial, religious, political, or social groups of people. However, the indictment did not clarify if the term "extermination" signified plain murder or if it implied a broader concept of genocide.

During the actual proceedings, the new term was not elaborated, although most of the prosecutors referred to genocide in their closing statements. The British chief prosecutor, Hartley Shawcross, listed additional aspects which had been part of the Nazi "policy of genocide": the annihilation of the mentally and physically disabled,[30] the slow death measures the Nazis had imposed on forced laborers from foreign countries,[31] and those policies aimed at reducing the birthrate in the occupied territories by sterilization, abortion, and separating men from women.[32] This physical and biological extermination of certain groups of people, particularly in the occupied territories but also in Germany, had not been an aim in itself. Shawcross advanced a sophisticated interpretation of the motivations of the Nazis that manifestly built on Lemkin's assumption of denationalization and Germanization as the core of the Nazi policy of genocide:

> Their aims went beyond mere Germanization, the imposition of the German cultural pattern upon other peoples. Hitler was resolved to expel non-Germans from the soil he required but that they owned, and colonize it by Germans ... Such were the plans for the Soviet Union, for Poland and for Czechoslovakia. Genocide was not restricted to extermination of the Jewish people or of the gypsies. It was applied in different forms to Yugoslavia, to the non-German inhabitants of Alsace-Lorraine, to the people of the Low Countries and of Norway. The technique varied from nation to nation, from people to people. The long-term aim was the same in all cases. [33]

Shawcross drew attention to the Nazi program of conquering "Lebensraum" for settlement reasons. This main tenet had led the German occupants to establish a regime based on Germanization on the one hand and on persecution and extermination on the other.

The French chief prosecutor concurred with Shawcross's opinion: "The conquest of living space, that is, of territories emptied of their population by every means including extermination—that was the great idea of the Party, the system, the state."[34] Auguste Champetier de Ribes named this strategy "the greatest crime of all, genocide, the extermination of the races or people at whose expense they intended to conquer the living space they held necessary for the so-called Germanic race."[35] At first glance, it seems as if both Shawcross and Champetier de Ribes shared the same opinion. But the French prosecutor already meant mass murder when he resorted to the terms extermination and genocide.[36]

Meanwhile, the Soviet chief prosecutor, General Roman Andreyevich Rudenko, introduced a third point of view. He attached more importance to the Nazi ideology. This "fascist racial ideology"[37] had implied murder, plunder, destruction of culture, and the extermination of people. Rudenko elucidated cultural and economic aspects. Thus, the Nazi extermination policy had hit different groups alike, political opponents of the Nazi regime, prisoners of war, forced laborers, concentration camp inmates, Jews, and other inhabitants of the occupied territories.[38] The aims of Nazi policy had not only been "world domination" but also "enslavement and genocide" per se.[39] This interpretation, which centered around the belief that the Nazi ideology had been based not so much on the strengthening of their own as on the sheer destruction of other peoples, clearly differed markedly from the British prosecutor's perspective, and owed much to the vastly different wartime experiences of the Allies but also to the Soviet interest to link genocide closely to fascism.[40]

Finally, the American chief prosecutor Robert H. Jackson hardly dealt with the concept of genocide at all. The focal point of his closing statement was not genocide but the conspiracy to overthrow the Treaty of Versailles through a war of aggression.[41] The application of the new term genocide did not figure prominently on Jackson's agenda and certainly no more than the "individual barbarities and perversions" upon which he touched fleetingly. His concern was the overarching, all-embracing "Nazi master plan."[42] Still, Jackson did not omit the policy of extermination in his closing statement: "The Nazi movement will be of evil memory in history because of its persecution of the Jews, the most far-flung and terrible racial persecution of all time."[43] None of the other Allied prosecutors had restricted the Nazi extermination program to the mass murder of the Jews as the worst of the Nazi crimes. Jackson's final emphasis was probably rooted in the same experience Telford Taylor retrospectively recalled: the sheer dimension of the mass murder of the European Jews came to full awareness only during the IMT's proceedings.[44]

In their verdict, the four Allied judges found that the main aim of the Nazis, i.e., the conquest of living space, had been amply proven by the prosecution. Therefore, they viewed the atrocities committed during the war as consequences rather than ends—but did not refer to these policies as a program of genocide:

> The evidence shows that at any rate in the East, the mass murders and cruelties were not committed solely for the purpose of stamping out opposition or resistance to the German occupying forces. In Poland and the Soviet Union these crimes were part of a plan to get rid of whole native populations by

expulsion and annihilation, in order that their territory could be used for colonization by Germans.[45]

This statement shows that the tribunal referred to another method of destruction which Lemkin had mentioned in his original account: the technique of forced displacement of populations. The four judges stressed in their judgment that "civilian populations ... of the Soviet Union and Poland" had fallen victim to systematic starvation, torture, slave labor, plunder, expulsion, and mass shootings.[46] At the same time, they elucidated the Nazi program of the Final Solution directed exclusively against the European Jews.[47] In the event, although the court adumbrated the various policies highlighted by Lemkin, neither the whole Nazi program of extermination in the occupied territories for settlement purposes, nor the mass murder of the European Jews, was explicitly labeled "genocide" in the IMT judgment. In this respect, the trial of major war criminals did not establish a precedent.

On the whole, the new term of genocide carried diverse meanings in the course of the IMT's proceedings. Genocide was used to characterize a broad policy program, composed of a set of crimes and of various "techniques" directed against several victim groups, and with the broad aim of gaining new "living space" for the purpose of colonization rather than being exclusively defined as a deliberate crime targeting an entire extermination of one single ethnic group. Predominantly, the prosecutors and the judges did not interpret the mass murder of Europe's Jews as being exclusively congruent with genocide in general, but understood the persecution and extermination of the Jews as part of the aggressive war and not only fueled by antisemitism.[48]

## The Polish Genocide Trials

If Lemkin's concept of genocide was marginal and its meaning unstable in the Nuremburg trials, it proved to be of great importance in some of the Polish war crimes trials. The Supreme National Tribunal of Poland (*Najwyższy Trybunał Narodowy,* NTN) was established to try the main Nazi perpetrators who had committed crimes in occupied Poland.[49] In particular, three cases are interesting in view of the definition and application of the term genocide in early war crimes trials: the cases against Arthur Greiser, *Gauleiter* of the Wartheland (June–July 1946), the case against Amon Leopold Göth, commandant of the concentration camp in Płaszów (August–September 1946), and the trial against Rudolf Höß, commandant of the Auschwitz concentration camp (March 1947). As the trials against Greiser and Göth had already been completed before the verdict of the IMT was handed down, the Polish judgments were the first to use the term genocide. While the trial against Greiser elucidated the main strands of Nazi occupation policy in the Wartheland, the trials against Göth and Höß focused on murder, torture, and ill-treatment of concentration camp inmates (Jews, Poles, and Soviet prisoners of war), as well as on forced labor and medical experiments.

Greiser was charged with the following offences: mass murder, ill-treatment and persecution of, and causing bodily harm to civilians and prisoners of war, "systematic destruction of Polish culture, robbery of Polish cultural treasures and Germanization of the Polish country and population, and illegal seizure of public [and private] property."[50] Additional accusations concerned the establishment of the ghetto of Łódź, and of the extermination camp at Chelmo, and various deportations of Poles and Jews to the so-called *Generalgouvernement*, as forced laborers to Germany, and of Polish children for the purpose of Germanization, and so forth. When the judges pronounced the sentence, they stated: "There were three ways of arriving at such a Germanization of the [Wartheland] …: by deportation of adult Poles and Jews, Germanization of Polish children racially suited to it, the new method of mass extermination of the Polish and Jewish population, and complete destruction of Polish culture and political thought, in other words by physical and spiritual genocide."[51] Interestingly, the Polish judges classified not only mass murder but also deportations as physical genocide. In addition, they included the aspects of cultural, political, and moral techniques in the Nazi program of persecution and extermination of the Polish and Jewish population.

In the trial against Göth, the prosecution claimed that genocide was a *crimen laesae humanitatis* (crime against humanity) and therefore *eo ipso* part of international criminal law.[52] The judges adopted the new term and declared: "This criminal organization did not reject any means of furthering their aim at destroying the Jewish nation. The wholesale extermination of Jews and also of Poles had all the characteristics of genocide in the biological meaning of this term, and embraced in addition the destruction of the cultural life of these nations."[53] Here, physical and biological extermination were blended, although the original aspect of cultural destruction played a prominent role. In the trial against Höß, neither the prosecution nor the judges employed Lemkin's term.[54] Even so, all three trials were classified as "genocide trials" by the UN War Crimes Commission, attesting to the broader definition of genocide favored by the Commission. Significantly, the UNWCC grouped yet another tribunal along with the said Polish trials: the case against Ulrich Greifelt before the Nuernberg Military Tribunal I.[55]

## The Concept of Genocide in the Race and Settlement Case

The Office of Chief of Counsel for War Crimes (OCCWC) under the direction of Telford Taylor clearly devised their prosecution strategy in the light of the IMT's outcome—but also modeled it on Lemkin's concept of genocide. Lemkin himself remained an active force behind the scenes, writing scores of memoranda to Taylor's staff advising the use of the term genocide in various planned trials and suggesting taking up other, specific trials.[56] The prosecutors used the new term genocide in several indictments and in the opening and closing statements of the trial series: in the Medical case, the Pohl case, the *Einsatzgruppen* case, the Ministries case, the High Command case, and most extensively in the Race and Settlement case.

In the so-called RuSHA trial, all fourteen defendants were officials of various SS organizations responsible for implementing the "new order" in Eastern Europe: the Main Office of the Reich Commissioner for the Strengthening of Germandom (*Stabshauptamt des Reichskommissars für die Festigung deutschen Volkstums,* RKF), the Race and Settlement Main Office of the SS (*Rasse- und Siedlungshauptamt der SS,* RuSHA), the Ethnic German Liaison Office (*Volksdeutsche Mittelstelle,* VoMi), and the *Lebensborn* society.[57] The prosecution subsumed about a dozen crimes under the counts of crimes against humanity and war crimes, such as kidnapping of "racially valuable" children, forcing "racially undesirable" pregnant women to undergo abortions, hampering reproduction of foreign nationals, sending persons who had had "interracial" sexual relationships to concentration camps, deporting foreign populations and resettling ethnic Germans (*Volksdeutsche*) on such lands, plundering of property, and for general participation in the persecution and extermination of the Jewish population.[58] The mere list of offenses attests to the significance attributed to Nazi racial population policy (*Volkstumspolitik*[59]) as a component on the persecution and extermination policy. The prosecutors stated that the object of the "systematic program of genocide" had been "to strengthen the German nation and the so-called 'Aryan' race at the expense of such other nations and groups by imposing Nazi and German characteristics upon individuals selected therefrom (such imposition being hereinafter called 'Germanization'), and by the extermination of 'undesirable' racial elements."[60]

In their Opening Statement on October 20, 1947, the prosecution offered their definition of genocide: "This program of genocide was part of the Nazi doctrine of total warfare, war waged against populations rather than against states and armed forces."[61] The foundations of the Nazi program of genocide had been laid by "theories of race and Lebensraum," the chief prosecutor James McHaney explained. Therefore the "General Plan East" (*General Plan Ost,* GPO) drafted by the defendant Konrad Meyer(-Hetling) on behalf of Himmler in 1942 played a decisive role in the prosecution's strategy. That plan of an ethnic reconstruction of Eastern Europe had been based upon displacement, expulsion, and mass killings of millions of Poles, Lithuanians, Belarusians, Russians, Ukrainians, and the entire Jewish populace in order to resettle ethnic Germans for "germanizing of the soil." The prosecutors identified the GPO as the core of the Nazi program of genocide: "It was a coordinated plan aimed at the destruction of the essential foundations of the life of national groups."[62] The prosecutors did not merely rely on Lemkin's original conceptualization of genocide; they quoted him directly and at some length:

> This destruction can be and was accomplished with the help of these defendants by a number of different means, which may be broadly classified as physical, political, biological, and cultural. They sought the "disintegration of the political and social institutions of culture, language, national feelings, religion, and the economic existence of national groups, and the destruction of the personal security, liberty, health, dignity, and even the lives of the individuals belonging to such groups."[63]

The RuSHA trial's prosecutors also reflected on the divergent notions of the term employed in Nuremberg and distinguished between their own use and that of the prosecutors in the *Einsatzgruppen* trial:

> In another courtroom of this same building, 23 leaders of the notorious Einsatzgruppen of the Security Police and SD are being tried for the mass annihilation of Jews and Russians. While a number of the defendants in this dock also participated in those very same crimes and others of similar nature, their main efforts were devoted to the destruction of national groups by other methods. The technique of these defendants was the mass deportation of oppressed peoples, the deprivation of their means of livelihood by the wholesale confiscation of property, the forced Germanization of citizens of occupied countries, and the destruction of their national culture, folkways, and educational facilities, the creation of conditions which increased the mortality rate and prevented increase of the population, and the kidnapping of children.[64]

In this case, the prosecutors assessed the annihilation of the Jews as a major crime but only as one crime amongst several that together constituted the "program of genocide" which in turn had resulted from the superordinated "master plan."[65] To that extent, they did not differ significantly from the predominant concept established in the IMT. Like that of Shawcross, the prosecutors' legal approach in Case 8 was marked by a succinctly moral emphasis reflecting Lemkin's philosophy: "These techniques of genocide, while neither so quick nor perhaps so simple as outright mass extermination, are by the very nature of things far more cruel and equally effective. If crimes such as these are allowed to go unpunished, the future of humanity is in far more danger than if an occasional murderer goes free. It is the enormity and far-reaching effects of these crimes that give this case its significance."[66]

In the closing statement, the prosecution team referred to other Nuremberg trials that had dealt with the Nazi program of genocide. Despite these parallels, the prosecutors identified a distinctive trait of the Race and Settlement case. Whereas the Medical, Pohl, and *Einsatzgruppen* cases had elucidated "primarily the negative side," the extermination of peoples, the Race and Settlement case unveiled "the

entire program of Germanization and genocide with all its ramifica-
tions."[67] The prosecutors emphasized that the Nazi policy of "strengthening Germanism" (or *Volkstumspolitik*) also had been a program of
genocide, composed of two intertwined elements:

> Genocide, as practiced by the Nazis, was a two-edged sword, both aspects
> of which were equally criminal. The positive side, according to the German
> concept, was the Germanization program by which they sought to strengthen
> themselves by adding to their population large groups of people selected
> from among the populations of the conquered territories, and by forcing the
> German language, culture, citizenship, and ideals upon those so selected.
> The negative side of this program, through which the so-called positive side
> was in equal measure accomplished, was the deliberate extermination and
> enslavement of the remaining population of these conquered territories.
> Thus, Germany would be strengthened by adding to its population, and its
> neighbors would be weakened by subtracting from their population, and the
> strength of Germany would thereby be proportionately increased.[68]

Predictably, the German defense counsels rejected all allegations that
defendants had participated in a systematic program of genocide. What
is more, the defense strategy built on the assertion that there was no
such thing as a crime of genocide in international law. Carl Haensel,
Greifelt's counsel, advanced the following argument: "An individual
cannot murder an entire people. If one wants to arrive at this legal construction, one has to start out from the premise that a people can only
be murdered by a people. Since, however, any penal guilt is the guilt of
an individual and thus the collective guilt cannot lead to punishment of
an individual, the individual cannot become guilty of genocide by leading his people to genocide."[69] Moreover, the defense lawyers argued that
the use of the term genocide lacked any positive legal basis and that,
therefore, the prosecution's charges contradicted the established maxim
of *nullum crimen sine lege, nulla poena sine lege*.[70] Finally, the defense
attorneys questioned whether relocation of population was a crime,
because past resettlements had allegedly been legal in most cases.[71] To
back up their argument, the German lawyers referred both to international agreements like the population transfer between Greece and
Turkey in the 1920s, and to the ongoing expulsions of Germans from
the Eastern territories, Poland, Czechoslovakia, and Hungary at that
time.[72] These points were quite obviously *tu quoque* ("You, too") arguments, but on the other hand they were not completely beside the point.

While the judges turned down all *tu quoque* arguments of the defense,
they indirectly agreed that the crime of genocide was not part of the
international law by refusing to integrate the term into their verdict.
The Nazi "genocide program," as the prosecution had called it, was
reduced to a "Germanization program." The judges, however, were convinced of the existence of a common plan of total Germanization and
Nazi domination in the occupied territories. They pointed out that the

program, which had been actively supported by the defendants, had been based on the following foundation: "The two-fold objective of weakening and eventually destroying other nations while at the same time strengthening Germany, territorially and biologically, at the expense of conquered nations."[73] The tribunal recognized the significance of the double character of the Nazi policy, i.e., the inseparability of the "positive" and "negative" measures and motifs.[74]

The Main Office of the RKF was seen as the "directing head of the Germanization program,"[75] while its leader Ulrich Greifelt had been, "with the exception of Himmler, the main driving force in the entire Germanization program" and "criminally responsible" for the "kidnapping of alien children; hampering the reproduction of enemy nationals; forced evacuations and resettlement of populations; forced Germanization of enemy nationals; the utilization of enemy nationals as slave labor; and the plunder of public and private property."[76] Other defendants were found equally guilty of committing these crimes. Undoubtedly, the judges viewed these crimes as parts of the Nazi extermination program: "the solution of the question of dealing with the so-called 'racially inferior' population was solved not so much by deportation as by the adoption of extermination measures, thus bringing about a speedier elimination of undesirable foreign elements by death."[77] The verdict mentioned not only physical but also biological extermination: "As a part of the gigantic program of strengthening Germany while weakening, and ultimately destroying, enemy nations, measures were taken to hamper and impede the reproduction of enemy nationals. These took the form of various decrees, all aimed at one purpose—to greatly reduce the birth rate among enemy nationals and thereby gradually bring about the destruction of the entire national group."[78] Later, these crimes would be included in the Genocide Convention, but the judges did not refer to the UN Resolution on Genocide from December 1946.

The count of the persecution and extermination of the Jews was subordinated to the other elements of the cases, such as punishments for sexual intercourse with Germans, the plundering of property, and the evacuations of enemy nationals. The judges stated: "Persecution upon racial grounds were directed particularly toward the Poles and Jews, and both the Poles and Jews were the victims of similar measures, as we have heretofore shown in this judgment."[79] This evaluation of the Nazi extermination policy clearly followed the notion of the prosecution, which had already described the destruction of the Jews as an aspect of the Nazi plan of conquering new living space. The judgment emphasized that the General Plan East had been "a drastic plan which in all its cruel aspects sought the reconversion of the East into a Germanic stronghold practically overnight."[80] The judges assumed that Konrad Meyer, the scientist who had drawn up the plan, was not guilty, but an executive tool. Instead, they held Himmler responsible for the murderous outcome of the "General Plan East" which resulted in a harsh extermination policy towards the native people.[81]

## Genocide in Other Cases before the Nuernberg Military Tribunals

Initially, Telford Taylor intended to follow Jackson's tracks and continue the conspiracy and aggressive war theory line of argument against the German defendants. Taylor did indeed regard this endeavor to link the waging of aggressive war, including the Nazi persecution and extermination policy, with militarism and the German industry as the heart of the matter at Nuremberg. Therefore, he focused on military leaders, state bureaucracy, and German business leaders for their support of the Nazis before and after the assumption of power.[82] Atrocities were mostly seen as products of aggression, war, and occupation. However, he also pursued a second, both more conventional and more straightforward approach to Nazi persecution and extermination policy, namely to convict perpetrators of atrocities.[83] This consideration was less concerned with re-educating German society or strengthening international law than with punishment. But if achieving convictions was a primary objective, then the individual's guilt would have to be proven beyond reasonable doubt, i.e., it had to be proven and to withstand scrutiny in international tribunals as well as in national criminal courts. That was the reason why the *Einsatzgruppen* case (and not the trial against the Reich Security Main Office, as planned in an early stage[84]) was implemented, because evidence of individual participation in crimes was abundant and unequivocal.[85]

In the Medical case, the prosecution team linked the crimes of human experiments, sterilization, castration, and "euthanasia" committed by German physicians in concentration camps and sanitariums to the broader Nazi policy of extermination and called these medical crimes "techniques of genocide."[86] The prosecutors tried to prove that these crimes had been testing grounds and predecessors of the mass-scale persecution and extermination policy in the occupied territories during World War II: "The thanatological knowledge [the science of producing death], derived in part from these [human] experiments, supplied the techniques for genocide, a policy of the Third Reich, exemplified in the 'euthanasia' program in the widespread slaughter of Jews, Gypsies, Poles, and Russians."[87] The prosecution similarly used the concept of genocide for the crime of sterilization: "They [the Nazis] were developing a new branch of medical science which would give them the scientific tools for the planning and practice of genocide. The primary purpose was to discover an inexpensive, unobtrusive, and rapid method of sterilization which could be used to wipe out Russians, Poles, Jews, and other people."[88] Strikingly, the prosecution team of chief prosecutor James

M. McHaney strongly emphasized the heterogeneity of the affected people. In the Medical case judgment, experiments and sterilizations were prominently marked as integral parts of a broader Nazi program, although this program was not labeled genocide.[89]

The extermination of diverse groups by means of physical and biological techniques was likewise confirmed in the indictment of the Justice case: "The Ministry of Justice participated in the Nazi program of racial purity pursuant to which sterilization and castration laws were perverted for the extermination of Jews, 'asocials,' and certain nationals of the occupied territories. In the course of the program thousands of Jews were sterilized. Insane, aged people, and sick nationals of occupied territories, the so-called 'useless eaters,' were systematically murdered."[90] Curiously, the judgment made no mention either of sterilization and "euthanasia" or of the murder of disabled people and so-called asocials. Nevertheless, it was in the Justice case that the new term genocide made its first appearance in a judgment formulated by any of the Nuremberg tribunals, even referring to the genocide resolution adopted by the General Assembly of the United Nations.[91] The judges of Case 3 defined genocide as Nazi racial persecution and extermination policy against Jews and Poles alike.[92]

McHaney had not only been chief prosecutor in the Medical but also in the three SS trials. Highlighting the instability of genocide's meaning, his interpretation of the Nazi persecution and extermination policy underwent slight but significant changes from case to case as he adapted the definition to suit the respective facts. In the Pohl case on the SS business and concentration camp system, the prosecution held the view that the Nazi extermination policy targeted different "groups considered racially inferior, such as the Poles, but the Jew was especially marked for destruction."[93] The American lawyers called the annihilation of the Jews, the deportations of thousands of people to concentration camps, the use of slave labor, and the confiscation of property a "war waged against populations" and therefore, a "crime of genocide."[94] But the Nazi policy towards the Jews had been somewhat special, the prosecution expounded: "The systematic and relentless annihilation of the Jewish people by the Nazis constitutes one of the blackest pages in the history of the civilized world."[95] Medical experiments, sterilization, "euthanasia", ill-treatment of the concentration camp prisoners (Jewish and others) and the extermination of the Jews were closely connected, the judges stated in their opinion.[96]

For all that, the verdict did not mention genocide. But Judge Michael A. Musmanno did in his concurring opinion, and set forth a definition of the new term, which differed from that of the three judges in the Justice case. In his concurring opinion, he described the extermination camps as absolute killing institutions and as manifestation of "the trend of modernity toward mechanization and assembly line method," ultimately leading to "genocide—a business so novel that a new name had to be coined for it. Genocide, the scientific extermination of a race."[97] Paraphrasing Lemkin, genocide in Musmanno's conceptualization stands for industrial mass killings of European Jewry.

The prosecution in the *Einsatzgruppen* case had charged the defendants with a "plan of genocide" that the Nazis had constantly enlarged during the war: "They [the *Einsatzgruppen*] were to destroy all those denominated Jew, political official, gypsy, and those other thousands called 'asocial' by the self-styled Nazi superman."[98] The motivation for this "crime of genocide" by the Nazis had been their racial ideology, and "the Jews were only one of the peoples marked for extermination in the Nazi program," the prosecution propounded.[99] In the closing statement, the prosecutors adhered to this opinion but added a further aspect: "It is only too well known that antisemitism was a cardinal point of Nazi ideology ... The war presented Himmler and Heydrich with what, to them, was a golden opportunity to carry these doctrines to their logical and terrible conclusion—the extermination of all Jews in Germany and in the countries overrun by the Wehrmacht."[100] The twofold narrative that the Nazi persecution and extermination policy had been directed against a range of groups of people, denominated "undesirables," but that the Jews had been especially affected,[101] had already gained acceptance in the course of the American Military Tribunals in 1947.[102]

As in the Pohl case, the *Einsatzgruppen* trial focused on the fact that first and foremost Jews had been killed, but also kept one eye on the murder of other victims: partisans, communist leaders, Romanies, mentally disordered, and so-called "Asiatic inferiors,"[103] as well as the killing of prisoners of war.[104] In principle, the judges declared, the charge in this case was murder.[105] Building on this premise, Military Tribunal II stated that the way in which the *Einsatzgruppen* had perpetrated "their homicidal duties, it appears that the Einsatz authorities now even set up a school in this new development of the fine art of genocide."[106] Musmanno and his colleagues called this particular method of mass murder "ultra-modern executions"[107] and saw them as a technique of genocide. They also identified especially the annihilation of the Jews in no uncertain terms as a "genocide program."[108] Judge Musmanno seems to have played an important role in emphasizing the special case of the Nazi mass murder of the European Jews and in referring to it as "industrialized" or engineered killing—a misleading trope, which historians would seize upon later.[109]

Yet another narrative became prevalent in 1948—not by chance in the aftermath of the Pohl and *Einsatzgruppen* cases. In the High Command and the Ministries cases, the two last trials before the NMT, the prosecutors and the judges adhered to the assumption that the "program of genocide and extermination" had mostly been perpetrated by the Security Police and SS. Genocide was therefore reduced to the extermination of the European Jews. During 1948, the broader definition of genocide as a policy composed of different techniques, directed against many groups of people, perpetrated by various agencies and layers of society, aiming not only at exclusion (extermination) but also at inclusion (Germanization), and acquisition of soil for settlement reasons, vanished. The Race and Settlement case did not displace this interpretation. Instead, the results of the other SS trials suited the political consensus of a re-emerging German society that gladly adopted the notion of the genocidal SS as an "alibi of the nation."[110]

The prosecutors in the High Command case denounced the *Einsatzgruppen* more than the Wehrmacht for being responsible for the coordinated mass murder: "The triggermen in this gigantic program of slaughter were, for the most part, the members of the so-called *Einsatzgruppen* of the SS ... The chief victims of this genocidal program were the Jews, and it can be conservatively estimated that nearly one million Russian Jews were slaughtered by the *Einsatzgruppen*."[111] The judges did not convict the Wehrmacht generals in total for committing genocide or participating in the Nazi extermination policy; they convicted single defendants solely for their knowledge of the mass murder of Soviet Jewry in the occupied territories.[112]

In the last of the twelve NMT, the Ministries case (starting in January 1948 and ending in April 1949), OCCWC lumped all remaining accused war criminals under investigation together in one trial. Initially, Taylor's team had planned individual cases against the Foreign Office members, against the bankers, against Gottlob Berger and Walter Darré, as well as against other ministers and undersecretaries. But time pressure and financial problems forced OCCWC to bring the war crimes trial program to an end.[113] Dirk Pöppmann has recently shown that the Ministries case started as a trial of the Nazi ministerial bureaucracy but ended as an SS trial.[114] The same gap between the interpretations of the prosecutors and the judges can be found in several of the NMT. However, the strategy of the prosecution itself changed in the course of the proceedings. While the team organized by chief prosecutor Robert M.W. Kempner stated in the indictment that all defendants had participated in a

> systematic program of genocide, aimed at the destruction of nations and ethnic groups within the German sphere of influence, in part by murderous extermination, and in part by elimination and suppression of national characteristics. The object of this program was to strengthen the German nation and the alleged "Aryan" race at the expense of such other nations and groups, by imposing Nazi and German characteristics upon individuals selected therefrom (such imposition being hereinafter called "Germanization") and by the extermination of "undesirable racial elements"[115]

at the end of 1947, when the indictment was filed, the prosecutors defined genocide as consisting of both Germanization *and* extermination. The detailed indictment comprised eight counts and seventy-five single elements of crimes, so that Nazi persecution and extermination policy against opponents of the occupation was dissociated from the "program for the extermination of all surviving European Jews."[116] In the Opening Statement, the Final Solution played a prominent role and all defendants were charged with taking part in this annihilation program.[117] Nevertheless, in their closing statement the prosecutors mentioned the "genocidal policy of the Third Reich" only once—and here they implied the extermination of the Jews alone and the special participation of Schellenberg and Berger in this program.[118]

Consequently, the judges did not use the new term genocide at all in their opinion. Moreover, they did not link the Germanization and resettlement program to the persecution and extermination policy. A process of decontexualizing the mass murder of the European Jews from the grand picture of Nazi policy in the occupied territories was thus well under way. Jews, Poles, Russians, Romanies, and other victims in the occupied territories were no longer perceived of as having been affected in similar ways. Instead, the persecution and extermination of the Jews was explained as an aim in itself: "Hitler made the Jewish persecution one of the primary subjects of his policy to gain and retain power."[119] A new analysis of the Nazi policy was now evolving and emanating from Nuremberg. The judges came to the conclusion that the members of the German Foreign Office had had only some knowledge of the extermination program by the *Einsatzgruppen* but "no jurisdiction or power to intervene." Event though the tribunal found that the diplomats had "played an essential part" in the deportation of Jews as slave labor and/or to the extermination camps, the judges cleared the diplomats of guilt at the Wannsee Conference and of planning the Final Solution: they "neither originated it, gave it enthusiastic support, nor in their hearts approved of it."[120]

According to the judges, the SS had had the greatest share in the extermination program. As a consequence, Berger, one of the highest-ranking SS officers in the Third Reich occupied center stage when the "mass murder charge" was brought up. He was convicted for his role in the destruction of the European Jews and sentenced to twenty-five years in prison.[121] Judge Powers elaborated on this issue in his dissenting opinion: "The handling of the so-called Jewish question was vested by Hitler exclusively in Himmler and his SS."[122] Additionally, he alleged: "The evidence by those who were on the inside of this terrible extermination program strongly tends to show that not over 100 people in all were informed about the matter."[123] Although a single man's opinion, Powers' elucidation positively represented an increasingly discernible tendency in the Nuremberg trials to restrict the meaning of genocide to the murder of the European Jews and to identify the SS as the main perpetrator. This new narrative would have major consequences in the respective realms of both history and the law.

## The Genocide Convention

Lemkin was not only involved in the American war crimes trials program, he also played a major part in the elaboration of the convention on genocide adopted by the United Nations.[124] In Lemkin's eyes, the Nuremberg trials could not have been a substitute for a universal, legally binding convention on genocide.[125] For different reasons, the definition of genocide in the eventual Genocide Convention was a reflection of the original concept rather than anything else. In fact, the prolonged process of drafting the convention mirrored the Nuremberg precedent insofar as the concept of genocide was significantly curtailed in successive steps. This development had started as early as December 1946 when the UN Resolution 96(I) had declared, "genocide is a denial of the right of existence of entire human groups, as homicide is the denial of the right to live of individual human beings." While this had clearly connoted mass murder, the resolution had also stated: "such denial of the right of existence ... results in great losses to humanity in the form of cultural and other contributions represented by these human groups."[126] The "denial of the right to existence" was used as a variable phrase for extermination but also differed from the interpretation of mass killings up to cultural destruction of "racial, religious, political and other groups ... entirely or in part." It had been Lemkin though who had drafted the first version of that resolution.[127] However, the General Assembly had implied that genocide was the murder of an entire human group (after specific criteria). While still keeping an eye on cultural destruction, the definition omitted the intention of denationalization as a state policy with all its political and socio-economic implications.[128]

Two years later the UN Convention on the Prevention and Punishment of the Crime of Genocide defined genocide in Article II:

> genocide means any of the following acts committed with intent to destroy, in whole or in part, a national, ethnical, racial, or religious group, as such: (a) Killing members of the group; (b) Causing serious bodily or mental harm to members of the group; (c) Deliberately inflicting on the group conditions of life calculated to bring about its physical destruction in whole or in part; (d) Imposing measures intended to prevent births within the group; (e) Forcibly transferring children of the group to another group.[129]

There is an ongoing debate between scholars from the legal and political sciences whether this definition is too narrow or too broad. From a historical perspective, though, it is of far greater interest to examine which parts of the original, broader concept were missing, and to ask which political interests were the reasons for this deliberate omission.

Prima facie, extermination was defined as biological or physical destruction. Culturally intended oppression or destruction of certain groups, for example prohibiting the use of native language, forced assimilation, destruction of cultural monuments and achievements—the complex of cultural genocide—was omitted.[130] But not completely: rendering the compulsory transfer of children illegal acknowledged that such policies did not only aim at the biological extermination of people but also at their cultural assimilation.[131]

Another major complex of the original empirical analysis on the Nazi "genocide" was absent—the relocation of population: forced emigration, deportation for forced labor purposes, deportation to ghettos and camps, resettlement and expulsion. The Nazi policy of relocating millions of people definitely caused "serious bodily harm," or even death as the Nazis had usually no regard for the plight of their victims. On the transports, in the camps, in segregated residential areas, the Nazis inflicted on these relocated people "conditions of life calculated to bring about [their] physical destruction" and associated with this they often "intended to prevent births." Paragraphs (b) to (d) of the Genocide Convention could surely also be intended measures in general and they were in the case of the Nazi policy of persecution and extermination without deportations and relocations, e.g. as a form of segregation policy in times of peace (conceivably also in a colonial setting) and as a form of occupation policy in times of war. However, without a designation of an actual act (deportation, segregation), paras (b) to (d) had little practical relevance.[132]

Lemkin's original concept had stated that such actions (or crimes) were based not only on racial ideology but also on concrete socio-economic interests: the Nazis sought to exterminate "undesired" groups of people *and* rob their property and possessions *and* partially exploit their manpower. Furthermore, Nazi persecution and extermination policy aimed at gaining new living space by annexing territories, making them "German," imposing National Socialist and German cultural patterns on these populations, deporting and murdering the native populace, and colonizing these regions with Germans. This means, the emphasis on genocide in the UN Convention, the reduction of "destruction" to mass killings "in whole or in part, [of] a national, ethnical, racial, or religious group," led to an—initially unintended—focus on just one single motivation, the intent to murder a group "as such." However, from a historian's perspective, the claim of an alleged, universally valid intent of genocides does not stand up to empirical examination.[133] But from a jurist's perspective, this specific intent distinguishes genocide from common murder.

The question why the negotiations of the Genocide Convention led to this inapplicable definition cannot be discussed at length here. The drafts of the Convention included several more measures aimed at the destruction of national and ethnic groups in addition to the obvious methods of killing.[134] It certainly requires little speculation to argue that a broader definition of "extermination" of certain groups of people would have put a lot of governments into serious trouble. Besides the

Soviet Union, which achieved the exclusion of the protection of political groups,[135] a range of countries and regimes pursued vested interests in obstructing a more far-reaching convention: colonial powers, apartheid states, democratic states with an indigenous minority "problem," and newly decolonized states with the objective of building a homogeneous nation all had obvious motives to discourage any move that would have made cultural, political, and socioeconomic discrimination or the destruction of minorities (including forcible population transfers and forced assimilation) an internationally criminal and punishable act.[136]

Instead of strengthening minority (or group) rights, the UN General Assembly decided to issue the Universal Declaration of Human Rights. The Genocide Convention and the Universal Declaration belong together and the latter explains to a certain extent why cultural genocide was left out of the former.[137] There were attempts to include minority rights in the Universal Declaration but finally, when the last version was promulgated, group rights were ignored. The idea of international protection of human rights and non-discrimination of individual persons differed very much from the interwar notion of the protection of minorities (in East Central and Southeast Europe). But the notion of international and global protection of minorities was ultimately dropped after World War II. The Genocide Convention—by all means a law for the protection of minorities—theoretically offered protection only to certain groups, i.e., none defined along political, social, or economic lines, from annihilation.[138] The shift from minority rights to individual human rights after 1945 "represented a considerable weakening of international will compared with the interwar League [of Nations]," as Mark Mazower has assessed the value of the Universal Declaration, because it "had no binding legal force."[139]

Scholars, apart from Lemkin, who were concerned with the protection of minorities by international law in future times, could see very clearly that these nationality conflicts or minority "problems" had not faded away in the aftermath of the war. Their claim for general principles sorted ill with the continuing population transfers in East Central and Southeast Europe[140] and the massive population exchanges between India and Pakistan—both forced migration processes—were accompanied by massive violence. But for Lemkin the coming into force of the Genocide Convention on January 12, 1951 was definitely a personal and institutional success.[141] In his unpublished manuscripts, though, he stuck to his original opinion that the Nazi genocide had been a broader policy with different techniques and victims groups. Lemkin noted: "The Nazi plan of Genocide was related to many people, races, and religions and it is only because Hitler succeeded in wiping out six million Jews, that it became known predominantly as a Jewish case."[142] Ultimately, Lemkin's thoughts and his actions seemed inconsistent,[143] although he just might have been very pragmatic.[144]

# Conclusion

The Nuremberg trials established several interpretations of the Nazi regime. Most ominous from today's perspective was that, during the years of the trial program, the planning of the Nazi persecution and extermination policy were reduced to a conspiracy of Hitler, Himmler, and Heydrich, and that perpetrators were effectively narrowed down to the SS. Equally crucial was that the mass murder of the European Jews was singled out from other Nazi mass violence. Institutional networks between the Nazi party and the state bureaucracy, economic interests of German industry, the cooperation between the Wehrmacht and the SS (Waffen-SS, Security Police and SD, as well as the regular police force) were poorly highlighted. Thus, connections between the persecution and extermination of the Jews and mass killings and ill-treatment of other people, forced labor, malnutrition and anti-guerilla warfare, Germanization, population and settlement policy, eugenics, racial policy, and antisemitism were insufficiently linked with one another.

Among historians in particular, the de-contextualization of the annihilation of the Jews from the larger framework of Nazi policy turned out to be efficacious, if misguided. Only a few studies professing an interest in the persecution and extermination of European Jewry were published between the end of the Nuremberg trials and Adolf Eichmann's trial in Israel, which would mark a turning-point in the Holocaust's rise to prominence in public memory.[145] Undoubtedly, these books, which all relied heavily on the Nuremberg evidence, were (and still are) all of great importance.[146] Although these studies concentrated on the Nazi policy toward the European Jews, the authors did not conceal that Nazi mass violence targeted also other groups of people. Nevertheless, their focus on the Jewish case considerably eased the triumph of the narrative of the Holocaust as *the* Nazi genocide, indeed, it helped construct this narrative.

Simultaneously, historical research on the Nazi policy in the annexed and occupied territories of Poland and the Soviet Union implicitly negated any connection between the population, Germanization and settlement policy, the destruction of Poles and other Slavic people on one hand and the extermination of the Jews on the other.[147] In addition, these studies drastically diminished the role of the German scientists,[148] the state bureaucracy, and the organization of the Reich Commissioner for the Strengthening of Germandom within the Nazi extermination policy.[149] At that time Polish historians entertained a broader perspective on the Nazi genocide. To them, the destruction of the Jews, the Poles, and the Germanization aims of the Nazi had all been intertwined.[150] It was not until the 1990s that historical research started to reassess Nazi population and settlement policies and re-connect these with the extermination policy, sparked by the studies of Götz Aly and Susanne Heim.[151]

The use of Lemkin's new term genocide within the Nuremberg trials varied and underwent massive changes between 1945 and 1949. Even in the IMT trial, the Allied prosecutors defined genocide in different ways. Shawcross followed Lemkin's original concept and interpreted the Nazi occupation policy as consisting of physical, biological, cultural, political, and economical persecution and extermination of populations. Jackson, by contrast, explicitly stressed the annihilation of the Jewish people and called the Nazi persecution of the Jews the most terrible racial crime in history. Two diverging interpretations of genocide thus were shaped in and emerged from the IMT arena.

Taylor's staff resorted to the concept of genocide in several of the NMT trials but with shifting implications. In the Medical, Pohl, *Einsatzgruppen*, and High Command cases, the American prosecutors focused on biological and physical methods of genocide, whereas in the Justice and Ministries cases genocide was conceptualized in a *temporally* broader manner. Here, the prosecution included the racial, political, and economical persecution of the Jews in Germany before 1939. At the same time, this interpretation was narrower because, *materially*, it focused exclusively on the Jewish case. Only in the Race and Settlement case did OCCWC's prosecutors apply genocide within a broader historical and sociological framework of oppression, persecution, and extermination of minorities and populations in occupied territories. Therefore, two interpretations of genocide came into existence during the NMT trials: one considered genocide as an overall policy of persecution and destruction of various groups of people, by various techniques, based not only on racial ideology but also on a plan of gaining living space. The other restricted genocide to the Nazi extermination policy towards the European Jews—one group of victims, one main group of perpetrators—the SS, and one ideological intent. These two, principally antagonistic lines of interpretation had already been formed during the IMT trial (even if that had not been clearly recognizable at the time) but were fully established during the NMT. Obviously, the dynamic development of these diverging interpretations followed the logic that arose from the chronology of the trials: after the Pohl, RuSHA, and *Einsatzgruppen* cases, the narrative that, above all, the SS had been the collective agent of genocide, was ultimately established. Coincidentally, such an interpretation fostered analyses and narratives that focused dominantly if not exclusively on the persecution and extermination of the European Jews.

The broader use of the term genocide mainly in the Race and Settlement case, the interpretation of genocide as a whole set of Nazi crimes not limited to mass killings, would have been impossible after the official codification of the definition of genocide in the Genocide Convention. A reduction of Lemkin's broad concept and a decontextualization from the specific Nazi crimes to transform it into a legal institution with universal force could be seen as a normal case of legislative evolution. At the same time, this process forecast the future problems historical analyses of phenomena of mass violence would face when dealing with this definition. The reason why the Genocide Convention defined genocide in a much narrower sense than Lemkin's original definition depended only partly on the perception of the persecution and mass murdering of the European Jews as the worst crime in history, because this perception had just slowly emerged in the course of the Nuremberg trials. The limitation of the concept of genocide to mass killings (and some other alleged subordinated elements of crimes) was by and large based on the both divergent and coalescing political interests of the members of the United Nations at that time.

The narrowing of the spectrum of Nazi atrocities in the Nuremberg trials and the legal formulation of the crime of genocide by reducing the original definition of the concept had a common denominator—the emerging Cold War. The diminishing scope of the term "genocide" in the course of "Nuremberg" was to a certain degree related to the changing interests of the American occupation policy in Western Germany. Although this development hardly affected the use of the genocide concept by the prosecution, the judges proved to be more concerned with historical and political changes.[152] West Germany's integration in the Western hemisphere, an important political tenet of US policy in the late 1940s, would have been much more difficult if the public service, the military elite, and the German industrialists had been convicted on charges of large-scale mass murder. The focus on the SS as the main perpetrator thus prevailed at an opportune moment.

## Notes

1. Raphael Lemkin, *Axis Rule in Occupied Europe: Laws of Occupation, Analysis of Government, Proposals for Redress* (Washington, DC, 1944), 79–95.
2. See Johannes Morsink, "Cultural Genocide, the Universal Declaration, and Minority Rights," *Human Rights Quarterly* 21 (1999): 1009–60; William A. Schabas, *Genozid im Völkerrecht* (Hamburg, 2003), 237; A. Dirk Moses, "The Holocaust and Genocide," in *The Historiography of the Holocaust*, ed. Dan Stone (New York, 2005), 533–55, here 535; Martin Shaw, *What is Genocide?* (Cambridge, 2007), 33–36; Bartolomé Clavero, *Genocide or Ethnocide, 1933–2007. How to Make, Unmake, and Remake Law with Words* (Milano, 2008), 57.
3. *New York Times*, July 2, 1947, 2.
4. *New York Times*, March 11, 1948, 10.
5. *Law Reports of Trials of War Criminals. Selected and Prepared by the United Nations War Crimes Commission [LRTWC]*, 15 vols (London, 1947–1949), here XIII, ix.
6. *Trials of War Criminals before the Nuremberg Military Tribunals under Control Council Law No. 10 [TWC]*, 15 vols (Washington, DC, 1950–1953), here XV, 1184–85; Introduction, RuSHA case, *TWC*, IV, 599.
7. *New York Times*, July 4, 1947, 4.
8. Preface, *TWC*, IV, iii–iv.
9. For an excellent summary on recent research on genocide, see Birthe Kundrus and Henning Strotbeck, "Genozid. Grenzen und Möglichkeiten eines Forschungsbegriffs—ein Literaturbericht," *Neue Politische Literatur* 51 (2006): 397–423. See also Donald Bloxham and A. Dirk Moses, "Changing Themes in the Study of Genocide,"

in *The Oxford Handbook of Genocide Studies*, eds. Bloxham and Moses (Oxford, 2010), 1–15.

10. Cf. Mark Levene, "Why Is the Twentieth Century the Century of Genocide?," *Journal of World History* 11 (2000): 305–36; A. Dirk Moses, "Conceptual Blockages and Definitional Dilemmas in the 'Racial Century': Genocide of Indigenous Peoples and the Holocaust," *Patterns of Prejudice* 36 (2002): 7–36; Christian Gerlach, "Extremely Violent Societies: an Alternative to the Concept of Genocide," *Journal of Genocide Research* 8 (2006): 455–71; Donald Bloxham, *The Final Solution: A Genocide* (Oxford, 2009).

11. Cf. Sybil Milton, "The Context of the Holocaust," *German Studies Review* 13 (1990): 269–83; Henry Friedlander, *The Origins of Nazi Genocide: From Euthanasia to the Final Solution* (Chapel Hill, 1995); Christian Gerlach, *Kalkulierte Morde. Die deutsche Wirtschafts- und Vernichtungspolitik in Weißrußland 1941–1944* (Hamburg, 1999); Götz Aly, *"Final solution:" Nazi Population Policy and the Murder of the European Jews* (New York, 1999); *National Socialist Extermination Policies: Contemporary German Perspectives and Controversies*, ed. Ulrich Herbert (New York, 2000); Michael Wildt, *Generation des Unbedingten. Das Führungskorps des Reichssicherheitshauptamt* (Hamburg, 2002); Götz Aly and Susanne Heim, *Architects of Annihilation: Auschwitz and the Logic of Destruction* (Princeton, 2003); Isabel Heinemann, *"Rasse, Siedlung, deutsches Blut": Das Rasse- und Siedlungshauptamt der SS und die rassenpolitische Neuordnung Europas* (Göttingen, 2003); *German Scholars and Ethnic Cleansing, 1919–1945*, eds. Michael Fahlbusch and Ingo Haar (New York, 2004); Wendy Lower, *Nazi-empire Building and the Holocaust in Ukraine* (Chapel Hill, 2005); Phillip T. Rutherfort, *Prelude to the Final Solution. The Nazi Program for Deporting Ethnic Poles, 1939–1941* (Lawrence, KS, 2007); Peter Longerich, *Heinrich Himmler. Biographie* (Munich, 2008).

12. See Schabas, *Genozid im Völkerrecht*, 71–74; Frank Selbmann, *Der Tatbestand des Genozids im Völkerstrafrecht* (Leipzig, 2003), 41–44.

13. See Dan Stone, "Raphael Lemkin on the Holocaust," *Journal of Genocide Research* 7 (2005): 539–50.

14. Other scholars have already analyzed how the Nuremberg trials dealt with the extermination of the European Jews and have, interestingly, come to different conclusions. Whereas Marrus considers that the IMT established the fact that the extermination of the European Jewry is "of great historical importance," Bloxham finds Nuremberg's legacy in this regard to be distorting rather than clarifying. See Michael R. Marrus, "The Holocaust at Nuremberg," *Yad Vashem Studies* 26 (1998): 5–41, here 40–41; Donald Bloxham, *Genocide on Trial. War Crimes Trials and the Formation of Holocaust History and Memory* (New York, 2001), 221–27.

15. Lemkin, *Axis Rule*, 79.

16. Actually, Lemkin did not coin the word but translated it into English or rather into a Greco-Latin derivative. The first mention of the word *Völkermord*, as far as it is known, was made by a German, August Graf von Platen, in his *Polish Songs* from 1831, which were a critique of the second division of Poland. To use the word *Völkermord* became quite prominent amongst the early German democrats in the mid-nineteenth century, whenever they denounced the oppression of the Polish nation. See *Geflügelte Worte: Zitate, Sentenzen und Begriffe in ihrem geschichtlichen Zusammenhang*, eds. Kurt Böttcher, Karl Heinz Berger, Kurt Krolop, Christa Zimmermann (Leipzig, 1981), 466.

17. Lemkin, *Axis Rule*, 81.

18. Ibid., 79–81.

19. Claudia Kraft, "Völkermorde im 20. Jahrhundert: Rafael Lemkin und die Ahndung des Genozids durch das internationale Strafrecht," in *Finis mundi: Endzeiten und Weltenden im östlichen Europa*, eds. Joachim Hösler and Wolfgang Kessler (Stuttgart, 1998), 91–110, here 101; John Cooper, *Raphael Lemkin and the Struggle for the Genocide Convention* (Basingstoke, 2008), 14–25; Stone, "Raphael Lemkin," 539.

On the protection of minorities in Europe, see: Mark Mazower, *Dark Continent: Europe's Twentieth Century* (London, 1998), 41–75; Martin Scheuermann, *Minderheitenschutz contra Konfliktverhütung? Die Minderheitenpolitik des Völkerbundes in den zwanziger Jahren* (Marburg, 2000); Carole Fink, *Defending the Rights of Others: The Great Powers, the Jews, and International Minority Protection, 1878–1938* (Cambridge, 2004).

20. A. Dirk Moses, "Lemkin, Culture, and the Concept of Genocide," in *The Oxford Handbook of Genocide Studies*, eds. Bloxham and Moses (Oxford, 2010), 19–41, here 22–25.
21. Josef L. Kunz, "The Future of the International Law for the Protection of National Minorities," *American Journal of International Law* 39 (1945), 89–95.
22. See Lemkin, *Axis Rule*, 82–90.
23. Daniel Marc Segesser and Myriam Gessler, "Raphael Lemkin and the International Debate on the Punishment of War Crimes (1919–1948)," *Journal of Genocide Research* 7 (2005), 453–68, here 461.
24. Lemkin, *Axis Rule*, 79.
25. See Stone, "Raphael Lemkin," 545.
26. After the Nuremberg trials and the declaration of the Genocide Convention, Lemkin still stuck with this opinion. In an unfinished manuscript on the Nazi crimes he discussed this Nazi driving force in a chapter entitled "Intent to Kill." See *Raphael Lemkin's Thoughts on Nazi Genocide. Not Guilty?*, ed. Steven L. Jacobs (Lewiston, 1992), 159–71.
27. See Segesser and Gessler, "Raphael Lemkin," 463; Jonathan Bush, " 'The Supreme … Crime' and Its Origins: The Lost Legislative History of the Crime of Aggressive War," *Columbia Law Review* 120 (2002), 2324–424, here 2368; Anson Rabinbach, "The Challenge of the Unprecedented—Raphael Lemkin and the Concept of Genocide," *Simon Dubnow Institute Yearbook* 4 (2005): 397–420, here 410; Cooper, *Raphael Lemkin*, 62–75.
28. Indictment, *Trial of the Major War Criminals before the International Military Tribunal [IMT]*, 42 vols (Nuremberg, 1947–49), here I, 43–44.
29. Ibid., 66–67.
30. Closing Statement of the British Prosecution, Hartley Shawcross, July 27, 1946, *IMT*, XIX, 509.
31. Ibid., 514–15.
32. Ibid., 498.
33. Ibid., 496–97. Lemkin's cited this passage of Shawcross's closing statement in length in his unfinished manuscript. This citation and the discussion about the motivation of the Nazis is part of the chapter "Intent to Kill." See *Raphael Lemkin's Thoughts*, 171. Dan Stone erroneously attributed Shawcross's citation to Lemkin; see Stone, "Raphael Lemkin," 544.
34. Closing Statement of the French Prosecution, M. Auguste Champetier de Ribes, July 29, 1946, *IMT*, XIX, 543.
35. Ibid., 561–62.
36. Ibid., 531.
37. Closing Statement of the Soviet Prosecution, Gen. Rudenko, July 29, 1946, *IMT*, XIX, 600.
38. Ibid., 574.
39. Ibid., 570.
40. This reading was not too dissimilar from Hannah Arendt's theoretical analysis of the Nazi totalitarian movement which, though, also applied to Stalin's Soviet Union. See particularly her chapter on the concentration camps: Hannah Arendt, *The Origins of Totalitarianism* (New York, 1951).
41. See, for example, Closing Statement of the American Prosecution, Robert Jackson, July 26, 1946, *IMT*, XIX, 406.

42. *Report of Robert H. Jackson, United States Representative to the International Conference on Military Trials, London 1945* (Washington, DC, 1949), 48. Cf. Bradley F. Smith, *The Road to Nuremberg* (New York, 1981); Marrus, "Holocaust at Nuremberg," 14.

43. Closing Statement Jackson, *IMT*, XIX, 404.

44. Telford Taylor, *Anatomy of the Nuremberg Trials: A Personal Memoir* (New York, 1992), xi.

45. Judgment, September 30, 1946, *IMT*, XXII, 480.

46. Ibid., 477–78, 484–85.

47. Ibid., 491–96. Cf. Marrus, "Holocaust at Nuremberg," 38.

48. Lawrence Douglas, "Film as Witness: Screening Nazi Concentration Camps before the Nuremberg Trials," *Yale Law Journal* 105 (1995): 477; Marrus, "Holocaust at Nuremberg," 39–40.

49. On the NTN trials, see Tadeusz Cyprian and Jerzy Sawicki, *Siedem procesów przed Najwyższym Trybunałem Narodowym* (Poznań, 1962); Janusz Gumkowski and Tadeusz Kułakowski, *Zbrodniarze hitlerowscy przed Najwyższym Trybunałem Narodowym* (Warsaw, 1965); Alexander V. Prusin, "Poland's Nuremberg: The Seven Court Cases of the Supreme National Tribunal, 1946–1948," *Holocaust and Genocide Studies* 24 (2010): 1–25. Excerpts of some NTN trials are published in English translation in the UNWCC's series, see *LRTWC*, VII, XIII, and XIV.

50. Trial of Artur [sic] Greiser, *LRTWC*, XIII, 71.

51. Judgment of the NTN, Trial of Greiser, *LRTWC*, XIII, 114.

52. Trial of Amon Leopold Goeth, *LRTWC*, VII, 7.

53. Judgment of the NTN, Trial of Goeth, *LRTWC*, VII, 9.

54. Trial of Rudolf Franz Ferdinand Hoess [Höß], *LRTWC*, VII, 11–26.

55. Foreword by Robert Wright, *LRTWC*, XIII, vii–ix. On the history of the UNWCC, see Robert Wright, *The History of the United War Crimes Commission and the Development of the Laws of War* (London, 1948); Arieh Kochavi, "Britain and the Establishment of the United Nations War Crimes Commission," *English Historical Review* 107 (1992): 323–49.

56. In January 1947, after the UN General Assembly had adopted the Resolution on the crime of genocide in December 1946, Lemkin wrote three memoranda on the crime of genocide and how it could be charged in the NMT trials, and sent them to OCCWC: "The Importance of the Genocide Concept for the Doctors Case," "The Participation of German Industrialists and Bankers in Genocide," and "Planning of a Special Trial on Abduction of Women into Prostitution." See Paul Weindling, *Nazi Medicine and the Nuremberg Trials: From Medical War Crimes to Informed Consent* (Basingstoke, 2004), 227–28, 230–31; Jonathan A. Bush, "The Prehistory of Corporations and Conspiracy in International Criminal Law: What Nuremberg Really Said," *Columbia Law Review* 109 (2009): 1094–262, here 1178–81 and 1258. See also Paul Weindling's contribution in this book.

57. For more details on the RuSHA case, about the individual defendants, and the strategies of the prosecution and defense, see: Heinemann, "*Rasse, Siedlung, deutsches Blut*," 565–80; Alexa Stiller, "Die Volkstumspolitik der SS vor Gericht: Strategien der Anklage und Verteidigung im Nürnberger RuSHA-Prozess, 1947–1948," in *Leipzig—Nürnberg—Den Haag: Neue Fragestellungen und Forschungen zum Verhältnis von Menschenrechtsverbrechen, justizieller Säuberung und Völkerstrafrecht*, ed. Helia-Verena Daubach (Düsseldorf, 2008), 66–86.

58. RuSHA case, Indictment, July 1, 1947, *TWC*, IV, 609–10.

59. The Nazi term *Volkstumspolitik* is literally translated as "ethnicity policy," but it was actually a racial population and settlement policy intertwined with the Nazi persecution and extermination policy. See: Alexa Stiller, "Grenzen des 'Deutschen': Nationalsozialistische Volkstumspolitik in Polen, Frankreich und Slowenien während des Zweiten Weltkrieges," in *Deutschsein als Grenzerfahrung: Minderheiten-*

*politik in Europa zwischen 1914 und 1950*, eds. Mathias Beer, Dietrich Beyrau, and Cornelia Rauh (Essen, 2009), 61–84.

60. RuSHA case, Indictment, July 1, 1947, *TWC*, IV, 610.
61. RuSHA case, Opening Statement of the Prosecution, October 20, 1947, *TWC*, IV, 622.
62. Ibid., 626.
63. Ibid., 626.
64. Ibid., 627. In fact, when two former staff members of the OCCWC compiled the trial materials for publication, they put the RuSHA and the *Einsatzgruppen* cases together in one volume because, from their point of view, these two trials belonged together and had shown two different aspects of the Nazi genocide program. See: 3rd Draft of the Preface, RuSHA case, Green Series, December 15, 1948, National Archives and Records Administration (NARA), RG 238, NM-70, Entry 159, Box 2, Folder 2.
65. RuSHA case, Opening Statement of the Prosecution, October 20, 1947, *TWC*, IV, 634, 637, 663, 687, 693–94. Interestingly, the passage on the persecution of the Jews in the Opening Statement is literally identical with one in the Opening Statement in the Pohl case. See Ibid., 666; Pohl case, Opening Statement of the Prosecution, April 8, 1947, *TWC*, V, 250–51. But this identical passage is hardly surprising because both prosecution teams were headed by James M. McHaney, Chief of the SS Division, Chief Prosecutor, and later Deputy Chief of Counsel in the Medical, the Pohl, the RuSHA, the Hostages, the *Einsatzgruppen*, and the High Command cases. Hans Froehlich and Daniel J. Shiller were also active in the preparation of the Pohl and RuSHA cases for trial and respective members of the prosecution counsel.
66. RuSHA case, Opening Statement of the Prosecution, October 20, 1947, *TWC*, IV, 626–27.
67. RuSHA case, Closing Statement of the Prosecution, February 13, 1948, *TWC*, V, 31.
68. Ibid.
69. RuSHA case, Opening Statement for Defendant Greifelt, Dr. Carl Haensel, November 20, 1947, *TWC*, IV, 701–702.
70. Carl Haensel (Greifelt's attorney), RuSHA Trial transcript, German translation, 1194–95; Karl Dötzer (Brückner's attorney), ibid., 1257; Kurt Behling (Meyer's attorney), ibid., 1295.
71. Werner Schubert (Lorenz' attorney), ibid., 1267.
72. Haensel, ibid., 1186, 1196; Dötzer, ibid., 1258.
73. RuSHA case, Opinion and Judgment, March 10, 1948, *TWC*, V, 90.
74. Ibid., 96.
75. Ibid., 100–2.
76. Ibid., 154–55.
77. Ibid., 97.
78. Ibid., 121.
79. Ibid., 152.
80. Ibid., 156.
81. Mechthild Rössler, "Konrad Meyer und der 'Generalplan Ost' in der Beurteilung der Nürnberger Prozesse," in *Der 'Generalplan Ost.' Hauptlinien der nationalsozialistischen Planungs- und Vernichtungspolitik*, eds. Mechthild Rössler and Sabine Schleiermacher (Berlin, 1993), 356–68.
82. See the chapter by Kim C. Priemel in this book.
83. The Medical and the *Einsatzgruppen* cases were primarily murder trials. See Weindling, *Nazi Medicine*, 170; Hilary Earl, *The Nuremberg SS-Einsatzgruppen Trial, 1945–1958. Atrocity, Law, and History* (New York, 2009), 81–82.
84. Ferencz recommended a concentration on Ohlendorf, the *Einsatzgruppen*, and the SD. See Intra-Office Memorandum from Ferencz to Section Chiefs, February 5, 1947, NARA, RG 238, NM-70, Entry 202, Box 3, Folder 1. Cf. Memorandum from Taylor to Ervin and others, February 6, 1947, printed in Bush, "Prehistory," 1262.

85. Bloxham, *Genocide on Trial*, 189–94; Earl, *SS-Einsatzgruppen Trial*, 76–82, 95.
86. Raphael Lemkin, "Genocide as a Crime under International Law," *The American Journal of International Law* 41 (1947): 145–51, here 147, footnote 6; Michael R. Marrus, "The Doctor's Trial in Historical Context," *Bulletin of the History of Medicine* 73 (1999): 106–23, here 116; Weindling, *Nazi Medicine*, 170, 179–87, 225–32.
87. Medical case, Opening Statement of the Prosecution, December 9, 1946, in *TWC*, I, 38.
88. Ibid., 48.
89. Medical case, Opinion and Judgment, August 19, 1947, *TWC*, II, 181, 183, 197, 278.
90. Justice case, Indictment, January 4, 1947, *TWC*, III, 20–21.
91. Justice case, Opinion and Judgment, December 3–4, 1947, *TWC*, III, 983.
92. Ibid., 1063–64, 1128, 1142, 1146, 1156.
93. Pohl case, Opening Statement of the Prosecution, April 8, 1947, *TWC*, V, 250–51.
94. Ibid., 250–51, 253, see also 232–33.
95. Ibid., 250–51.
96. Pohl case, Opinion and judgment, November 3, 1947, *TWC*, V, 971–80.
97. Pohl case, Concurring opinion by Judge Musmanno, November 3, 1947, *TWC*, V, 1135.
98. *Einsatzgruppen* case, Opening Statement of the Prosecution, September 29, 1947, *TWC*, IV, 30–31.
99. Ibid., 32–33.
100. Ibid., 369–70.
101. On the presupposition of intent in the *Einsatzgruppen* case, see Bloxham, *Genocide on Trial*, 204–6; Earl, *SS-Einsatzgruppen Trial*, 211–16.
102. Further work on this issue needs to be done.
103. *Einsatzgruppen* case, Opinion and Judgment, April 8–9, 1948, *TWC*, IV, 415–16.
104. "The extermination program on racial and political grounds also extended to prisoners of war." Ibid., 441.
105. Ibid., 411.
106. Ibid., 450.
107. Ibid., 450.
108. Ibid., 469–70.
109. On Musmanno, see the chapter by Earl in this book.
110. This phrase goes back to Gerald Reitlinger, *The SS: Alibi of a Nation 1922–1945* (Melbourne, 1956). See the chapter by Jan Erik Schulte in this book.
111. High Command case, Opening Statement of the Prosecution, February 5, 1948, *TWC*, X, 138–39. Cf. also High Command case, Closing Statement of the Prosecution, August 10, 1948, *TWC*, XI, 347, 353, 364. On the High Command case in general, see Valerie G. Hebert, *Hitler's Generals on Trial. The Last War Crimes Tribunal at Nuremberg* (Lawrence, KS, 2010).
112. High Command case, Judgment, October 27–28, 1948, *TWC*, XI, 462–697, in particular 547–49.
113. Telford Taylor, *Final Report to the Secretary of the Army on the Nuernberg War Crimes Trials under Control Council Law No. 100* (Washington, DC, 1949), 76. For a general overview, see Frank Buscher, *The U.S. War Crimes Trial Program in Germany, 1946–1955* (New York, 1989).
114. Dirk Pöppmann, "Der Wilhelmstraßenprozess—ein Ministerial- oder SS-Verfahren?," paper presented at the conference "Negotiating the Past: German-American Perspectives in the U.S. War Crimes Trials in Nuremberg, 1946–1949," at the European University Viadrina, Frankfurt, April 23–25, 2009.
115. Ministries case, Indictment, November 4, 1947, *TWC*, XII, 44.
116. Ibid., 45–49.
117. Ministries case, Opening Statement of the Prosecution, January 6, 1948, *TWC*, XII, 176, 204, 219, 232.

118. Ministries case, Closing Statement of the Prosecution, November 9, 1948, *TWC*, XIV, 41.

119. Ministries case, Judgment, April 11–13, 1949, *TWC*, XIV, 470.

120. Ibid., 472–78.

121. Ibid., 541, 48, 666–67.

122. Ministries case, Dissenting Opinion of Judge Powers, April 13, 1949, *TWC*, XIV, 910–11.

123. Ibid., 910. For that reason, Powers found von Weizsäcker, Woermann, Steengracht von Moyland, Veesenmayer, Dietrich, Schwerin von Krosigk, and Puhl not guilty of taking part in the extermination of the Jews. See ibid., 909–31.

124. Cooper, *Raphael Lemkin*.

125. Weindling, *Nazi Medicine*, 228.

126. United Nations Resolution 96 (I). The Crime of Genocide, December 11, 1946, http://www.un.org/documents/ga/res/1/ares1.htm (May 2010).

127. Lemkin, "Genocide as a Crime," 148–50.

128. Shaw, *What is Genocide?*, 27, 33–36; Clavero, *Genocide or Ethnocide*, 39, 45.

129. Convention on the Prevention and Punishment of the Crime of Genocide, adopted by Resolution 260 (III) A of the UN General Assembly on December 9, 1948, Entry into force: January 12, 1951, *United Nations Bulletin* 5 (1948): 1012–15.

130. Josef L. Kunz, "The United Nations Convention on Genocide," *The American Journal of International Law* 43 (1949): 738–46, here 742.

131. Clavero, *Genocide or Ethnocide*, 53–56. Cf. Robert van Krieken, "The Barbarism of Civilization: Cultural Genocide and the 'Stolen Generations'", *British Journal of Sociology* 52 (1999): 295–313; *Genocide and Settler Society: Frontier Violence and Stolen Indigenous Children in Australian History*, ed. A. Dirk Moses (New York, 2004); Ward Churchill, *Kill the Indian, Save the Man: The Genocidal Impact of American Indian Residential Schools* (San Francisco, 2004).

132. The original concept of Lemkin's "genocide" covered what has become known as "ethnic cleansing" since the 1990s. However, the Genocide Convention does not include population relocations in any way. Nowadays scholars differentiate between both acts by referring to the intent: while the intention of genocide is the total physical and biological destruction of a group of people, ethnical cleansing intends "only" the expulsion of a supposedly ethnically homogeneous population. See Schabas, *Genozid im Völkerrecht*, 265; Norman M. Naimark, *Flammender Hass. Ethnische Säuberungen im 20. Jahrhundert* (Munich, 2004), 12. The question remains if this difference is not only theoretically construed for legal reasons but historically hard to detect for both acts occur simultaneously and are often intertwined. Or, as Lemkin suggested in *Axis Rule*, what we call genocide and ethnic cleansing principally pursue an identical intention.

133. On the problematic issue of the decision-making process to commit genocide within historical analyses, see Birthe Kundrus, "Entscheidung für den Völkermord? Einleitende Überlegungen zu einem historiographischen Problem," *Mittelweg* 36, 6 (2006): 4–17.

134. First Draft of the Genocide Convention by the UN Secretariat, [May] 1947 (UN Doc. E/447), and Second Draft of the Genocide Convention, Ad Hoc Committee of the Economic and Social Council (ECOSOC), April 5, 1948 and May 10, 1948 (UN Doc. E/AC.25/SR.1 to 28), http://www.preventgenocide.org/law/convention/drafts/ (May 2010). For more details, see: Kunz, "UN Convention on Genocide," 738–46; Morsink, "Cultural Genocide;" Schabas, *Genozid im Völkerrecht*, 75–137; Matthew Lippman, "A Road Map to the 1948 Convention on the Prevention and Punishment of Genocide," *Journal of Genocide Research* 4 (2002): 177–95.

135. On the other hand, the communist delegations favored a cultural genocide paragraph. See Morsink, "Cultural Genocide."

136. Some authors hint to these diverse political interests. Cf. Morsink, "Cultural Genocide;" Schabas, *Genozid im Völkerrecht*, 239–45, 258–60; Anson Rabinbach,

"Challenge of the Unprecedented," 402; Calvero, *Genocide and Ethnocide*, 54–55. It should also be noted that Pakistan brought up the charge of genocide against India, because of India's mistreatment towards Moslems, before the Security Council several times in 1948. See Cooper, *Raphael Lemkin*, 127.

137. Morsink, "Cultural Genocide;" Johannes Morsink, *The Universal Declaration of Human Rights: Origins, Drafting, and Intent* (Philadelphia, 1999).

138. Joseph B. Schechtman, "Decline of the International Protection of Minority Rights," *The Western Political Quarterly* 4 (1951): 1–11; Josef L. Kunz, "The Present Status of the International Law for the Protection of Minorities," *American Journal of International Law* 48 (1954): 282–87, here 284.

139. Mark Mazower, "The Strange Triumph of Human Rights, 1933–1950," *Historical Journal* 47 (2004): 379–98.

140. Kunz, "Future of the International Law," 94–95; Hans Rothfels, "Frontiers and Mass Migration in Eastern Central Europe," *Review of Politics* 8 (1946): 37–67.

141. On Lemkin's campaign for ratification of the Genocide Convention, see Cooper, *Raphael Lemkin*, 173–88.

142. Lemkin's draft on "The Hitler Case", n.d., cited in Rabinbach, "Challenge of the Unprecedented," 408; Stone, "Raphael Lemkin," 546.

143. On Lemkin's inconsistencies, see Clavero, *Genocide or Ethnocide*, 57.

144. Moses, "Lemkin, Culture, and the Concept of Genocide," 37–38.

145. On the development of Holocaust memory in American Society, see: Peter Novick, *The Holocaust in American Life* (Boston, 1999), 103–24; Lawrence Baron, "The Holocaust and American Public Memory, 1945–1960," *Holocaust and Genocide Studies* 17 (2003): 62–88.

146. See: Léon Poliakov, *Bréviaire de la haine: Le IIIe Reich et les juifs* (Paris, 1951) [*Harvest of Hate: The Nazi Program for the Destruction of the Jews of Europe* (Syracuse, 1954)]; Gerald Reitlinger, *The Final Solution: the Attempt to Exterminate the Jews of Europe 1939–1945* (London, 1953); *Das Dritte Reich und die Juden: Dokumente und Aufsätze*, eds. Léon Poliakov and Joseph Wulf (Berlin, 1955); Wolfgang Scheffler, *Judenverfolgung im Dritten Reich: 1933–1945* (Berlin, 1960); Gerhard Schoenberner, *Der gelbe Stern: die Judenverfolgung in Europa 1933 bis 1945* (Hamburg, 1960) [*The Holocaust: The Nazi Destruction of Europe's Jews* (Edmonton, 1969)]; Raul Hilberg, *The Destruction of the European Jews* (New York, 1961).

147. Robert L. Koehl, *RKFDV: German Resettlement and Population Policy 1939–1945. A History of the Reich Commission for the Strengthening of Germandom* (Cambridge, 1957). In contrast, see Ihor Kamentsky, *Secret Nazi Plans for East Europe. A Study of Lebensraum Policies* (New York, 1961).

148. Helmut Heiber, "Der Generalplan Ost," *Vierteljahreshefte für Zeitgeschichte* 6 (1958): 281–325.

149. Hans Buchheim, "Rechtsstellung und Organisation des Reichskommissars für die Festigung deutschen Volkstums," in *Gutachten des Instituts für Zeitgeschichte* (Munich, 1958), 239–79; Martin Broszat, *Nationalsozialistische Polenpolitik 1939–1945* (Stuttgart, 1961).

150. Tadeusz Cyprian and Jerzy Sawicki, *Nazi Rule in Poland 1939–1945* (Warsaw, 1961); Janusz Gumkowski and Kazimierz Leszczyński, *Poland under Nazi Occupation* (Warsaw, 1961); *Genocide 1939–1945. War Crimes in Poland*, eds. Szymon Datner, Janusz Gumkowski and Kazimierz Leszezyński (Poznań, 1962).

151. Aly and Heim, *Architects of Annihilation*; Aly, *"Final Solution."*

152. Jonathan Friedman, "Law and Politics in the Subsequent Nuremberg Trials, 1946–1949," in *Atrocities on Trial. Historical Perspectives on the Politics of Prosecuting War Crimes*, eds. Patricia Heberer and Jürgen Matthäus (Lincoln, NE, 2008), 75–101, here 92f.

## CHAPTER 5

# THE SS AS THE "ALIBI OF A NATION"?
## NARRATIVE CONTINUITIES FROM THE
## NUREMBERG TRIALS TO THE 1960S

*Jan Erik Schulte*

⟨◦ss⟩

### Introduction

In the judgment of the Nuremberg International Military Tribunal
(IMT) the *Schutzstaffel* (SS or Protective Squad) of the National Socialist Party was named a criminal organization. Even before the verdict
was delivered, Allied propaganda,[1] the media[2] and especially the testimonies during the IMT proceedings had made clear that the SS was
responsible for major crimes and atrocities of the Third Reich. It therefore came as no surprise that SS men and their crimes were at the
center of successive Allied war crimes trials. Notably, at the location of
the former Dachau concentration camp, US authorities initiated 489
trials against 1,672 defendants of whom the majority were SS men,
including concentration camp guards and *Waffen SS* soldiers. More than
400 death sentences were passed. Of these some 300 were carried out.[3]

When the US Chief of Counsel for War Crimes decided to stage major
follow-up proceedings to the International Military Tribunal against
the major war criminals, the SS figured prominently on his agenda.
Indeed, according to Telford Taylor, Chief of Counsel for War Crimes,
at least three, i.e. one out of four, of the so-called Nuremberg Military
Trials (NMT) could be labeled as SS trials.[4] These included the so-called
Pohl (Case 4), RuSHA (Case 8), and *Einsatzgruppen* trials (Case 9).

Other Nuremberg proceedings dealt with individual SS members and with crimes that were attributed to the SS, notably the Medical trial with its score of "SS physicians," and the Ministries case in which the high-ranking officers Gottlob Berger and Walter Schellenberg featured prominently. The first of the "all SS" trials was that of Oswald Pohl and his fellow defendants from the former SS Economic and Administration Main Office. From 1942 to the end of the war, Pohl's apparatus had been responsible for the concentration camp system, including Auschwitz, for the exploitation of concentration camp labor and for collecting and distributing the valuables stolen from Jewish victims of the Holocaust.

In contrast to other groups of NMT defendants, few of the former SS officers escaped heavy sentences at the end of the trials. In the Pohl case, four defendants were sentenced to death.[5] Given the already established information about atrocities committed by the SS, both judges and prosecution counsels conceived of the SS officers as major perpetrators. Although the Chief of Counsel's office set out to prove individual criminality, it appeared that the prosecution's portrayal of the SS as a homogeneous and all-powerful elite was especially well received by the tribunals. Not only individuals but the SS as a whole seemed to stand trial in several of the Nuremberg Subsequent Trials.

The prosecution's strategy proved successful, not only in obtaining severe sentences for the SS defendants. It seems that the image of the SS created by the prosecution, the courts, the defendants, and some of the witnesses also helped to establish a major and seemingly coherent set of narratives about the character and the history of the SS. These narratives, it will be shown, were prominent in popular and academic publications from the end of the Nuremberg trials at least up to the 1960s.

Although there were varied reasons for creating and supporting these narratives, e.g. the depiction of the SS as a coherent, uniform organization, of the Reich Leader SS Heinrich Himmler as the omnipotent arch villain, or of the SS as the Third Reich's evil force, they intentionally or unintentionally helped to distance the SS from the rest of German society. Unlike the plethora of details that were uncovered and presented during the trials, the major narratives which dominated the proceedings and public perception did not help in clarifying the historical role of the SS and other actors in Nazi Germany. For the time being the trials in fact closed the door for a broader debate on the Nazi past rather than opening it.

The present article asks how these narratives were established and of which elements they were made up. In addition, it analyzes the relevance of these narratives in the formation of a broader representation or historical consciousness of the Nazi past in West Germany. Therefore, the article will trace the development of the images of the SS which were first created during the Nuremberg trials and subsequently repeated in various publications. Starting with a short evaluation of the IMT judgment of the SS, it will analyze the background to and the reasoning in the Chief of Counsel's prosecution strategy during the subsequent Nuremberg trials and especially with regard to the SS trials. The Pohl case will be taken as a major example to illustrate the dynamics of the court procedure. Here, the parties' various strategies of presenting the SS will be reconstructed. Finally, the article will examine which images and which aspects of the trials came to dominate post-1949 on the SS, and what purpose these publications explicitly or implicitly pursued.

## SS Criminality and Preparations for the Subsequent Trials

It is often overlooked that the trial of the major war criminals, which took place in Nuremberg from November 14, 1945 to October 1, 1946, involved not only individuals as defendants. In addition to twenty-two high-ranking officials of the Third Reich, the prosecution indicted various National Socialist organizations. These were accused of having been criminal associations. Each of these organizations had its own defense counsel. Three of these entities the tribunal did not find to be entirely criminal in the end: the *Sturmabteilungen* (SA or Storm Troopers), the Reich Government, and the *Generalstab* and the High Command of the Wehrmacht.[6] However, in their verdict, the four Allied judges declared the following entities to be criminal organizations: first, the corps of the political leaders of the Nazi Party; second, the *Geheime Staatspolizei* (Gestapo or Secret State Police) as well as the SS-*Sicherheitsdienst* (SD or Security Service), both of which had been under the supervision of Heinrich Himmler, Reich Leader of the SS; and third, the SS as a whole.

The SS therefore was seen to have stood at the center of National Socialist criminality. There were some exceptions, notably the *Reiter-SS* (Mounted SS) and the *Waffen SS* conscripts who had joined in the later stages of the war. But overall, the verdict perceived the SS as the most heinous organization of National Socialist Germany. In this sense, the judges followed the prosecution's lead. In his opening address at the beginning of the IMT, Robert H. Jackson, US Chief of Counsel, had already suggested that the SS belonged to "the worst of the [Nazi] movement."[7] On November 21, 1945, he further pointed out that the majority of those who had worked for the SS had been both volunteers and ideologically committed to the SS goals: "Except for a late period when some compulsory recruiting was done in the SS, membership in all these militarized formations was voluntary. The police organizations were recruited from ardent partisans who enlisted blindly to do the dirty work the leaders planned."[8]

Clearly, in the IMT verdict those crimes that were most closely associated with National Socialist barbarity were also most closely linked to the SS: the extermination of the Jews, the concentration camps, terror against civilians in the occupied territories, forced labor, and the maltreatment and killing of prisoners of war.[9] The judgment reads: "It is impossible to single out any one portion of the SS which was not involved in these criminal activities."[10] While the judges declared that knowledge of the SS crimes had been widespread, the SS in itself was seen as an essentially homogeneous organization, an elite group with a strong and unifying ideological belief:[11]

> It must be recognized, moreover, that the criminal activities of the SS followed quite logically from the principles on which it was organized. Every effort had been made to make the SS a highly disciplined organization composed of the elite of National Socialism ... Himmler also indicated his view that the SS was concerned with perpetuating the elite racial stock with the object of making Europe a Germanic continent and the SS was instructed that it was designed to assist the Nazi Government in the ultimate domination of Europe and the elimination of all inferior races. This mystic and fanatical belief in the superiority of the Nordic German developed into the studied contempt and even hatred of other races which led to criminal activities of the type outlined above being considered as a matter of course if not a matter of pride.[12]

The Tribunal's verdict prepared the stage for the prominence of the SS in the Nuremberg Subsequent Trials. Without question, the SS was bound to be on center stage whenever National Socialist criminality was being prosecuted. At the same time, the IMT's rhetoric also set the tone for the arguments which would dominate the NMT procedures.

Before contemplating the subsequent trials, the Allies had already discussed plans for a second international trial. Although there seems to have been a tentative agreement on this scheme, both the British and the Americans were reluctant to follow up the idea, and Jackson in particular favored trials by the individual occupying powers. While the French were still pursuing the idea of a second international trial, the American and the British governments had made up their minds by mid-1946. However, it was only in early 1947 that the United States informed the other powers that no second international trial would take place. By that time US preparations for the subsequent trials were already in full swing.[13]

Jackson's successor Telford Taylor, the new Chief of Counsel, became responsible for the subsequent proceedings which were to be held in Nuremberg. Initially, the main focus was to be on the indictment of the industrialists or, in Taylor's words, "future trials ... would emphasize the economic case."[14] That notwithstanding, the SS still figured prominently in Taylor's trial preparations. One of the four prosecution divisions which prepared the different cases was entirely devoted to the SS cases. This "SS Division" was headed by New York attorney James McHaney.[15] At the Berlin Branch of the Office of Chief of Counsel, where the documents representing different National Socialist institutions were assessed, McHaney's group "was larger than any other group."[16]

However, according to Benjamin Ferencz, head of the Berlin Branch, the group which was "responsible for gathering evidence against members of the SS" had many inexperienced analysts. Their task was overwhelming as there was "an almost inexhaustible amount of material to be examined by this group."[17]

Because criminal activity, potential defendants, and documents seemed to be abundant, seven cases against SS members were contemplated. Of these cases three actually went to court. The first was the so-called Medical case (Case 1).[18] In the strict sense, this was not an SS case. Only a portion, albeit a large one, of the defendants were former SS members. It was primarily the medical profession, not the SS as an organization that stood trial.[19] This was different in the Pohl case (Case 4) and in the Race and Settlement aka RuSHA case (Case 8).[20] In both these trials, almost all defendants were former SS members, and specific sub-divisions of the SS stood at the center of the trials. A case against Himmler's aide-de-camp Karl Wolff and his office, another against Hans Jüttner, a general of the Waffen SS and head of the SS *Führungshauptamt*, as well as one against Gottlob Berger and the SS Main Office were planned.[21] The Office of Chief of Counsel also intended to prosecute officials of the Reich Security Main Office (RSHA), which had included the Gestapo and SD. Yet it seems that little research capacity was actually assigned to this task.[22] In the further course of the preparations, which were hampered by financial and time restrictions, Taylor was not too keen to go ahead with the RSHA case. When finally the reports of the SS *Einsatzgruppen* were evaluated and the monstrosity of their criminal behavior became known, the planned proceeding was basically transformed into a trial against the leaders of the *Einsatzgruppen* (Case 9).[23]

Out of the fifty-six defendants in the three SS cases (4, 8, and 9), fifty-four had been SS officers.[24] The exceptions were Hans Hohberg, a civilian and business manager, who had held a prominent position in Pohl's economic empire, and Inge Viermetz, a female *Lebensborn* official who, because of her sex, had been barred from SS membership. Also, ten out of twenty-three defendants in the Medical trial were former SS men, mostly senior SS officers.[25] In the Justice case (Case 3), three defendants had been members of the SS, one a so-called supporting member (*Förderndes Mitglied*), another an advisor to the SD.[26] And finally, the economic cases featured a number of members of the notorious Circle of Friends of the Reich Leader SS (Himmler) where the industrialists had socialized with the likes of Pohl, *Einsatzgruppen* Leader Otto Ohlendorf and Wolfram Sievers of the SS's *Ahnenerbe* Institute.[27] Three of the defendants in the Flick, IG Farben, and Krupp cases were actually former members of the SS, and three more had been supporting members of the SS.[28] The so-called Ministries case (Case 11), an amalgamation of previously independent trials, included both full-time and part-time SS members. Among those investigations, which were merged in order to at least prosecute some of those singled out for the planned but aborted proceedings, was the case against the SS Main Office with its main defendant, former SS General Berger. The same happened to Walter Schellenberg, Heinrich Himmler's chief of espionage. Richard Walther Darré, National Socialist Minister of Agriculture, had been a high-ranking SS general, too, and in the early 1930s had reputedly been the prime ideologist of the SS. Thus, a solid majority of fourteen out of twenty-one defendants in Case 11 boasted SS ranks.[29] Although a variety of crimes were presented in court, historian Dirk Pöppmann argues that SS criminality and membership stood firmly at the center of the Ministries trial.[30] The same might be said of the whole NMT series, at least from a formal perspective. A total of eighty-four of the 185[31] defendants at the Subsequent Trials, i.e. over forty-five percent, had in fact been SS members—far more than Taylor estimated in his account of the war crimes program.[32]

Therefore, it seems that organizational affiliations had a strong influence on the selection of the defendants. Already in the trial against the major war criminals, the accused officials had not necessarily been regarded solely as individuals. At least some defendants had been singled out because, apart from their personal position at the top of the Nazi hierarchy, they represented various important structures and prominent institutions of the Third Reich.[33] Ernst Kaltenbrunner, as the last head of the RSHA undoubtedly a major figure in the SS, had basically been indicted as a substitute for Himmler, who had committed suicide after being captured by Allied military personnel, and as *the* representative of the SS.[34]

The strategy of selecting the defendants because of their organizational affiliation became even more prominent in the subsequent trials.[35] In turn, this approach eventually helped to create a homogeneous image of the SS. For the US Chief of Counsel, aiming at institutions rather than at individuals had two advantages. First, the prosecution could continue to focus on proving that there had been a collective criminal plan. The charge of a "general conspiracy"[36] to wage a "war of aggression" and therefore to commit a "crime against peace" was important at the IMT proceedings. And although the IMT judges did not follow the prosecution's argument and were reluctant to convict the defendants on this count, the basic idea of the concept was transferred to the NMT.[37] In seven of the twelve subsequent cases, the indictment included the "common plan or conspiracy" charge. However, unlike the IMT, in the NMT the conspiracy charge was linked to "war crimes and crimes against humanity."[38] With its focus on a common criminal plan, the prosecution intended to first prove the collective guilt of a group, and only secondly and indirectly the individual guilt of the defendants.[39] As a follow-up to the IMT, it was not so much individuals but major structures of the Third Reich that were put on trial.[40] However, the overall shape of the cases did not prevail in court. The charge of "common design or conspiracy" was only integrated into the first of the SS trials, the Pohl trial, but not into the RuSHA and the *Einsatzgruppen* trials. Again, the judges did not follow the prosecution's argument and dismissed the conspiracy charge.[41] In the case against the leaders of the *Einsatzgruppen*, it appears that there was no necessity to include a collective charge, because the criminal actions of the individuals concerned indicated a clear case of first degree murder anyway.[42]

Therefore, the second advantage in the prosecution's focus on institutions rather than on individuals seems to have had a practical side. Apparently, whenever the evidence for incriminating individuals was strong, as in the *Einsatzgruppen* case, a detour via the "common design" charge was not seen as necessary for proving the guilt of the defendants.[43] In other cases, the prosecution followed a different aim: "Responsibility for participation in the conspiracy would be first fixed on" the group. This then "would offer the greatest scope for the introduction of evidence" for "individual guilt as well."[44] Moreover, it was obvious from the outset that both time and personnel were limited. In May 1946 Taylor thought that the program had to be finished in one year. Focusing on groups did help to pool scarce resources.[45]

As a consequence, on May 26, 1946, Taylor decided to follow the so-called "institutional approach."[46] He stated: "These trials would each cover only a single and homogeneous type of activity."[47] In October 1946 this decision was confirmed. In a memorandum Benjamin Ferencz informed his Berlin Branch section chiefs about a meeting with Taylor on September 21, 1946. Ferencz wrote:

> It was there decided that henceforth there will be an 'institutional approach' to the prosecution. This means that any persons named either as defendants or targets are to be considered as guides for research purposes rather than as definitely determined objectives. Information should be gathered about any or all persons involved in the particular agency being examined.[48]

Thus, notwithstanding a specific focus on certain major figures, various groups rather than individuals were the prime targets of the prosecution both before and during the trials.

## An Exemplary Case: the Pohl Trial

Early on, Oswald Pohl and his former subordinates were shortlisted as defendants in the subsequent trials. By the end of August 1946, the preparations for what would become the Pohl trial were a "top priority matter" for the Office of Chief of Counsel.[49] The case appears to have been the spearhead for the SS trials.[50] In a prosecution document, the Pohl trial was listed as second only to the Medical case. The latter was the first one brought to court, mainly because the preparations were so well advanced and, from the point of view of the prosecution, the trial seemed rather straightforward.[51] The Pohl case was supposed to prepare for follow-up proceedings targeting various other SS main offices.[52] Yet, it was not only envisaged as the first of the trials against the major offices of the SS hierarchy. The Pohl case also pointed to the core of SS criminality. The main offences which the IMT had attributed to the SS had also been committed by Pohl and his associates from the SS Economic and Administration Main Office (*SS-Wirtschafts-Verwaltungshauptamt* or WVHA). As early as late May 1945, the prosecution had already regarded the WVHA as one of the institutions established specifically for the perpetration of crimes. Thus, since the immediate aftermath of the war the WVHA case was conceived of in terms of its support of the conspiracy charge.[53]

Oswald Pohl had been one of the highest-ranking SS generals and a key figure among the heads of the SS main offices.[54] The Office of Chief of Counsel regarded him as "one of Himmler's very top assistants."[55] Born in 1892, the former navy paymaster joined the SS in 1934 and became Himmler's chief administrative official. In 1942 he was promoted to the rank of Lieutenant General of the SS and Waffen SS (*Obergruppenführer und General der Waffen-SS*). Also in 1942, the WVHA was established. It combined various offices which had previously been under Pohl's command. The WVHA was subdivided into several branches. Office Groups (*Amtsgruppen*) A and B were responsible for the administration of the Waffen SS, especially budget, payment, uniforms, food, and housing. These sections also included the office for the administration of the so-called General SS, the volunteer formation of the SS. Office Group C supervised all building activities of both the SS and the German police, including the concentration camps. On March 16, 1942, the former Inspectorate of Concentration Camps was incorporated into the WVHA as Office Group D—Concentration Camps. However, even before that date, Pohl and his agencies had administered forced labor from the concentration camps. Office Group W (Economic Enterprises) was an amalgamation of small and medium-size businesses. Most of these enterprises were dependent on workers from the concentration camps. The brick factories and the quarries of the German Earth and Stone Works exploited several thousand camp inmates. From 1942 onwards, concentration camp prisoners were increasingly exploited to sustain the war economy. They were used as forced laborers at many of the big combines in the German armaments industry, most notoriously at IG Farben's Monowitz plant near Auschwitz. Furthermore, members of Pohl's staff supervised the plundering of valuables from Jews who were deported to both Auschwitz and the "Operation Reinhardt" extermination camps in occupied Poland.[56]

In the early stages of the Pohl trial, it became literally visible that the wartime organization of the WVHA had been transformed into a significant structural element for selecting the defendants. Even in the dock they were seated not according to rank or name but according to their former affiliation with the different sub-organizations of the WVHA. Thus four former members of Office Group A were seated beside Pohl. Following in subsequent order were officials of Office Groups B, C, D, and W.[57] As the prosecution wanted to differentiate between the various branches of the WVHA, defendants had to be selected for each individual Office Group. Because of this, two relatively minor SS officers had to represent the concentration camp section (Office Group D) as higher ranking officers were either dead or had to stand trial in other courts.[58] The Office Group's chief dentist, SS Lieutenant Colonel Dr Hermann Pook, and the deputy head of the concentration camp labor allocation office, SS Major Karl Sommer, served as examples for their branch and as substitutes for those men who were unavailable.[59] The institutional approach's impact as a major driving force behind the organization of the Pohl case could not have been clearer.

The trial began with the filing and serving of the indictment on January 13, 1947. Three months later, in his opening address, the Chief of the SS Division McHaney developed the prosecution's strategy. He portrayed the SS as a homogeneous, criminal, and omnipotent organization: "Let there be no mistake about that," he said, "Himmler was eminently successful in making the SS an all-powerful elite ... It has been said with considerable truth that the SS was a state within a state."[60] McHaney not only reiterated major IMT conclusions regarding the SS. He also added the notion of the SS as "a state within a state." In doing so, he dissociated the SS from the rest of the German bureaucracy, state and party organizations, and implicitly from German society. McHaney may have been influenced by the arguments and the language found in Eugen Kogon's book *The SS State* which had been published just before the start of the trial and which McHaney quoted in his opening address.[61] Kogon also appeared as a witness in the Pohl trial, but his testimony focused mainly on his own experience as a former prisoner in Buchenwald concentration camp. In contrast, in his book, Kogon assumed a much wider perspective. He not only coined the term "SS State" but also described the SS perpetrators as degenerate, psychologically warped human beings. For Kogon, the guards and other perpetrators clearly represented the fringes and not the mainstream of German society.[62]

Furthermore, McHaney's argument stood in the tradition of the Third Reich's conceptualization by Franz Neumann, an exiled German, a key figure in the Research & Analysis branch of the Office of Strategic Services (OSS) and author of the most authoritative study on Nazi Germany at the time,[63] *Behemoth. The structure and practice of National Socialism 1933–1944*, the first version of which had been published in 1942.[64] While stressing the interaction of the various powers, Neumann nonetheless drew a clear line between the National Socialist Party, including the SS, and the other pillars of the Nazi state. In this respect, Neumann differed from the interpretation by Ernst Fraenkel, another émigré academic, whose earlier book *The Dual State* had emphasized the intersection of the different ruling circles.[65] As the leading OSS expert on Nazi Germany, Neumann played a significant role in preparations for the war crimes trials.[66] Even if, as Taylor suggested, Neumann's studies were not directly used for preparing individual cases, they provided some badly needed background information on the functioning of the Nazi state.[67] And they provided an interpretative framework which structured both investigations and actual accusations.[68] At the time, Kogon's and Neumann's studies were seen as among the most reliable analyses of the SS and Nazi Germany.

Still, McHaney's primary task was to achieve convictions, not to delve into the depths of academic analysis. His argument therefore was not necessarily an accurate representation of the US counsel's private perception of the SS. McHaney portrayed the SS in the way that seemed best for winning the case. Of course, the prosecution was by no means ignorant of the fact that the SS had been much more an integral part of German state and society than the American lawyers argued in court. Indeed, the "old story of 'empire within an empire'," as one prosecution official wrote in May 1946, was obviously not really bought into by Taylor's staff.[69]

In any case, the defense knew how to react to the prosecution's strategy. If Himmler and the SS were an all-powerful and overwhelming organization, then the defendants had to support this view by presenting themselves as powerless individuals and as small cogs in a big wheel. This happened exemplarily in the case of Pohl's old friend and temporary deputy Georg Lörner. His defense counsel Carl Haensel portrayed him with the following words: "The basis of this character is that of a simple, honest man, yes one could even say of a 'petit bourgeois' whom fate threw into a time which he could not tackle."[70] Haensel suggested, Lörner "was perhaps located very far in the background; however, from his position in the background he was not able to overlook the things which took place within the huge field of task of the WVHA."[71] In contrast to Lörner, Pohl was "an organizational genius."[72] And while the former main office chief was not really blamed, it was implied that only he could have overlooked the whole organization while a "man like Lörner" could not have seen "further than the particular task he was assigned to."[73]

For obvious reasons, the old party and SS comrades tried to diminish their involvement with the SS. Only Pohl seemed to have had a comprehensive overview of the activities of the WVHA and the SS. The WVHA business managers principally took the same stand but, in contrast to the old comrades, put much more blame on Pohl personally. According to their testimonies, he had been the main culprit and the sole ruler of his SS economic empire. The SS managers, in turn, had allegedly only followed his orders.[74] As a result, Pohl implicitly turned into a "little Himmler." At the same time, the business managers tried to distinguish between the economic enterprises and the other activities of the WVHA.

Former SS business manager and SS Captain (*Hauptsturmführer*) Leo Volk explained that there had been only one link between the WVHA's economic organization and the SS: Pohl himself.[75] As soon became obvious, at least some of the SS managers had a well-devised defense strategy which was fully developed well before the beginning of the trial.[76]

This strategy implied nothing less than an early attempt to disassociate a fraction from the (whole of the) SS as such, claiming that a specific, small division had not been truly connected with, much less thoroughly integrated in, the comprehensive organization. A similar strategy was adopted by the veterans of the Waffen SS. Their defense narrative was introduced to the court proceedings with the help of assorted witnesses. In the Pohl trial, former Waffen SS General Felix Steiner, a witness for the defense, virtually testified on his own account. He claimed that the Waffen SS had been a purely military organization without any political relevance.[77] Wrongly, but trenchantly, defendant Volk seconded Steiner's narrative. For Volk the Waffen SS had been part of the Wehrmacht, thereby belonging to the German Reich rather than to the SS (as a party organization).[78] While Steiner's argument was more balanced, he nonetheless stuck to the deliberations of Waffen SS veterans during the IMT trial.[79] In this respect, the rising master narrative of the Waffen SS was not born at the Pohl trial, but it was reinforced through Steiner's testimony.

The ostensibly most comprehensive characterization of the SS was given by former SS General Karl Wolff who appeared as a defense witness. Wolff had been Himmler's adjutant before the war, the SS liaison to Hitler during the war, and the highest representative of the SS in Italy by the end of the war. In Italy, he had negotiated an early surrender of the German troops on the Southern Front with Allen Welsh Dulles, an influential OSS representative in Switzerland during World War II.[80] Telford Taylor himself was involved in the scheme to prevent Wolff from being charged with war crimes in the post-World War II period, in turn calling him into the witness stand for the prosecution in several trials.[81] Tellingly, despite Wolff's own indications in the Pohl trial that he had not only known of, but had also been involved in, the persecution of the Jews, neither the prosecution nor the trial judges pursued this lead.[82]

Wolff assisted the prosecution's portrayal of the SS as an all-powerful organization and of Himmler as its omnipotent head. For the former adjutant, the SS had been designed as an elite organization and a military guard.[83] Wolff argued that the SS, as a closely-knit organization, had been hard to leave, suggesting that once one had entered the SS there had been almost no way out. According to Wolff, Himmler had been the undisputed and sole ruler of the SS. There had been neither deputies nor meetings of the higher SS leaders. Conveniently and with a self-absolving hint, Wolff had, as he said, only realized bit by bit that Himmler had built his influence on a divide-and-rule strategy.[84]

Apparently, the tribunal accepted the main arguments regarding the role of Himmler and the SS in the Third Reich. In his concurring opinion, Judge Michael A. Musmanno spoke of the "absolutely slavish loyalty to Hitler" by the SS as an organization as well as by its membership. According to him, even the thoughts of the SS men had been "chained" to Hitler[85]—an explanation which echoed the Tribunal's findings that "under the hypnotism of the Nazi ideology, the German people readily became complaisant to this strange and inhuman system."[86] In Musmanno's reading, Himmler, whom he saw as the super-ego of the SS,[87] turned out to be a psychopath: "That Himmler was a psychopathic degenerate must now be obvious to all the German people."[88]

Such sweeping conclusions, which were deficient in differentiation, were hardly surprising in the light of the interpretative consensus shared by prosecution and defense. Both had created the image of the SS as an externally as well as internally coercive organization and of Himmler as "the incarnation of all evil" and the undisputed ruler of the SS.[89] The focus on organizational responsibility blurred the picture of individual guilt with which the proceedings and the judgment had dealt in detail. In effect, the dominant narratives diminished the individual freedom of action and the responsibility of almost all SS members. Consequently, the focus on Himmler as head of the organization credited him with having been the only protagonist acting on his own will and thus the ultimately guilty individual in the SS. With the exception of the Reich Leader SS, the prosecution's institutional approach had glossed over individual actions and culpability. And, because the tribunal accepted the explanations about the general character of the SS it was given during the proceedings, it in turn lent them additional credit. While it is questionable whether this portrayal of the SS helped the individual defendants to avoid severe sentences, it nonetheless became an important element in the consolidation of postwar narratives about the SS.

The characterization of the SS established in the Pohl case was also prominent in other Nuremberg trials, especially those where the tribunals had to sit in judgment mainly over former SS officers. Here again, the prosecution focused strongly on Himmler as the arch villain. Increasingly, the SS looked like a one-man-show. In line with its general strategy, the prosecution in the Medical case argued that there had been a "conspiracy and a common design ... to commit the criminal [human] experiments."[90] Taylor singled out Himmler as the person who had been directly and personally responsible for that conspiracy. By providing victims for the medical experiments, the leader of the SS had "enhanced the prestige of his organization and was able to give free reign to the Nazi racial theories of which he was a leading protagonist and to develop new techniques for the mass extermination which were dear to his heart."[91] In his brief history of the SS in the RuSHA case, McHaney accentuated that the SS had essentially been of Himmler's doing: "The subsequent development of the SS was based primarily upon the tremendous increase in power of Himmler. Wherever Himmler went, the SS went with him."[92]

The SS, it seemed, was a homogeneous and totally secluded organization. In the *Einsatzgruppen* trial, chief prosecutor Ferencz merely reiterated this notion of the SS as a "state within the state." Treating this notion as if it was a commonplace and without going into further detail, Ferencz added the weight of his "own" case to the image created among his colleagues. Thus he said: "During the last years the world has learned much about this 'state within the state' which was formed by the SS. Much about this new aristocracy of 'blood and elite' need not be repeated here."[93] Hardly surprising, McHaney in the RuSHA trial also revisited the argumentative lines he had been using in the Pohl case, particularly the trope of SS omnipotence: "Through infiltration, the SS gained influence in every branch of German life."[94]

Last but not least, the SS appeared as the major evil force behind the principal criminal acts. Especially the portrayal of the *Einsatzgruppen*— which "were part of the SS"[95]– strengthened the picture of the SS as the main perpetrator of National Socialist crimes. This perception was underlined by the court's judgment in the *Einsatzgruppen* trial. It read: "One of counsel has characterized this trial as the biggest murder trial in history. Certainly never before have twenty-three men been brought into court to answer to the charge of destroying over one million of their fellow human beings."[96] The RuSHA trial also subscribed to putting the ultimate blame on the SS. For the prosecution McHaney stated: "These ruthless aims [for genocide] needed ruthless executioners. Hitler found them in Heinrich Himmler and the SS."[97]

It is a great though not uncommon misunderstanding to expect a legal trial to bring forward historical truth.[98] Depending on the view of the parties to the trial (prosecution, defense counsel, and defendants), the aim of the proceedings is to obtain or to avoid guilty verdicts. Everything else has to be subordinated to these goals. However, due to the educational purpose that the Nuremberg trials were intended to serve according to the US prosecution,[99] the court proceedings were vested with additional, historical significance.[100] Thus, the statements made in court gained in terms of gravity, not only as part of the struggle over individual guilt but also as discursive patterns on historical truth. This might be one explanation why the factual findings and the historically-minded narratives presented during the Nuremberg Subsequent Trials would soon become canonized historical opinion.

## The Aftermath of the Trials: Refining Established Narratives

The Nuremberg Subsequent Trials became a catalyst for depictions and analyses of the SS which dominated the historical and political discourse up to the 1960s.[101] Some views emerged during the trials; others were reinforced by the proceedings. The image of the criminal and mentally ill "outsider" which Judge Musmanno had emphasized in his final word on the Pohl trial referring to Himmler, became a commonplace in post-war Germany.[102] Kogon's book *Der SS-Staat*, cited by McHaney in the Pohl case, was most influential in promoting this view. Even before the NMT, Kogon's first edition had been widely read and had sold 35,000 copies by the time the Pohl trial started. The second edition, which was printed while the trial proceeded, numbered a staggering 100,000 copies.[103] A survivor of the Buchenwald concentration camp and a distinguished intellectual, Kogon depicted the SS as a bunch of criminals and psychopaths. Building on his own experiences as a prisoner, he provided a psychological sketch of the prototypical SS camp guard,[104] thereby paving the way for the successful dissemination of the *topos* of the pathologic, notoriously criminal Nazi perpetrator.[105] West Germany's media and historical literature were not alone in following this lead. In fact, this psychologizing pattern was also prominent in East Germany. In particular, the 1950s' trials of female concentration camp guards unleashed a language that portrayed the defendants as inhuman beasts, and therefore as standing outside of society.[106]

Obviously, in the eyes of an interested audience, the criminal "outsider" differed from the ordinary German which allowed isolating guilt to leading figures of the SS and exculpating most others.[107] The NMT trials made it clear that Himmler was the main person responsible for the acts of the SS. He was depicted as the "ruthless executioner" of SS atrocities. Subsequent publications resorted to the adjective "evil" when Himmler was characterized.[108] Himmler became the ultimate villain who had been far removed from the rest of society and against whom nobody could possibly have rebelled.[109] In addition to Himmler, Reinhard Heydrich, chief of the Reich Security Main Office, appeared as "Hitler's most evil henchman"[110] and thus became the second notorious (and conveniently dead) arch criminal. Simultaneously, the top ranking SS men were described as the oppressors of the German people, as seducers of the majority of the SS men and—like the rest of the leading Nazi circles—as abnormal individuals.[111] Thus, a huge gap was created between the criminals-cum-main culprits on one side versus society at large and the ordinary SS man, including higher echelons of the SS and police, on the other side.[112] Of course, it was not only the Nuremberg legacy that provoked such concentration on the SS. It also suited the picture that postwar German society had formed about the past.[113]

During the Nuremberg trials, the SS—like Himmler personally—became the incarnation of Nazi criminality and atrocities. The genocide against the Jews was seen as the ultimate SS crime. Especially the case against Otto Ohlendorf and the *Einsatzgruppen* members helped to bolster this image. Based on the documents gathered for the Nuremberg trials, this view was disseminated through various publications. Books, like *Macht ohne Moral*, a documentation on the SS published in 1957, *Eichmann und Komplizen* by former US Deputy Chief of Counsel Robert M.W. Kempner in 1961, and *SS im Einsatz*, published in East Berlin in 1964, while educational in character, were nonetheless narrowly focused on the SS.[114] Unintentionally, the NMT's focus on SS criminality and the wealth of documents the trials had produced helped various parts of German society and ruling circles avoid public scrutiny.[115]

The IMT's and NMT's portrayal of the SS as a homogeneous and elite[116] organization had proven to be rather effective in prosecuting and convicting former SS members, but it had come at a price. By changing the argument only slightly, it provided an ideal defense strategy, both in the courtroom and in the face of a larger public. If Himmler was the ultimate ruler of the SS, and the SS itself was a hierarchic and monolithic institution, the individual had no independent role to play. Viewed from this angle, the bulk of SS members remained faceless or even mutated into the victims of a vicious few. In his Hitler biography from 1963 Hans Bernd Gisevius supported this view when he called the agents of the Gestapo "Roboter" ("robots").[117] Perhaps unwittingly, Kempner also reflected this view. On the cover of the dust sleeve to his book *SS im Kreuzverhör* appeared a photograph of a group of SS generals with almost featureless faces (Figure 5.1).[118]

**5.1** Sketches of Nuremberg: Robert M.W. Kempner's selection of documents from the SS trials (1964)

*[publishing house no longer existent; no copyright holder identified]*

Another narrative, although it did not correspond entirely with the image of the homogeneous SS, was no less successful: the Waffen SS as an organization which had led an independent existence apart from that of the other SS branches. This narrative, as has been shown above, had emerged from Nuremberg's Palace of Justice. Based on their accounts during the trials, former SS generals tried to establish their view of the past during the 1950s and 1960s. They focused on the military performance of the Waffen SS and its structural similarity to the Wehrmacht. Hence, Himmler was portrayed as the usurper of a military position for which he had been unqualified.[119] Accordingly, the veterans claimed, he had never actually commanded the Waffen SS. Likewise, the professed character of the Waffen SS as a strictly military organization was not to be stained by the inclusion of the concentration camp guards: that had been a mere aberration for which Himmler was blamed.[120] In particular, the highly successful books of Paul Karl Schmidt, alias Paul Carell, helped to incorporate the Waffen SS into the broader narrative of the Wehrmacht in World War II. For Carell, a former high-ranking SS officer and Foreign Office press chief, the Waffen SS had been the elite guard and the "praetorians" of the German military arm. In his best-selling books *Operation Barbarossa* and *Scorched Earth*, he focused exclusively on the spectacular military deeds of the Waffen SS whilst omitting its murderous actions.[121] The world view of some of the veteran generals culminated in the declaration that ordinary Waffen SS soldiers had been "Soldaten wie andere auch" ("soldiers like others"), a phrase which was coined by the First Chancellor of the Federal Republic of Germany, Konrad Adenauer.[122] This formula also featured in the title of a prominent book which was authored by former SS General Paul Hausser and published in 1966.[123] Hausser, according to his peers, the 'senior' of the dissolved Waffen SS, was perhaps the most influential spokesperson for the reintegration of its members into German society.[124]

The myth of the Waffen SS as an independent organization, which had had nothing to do with the criminality of the Gestapo or the concentration camp guards, remained prominent well into the 1960s. It was reiterated in the introduction to Heinz Höhne's series of articles *Der Orden unter dem Totenkopf* in the German news magazine *Der Spiegel* (see Figure 5.2).[125] Still, the IMT verdict on the criminality of all parts of the SS had not been inconsequential. It did help to differentiate between the Wehrmacht and the SS in Federal Republic court procedures and administrative decisions.[126] In particular, it precluded the mass integration of former Waffen SS members in the West German *Bundeswehr*.[127] While the veterans' self-stylization was ever-present in public debates, the legal and administrative reintegration of the Waffen SS in German postwar society was seriously hampered, all the more the veterans could not expect help from their Wehrmacht comrades in organizational terms. If the Wehrmacht veterans were to preserve the myth of their own institution's clean hands, they had to draw a clear line between the

Waffen SS and themselves.[128] Thus both images created at Nuremberg, one apologetic, the other accusatory—although being mutually exclusive—remained in place: popular narratives followed the lead given by the veterans of the Waffen SS but already in the 1950s German politics accepted the consequences of the Nuremberg judgment insofar as it applied to the Waffen SS, if only reluctantly and certainly not least because of foreign pressure.[129]

What the Waffen SS failed to achieve, the German police accomplished. Not convicted as an organization in the Nuremberg trials, its former members—like the Waffen SS veterans—tried to draw a line between the SS proper and the police. In October 1949, only weeks after the first cabinet of the new Federal Republic of Germany was sworn in, the former deputy chief of the Reich Criminal Office, ex-SS Colonel (*Oberführer*) Paul Werner, pleaded for the re-employment of former detectives by the new police forces. Coming to Werner's support, his former subordinate Bernd Wehner published a thirty-article series on the Nazi criminal police in *Der Spiegel*, starting in September 1949.

**5.2** The SS as the "black order": *Der Spiegel* cover accompanying Heinz Höhne's serial (1966)

*Spiegel-Verlag Rudolf Augstein GmbH & Co. KG, Hamburg*

Wehner argued that the criminal police of the Third Reich had been a professional organization more or less independent of Himmler and Heydrich towards whom the majority of the policemen had felt fear and loathing. In contrast to the Waffen SS, the reputation of the veteran police remained by and large untarnished in the view of German society and the administration. And indeed, the majority of former police members especially of the uniformed police (the so-called Order Police) were re-employed.[130] In 1951 Wehner himself was hired as a police officer, and in 1954 he was promoted to head of the criminal police in Düsseldorf, capital of the German state of North-Rhine Westphalia.[131]

Perceived as an institution outside of both German society and state, the SS was ideally described by the phrase "a state within a state." While US prosecution officials clearly did not wholeheartedly subscribe to this themselves, it nonetheless was reiterated during the Nuremberg Subsequent Trials. Kogon's title *Der SS-Staat* helped this term to grow into a commonplace characterization of the SS.[132] The ahistorical *topos* of the SS as a "Black Order"[133] fortified the idea of the secretive, exclusive, and distant institution. Even scientific studies, which for analytical reasons had to differentiate between the various powers or groups of the Nazi state, frequently helped to underscore this image. Not cooperation but differentiation and usurpation were perceived to characterize the relationship between the SS and other ruling circles of National Socialist Germany.[134]

The criminals, the vicious few, the faceless mass, and the isolated institution were some of the tropes which were prominent in depictions of the SS at least until the 1960s. However, the 1950s also saw a first wave of historical studies qualifying the notion of the SS as a homogeneous and elitist organization. In 1956, US author Gerald Reitlinger in particular criticized the Allied Nuremberg lawyers for having misunderstood the character of the SS. According to him, the SS had hardly been a "state within a state." Rather, it had depended "on the co-operation of the entire German bureaucracy."[135] Whilst revising some of his older arguments made in his earlier book on the Final Solution, Reitlinger argued:

> It is not realized that the massive machinery, by which more than four million Jews were dragged from their homes to die in often very distant concentration camps, ghettos, and gas chambers, could never have been secret and could not have happened at all without the minute interlocking of the Ministry of the Interior, the Ministries of Transport, Finance, and Economics, the two High Command Offices ... The first Nuremberg Tribunal set itself the task of judging the SS in bulk and deciding whether it was a criminal organization ... It judged affirmatively and through this judgment membership of the SS constituted some degree of complicity in the atrocities that had been committed. Psychologically it was the most dangerous of errors. If such a judgment were to be made at all, it should have been made on the German nation as a whole, instead of providing the German nation with a convenient scapegoat.[136]

For Reitlinger the focus on the SS, which had resulted from the Nuremberg trials, bore all the marks of an "Alibi of a Nation." In a similar vein, Edward Crankshaw saw the Gestapo as a "universal scapegoat." In his book about the Gestapo he disputed the idea of just a few people being responsible for its crimes.[137] As noted in more recent studies, there had already been a shift by the mid or late 1950s in how West German society tried to come to terms with its past.[138] Still, the findings of Robert L. Koehl, Reitlinger, Crankshaw and others[139] did not immediately affect the common perception about the SS. It took a few more years and yet other trials, including those of Adolf Eichmann and the first Frankfurt Auschwitz trial, before a profound revision of public opinion began.[140] In 1967 Heinz Höhne, in his monograph on the history of the SS, implicitly backed Reitlinger's argument. Like Reitlinger, Höhne concluded that the SS was far from being a monolithic omnipotent organization, but had become an alibi of the Germans.[141] And although Höhne integrated some well-established, popular images of the SS in his book in the 1960s, he and others set out to destroy the notion of the SS as a homogeneous organization and as the collective agent which bore the brunt of, if not sole responsibility for the National Socialist crimes—and, on the whole they were successful.[142]

## Conclusion

The overall strategy of the prosecution, especially in the Nuremberg Subsequent Trials, promoted certain images of the SS. For different reasons other parties to the trials, the tribunals, the defense, and the witnesses, adopted and supported these images. They wanted either to highlight the criminality and responsibility of Himmler and the SS or to diminish the individual acts and accountability of the former SS officers turned defendants. In the short run, and in the narrow context of the trial as a judicial proceeding, the prosecution's limitation to the "institutional approach" proved to be successful, especially in the SS trials. Former SS men in particular received severe sentences. In the long run, though, the judicial success turned out to be a mixed blessing. In the broader context of the trials as educational endeavors, the prosecution's strategy backfired. Contrary to the prosecution's professed intention, its interpretative strategy helped to establish the SS as a scapegoat for various societal groups and institutions of National Socialist Germany.

Building on the rhetoric and the documents of the Nuremberg trials, and based on diverse motivations, a number of exculpatory narratives about the SS emerged. SS men were depicted as abnormal, i.e., untypical, Himmler was perceived of as all-powerful, and Nazi atrocities were described as an exclusive domain of the SS, while the Waffen SS had had nothing to do with the SS proper. In short, the SS was portrayed as a homogeneous, secluded, ideologically, economically, and politically self-sustaining organization which had existed completely isolated from the rest of German society. Hence, the SS and its crimes had had nothing to do with ordinary Germans and society's traditional institutions, such as the Wehrmacht or the ministerial bureaucracy. As a legacy of the Nuremberg trials, these narratives proved to be very persistent. At least in Germany they went well with the broad historical consensus of a postwar society which was very much concentrated on the task of economic reconstruction and reintegration into the international community. It took some twenty years before these interpretations and conceptualizations were effectively challenged. And it would take another twenty years before broad historical research started looking beyond the documentary and narrative legacy of the Nuremberg trials.[143] But to this day some of the narratives, such as the homogeneous SS "order" or the SS as a state-within-a-state,[144] certainly the image of the Waffen SS as a purely military and elite organization,[145] are very much alive in the booming genre of popular historical writings.

## Notes

1.  "Gedanken des Führers über die Waffen SS"/"Hitlers Freibrief für die SS," Allied aerial leaflet 1943, Wewelsburg District Museum (Germany), inventory No. 2910 and 8870; Bernd Wegner, "Anmerkungen zur Geschichte der Waffen-SS aus organisations- und funktionsgeschichtlicher Sicht," in *Die Wehrmacht. Mythos und Realität*, eds. Rolf-Dieter Müller and Hans-Erich Volkmann (Munich, 1999), 405–19, here 406.
2.  See "SS Women Guards declared brutal," *The New York Times*, November 13, 1944, 3; "Urges Executions of 1,500,000 Nazis," *New York Times*, May 23, 1945, 11; James MacDonald, "Arch Criminal Dies," *New York Times*, May 25, 1945, 1.
3.  Ute Stiepani, "Die Dachauer Prozesse und ihre Bedeutung im Rahmen der alliierten Strafverfolgung von NS-Verbrechen," in *Der Nationalsozialismus vor Gericht. Die alliierten Prozesse gegen Kriegsverbrecher und Soldaten 1943–1952*, ed. Gerd R. Ueberschär (Frankfurt a.M., 1999), 227–39; *Dachauer Prozesse. NS-Verbrechen vor amerikanischen Militärgerichten in Dachau 1945–1948*, eds. Ludwig Eiber and Robert Sigel (Göttingen, 2007); Lisa Yavnai, "Military Justice: War Crimes Trials in the American Zone of Occupation in Germany, 1945–1947," in *The Nuremberg Trials. International Law Since 1945*, eds. Herbert R. Reginbogin and Christoph J.M. Safferling (Munich, 2006), 191–96; Lisa Yavnai, "US Army War Crimes Trials in Ge-rmany, 1945–1947," in *Atrocities on Trial. Historical Perspectives on the Politics of Prosecuting War Crimes*, eds. Patricia Heberer and Jürgen Matthäus (Lincoln/London, 2008), 49–71.
4.  Telford Taylor, *Final Report to the Secretary of the Army on the Nuernberg War Crimes Trials under Control Council Law No. 10* (Washington, DC, 1949), 70; Telford Taylor, *Die Nürnberger Prozesse. Kriegsverbrechen und Völkerrecht* (Zurich, 1951), 52.
5.  Johannes Tuchel, "Fall 4: Der Prozeß gegen Oswald Pohl und andere Angehörige des SS-Wirtschafts-Verwaltungshauptamtes," in *Der Nationalsozialismus vor Gericht. Die alliierten Prozesse gegen Kriegsverbrecher und Soldaten 1943–1952*, ed. Gerd R. Ueberschär (Frankfurt a.M., 1999), 110–20, here 116.
6.  Bradley F. Smith, *Reaching Judgment at Nuremberg* (London, 1977), 166.

7.  *Trial of the Major War Criminals before the International Military Tribunal, Nuremberg 14 November 1945–1 October 1946, 42 vols [IMT]* (Nuremberg, 1947–49), here II, 151.

8.  Ibid.

9.  *IMT*, XXII, 511; see also 514f.

10. Ibid., 515.

11. Smith, *Reaching Judgment at Nuremberg*, 166.

12. *IMT*, XXII, 516.

13. Donald Bloxham, "'The Trial That Never Was': Why there was no Second International Trial of Major War Criminals at Nuremberg," *History. The Journal of the Historical Association* 87 (2002): 41–60. Hilary Earl especially draws attention to the beginning of the Cold War differences between Soviets and Americans; see Hilary Earl, *The Nuremberg SS-Einsatzgruppen Trial, 1945–1958. Atrocity, Law, and History* (Cambridge, 2009), 25–39.

14. Summary of points covered in an OCC-OMGUS meeting, May 28, 1946, NARA, RG 238, Entry 159, Box 1, Folder "subsequent proceedings basic politics." For the prosecution's motives, see Kim C. Priemel in this volume.

15. Chart "Office of Chief of Counsel for War Crimes," October 28, 1946, NARA, RG 238, Entry 159, Box 1, Folder "Chart OCCWC."

16. Benjamin Ferencz to Taylor, September 21, 1946, NARA, RG 238, Entry 159, Box 4, Folder "Mr. Ference" [sic].

17. Ibid.

18. For a brief account, see Wolfgang U. Eckart, "Fall 1: Der Nürnberger Ärzteprozeß," in *Der Nationalsozialismus vor Gericht. Die alliierten Prozesse gegen Kriegsverbrecher und Soldaten 1943–1952*, ed. Gerd R. Ueberschär (Frankfurt a.M., 1999), 73–85; now Paul Weindling, *Nazi Medicine and the Nuremberg Trials: From Medical War Crimes to Informed Consent* (Hampshire/New York: 2004); for a different evaluation of the trial, see Michael R. Marrus, "The Nuremberg Doctors' Trial and the Limitations of Context," in *Atrocities on Trial. Historical Perspectives on the Politics of Prosecuting War Crimes*, eds. Patricia Heberer and Jürgen Matthäus (Lincoln/London, 2008), 103–22.

19. Regarding the prominence of the SS in this case, see Opening Statement of the Prosecution by Brigadier General Telford Taylor, December 9, 1946, *Trials of War Criminals before the Nuernberg Military Tribunals under Control Council Law No. 10 (TWC), Nuernberg Oct 1946–Apr 1949*, 15 vols (Washington, DC, 1951), here I, 32–36.

20. Detlef Scheffler, "Fall 8: Der Prozess gegen das SS-Rasse- und Siedlungshauptamt ('RuSHA-Case')," in *Der Nationalsozialismus vor Gericht. Die alliierten Prozesse gegen Kriegsverbrecher und Soldaten 1943–1952*, ed. Gerd R. Ueberschär (Frankfurt a.M., 1999), 155–63; Alexa Stiller, "Die frühe Strafverfolgung der nationalsozialistischen Vertreibungs- und Germanisierungsverbrechen: Der 'RuSHA Prozess' in Nürnberg 1947–1948," in *Krieg und Verbrechen. Situation und Intention: Fallbeispiele*, ed. Timm C. Richter (Munich, 2006), 231–41; Alexa Stiller, "Die Volkstumspolitik der SS vor Gericht: Strategien der Anklage und Verteidigung im Nürnberger 'RuSHA-Prozess', 1947–1948," in *Leipzig—Nürnberg—Den Haag: Neue Fragestellungen und Forschungen zum Verhältnis von Menschenrechtsverbrechen, justizieller Säuberung und Völkerstrafrecht*, ed. Helia-Verena Daubach (Düsseldorf, 2008), 66–86.

21. List, undated, copy white on black, NARA, RG 238, Entry 191, Box 2, Folder "SS General." For the intelligence maneuvers which allowed Wolff to serve as a witness in a number of trials without being charged himself, see Kerstin von Lingen, "Conspiracy of Silence: How the 'Old Boys' of American Intelligence Shielded SS General Karl Wolff from Prosecution," in *Holocaust and Genocide Studies* 22 (2008): 74–109.

22. Benjamin Ferencz to Taylor, September 21, 1946, NARA, RG 238, Entry 159, Box 4, Folder "Mr. Ference" [sic].

23. Earl, *SS-Einsatzgruppen Trial*, 77–79.
24. 17 out of 18 in the Pohl case, 13 out of 14 in the RuSHA case, and all 24 defendants in the *Einsatzgruppen* case. Mathias Graf held the lowest rank as SS Untersturm-führer or 2nd lieutenant in the *Einsatzgruppen* trial. Cf. Indictment, *TWC*, IV, 15.
25. Karl Brandt, Karl Grenzken, Karl Gebhardt, Rudolf Brandt, Joachim Mrugowsky, Helmut Poppendick, Wolfram Sievers, Viktor Brack, Waldemar Hoven, and Fritz Fischer. Cf. Indictment, *TWC*, I, 7–10.
26. Josef Altstötter, Karl Engert, and Günter Joel were SS members, Oswald Rothaug collaborated with the SD, Hermann Cuhorst was a sponsoring member. Cf. Indict-ment and Judgment, *TWC*, III, 15f., 1134–44, 1157f., 1170–77.
27. Notably in the Flick and Farben trials, but also in the Ministries case (Karl Rasche of Dresdner Bank); cf. Ralf Ahrens, *Die Dresdner Bank 1945–1957. Konsequenzen und Kontinuitäten nach dem Ende des NS-Regimes* (Munich, 2007), 101–14.
28. Former SS members were Otto Steinbrinck (Flick case), Heinrich Bütefisch, and Erich von der Heyde (IG Farben case); whereas Christian Schneider (IG Farben case), Alfried Krupp and Friedrich Wilhelm Janssen (Krupp case) had been support-ing members. Cf. Indictments, *TWC*, VI, 12; *TWC*, VII, 12–14; *TWC*, IX, 8f.
29. Ernst v. Weizsäcker, Wilhelm Keppler, Ernst Wilhelm Bohle, Ernst Woermann, Edmund Veesenmayer, Hans Heinrich Lammers, Wilhelm Stuckart, Richard Wal-ther Darré, Otto Dietrich, Gottlob Berger, Walter Schellenberg, Karl Rasche, Paul Körner, and Hans Kehrl. Cf. Indictment, *TWC*, XII, 14–20.
30. Dirk Pöppmann, "Der Wilhelmstraßenprozess—ein Ministerial- oder ein SS-Ver-fahren," paper presented at the conference Negotiating the Past: German-American Perspectives in the US War Crimes Trials in Nuremberg, 1946–1949, Frankfurt/Oder (Germany), April 23–25, 2009.
31. Taylor, *Final Report*, 55.
32. According to Taylor there were "more than 60" ("mehr als 60") SS Officers and oth-ers associated with the SS. Cf. Taylor, *Nürnberger Prozesse*, 67.
33. Ibid., 112.
34. Smith, *Reaching Judgment at Nuremberg*, 166; Peter Black, *Ernst Kaltenbrunner. Vasall Himmlers: Eine SS-Karriere* (Paderborn, 1991), 285f.; Taylor, *Nürnberger Prozesse*, 112, 117.
35. For the Ministries case, see Dirk Pöppmann, "Robert Kempner und Ernst von Weizsäcker im Wilhelmstraßenprozess. Zur Diskussion über die Beteiligung der deutschen Funktionselite an den NS-Verbrechen," in *Im Labyrinth der Schuld. Täter, Opfer, Ankläger*, eds. Irmtrud Wojak and Susanne Meinl (Darmstadt, 2003), 163–97, here 183f.; for a single defendant, Karl Rasche, see Ahrens, *Die Dresdner Bank*, 101, 103, 106.
36. Cited in Bloxham, "The Trial That Never Was," 44.
37. Taylor, *Final Report*, 70f.; Kim C. Priemel, *Flick. Eine Konzerngeschichte vom Kai-serreich bis zur Bundesrepublik*, 2nd edn (Göttingen, 2008), 619.
38. Indictment, *TWC*, V, 201.
39. L.M. Drachsler to J.E. Heate, Intra-Office Memorandum, September 28, 1946, NARA, RG 238, Entry 159, Box 4, Folder "Mr. Drachsler." See a similar argument made by Jackson, cited in Bloxham, "The Trial That Never Was," 44.
40. See Taylor's Opening Statement in the Flick trial (Case 5), quoted in Priemel, *Flick*, 635; Rudolf Wassermann, "Fall 3: Der Nürnberger Juristenprozeß," in *Der Nationalsozialismus vor Gericht. Die alliierten Prozesse gegen Kriegsverbrecher und Soldaten 1943–1952*, ed. Gerd R. Ueberschär (Frankfurt a.M., 1999), 99–109, here 99f.
41. Taylor, *Final Report*, 70f.
42. Earl, *SS-Einsatzgruppen Trial*, 90–92.
43. This is clearly shown by the sequence of events in the *Einsatzgruppen* case. In the trial, which started on July 3, 1947, the prosecution did not use the conspiracy charge, although the joint session of the three tribunals of the Medical, Justice and

Pohl trials, which led to the dismissal of the conspiracy charge, was only held on July 9, 1947. Taylor, *Final Report*, 71.

44. In this specific memo, the author is focusing exclusively on the industrialist cases. Cf. L.M. Drachsler to J.E. Heath, Intra-Office Memorandum, September 28, 1946, NARA, RG 238, Entry 159, Box 4, Folder "Mr. Drachsler."

45. Summary of points covered in an OCC-OMGUS meeting, May 28, 1946, NARA, RG 238, Entry 159, Box 1, Folder "subsequent proceedings basic politics"; Taylor, *Final Report*, 76.

46. L.M. Drachsler to J.E. Heath, Intra-Office Memorandum, September 28, 1946, NARA, RG 238, Entry 159, Box 4, Folder "Mr. Drachsler."

47. Summary of points covered in an OCC-OMGUS meeting, May 28, 1946, NARA, RG 238, Entry 159, Box 1, Folder "subsequent proceedings basic politics."

48. Benjamin Ferencz, "Intra-Office Memorandum," October 2, 1946, NARA, RG 238, Entry 205, Box 1, Folder "No. 6."

49. Memo to Dr Edmund Schwenk, August 29, 1946, NARA, RG 238, Entry 202, Box 2, Folder (3) "Various Correspondences August 1946–January 1947." I would like to thank Kim C. Priemel for sharing the content of this document with me.

50. Cf. Opening Statement for the Prosecution by James M. McHaney, April 8, 1947, Bundesarchiv (BArch), AllProz 1, XLI Pohlprozess, A 2, 19.

51. Weindling, *Nazi Medicine*, 106f., 125.

52. List, undated, copy white on black, NARA, RG 238, Entry 191, Box 2, Folder "SS General."

53. Outline of Project, Principal Nazi Organizations Involved in War Crimes, May 31, 1945, NARA, RG 239, Entry 45, Box 1, Folder "R & A No. 3113, Exhibit A." This document was brought to my attention by Kim C. Priemel.

54. SS main offices were created in 1935; see Robert L. Koehl, *The Black Corps. The Structure and Power Struggles of the Nazi SS* (Madison, WI., 1983), 109–30.

55. Memo to Dr Edmund Schwenk, August 29, 1946, NARA, RG 238, Entry 202, Box 2, Folder (3) "Various Correspondences August 1946–January 1947."

56. Jan Erik Schulte, *Zwangsarbeit und Vernichtung: Das Wirtschaftsimperium der SS. Oswald Pohl und das SS-Wirtschafts-Verwaltungshauptamt 1933–1945* (Paderborn, 2001); Michael Thad Allen, *The Business of Genocide. The SS, Slave Labor, and The Concentration Camps* (Chapel Hill/London, 2002); Hermann Kaienburg, *Die Wirtschaft der SS* (Berlin, 2003).

57. Military Tribunal No. II. Court Room No. 2, Room 581, Oswald Pohl and Others, Case No. 4, NARA, RG 238, Entry 191, Box 3, Folder "Chart, Case # 4—Military Tribunal # 3."

58. Schulte, *Zwangsarbeit und Vernichtung*, 429, 434f.

59. See Annette Weinke, *Die Nürnberger Prozesse* (Munich, 2006), 73.

60. Opening Statement James M. McHaney, *TWC*, V, 211.

61. Ibid., p. 212. Quotation from Eugon Kogon, *Der SS-Staat. Das System der deutschen Konzentrationslager* (Munich, 1946), 296.

62. Kogon, *Der SS-Staat*, 288–92, 300, 302f.

63. Petra Marquardt-Bigman, *Amerikanische Geheimdienstanalysen über Deutschland 1942–1949* (Munich, 1995), 70f.

64. Franz L. Neumann, *Behemoth. Struktur und Praxis des Nationalsozialismus 1933–1944*, 2nd edn, ed. Gert Schäfer (Frankfurt a.M., 1993), 99.

65. Ernst Fraenkel, *Der Doppelstaat* (Frankfurt/Köln, 1974) (1st edn, 1941).

66. Cf. Barry M. Katz, "The Frankfurt School Goes to War," *The Journal of Modern History* 59 (1987): 439–78, here p. 448, 467–73; Joachim Perels, "Fast vergessen: Franz L. Neumanns Beitrag zur Konzipierung der Nürnberger Prozesse. Eine Erinnerung aus Anlaß seines 100. Geburtstages," *Kritische Justiz* 34 (2001): 117–25; Tim B. Mueller, "Nürnberg, die intellektuelle Emigration und der Kalte Krieg," paper presented at the conference Negotiating the Past: German-American Per-

spectives in the US War Crimes Trials in Nuremberg, 1946–1949, Frankfurt/Oder (Germany), April 23–25, 2009; Priemel, *Flick*, 619.

67. Michael Salter, *Nazi War Crimes, US Intelligence and Selective Prosecution at Nuremberg* (Abingdon, NY, 2007), 258f.

68. Cf. the contribution by Kim C. Priemel in the present volume.

69. Report "Individual Responsibility of Prof. Dr. Karl Brandt," handwritten note, May 1946, NARA, RG 238, Entry 191, Box 2, Folder "Individual Responsibility of Prof. Dr. Karl Brandt."

70. Opening Statement for Defendant Georg Lörner, Carl Haensel, May 14, 1947, *TWC*, V, 280.

71. Ibid. As counsel for the main defendant Ulrich Greifelt in the RuSHA case, Haensel followed a similar defense strategy; see Stiller, "Volkstumspolitik," 76.

72. Opening Statement for Defendant Georg Lörner, Carl Haensel, May 14, 1947, *TWC*, V, 279.

73. Ibid.

74. Interrogation Volk, July 25, 1947, Pohl trial (Case 4), NARA, RG 238, M-890, Reel 23, 4998, 5002.

75. Ibid., 4999; Opening Statement by Dr Bracht on behalf of defendant Karl Mummenthey, May 15, 1947, BArch, AllProz 1, XLI Pohlprozess, A 18, 1246; Prosecution Closing Statement by Jack W. Robbins, September 17, 1947, BArch, AllProz 1, XLI Pohlprozess, A 97, 7461f.

76. Walter Naasner, *SS-Wirtschaft und SS-Verwaltung. 'Das SS-Wirtschafts-Verwaltungshauptamt und die unter seiner Dienstaufsicht stehenden wirtschaftlichen Unternehmungen' und weitere Dokumente* (Düsseldorf, 1998), 10f., 15–19. Similarly, at the *Einsatzgruppen* trial there was an attempt to coordinate the defense strategy. See Earl, *Einsatzgruppen Trial*, 198.

77. Interrogation Steiner, September 2, 1947, Pohl trial (Case 4), NARA, RG 238, M-890, Reel 25, 7132f.

78. Interrogation Volk, July 25, 1947, Pohl trial (Case 4), NARA, RG 238, M-890, Reel 23, 5000.

79. *IMT*, XX, 354f., 357f., 365–68.

80. Katherine Schiemann, "Der Geheimdienst beendet den Krieg. 'Operation Sunrise' und die deutsche Kapitulation in Italien," in *Geheimdienstkrieg gegen Deutschland. Subversion, Propaganda und politische Planungen des amerikanischen Geheimdienstes im Zweiten Weltkrieg*, eds. Jürgen Heideking and Christoph Mauch (Göttingen, 1993), 142–65.

81. In his final report, Taylor is conspicuously vague with regard to Wolff not being charged by US authorities. See Taylor, *Final Report*, 78.

82. Cf. Kerstin von Lingen, *SS und Secret Service. 'Verschwörung des Schweigens': Die Akte Karl Wolff* (Paderborn, 2010), 30, 136–71, 194. See also Salter, *Nazi War Crimes*, 131–34.

83. Wartime Allied newspaper reports called the Waffen SS "Elite Guard." Cf. "SS General Promoted," *New York Times*, March 18, 1945.

84. Interrogation Wolff, June 3, 1947, Pohl trial (Case 4), NARA, RG 238, M-890, Reel 23, 2102–4, 2122f. See also Stiller, "Volkstumspolitik," 83.

85. *TWC*, vol. V, 1069.

86. Opinion and Judgment of the United States Military Tribunal II, November 3, 1947, *TWC*, V, 967.

87. *TWC*, V, 1069.

88. Ibid., 1071. See also Musmanno's stance in the *Einsatzgruppen* trial, where he labeled Otto Ohlendorf, the main defendant, a schizophrenic personality. Cf. Klaus Michael Mallmann, "Dr. Jekyll & Mr. Hyde. Der Täterdiskurs in Wissenschaft und Gesellschaft," in *Die Gestapo nach 1945*, eds. Klaus-Michael Mallmann and Andrej Angrick (Darmstadt, 2009), 292–318, here 292.

89. Final Statement by Dr Fröschmann on behalf of defendant Karl Mummenthey, September 20, 1947, BArch, AllProz 1, XLI Pohl-Prozess, A 100, 7827.

90. Opening Statement Telford Taylor, December 9, 1946, *TWC*, I, 68.

91. Ibid., 69.

92. Opening Statement for the Prosecution in the RuSHA case, James M. McHaney, October 20, 1947, *TWC*, IV, 628.

93. Opening Statement Benjamin Ferencz, September 29, 1947, *TWC*, IV, 35f.

94. Opening Statement for the Prosecution, James M. McHaney, October 20, 1947, *TWC*, IV, 629.

95. Opening Statement Benjamin Ferencz, September 29, 1947, *TWC*, IV, 36. Although established by the Reich Security Main Office, headed by Reinhard Heydrich, the *Einsatzgruppen* consisted of officials from various quarters of the SS and police complex. They included Gestapo, Criminal Police and Security Service members, officers of the Order Police and Waffen SS soldiers.

96. Judgment, *TWC*, IV, 412.

97. Cf. Opening Statement of the Prosecution, James M. McHaney, October 20, 1947, *TWC*, IV, 627. Also in the Ministries case, the SS was depicted as the organization mainly responsible for the National Socialist crimes. Cf. Opening Statement for the Prosecution, William Caming, January 6, 1948, *TWC*, XII, 173–80 *et passim*.

98. Martha Minow, *Between Vengeance and Forgiveness. Facing History after Genocide and Mass Violence* (Boston, 1998), 47, 51; Michael Wildt, "Differierende Wahrheiten. Historiker und Staatsanwälte als Ermittler von NS-Verbrechen," in *Geschichte vor Gericht. Historiker, Richter und die Suche nach Gerechtigkeit*, eds. Norbert Frei, Dirk van Laak and Michael Stolleis (Munich, 2000), 46–59.

99. Earl, *SS-Einsatzgruppen Trial*, 2, 13, 21.

100. Lawrence Douglas argues that didactic aspects are inherent to all trials. See Lawrence Douglas, *The Memory of Judgment. Making Law and History in the Trials of the Holocaust* (New Haven/London, 2001).

101. For other exculpatory narratives stemming from the Nuremberg trials, see Pöppmann, "Robert Kempner und Ernst von Weizsäcker," 184f.; Ahrens, *Die Dresdner Bank*, 144.

102. Gerhard Paul, "Von Psychopathen, Technokraten des Terrors und 'ganz gewöhnlichen' Deutschen. Die Täter der Shoah im Spiegel der Forschung," in *Die Täter der Shoah. Fanatische Nationalsozialisten oder ganz normale Deutsche?*, ed. Gerhard Paul (Göttingen, 2002), 13–90, here 17.

103. Testimony Kogon, April 21, 1947, Pohl trial (Case 4), NARA, RG 238, M-890, Reel 19, 752.

104. Kogon, *Der SS-Staat*, *passim*; Volkhard Knigge, "'Die organisierte Hölle'. Eugon Kogons ambivalente Zeugenschaft," in *50 Klassiker der Zeitgeschichte*, eds. Jürgen Danyel, Jan-Holger Kirsch and Martin Sabrow (Göttingen, 2007), 24–28.

105. Hugh R. Trevor-Roper, *The Last Days of Hitler* (New York, 1947), 234; Karl Otto Paetel, "Die SS. Ein Beitrag zur Soziologie des Nationalsozialismus," *Vierteljahreshefte für Zeitgeschichte* 1 (1954): 1–33; Gerald Reitlinger, *Die Endlösung. Hitlers Versuch der Ausrottung der Juden Europas 1939–1945* (Berlin, 1956) (1st English edn, 1953), 215; Golo Mann, *Deutsche Geschichte des 19. und 20. Jahrhunderts* (Frankfurt a.M., 1958), 930.

106. Insa Eschebach, "NS-Prozesse in der sowjetischen Besatzungszone und der DDR. Einige Überlegungen zu den Strafverfahren ehemaliger SS-Aufseherinnen des Frauenkonzentrationslagers Ravensbrück," *Beiträge zur Geschichte der nationalsozialistischen Verfolgung in Norddeutschland* 3 (1997): 65–74, here 71f.; Alexandra Przyrembel, "Transfixed by an Image: Ilse Koch, the 'Kommandeuse of Buchenwald,'" *German History* 19 (2001): 369–99; *'Bestien' und 'Befehlsempfänger': Frauen und Männer in NS-Prozessen nach 1945*, eds. Ulrike Weckel and Edgar Wolfrum (Göttingen, 2003).

107. Cf. Paul, "Von Psychopathen," 17.
108. Felix Steiner, *Die Armee der Geächteten*, 3rd edn (Göttingen, 1963), 239.
109. Golo Mann saw Himmler as the "Oberhenker" ("chief hangman"). Cf. Mann, *Deutsche Geschichte*, 944.
110. Cf. Charles Wighton, *Heydrich. Hitler's Most Evil Henchman* (Philadelphia/New York, 1962).
111. Jan Erik Schulte, "'Namen sind Nachrichten': Journalismus und NS-Täterforschung in der frühen Bundesrepublik Deutschland," in *Public History. Öffentliche Darstellungen des Nationalsozialismus jenseits der Geschichtswissenschaft*, eds. Frank Bösch and Constantin Goschler (Frankfurt a.M., 2009), 24–51, here 34.
112. Mallmann, "Dr Jekyll & Mr. Hyde," 293.
113. See, e.g., Norbert Frei, *Vergangenheitspolitik. Die Anfänge der Bundesrepublik und die NS-Vergangenheit* (Munich, 1996); Jeffrey Herf, *Zweierlei Erinnerung. Die NS-Vergangenheit im geteilten Deutschland* (Berlin, 1998), 194–394.
114. Reimund Schnabel, *Macht ohne Moral. Eine Dokumentation über die SS* (Frankfurt a.M., 1957); Robert M.W. Kempner, *Eichmann und Komplizen* (Zurich, 1961); *SS im Einsatz. Eine Dokumentation über die Verbrechen der SS* (Berlin/Ost, 1964).
115. Paul, "Von Psychopathen," 17.
116. Even in critical historical studies like George H. Stein, *The Waffen SS. Hitler's Elite Guard at War, 1939–1945* (Ithaca, NY, 1966) the SS, or at least a portion of the organization, was still labeled as 'elite'.
117. Hans Bernd Gisevius, *Adolf Hitler. Versuch einer Deutung* (Munich, 1963), 217.
118. Robert M.W. Kempner, *SS im Kreuzverhör* (Munich, 1964).
119. Paul Hausser, *Waffen-SS im Einsatz*, 3rd edn (Göttingen, 1953), 10; Steiner, *Die Armee der Geächteten*, 58–65.
120. Steiner, *Die Armee der Geächteten*, 238f. In contrast Stein, *The Waffen SS*.
121. Paul Carell, *Unternehmen Barbarossa. Der Marsch nach Russland*, 2nd edn (Frankfurt/Berlin, 1980 [1st edn 1963]), 125, 161 *et passim*; Paul Carell, *Verbrannte Erde. Schlacht zwischen Wolga und Weichsel*, 2nd edn (Frankfurt/Berlin, 1982 [1st edn 1966]), 161–63 *et passim*; Wigbert Benz, *Paul Carell. Ribbentrops Pressechef Paul Karl Schmidt vor und nach 1945* (Berlin, 2005), 91–100; Christian Plöger, *Von Ribbentrop zu Springer: Zu Leben und Wirken von Paul Karl Schmidt alias Paul Carell* (Marburg, 2009), 340–42.
122. Bert-Oliver Manig, *Die Politik der Ehre. Die Rehabilitierung der Berufssoldaten in der frühen Bundesrepublik* (Göttingen, 2004), 566; Karsten Wilke, *Die "Hilfsgemeinschaft auf Gegenseitigkeit" (HIAG) 1950-1990. Veteranen der Waffen-SS in der Bundesrepublik* (Paderborn, 2011), 137.
123. Paul Hausser, *Soldaten wie andere auch. Der Weg der Waffen-SS* (Osnabrück, 1966).
124. Georg Meyer, "Soldaten wie andere auch? Zur Einstellung ehemaliger Angehöriger der Waffen-SS in die Bundeswehr," in *Festgabe Heinz Hürten zum 60. Geburtstag*, ed. Harald Dickerhof (Frankfurt a.M., 1988), 545–95, here 550f.; Manig, *Die Politik der Ehre*, 518; Wilke, *Die "Hilfsgemeinschaft auf Gegenseitigkeit"*, 39f. *et passim*.
125. "Hausmitteilung," October 10, 1968, *Der Spiegel* 42 (1966): 3.
126. Karsten Wilke, "Geistige Regeneration der Schutzstaffel in der frühen Bundesrepublik? Die 'Hilfsgemeinschaft auf Gegenseitigkeit der Angehörigen der ehemaligen Waffen-SS,'" in *Die SS, Himmler und die Wewelsburg*, ed. Jan Erik Schulte (Paderborn, 2009), 433–48, here 442.
127. Meyer, "Soldaten wie andere auch?"
128. Oliver von Wrochem, "Die Stunde der Memoiren: Militärische Eliten als Stichwortgeber," in *Public History. Öffentliche Darstellungen des Nationalsozialismus jenseits der Geschichtswissenschaft*, eds. Frank Bösch and Constantin Goschler (Frankfurt a.M., 2009), 105–29, here 111; Manig, *Die Politik der Ehre*, 440, 596. For an exemplary study of how the old Wehrmacht elite campaigned to rehabilitate their

organization, see Oliver von Wrochem, *Erich von Mannstein: Vernichtungskrieg und Geschichtspolitik* (Paderborn, 2006).

129. Manig, *Die Politik der Ehre*, 431, 537–39, 587, 597 *et passim*. For the veterans of the Waffen SS see Wilke, *"Hilfsgemeinschaft auf Gegenseitigkeit"*.

130. Patrick Wagner, *Volksgemeinschaft ohne Verbrecher. Konzeption und Praxis der Kriminalpolizei in der Zeit der Weimarer Republik und des Nationalsozialismus* (Hamburg, 1996), 10f.; Patrick Wagner, *Hitlers Kriminalisten. Die deutsche Kriminalpolizei und der Nationalsozialismus* (Munich, 2002), 7-11, 149-86; Stefan Noethen, *Alte Kameraden und neue Kollegen. Polizei in Nordrhein-Westfalen 1945–1953* (Essen, 2003); Schulte, "Namen sind Nachrichten," 26–37.

131. Noethen, *Alte Kameraden*, 382.

132. Alan Bullock, *Hitler. Eine Studie über Tyrannei* (Düsseldorf, 1961), 731.

133. Karl O. Paetel, "Der Schwarze Orden. Zur Literatur über die SS," *Neue Politische Literatur* 3 (1958): 263–78.

134. Hannah Arendt, *Elemente und Ursprünge totaler Herrschaft. Antisemitismus, Imperialismus, Totalitarismus*, 7th edn (Munich/Zurich, 2000), 804 *et passim*; Hans Buchheim et al., *Anatomie des SS-Staates*, 4th edn, 2 vols (Munich, 1984).

135. Gerald Reitlinger, *The SS. Alibi of a Nation, 1922–1945*, 2nd edn (New York, 1968) (1st edn, 1957), 452.

136. Ibid.

137. Edward Crankshaw, *Die Gestapo* (Berlin, 1959) (1st English edn, 1956), 8–10, 226.

138. Alaric Searle, "Revising the 'Myth' of 'Clean Wehrmacht': Generals' Trials, Public Opinion, and the Dynamics of Vergangenheitsbewältigung in West Germany, 1948–60," *German Historical Institute London, Bulletin* 25 (2003): 17–48.

139. See Robert L. Koehl, *RKFDV: German Resettlement and Population Policy 1939–1945. A History of the Reich Commission for the Strengthening of Germandom* (Cambridge, MA, 1957); Robert L. Koehl, "The Character of the Nazi SS," *Journal of Modern History* 34 (1962): 275–83; Hans Buchheim, "Die SS in der Verfassung des Dritten Reiches," *Vierteljahreshefte für Zeitgeschichte* 3 (1955): 127–57; Ermenhild Neusüß-Hunkel, *Die SS* (Hannover/Frankfurt a.M., 1956).

140. *'Gerichtstag halten über uns selbst ...' Geschichte und Wirkung des ersten Frankfurter Auschwitz-Prozesses*, ed. Irmtrud Wojak for the Fritz Bauer Institute (Frankfurt/New York, 2001); Michael Wildt, *Generation des Unbedingten. Das Führerkorps des Reichssicherheitshauptamtes* (Hamburg, 2002), 16f.; Edgar Wolfrum, "Die beiden Deutschland," in *Verbrechen erinnern. Die Auseinandersetzung mit Holocaust und Völkermord*, eds. Volkhard Knigge and Norbert Frei (Munich, 2002), 133–49, here 138; Schulte, "Namen sind Nachrichten," 26–37.

141. Heinz Höhne, *Der Orden unter dem Totenkopf. Die Geschichte der SS* (Bindlach, 1990) (1st edn, 1967), 12.

142. Jan Erik Schulte, "Zur Geschichte der SS. Erzähltraditionen und Forschungsstand," in *Die SS, Himmler und die Wewelsburg*, ed. Jan Erik Schulte (Paderborn, 2009), XI–XXXV, here XV. In 1961 Raul Hilberg published his masterpiece on the destruction of the European Jews. It was based on the Nuremberg trials' documents and drastically broadened the group of those responsible for the Holocaust. However, it was widely ignored for 20 years. Cf. Raul Hilberg, *The Destruction of the European Jews* (Chicago, 1961); Raul Hilberg, *Unerbetene Erinnerung. Der Weg eines Holocaust-Forschers* (Frankfurt a.M., 1994).

143. Christoph Cornelißen, "Erforschung und Erinnerung—Historiker und die zweite Geschichte," in *Der Nationalsozialismus—Die zweite Geschichte. Überwindung, Deutung, Erinnerung*, eds. Peter Reichel, Harald Schmid and Peter Steinbach (Munich, 2009), 217–42, here 236–38.

144. For example, Guido Knopp, *Die SS. Eine Warnung der Geschichte* (Munich, 2002), 9.

145. See, e.g., Tim Ripley, *Hitler's Praetorians. The History of the Waffen-SS 1925–1945* (Staplehurst, 2004) or the numerous books by Jean Mabire in French and by Rolf Michaelis in German.

## CHAPTER 6

# TALES OF TOTALITARIANISM

## CONFLICTING NARRATIVES IN THE INDUSTRIALIST CASES AT NUREMBERG

*Kim C. Priemel*

⟡⟡⟡

In 1995, Celia Goetz was invited to a panel celebrating the fiftieth anniversary of the Nuremberg trials. Sitting alongside other participants in the trials, such as Telford Taylor and his former deputy Drexel A. Sprecher, Goetz took a decidedly critical stand towards the legacy of the so-called Subsequent Proceedings. "I have grave reservations about the usefulness of Nuremberg as a precedent," she told the audience. In her eyes at least those cases conducted by the US authorities under Control Council Law No. 10 had been "a flawed precedent."[1] This harsh verdict might come as a surprise because the Allied proceedings against the Third Reich's elites are usually held to be a landmark achievement in the development of international law.[2] Criticism of Nuremberg (which in fact is abundant) is usually applied to the subsequent unsatisfactory adoption of the Nuremberg principles, rather than to the direct accomplishments of the 13 trials from 1945 to 1949.[3]

Even so, Goetz's reservations are explicable in the light of her own experiences and, in fact, her disappointments as a member of the prosecution in the trials of German industrialists. The results of the proceedings in which she had participated, notably the Flick and Krupp cases, had not lived up to the prosecution's expectations. The tribunals had dismissed half of the counts, and the sentences delivered had been among the most lenient of all cases tried—"absurdly light" in the eyes of another frustrated prosecutor, William A. Zeck. Both Zeck and Goetz directed their criticism mostly at the fact that the tribunals had accepted the concept of necessity as an exonerating argument in favor of the indicted industrialists, thereby allowing the defendants to get away with but a small degree of historical blame.[4]

These exemplary remarks of two of the American staff directly lead to the core of what the Subsequent Nuremberg Trials tried to establish: which social groups bore responsibility for the different Nazi crimes. In contrast to the International Military Tribunal (IMT) that—despite Robert Jackson's professed intention to teach the world and especially the German public a lesson about the workings of the Third Reich[5]—had focused on the remaining big shots of the Nazi state, party and military elite, the later Proceedings followed a much more elaborate pattern. The design of the twelve *Trials of War Criminals Before the Nuernberg Military Tribunals Under Control Council Law No. 10*, as they were formally known, was meant to reveal the fabric of the dictatorship and the share of responsibility for its crimes among the different strata of German society. The industrialist cases clearly stood out in this configuration for five reasons.

First, the failure to incorporate bankers and industrialists in the IMT contributed crucially to the decision to launch another series of trials. Second, most of the businessmen who would ultimately be indicted were formally independent from both state and party offices. Complemented by lawyers and doctors, these cases against specific, *civilian* professions targeted the broad social responsibility for the Third Reich's deeds beyond the easily administered—and, not least among the German population, rather willingly accepted—guilt of the highest echelons of the Nazi state that had stood trial before the IMT.[6] For these reasons, Nuremberg's (re-)educational tenets were closely linked to the outcome of the industrialist trials: while indicting generals, security police officers, and even government officials seemed more conventional after the IMT, indicting industrialists clearly did not. Third, from the American perspective, the codes and manners of German corporate culture, such as cartels and universal banking, then both outlawed in the United States, epitomized illiberal traditions of German authoritarianism and economic feudalism that were believed to correlate with Prussian militarism and National Socialism. Bringing businessmen to trial therefore promised to hit at the heart of the Third Reich. As a result of these three strands of reasoning, the industrialist cases were, fourth, not only essential in expediting the overall idea of combining punishment, re-education, and a reform of international law but were also supposed to vindicate the concept of conspiracy whose performance on the IMT stage had been rather poor. Fifth, the economic cases stood out among the Subsequent Proceedings in terms of sheer size: the number of trials, the length of the proceedings, and the amount of transcripts and documents.[7]

The Nuremberg courtroom served as the stage where these readings were formulated in coherent narratives and presented to the tribunals, the defendants and their lawyers as well as to an international and, more importantly, a German audience. The American prosecutors produced their own theory or rather theories of the cases and, in doing so, their conceptions of the Third Reich and National Socialist crimes. In the setting of the criminal trial, these theories therefore had to fulfill a double purpose, which at the same time, implied a double strain on the quality of arguments and evidence. They needed to be phrased in a way that would be acceptable to the judges and convincing to both contemporary spectators and posterity. If the success of the trials thus depended on their being properly read then they needed to be well written.[8]

However, prosecutors were but one party in the proceedings. Other protagonists had stakes in the process of devising and composing trial accounts, among them the judges and the witnesses. Mostly, however, it was the defendants and their counsel who served not only as the procedural opponents but who came up with their own explanations and interpretations, defying the storyline told by the prosecution. Out of the confrontation between these conflicting narratives, a communicative, dialectic process of anticipation and reaction developed, causing intense "representational struggles," which can be traced through trial briefs and outlines, opening and closing statements, cross-examinations, evidence, and rebuttals.[9]

Likewise, the defendants and their attorneys quickly moved away from a reactive position of pure defense. Beyond the deflection of the prosecution's charges, the German protagonists reached out for historical narratives that would not only rehabilitate the Nuremberg defendants but serve as a "usable past" for a postwar society in which perpetrators and bystanders were ever-present.[10] Here again, the industrialist cases played a pioneering role in terms of scale and scope of the arguments developed at Nuremberg. The courtroom served as a catalyst for prominent interpretative patterns which would be adopted and refined for several decades, among them the *topoi* of apolitical professionalism, totalitarian tyranny, the tragedy of patriotism, and the self-victimization of German elites. In the end, the German reading of the Third Reich emanating from the Palace of Justice proved to be no less comprehensive than the ambitious tenets of the prosecution, though with diametrically opposed conclusions.

## Commerce and Crime: Conceptualizing the Charges

The idea to hold German business to account for its alleged cooperation with the Nazi regime did not come out of the blue. Given that plans about what to do with occupied Germany were formulated rather belatedly, economic questions played an important role early on. These were put forward from three different angles. In the context of strategic bombing, Allied offices tried to evaluate the capacities of the German war economy and assembled information on industrial clusters, impor-

tant plants, and leading companies, which resulted in practical hand-
books such as the sarcastically dubbed *Bomber's Baedeker* or the famous
Strategic Bombing Surveys.[11] In a long-term perspective, deindustriali-
zation was discussed as a precondition for demilitarization. This concept
was backed by a range of protagonists including Robert Vansittart and
Henry Morgenthau, Jr.—despite the rather different patterns underlying their respective analyses—and met with sharp criticism from a
no less articulated group which included the US War Department and
the Office of Strategic Services, in particular the Research & Analysis
Branch with its core of German émigrés.[12] Finally, Allied declarations
that war criminals would be punished left sufficient room for interpretation as to who would be held legally responsible.[13] That a great number
of German crimes were of a distinctly economic character was obvious:
the employment of forced laborers and concentration camp inmates,
spoliation and plunder in occupied Europe, or the "Aryanization" of
Jewish firms featured easily on any list of Nazi crimes.[14] And that did
not even tackle the question of what role private business might have
played in Hitler's rise to power and in the preparation for war by boost-
ing rearmament and violating the restrictions of the Versailles Treaty.
Accordingly, various offices in the US administration conceived of businessmen as possible war criminals by 1944, although the way in which
retribution would be delivered was as yet unclear.[15]

Between these complementary perspectives on the economic dimension of Nazi rule, hardly any strict differentiation was made until the
summer of 1945. The data collected by the OSS and British intelligence,
later by various offices of military government, catered to all needs—
economic planning, security concerns, legal investigations.[16] From the
Allied perspective this was not only convenient but also consequent:
if the huge German combines had enabled the Nazi regime to start
a war of unprecedented quality, then the dismantling of both actual
plants and corporate structures along with the punishment of the leading personnel were but different facets of the same policy of disabling
the German threat to peace once and for all. Accordingly, those US
offices which were dealing with the deconcentration and decartelization
of German business also provided incriminating information on individual companies, and detailed the links between German state agencies
and private business in the wartime economy so that their research was
soon marked by a "twofold perspective."[17] Thus, in late 1945, Russell A.
Nixon, who headed the OMGUS Division of Investigation of Cartels and
External Assets, declared that the investigation of the six leading German banks would also produce findings "for the indictment and trials of
the banks as war criminals."[18] A few weeks later, Lucius D. Clay charged
the Cartels and Industry Branches of the OMGUS Economic Division
with furnishing the Public Safety Division with a list of business leaders
most prominently associated with the Nazi regime—which proved to be
also a list of potential defendants.[19]

By that time, decision making on the war crimes issue had advanced considerably with the preparations of the IMT being well under way. Economy clearly mattered in this respect. Senator Harley Kilgore's well-known Subcommittee on War Mobilization played a key role in this development, trying to determine which individuals in the Third Reich's economy bore particular responsibility and inquiring into German-American business connections. Despite the obvious empirical and analytical shortcomings of its findings, the committee proved highly influential, not so much because of the rather arbitrary list it came up with in October 1945, naming 42 businessmen who allegedly had "shared guilt in the crimes committed by the Nazis against the rest of world,"[20] but with an eye to both the publicity it gave the economic issue and the evidence that it produced—a large amount of which would feed into the Nuremberg prosecution's research efforts.[21]

Of even greater significance was the appointment of Supreme Court judge Robert H. Jackson as US chief prosecutor. Jackson soon became the driving force in the process of drawing up the IMT and was determined to put the industrial complicity in the planning and waging of aggressive war on display. Behind this was the idea of a Nazi conspiracy to launch a war in order to achieve domination over Europe and, ultimately, the world, which had included the perpetration of war crimes and crimes against humanity as ruthless means of German aggression. This catch-all conceptualization, which would serve as the argumentative backbone of the IMT, was as much tactically motivated as it articulated a specific reading of National Socialism. The idea that a conspiracy had been drawn up years before the war which resulted in a master plan for aggression, occupation, and mass murder which had then be implemented by criminal organizations offered a number of advantages, namely to bridge potential gaps between preconceptions of historical responsibility on the one hand and individualized proof on the other. Moreover, once organizational guilt was established it would be easy to deal with the enormous numbers of second and third tier perpetrators, not to speak of the rank and file.[22] Beyond these pragmatic considerations, the conspiracy concept implied a heightened susceptibility to the relations between the business elite and Nazi top officials. Who else could have provided Hitler's regime with the armaments to wage a war of aggression despite the restrictions of the Versailles Treaty? How could the exploitation of occupied Europe have been managed without the economic expertise of German industry and finance? And who else had run the Reich's war economy with stunning efficiency against an overwhelming coalition to the very end of the war?[23]

Therefore, when Jackson assigned the task of proving the existence of a Common Plan to OSS, whose head, William J. Donovan, became Jackson's deputy, the Chief of Counsel explicitly ordered that the economic instruments "by which Germany secured to herself important technological and military advantages" would be covered.[24] That was precisely what several

drafts on "Nazi Plans to Dominate Europe," which were drawn up by
the R&A section in summer 1945, did. Consistently, they pointed out the
"full-scale collaboration of the German industrialists, whose enterprises
and holdings provided the nuclei of expansion," who had supported "the
Nazi movement prior to Hitler's ascent to power," and who were rewarded
with the spoils of war and access to unlimited labor power.[25] This account
resonated with Franz Neumann's conceptualization of four pillars—party,
administration, military, and business—on which the Third Reich was
standing.[26] This distinct echo was hardly surprising given that he was the
head of the R&A Central European Section where his groundbreaking
*Behemoth* significantly influenced wartime studies of the German economy and private business, and that he would soon serve as a consultant
to the Chief of Counsel in Nuremberg.[27] And beyond the general patterns
outlined in *Behemoth*, the book also listed individual, identifiable names.[28]

Most of these names would reappear in a memorandum from Jackson's staff member Francis Shea in July 1945. Shea listed a set of candidates for prosecution which were drawn from the ranks of both state and
private economic administration: Hjalmar Schacht, Albert Speer, Fritz
Sauckel, Walther Funk, and Paul Körner from the former, and Hermann
Schmitz, Kurt von Schröder, Friedrich Flick, Hermann Röchling, and
Alfried Krupp from the latter.[29] These ten men were said to represent an
"economic gang" which had shared knowledge of and participated in the
Nazi plans for war, providing funding to the party, increasing armaments
production, and striving for autarchy. Evidence of confiscation of Jewish property, of looting occupied countries, and of industrial reliance on
forced labor illustrated the deep implication in actual war crimes.[30] However, as a result of Allied fears of a lengthy trial and the unwillingness
to delay the proceedings if judicially reliable evidence had to be procured
from provenances other than the easily available governmental records,
the latter half of Shea's list soon boiled down to Krupp. And even that
idea, due to the oft-reported blunder of confusing father and son, came to
naught so that no private businessman was eventually tried by the IMT.[31]

Despite this letdown, the Allied prosecutors did not drop the idea of
indicting bankers and industrialists altogether. The option of staging a
second IMT which would deal exclusively with businessmen had become
more likely with the British chief prosecutor's commitment to such an
undertaking in October 1945.[32] While this had been strongly motivated by
the wish to avoid any further discussion about the first tribunal and get
things going, there had also been considerable agreement in the British
delegation that there was damning evidence incriminating German business which could not be ignored.[33] A flurry of briefs, summaries, and biographical sketches on Krupp, Flick, Röchling, Schröder, and the directors
of IG Farben outlined the manifold ways in which German companies had
contributed to Nazi criminality.[34] The lists of likely defendants which circulated in the first half of 1946 all built on Shea's work with some minor
changes, including the focus on Paul Pleiger, the former head of the

Reichswerke Hermann Göring, and contemplations to put more than just one Farben director in the dock. However, British and US inclinations to a second international tribunal fell markedly as the IMT progressed, for a number of reasons, including growing fears that the rather weak case against Schacht might serve as an unwelcome precedent. No less important were misgivings between the Allies, particularly Western qualms of a Soviet-dominated, anti-capitalist show trial, the expected drop of public interest in what "would inevitably be an anti-climax," and a range of organizational and financial worries, especially on the British part.[35]

These doubts were shared by Jackson who advised in no uncertain terms against a second IMT.[36] Yet, that did neither mean that he was opposed to follow-up investigations nor that he did not want to see businessmen tried. Quite the contrary, Jackson's statements both to Truman and before the Tribunal betrayed a strong belief in the theory of a party-military-industrial complex as the backbone of the Third Reich. A draft indictment by Drexel Sprecher from June 1946, arguing that the NSDAP had been "the instrument of cohesion among the defendants and their co-conspirators" in the military and civilian offices, clearly breathed that spirit.[37] But in contrast to the British lack of action, the US delegation planned on making full use of the competences provided by CCL 10 on December 20, 1945. Preparations for zonal trials were pursued along with those for a possible second IMT which Taylor, who was put in charge of OCCWC, deemed possible as late as fall 1946. Therefore, investigations for both options overlapped organizationally and materially: if the 'IMT 2' did not happen, the research at least would not be in vain. Investigations for zonal proceedings focused on the very same people who would have appeared in the IMT dock but broadened the scope. Planned as a series of trials, this concept would allow indicting not only select, prominent representatives of German business but targeting the complex administrative machinery behind them, i.e., executive and supervisory boards, corporate administration, and industrial organizations which had managed the war economy. It was thus in the NMT that the promise of a both broad and in-depth analysis of the causes and crimes of Nazi rule, which the IMT had not lived up to, was supposed to be fulfilled.[38]

## The Industrialist Cases in the NMT

### *The Prosecution's Case*

The choice of defendants documented this new ambition. The men destined to stand trial before an 'IMT 2' were set candidates but much more could now be done in separate trials of IG Farben, Flick, or Krupp (as the British preferred extraditing Alfried Krupp and his associates over trying them in a CCL 10 tribunal in their own zone[39]). The number of targeted individuals and companies surged rapidly, with the lists of possible defendants going into the hundreds.[40] Several heavy industrial trusts were listed, among them Reichswerke and Röchling, though the latter case was soon handed over to the French who undertook the only NMT outside the American zone, the fourteenth Nuremberg Trial in all but name.[41] The top three electrical industry combines, Siemens, AEG and Bosch, came into the prosecutors' focus along with the "Big Six" banks. Selection criteria focused on the size of the corporations and their market share in different sectors rather than on formal party affiliation of their management. Tellingly, Kurt von Schröder—the private banker who had hosted the fateful meeting between Hitler and Papen in 1933—disappeared from tentative lists discussed among the US prosecutors in the following weeks despite his reputation as Hitler's door-opener to power. But by now the fact that the private banks "did not have the economic importance in Germany that the 'Big Six' had," mattered more than individual notoriety.[42]

Much attention was therefore paid to cartel and corporatist structures in choosing suitable candidates. Top representatives of the semi-public, self-governing *Wirtschaftsgruppen* and *Reichsvereinigungen* featured prominently on the 1946 lists, often grossly overestimating the actual influence of organizations or individuals.[43] Significantly, a memorandum on Ernst Poensgen, who had served as chief executive of Vereinigte Stahlwerke AG and *Wirtschaftsgruppe Eisen schaffende Industrie*, stated that he had

> had personal knowledge of German plans of aggression before they were put into effect, furthermore he actively collaborated in their formulation and execution by taking a prominent part in economic conferences with the Economic Ministry, the Reichsmarschall and generals Thomas and von Hanneken. In the conferences the economic side of the conspiracy was always discussed and not a single major economic decision was taken without consulting him as Head of the strongest economic group.[44]

Despite these charges, Poensgen would not appear in the defendants' dock as it turned out. For a variety of reasons—difficulties in recruiting competent judges, a growing awareness that the length of both investigations and trials had been underestimated, budgetary pressures, and thinning enthusiasm for trials in the wake of the Cold War—Taylor had to cut back his ambitious program in successive steps. By late 1947, twelve out of twenty trials which had been in planning in February were left. The final tableau, however, gave evidence to the emphasis on economic affairs. Three trials would deal with proprietors and managers of individual combines (Flick, IG Farben, Krupp), a fourth—a merger of several dropped cases, among them those against Dresdner Bank, Reichswerke, and the Reich economic bureaucracy—also purported a strong interest in industry and finance ("Ministries case").[45]

The selection of defendants from the multitude of available candidates was one thing, the search for unassailable evidence another, the preparation of a general line of argument a third. While the first two progressed satisfactorily since late 1946—although it proved to be much more difficult to find witnesses for the "Slave Labor" charge than expected[46]—the true challenge was to find a coherent narrative which would provide a framework for all cases without obscuring the individual dimension. A range of suggestions and concepts circulated among Taylor's staff, which despite some variations, were broadly similar in their perspectives on the relations between Nazism and big business.[47] This was by and large because most prosecutors built their assumptions and analyses on a common compilation of both theoretical and empirical writings—not only *Behemoth*, but also Lemkin's *Axis Rule*, Otto Nathan's account of *The Nazi Economic System*, Sheldon Glueck's inclusion of economic actors in his conceptualization of war crimes, or the study on forced labor of the International Labor Organization, authored by John H.E. Fried who would soon serve as Special Legal Consultant to the Nuremberg tribunals.[48] Due to the greater scope of the NMT, these works were exploited much more thoroughly than they had been for the IMT. Abstracts and copies were circulated among researchers and prosecutors, and in May 1946 Sprecher recommended: "Where you have no original documents or other qualified evidence to support a known factual point, ... cite secondary sources ... as if it [sic] were an original source."[49]

Accordingly, there was broad agreement that the trials of industrialists and financiers were to show that the German business elite had been actively involved in planning and implementing aggressive war. Along with the Party and the Wehrmacht, big business was held responsible collectively for the Common Plan. It had—here was some leeway for individual variations—either helped to bring National Socialism into power in the first place or joined the conspiracy once Hitler was in power, from then on implementing and benefiting from Nazi crimes. There were some differences in terms of the language that was used among the staff, especially in the case of Abraham Pomerantz, short-time deputy head of the economic trials branch, whose memoranda endorsed a crude *condottiere* motif in which Hitler figured as industry's "political arm and puppet."[50] But overall there was a broad consensus on these points.

However, there was no way of bringing the general message home without winning judgments in the particular cases. Therefore a strategy was required which would prove the accused individuals guilty without individualizing the responsibility and thus letting the respective companies as well as the broader German economic system off the hook. The solution to this threefold challenge was provided by the "institutional approach" in the last summer days of 1946. Building on earlier discussions, analyst Leonard Drachsler presented a 31-page outline for an indictment of the industrialists which would pertain to all cases.[51] In short, the defendants were supposed to appear in the dock "as officers of the leading German economic institutions, as corporate officials of their own organizations and as individuals." Thus, the aim of each trial would be "to demonstrate symbolically the common guilt not alone of, say, the Krupp and Farben executives as individuals, but of all important executives in German industry who participated and supported the Nazi conspiracy" or, even more generally, "the guilt of the Nazi economic system as a willing and enthusiastic instrument of a criminal state whose goal was aggressive war."[52] In early October, the head of the Berlin section, Benjamin Ferencz, informed all staff that the institutional approach had been adopted for the whole prosecution. "Conspiracy" and "aggressive war"—the two legal concepts which had marked the IMT—were thus also at the heart of the industrialist cases, but not the concept of criminal organizations. Although Taylor endorsed Drachsler's general blueprint, he decided to drop the latter idea as it had proven of little worth in the IMT and was not essential to the institutional approach. Instead the prosecution would focus on "the 'unified conspiracy' element" in order to "devise some technique and sequence that will make them [trials] all hang together."[53]

The setting of the three industrialist trials amply illustrated the institutional approach. The very fact that the trials were not ordered by type and enormity of crimes but by firms showed that companies were aimed at just as much as managers, even if corporate liability formally was not at stake and despite the professed belief that "the corporate entity, the legal person [...] did not commit crimes. It was merely the instrumentality of the men who guided and directed it."[54] However, the prosecutions' choice of a "total concern approach," tracing responsibility on different levels of decision making instead of targeting only the head office,[55] clearly contradicted such statements. While this was less obvious in the Flick case, where only one of the six defendants represented the plant level, the Farben and Krupp line-ups were more straightforward in that respect. The twelve Krupp defendants ranked from the sole proprietor, Alfried Krupp von Bohlen und Halbach, to the head of the foreign labor camps, Hans Kupke; the majority had been (deputy) members of the executive board. In the largest of the purely economic cases, the Farben trial, the twenty-three defendants were chosen from diverse places and offices, representing the major components of the trust (Bayer, BASF, Hoechst), different functional levels (finance, technical, trade and marketing, etc.) and various hierarchical levels, while the majority was again recruited from the executive board. The perception that not only individuals stood trial was shared by the defendants who explicitly thanked those who "had the courage to testify for Farben," and stressed that "the escutcheon of our enterprise, the IG, is clear."[56] Particularly remarkable was the indictment of Carl Krauch as lead defendant. The fact that Krauch, following his appointment as plenipotentiary of chemical production, had shifted to Farben's supervisory board, where actual competences were difficult to determine, was perceived as an asset rather than a problem: Krauch seemed to provide a perfect example for the blurred boundaries between business and state administration which the prosecution deemed typical of German industry.[57]

If the institutional approach in the case of IG Farben was strongly marked by the alleged proximity if not near-identity of the Four Year Plan on the one hand and IG Farben on the other, this was but the tip of the iceberg. Fully twenty pages of the printed indictment were devoted to a list of all posts and positions held by the defendants, financial-industrial or political, civil, and military in character, which had supposedly been used to participate in crimes against peace, war crimes, and crimes against humanity.[58] Such positions were also presented as proof of incriminating 'private-public partnerships' in the Krupp and Flick cases. Besides the *Reichs-* and *Wirtschaftsgruppen*, strong emphasis was placed on the *Reichsvereinigungen Kohle* (RVK) and *Eisen* (RVE). These were thoroughly investigated—though insufficiently understood—in the pre-trial phase and conceived of as compulsory top cartels through which the wartime economy had been organized, occupied Europe exploited, and industry's demands for cheap forced labor transmitted to compliant state agencies. While this argumentation mistook a by and large executive organization for a policy-making agency, it offered a threefold advantage. It assigned responsibility for the "slave labor program" as identified by the IMT to those top managers who had been remote from the day-to-day operations at plant level; it linked the Third Reich's economic system with its Imperial predecessors, highlighted by Taylor's reference to Ludendorff's consultations with Gustav Krupp and Carl Duisberg (Farben) during World War I;[59] and it phrased the charges in an anti-cartel language which was familiar to the judges and an American audience.[60]

The picture of Farben drawn by the prosecutors was that of an industrial giant that had dominated global markets for chemical products and raw materials for a long time and had hampered the productive capacities of Germany's enemies by means of espionage and one-sided trade agreements.[61] A significant portion of the trial was dedicated to such "Propaganda, Intelligence, and Espionage Activities" in which Farben's notorious *Verbindungsstelle W* had apparently played a key part by providing essential information to the Wehrmacht, coordinating armaments efforts, and participating in the planning of aggression and war crimes.[62] With an eye to the latter charge, specific attention was paid to Farben's plans to exploit the opportunities offered by German military expansion which had been a part of a more general debate, driven by the euphoria of victory in the west, among the Third Reich's political and economic elites what a postwar Europe under German hegemony should look like.[63] This "New Order," however, was now depicted as a genuine Farben venture, "a complete exposition of projects which Farben had developed since World War I and hoped to accomplish through German aggrandizement."[64]

This picture of plans for territorial expansion preceding the advent of National Socialism bore a striking resemblance to the concept of a double conspiracy which was the prosecution's main theme in the Krupp case. Here, the prosecutors claimed that up to 1933 two separate conspiracies had existed, one by the Nazi Party, the other a "Krupp conspiracy," which were fused after Hitler's assumption of power as their aims were essentially the same: rearmament and militarization, war and conquest.[65] This was not only a judicial ruse in order to try all defendants on all four counts, i.e. conspiracy, aggressive war, spoliation, and slave labor, despite the fact that most of them had not held senior positions in the 1920s, including Alfried Krupp von Bohlen und Halbach. In a pre-emptive move Taylor assured the tribunal that the son was not to be charged with the sins of the father, and that the prosecution did not intend to try the industrial icon Krupp either. Alfried Krupp & Co., Taylor and his team argued, were the right defendants in the right trial as they had joined the said Krupp conspiracy one by one and had finally executed and benefited from the long-prepared crimes.[66]

Taylor's essay in prophylaxis correctly anticipated the defense's future attack pattern but was hardly credible in the light of the larger picture painted by the prosecution. Taylor himself not only quoted Jackson's apodictic statements before the IMT that Krupp had a century-old reputation as an enemy of peace but continued in a not too dissimilar vein by placing the charges against the defendants in the broader context of the corporate history. According to the arguments that the prosecution presented at great length in the first weeks of the trial, Krupp was, by tradition, first and foremost an armaments maker whose rapid growth had been deeply intertwined with the Prussian-German wars in the nineteenth century and the imperialist ambitions of the Wilhelmine Empire. Out of this alliance with the reactionary, illiberal and anti-democratic forces in German politics, so the story went, as well as due to the resentment of the Versailles Treaty which curtailed its business ambitions, Krupp had deliberately circumvented the disarmament obligations in the 1920s, already preparing for the next war. Hitler had merely offered the best chance to fulfill these ambitions, and their alliance had been to their mutual benefit. While the Nazi regime had relied heavily on Krupp's expertise in preparing for war as well as on its party funding resources, the company had prospered and had been given special favors, notably the *Lex Krupp* which had provided for a tax-saving transformation of the joint stock corporation into a personal firm in 1943.[67]

This did not only read like a business history—it was. The prosecution's general interpretation relied heavily on *The Lords of Essen* by émigré journalist Bernhard Menne, which was offered as background information, though not as evidence, to the tribunal.[68] Menne's account was highly biased but well informed, as he had in turn used the massive amount of historical writings and records published by the Krupp combine.[69] As a consequence the Krupp trial became not only a judicial struggle over assorted war crimes and the relations between state and business in the Third Reich but also about Krupp's corporate identity. The first document book offered by the defense would assemble a collection of documents titled *Krupp 1812 bis 1918. Entwicklung und Geist* [Evolution and Spirit], followed by an affidavit of the company archivist, historical photographs, and a wide range of similar documents which bore little significance for the charges.[70]

The Flick history was by no means as impressive in terms of length—the combine's founder had started his career just before World War I—and for the greater part of the interwar decade Flick had not been in the same league as Farben or Krupp. On the other hand, the combine proved to be an interesting representative from the prosecution's perspective for precisely these reasons. Flick represented the case of a beneficiary of the Nazi regime whose "meteoric rise to power in German finance and industry is unparalleled in modern times."[71] The fact that this growth had resulted from rearmament and "Aryanization" and that Flick had also been among the first to reach out for expansive opportunities in the occupied countries made him an even better choice. What was more, apart from Krupp he had been the only industrialist with a seat in both RVE and RVK, and he had also been a member of the *Freundeskreis of the Reichsführer SS* and an alleged confidant of Hermann Göring. That way, a great number of connections between business and state or party agencies could easily be drawn out. Flick's ideological stance was secondary to the ruthless tactics he had employed and the lack of scruples he had shown when benefiting from Nazi crimes. In fact, at least some investigators found Flick's political expediency particularly disturbing as they perceived some similarities to US business practices, amply illustrated in such characterizations of Flick as a "modern self-made German Robber Baron."[72]

To draw out such similarities, though, was not what the prosecution had in mind. Instead, prosecutors like Pomerantz and Taylor, as well as the deputy Minister of War, Howard Petersen, agreed that Flick & Co. were to stand trial not "because of their business ambitions" but for the ways in which these had been pursued, i.e., aiding of, abetting in, and benefiting from criminal policies of the Nazi regime.[73] Implicit in the Flick indictment was thus a charge of violating essential principles of good business conduct, notably in the slave labor and spoliation counts but most of all in the "Aryanization" section. The latter did not only turn out to be the best-proven charge in the trial by far, it also substituted the conspiracy and crimes against peace count which was not formally brought against Flick and his associates. However, the argument was very much present throughout the trial, e.g., when "Aryanization" was discussed as a means of both eliminating interior ideological enemies and strengthening the German rearmaments effort, or when the armaments boom's effects on Flick's growth were, quite literally, exhibited.[74]

Finally, as Flick was the first of the Industrialist cases, the prosecution, in an endeavor to put the Third Reich's structures on display, stressed the representative character of the defendants as "leading representatives of one of the two principal concentrations of power in Germany ... Krupp, Flick, Thyssen, and a few others swayed the industrial group; Beck, Fritsch, Rundstedt, and other martial exemplars ruled the military clique. On the shoulders of these groups Hitler rode to power, and from power to conquest."[75]

### Making Martyrs: the Defense Narrative

German business had a rather early start in digging up defensive lines. The first efforts to establish interpretations of the relations between National Socialism and private business dated back to the dying days of the Third Reich and where tailored for the domestic as well as for an international audience. Although the scope of the war crimes trials was not yet foreseeable, these labors articulated an obvious urge to explain and legitimate business conduct in the preceding years. These early memoranda, essays, and autobiographical accounts already claimed interpretative sovereignty over the very recent past and thus laid the basis for the contest to come. Moreover, while comprising the germs of the apologetic PR strategies of the next decades, they also aimed at a "coherent and consequential framework of self-perception and self-presentation."[76] These efforts were not halted by the large-scale arrests of leading businessmen in the first six months of occupation either.[77] Instead, the shared experience of individual hardship and social derangement helped to shape common narratives. In the prisons reserved for the higher echelons of business and state bureaucracy[78] and in the Nuremberg courtroom, a distinct reading of the Nazi years emerged along with the "new industrialist" who would soon reintegrate into democratic, free-marketing West German society.[79]

While some representatives of German business displayed a surprising degree of carefreeness in the first weeks of occupation, not worrying too much what the new authorities might think about their previous political allegiances,[80] others looked out for justifications of their contributions to re-armament, expansion, and the use of forced labor. In May 1945, Krupp director Eduard Houdremont authored a memorandum which drew a picture of a tight dictatorship which had suppressed and disadvantaged industry systematically. Houdremont recalled recurrent clashes between private business and the state-run economic organizations. In short, Krupp had been liberated by the Allied forces and was now looking forward to a return to normal business and cooperation with the enemies-turned-partners.[81] Another account was drafted in June by Walter Rohland, chief executive of Vereinigte Stahlwerke, who had made full use of the career opportunities the war economy had offered. Rohland's ambitions went beyond the salvation of his own company when he defended participation in the German efforts with a patriotic sense of duty, and called for cooperation for the sake of reconstruction and anti-Soviet unity. Rohland also anticipated one of the key questions of industrial deconcentration when he demanded that the vertical integration of German combines had to be preserved by all means. Complicity between Party and industry was vehemently denied in yet another account authored by Poensgen and edited by Rohland.[82]

A particularly comprehensive report was drafted by Siemens' executive board. With "a combination of truths, half-truths and inaccuracies" the managers argued that the "House of Siemens" had always focused on a strictly peaceful product assortment and deviated from this course only under Nazi pressure. Likewise, the company had consistently maintained traditional—i.e. honorable—business ethics, including a good track-record on social policy which had motivated a firm if unsuccessful objection to the exploitation of forced labor. Finally, the argumentative potential of Siemens' indispensability for the postwar economy was not lost on its management and thus duly pointed out to the Allied audience it had in mind.[83]

Meanwhile in the Flick combine, preparations took a little longer to get going. Some minor notes and biographical sketches were drawn up in the spring of 1945[84] but full-blown memoranda like that of Houdremont were put to paper only in August. By that time Flick had been arrested and transferred to the OMGUS Decartelization branch, and a *Stars and Stripes* article had been published announcing the Allied intention to try prominent industrialists for their responsibility in planning and launching aggressive war. Flick and his subordinates reacted immediately, commissioned legal advice from the deceased regime's *Kronjurist* Carl Schmitt,[85] and sat themselves down to draw up a series of multipage essays dealing with the corporate history and the career of founder Friedrich Flick.[86] These writings were neatly summed up by a concise, yet comprehensive memorandum which lodged formal protest against Flick's continued arrest, the sequestrations in the Eastern zone, and the "violent campaign" in the press denouncing the tycoon as a war criminal. As in the cases of Krupp and Siemens, there was also a thinly-veiled warning that legal prosecution of businessmen would have negative repercussions for German reconstruction.[87]

In regard to their own specific case, the managers showed some acuity in figuring out what charges the Allies would bring against the combine.[88] Their pre-emptive justifications paid most attention to potential charges such as "Aryanization," spoliation, and complicity in preparing the war by means of armaments production. In sketching the lines along which a future defense would be organized, the managers and their lawyers also provided an interpretative framework for state-business relations in the Third Reich which laid claim to general validity. Firstly, "Aryanizations" were turned into ordinary transactions which had been either negotiated in a professional, dignified way and "at reasonable and regular prices," untinged by the racist policies of the Nazi regime. Or they had been "ordered by superior political authorities" and "under political pressure." In contrast, Flick and his staff credited themselves with financial help which they claimed to have offered to Jewish friends and partners. Secondly, active participation in the territorial expansion was flatly denied or described as a sort of heroic undertaking "in order to prevent a monopoly of the Reichswerke."[89]

Finally, the reproach that business had been complicit with the Nazi regime was completely mistaken, as the industrialists would have it. Not only had "Flick stood aloof from the party racket" personally, the NSDAP as such had been a lower class party strongly hostile to the economic elites. Therefore, the combine's staff had neither known about the war to come, nor had it had any power to stop it. To expect such a behavior was perceived as a breach of international law—*nullum crimen, nulla poena sine lege*—and a blatant misreading of the Third Reich: this had not been a cozy democracy such as those of the Western Allies but a "leviathan State which claimed the total domination of the individual in all provinces of public and private life and enforced this claim through a system of honour."[90] There was more than just slight irony in the fact that the future defendants, helped by Schmitt, invoked the Leviathan as a defense figure against a prosecution whose analysis of the Third Reich was informed by the very Behemoth which Schmitt's former student Neumann had described so powerfully.

The totalitarian paradigm was thus booked to appear on the Nuremberg stage,[91] and by late 1946 it became foreseeable that the first scene would feature Flick and his top managers as the main protagonists. Not Krupp but Flick would set the precedent for the US war crimes trials against industrialists and implement the institutional approach favored by Taylor's team. This was almost immediately understood by the defendants. As Otto Steinbrinck, Flick's former right hand, argued, the indictment in Case 5, as the trial soon became known, went beyond individual deeds and responsibilities, aiming at countless German entrepreneurs and executives and the ways in which these had run their business and contributed to "economic self-administration." Case 5 would be no private affair of Flick and his fellow defendants but *the* pioneering trial determining the fate of German industry.[92]

Pathetic or not, Steinbrinck's analysis had a point, and a significant number of industrialists shared his opinion. Therefore, by early 1947 Flick's trial team was by and large financed by the Ruhr heavyweights, and strategies for the three industrialist cases were centralized in the so-called *Industriebüro* which was funded by German steel.[93] Synergies showed on various levels. The documents introduced by the Flick defense counsel in Case 5 were literally recycled in the Krupp, partly also in the Farben trials.[94] This was greatly helped by the fact that the core of the defense counsel in all industrialist cases—including the Röchling trial in the French zone of occupation—was identical. Combining company lawyers with seasoned IMT attorneys who had adapted masterly to common law procedures and its adversary style, especially in cross-examinations of witnesses for the prosecution who were scrutinized harshly, the Flick defense counsel re-sampled their evidence, witnesses, and arguments in the trials of Farben and Krupp.[95]

Unsurprisingly, the general pattern of the defense counsel's reasoning was virtually the same in all three cases. Full use was made of the standard arguments of *nullum crimen, nulla poena* and *tu quoque*, conjuring the well-known images of victors' justice and collective guilt. Especially *tu quoque* was exhorted time and again in order to point out that industry had not known about the regime's intentions to go to war until 1939, no different from the Allies who had shaken hands with Hitler in Munich.[96] Hence, business in the Allied countries would not have behaved any differently under the same circumstances, as it had indeed patriotically supplied arms and war-essential materials to their respective countries. Lurking behind this argument was, in a less than subtle way, the image of the apolitical expert who had merely done his duty in times of national need and who had fallen victim of a tragic combination of patriotic "sacrifice and terrorist force, the intermingling of faith, self-deception, and betrayal."[97] *Tu quoque* also played a manifest role when it came to alleged Allied programs of forced labor and dismantling policies which were described as equivalents to the slave labor and spoliation counts.[98] While these issues were used to attack the American prosecution, the defense also appreciated the potential of the changed political climate from 1947 onwards. The attack by one of the Krupp lawyers on the trial's attempt "to hit the entire German industry," diagnosing a "painful resemblance" to Andrey Vyshinsky's attacon "capitalist monopolistic combines" before the UN General Assembly, was representative for all industrialist trials. To co-counsel Walter Siemers, the whole venture was nothing but "an anti-capitalist crusade."[99]

References to the growing bloc formation also echoed during the cross-examinations of former forced workers from Eastern Europe. These were treated with no empathy whatsoever and tricked into contradictory statements time and again, denouncing their evidence as deliberately false.[100] While the prosecution had called them into the witness stand to illustrate the plight of the victims, the defense counsel turned their narratives upside down, claiming that the defendants had done their utmost to take good care of their workers, in line with their traditions of social welfare and especially in the light of wartime conditions. The meaning of forced labor was reversed so far as to imply that these workers had been forced on the German employers. Responsibility was assigned to lower-level clerks—though to a lesser degree in the Krupp case where Kupke, Lehmann, and Bülow had been too closely involved in these issues and where the notion of corporate welfare did not go well with such a strategy—but most of all to state, party, and Wehrmacht agencies.[101]

There was more than just a slight ring of self-victimization in these accounts. In fact, the self-depiction as collaborators of the regime *malgré eux* was the starting point rather than the end of the industrialists' revamping efforts. True to their memoranda of summer 1945, the businessmen in the dock presented themselves as mere executives of the regime's will which had crushed any opposition; the specters of the Gestapo and the concentration camps had hung above all board meetings since the late 1930s. That this was rather inconsistent with the affirmed lack of knowledge when it came to Nazi crimes associated with the camps did not seem to bother the German lawyers or their clients.[102] Instead, many went far beyond that and testified on their implications in oppositional schemes which had mostly been unheard of so far, apart from the case of the former Krupp executive Ewald Löser whose attorney duly went at great length in describing his association with the Goerdeler circle.[103]

If the industrialists had been under pressure from a regime whose socialist suffix was repeatedly emphasized, but still had tried to alleviate its wrongs, someone else would have to be identified as Hitler's supporters. Easy choices were the well-known cases of Emil Kirdorf and Fritz Thyssen, who were portrayed as deplorable but utterly unrepresentative exceptions to the rule. The brunt of the guilt, however, was assigned to the working class. In a vulgarized adaptation of Ortega y Gasset's *Revolt of the Masses*, a triad made up by defendants, attorneys, and witnesses for the defense argued that the trade unions and workers had not only failed to resist the Nazi regime but had actively backed Hitler. The gospel according to lawyer Rudolf Dix maintained that Hitler had risen from the ranks of the proletariat to become its messiah. And against the irresponsible masses a bourgeois business elite had been nothing but helpless.[104]

Within this common framework, each defense counsel team developed specialized narratives in response to the prosecution's allegations—the ruthless tycoon Flick, the Farben octopus, and canon king Krupp—but also in line with traditional modes of self-perception and self-description. Thus, Flick and his managers, helped by their lawyers, spent much time on disclaiming all contentions that they had collaborated particularly closely with state and party authorities in the course of "Aryanization" or spoliation. The retrospective dissociation from private-public partnerships of any kind built on a firmly established discourse inside the combine which went back to the notorious Gelsenberg affair in 1932, when Flick had successfully blackmailed the Reich authorities into taking over his crumbling industrial empire, effectively saving his industrial career. Ever since, he had faced criticism for fostering "cold socialization" and entertaining intimate ties with state agencies. The deals with the Reichswerke in the late 1930s and during the war had hardly helped to improve this reputation. Therefore, the takeover of expropriated Jewish property in exchange for soft coal mines was labeled a "rape of German industry" in the preparatory stages before the trial.[105] Flick himself claimed that, being a good merchant, he had not only delayed state action as long as possible in order to conduct an ordinary private take-over bid, but had become a guardian of Jewish interests on the one hand and a victim of the Reichswerke's unscrupulous expansion on the other.[106]

The self-description as apolitical professionals who had remained loyal to traditional business ethics was taken up in the Farben and Krupp trials but assumed distinct shapes. In Case 6, the Farben directors and their defense counsel chose science and technology as the pervading themes of their argument. With regard to their company's—and, implicitly, their own—honor, the manifold achievements in medical and pharmaceutical progress undertaken by Farben chemists were brought to mind. Countering Taylor's denunciation of Farben's scientific feats as "malignant alchemy," the defense did not grow tired of recounting the concern's triumphs in the service of mankind. This led to bizarre moments such as Karl Hoffmann's opening statement for Otto Ambros, a key figure in the IG's venture at Auschwitz-Monowitz. In a strange kind of spoken verse, Hoffmann recited, "Aspirin and Pyramidone, Gardan and Compral, Evipan, Luminal and Veronal, Novalgine and Novocain," concluding that these had "brought healing and the alleviation of pain to millions of human beings throughout the earth."[107] It was this pure and noble science, the defendants claimed, which they had tried to keep aloof from the grip of totalitarian rule—"to rescue science from Hitler"—sincerely, if unsuccessfully in the end.[108] How strongly the defendants conceived of themselves in terms of scientists and technicians was emblematically formulated in Krauch's self-depiction as "technical man" who was not even above, but in a world entirely apart from that of politics.[109]

*Homo faber* was also evoked by the Krupp defendants, notably Houdremont and Erich Müller (*"Kanonen-Müller"*) who stressed their technical expertise and their pride in being engineers. This individual presentation went well with the second strand of reasoning devised by the defense, Krupp's famous reputation for technical excellence. The American focus on the company's career as an armaments manufacturer was contested by pointing to its many achievements in civilian products and the immeasurable good these had done civilization. Reaffirming the primacy over writing Krupp's corporate history, the defense contended that

[t]he reputation of Krupp crucible steel existed before one Krupp cannon was made. Krupp steel technology arose not as a result of production of cannons, but the quality of the steel developed in the Krupp plants led among other things to ... the application of Krupp steel products for military purposes. Krupp was, as the name of the Essen factory clearly intimates, first and foremost a steel plant ... .[110]

In addition, the second pillar of Krupp corporate identity, its welfare tradition which had been disputed by the prosecution, was rhetorically reinstalled. According to attorney Wolfgang Pohle, the defendants had maintained "the widest consideration traditional in this firm for the welfare of the people employed in it," including foreign laborers. The only reason why their endeavors had been less successful than intended was the "subtle system of secret organizations of security services and police and ... the many-branched Party and its numerous affiliations [which] watched over the carrying out of the dictatorial will of the State in the works. Rebellion against it meant detriment, dismissal, loss of freedom, the concentration camp, or death."[111]

### What the Audience Said: the Verdicts

The first audience which literally had to judge the persuasiveness of the competing narratives offered by prosecution and defense were the three tribunals. The results proved to be mixed blessings for both sides. Taylor's staff suffered significant defeats in all three cases, in particular in the wholesale rejection of the aggressive war and conspiracy counts. In the Farben case the American investigators failed to prove that the chemical trust had played a key role not only in executing but in formulating plans for war and expansion. Even Judge Hebert, who was far more sympathetic to the prosecution's arguments than his two colleagues found in his dissenting opinion—despite the credible evidence for the defendants' "sympathy and support of the Nazi regime and ... reckless disregard of the consequences, under circumstances strongly suspicious of individual knowledge of Hitler's ultimate aim to wage aggressive war"—that the proof had not met "the extraordinary standard" exacted by the IMT. Especially in the light of the precedents Schacht, Speer, and Dönitz, who had all been acquitted of crimes against peace, none of the judges bought into the concept of a conspiracy between party, army, and industry.[112]

In the Krupp case, the German lawyers easily assailed the double conspiracy construct which was duly dismissed by the court. Again, a special—though concurring—opinion tended to go along with the prosecution's general stance when Judge Wilkins stated that he had heard "a strong *prima facie* case, as far as the implication of Gustav Krupp and the Krupp firm is concerned." But Gustav Krupp was not on trial, nor was, for that matter, the Krupp firm. Therefore, Wilkins—his discernible conviction that Krupp had been instrumental in launching the war notwithstanding—accepted his colleagues' stand. Much more forthright was Presiding Judge Anderson, who filed yet another concurring opinion in which he lambasted the prosecution's efforts to hold private citizens and non-combatants accountable for their state's deeds. The Krupp conspiracy was flatly rejected.[113]

As the count of crimes against peace had not formed part of the Flick indictment, it could not be refused by the judges in the first industrial trial. Still, their decision anticipated the line of the two later tribunals. The "Aryanization" count, which had been the functional equivalent of the aggressive war charge and the formidably proven centerpiece of the prosecution's argument, was rebuffed as the tribunal declared its incompetence under CCL 10 to deal with pre-1939 crimes unrelated to the war. Given that the law did not declare such a limit—quite the contrary[114]—this was a huge disappointment from the prosecution's perspective. Worse, the judges added that in their eyes, "Aryanization" hardly qualified as a crime against humanity. The heaviest blow delivered by the judgment, however, was the acceptance of the defense argument of necessity. The judges in the Flick tribunal accepted the defendants' claim that they had acted under duress when employing forced labor, and thus set a precedent for the following cases. Both in the Farben and in the Ministries cases, necessity would work to the benefit of the men in the dock. In no other instance did the totalitarian picture of the Third Reich drawn by the defendants and their counsel prove as decisive as in the argument of necessity.[115]

Still, the tendency of the NMT courts to come to less than unanimous findings limited the impact of the precedent as the following trials showed. In his dissenting opinion, Hebert left little doubts that he had failed to see any significant pressure put on the Farben directors and certainly none to justify the construction of Monowitz. Auschwitz clearly weighed heavily on Hebert's mind, and his long comment suggested that the prosecutors' decision not to go for the somewhat easier conviction on counts such as aiding and abetting in mass murder but for the rather academic analysis of the Third Reich had lost them the case.[116]

In contrast to Hebert's minority vote which was filed months after the trial had been finished and therefore had little practical significance, the Krupp decision delivered a blow to the visibly grown confidence of the German side. Just as the Flick and Farben tribunals had done earlier, the judges firmly based their findings on the idea that a fair trial necessarily implied that individual guilt could not be substituted by mere membership in boards and associations, thereby effectively rejecting the essence of the institutional approach. But the Krupp judges refused to adopt the necessity argument of the preceding case unreservedly and scrutinized the evidence as to what proof it offered. The devastating result for Krupp and his managers was that the tribunal rejected the whole argument in no uncertain terms. It could see no credible information that either the Krupp company or its management had suffered from any significant pressure. Quite the contrary, the judges endorsed the image of the Essen-based combine as an exceptionally privileged firm which had been highly favored by the regime, not oppressed by it.

While this suggested a preordained verdict which had emancipated itself insufficiently from the Krupp myth, it was not the most important part of the judgment. Nor were the singularly harsh sentences imposed on the defendants, including long terms in prison and the only case in which private property was confiscated. What mattered most was the general stance that the tribunal assumed in discussing necessity. In a long section, the judges expressed their utter disbelief that the fear of reprisals, if Krupp had objected to the use of forced labor, had any basis in reality. More damning, the judgment expressed bewilderment that the Krupp managers, even now, thought the loss of their jobs or even the unlikely event of arrest more important than the lives of thousands of forced laborers. As a rule, any claim to necessity would have had to prove that the remedy had not been disproportionate to the evil—and this had not been the case.

> in all fairness it must be said that ... the defendants, in a concentration camp, would not have been in a worse plight than the thousands of helpless victims whom they daily exposed to danger of death, great bodily harm from starvation, and the relentless air raids upon the armament plants; to say nothing of involuntary servitude and the other indignities which they suffered. The disparity in the number of the actual and potential victims is also thought provoking.[117]

This passage made the Krupp judgment the high water mark of the industrialist trials from the perspective of the OCCWC, where anger and frustration prevailed the more cases were closed. In April 1948, Benjamin Ferencz reported to Sheldon Glueck that "things in Nuremberg are going very badly" and that "the defendants have succeeded in putting the prosecution on the defensive," referring among other things to the dismissal of Count 1 in the Krupp case.[118] In contrast, the defense had clearly felt on the winning side after the Flick and Farben cases and was therefore downright shocked when the Krupp judgment was delivered. Not for long though. The far-reaching implications were soon understood and a massive wave of support was organized with the help of the Nuremberg *Industriebüro* and its supporters in West German industry. Backing up Krupp was declared "a matter of honor" for all of German industry. Business associations, chambers of commerce, and individual companies all rallied to Krupp's support, with the Flick and Farben defendants swiftly joining the bandwagon, reiterating the same arguments the defense had presented in Nuremberg.[119] Though formal requests for clemency and appeal were unsuccessful, in the medium term the aggressive campaign against the imprisonment of the NMT defendants did not get lost on the US authorities, and in 1950 and 1951 those industrialists who had been sentenced to prison beyond the time served were released by High Commissioner John J. McCloy.[120]

# By Way of a Conclusion: the After-life of the Nuremberg Narratives

Nuremberg's character as a focal point for the formulation of historical narratives may be understood quite literally. Diverse but inter-related discourses such as the international cartel debate, Imperialism studies, and the concept of totalitarianism converged between 1944 and 1949, were bound together in the broad analysis of the Third Reich which stood at the heart of the NMT, and then diffused into a wide array of follow-up proceedings. These included further judicial action, notably in the fields of de-concentration, restitution, and compensation. Here, the same lines of confrontation which had dominated in the Nuremberg arena would be restaged, often featuring the same cast of protagonists. Although Flick, Farben, and Krupp were not the only objects of Allied de-concentration policy, they were those to whose fate the occupation authorities paid particular attention. Policy objectives were rooted in the same debate on cartels and monopolies which had informed the Allied discussions whether or not to put businessmen on trial. The link between war crimes proceedings and restructuring German industry was made explicit in the two laws No. 75, promulgated near-identically in the British and US zones, which demanded that no property rights be granted to those who had furthered Nazi schemes for aggressive war.[121]

Accordingly, in their efforts to negotiate a milder de-concentration plan, Flick's American attorneys repeatedly stressed that Flick had not

**6.1** Memorabilia: Picture book on Case 5 for the defendants and their counsel (the picture on the right shows Telford Taylor; the caption reads: "For all they that take the sword shall perish with the sword [Matthew 26:52] / For they have sown the wind, and they shall reap the whirlwind [Hosea 8:7] / The road from Nuremberg to Korea implies the gallows for Taylor and halos on some of Landsberg's graves."

*Landesarchiv Nordrhein-Westfalen, Düsseldorf, RWN 218, No. 638.*

been indicted on the aggressive war count, nor had he supported the regime in any other way. Again, affidavits and letters of recommendation were commissioned to prop up Flick's anti-Nazi credibility and point out his key role in German reconstruction.[122] Likewise, the totalitarian narrative would soon reappear as Flick had to face demands for restitution of "Aryanized" property. While the Jewish victims made full use of the Nuremberg documents, Flick pointed at his acquittal. Moreover, he and his lawyers effectively turned the defensive argument of a dictatorial regime which had pressurized the combine's management into submission into a means of attack, hoping to regain some of the assets Flick had sold to the Reichswerke in 1939/40. In the end, Flick indeed got the better of both the victims and his former accomplices.[123]

All three corporate defendants were also confronted with demands for compensation by former forced laborers. The Flick managers, before and after the death of the patriarch, doggedly refused to accept any responsibility whatsoever, continuing their defense line that the state agencies alone were to blame. Benjamin Ferencz, by now representing the Jewish Claims Conference (JCC) against Flick, observed sarcastically the "interesting phenomenon of history and psychology that very frequently the criminal comes to see himself as the victim."[124] Krupp, in contrast, struck a deal with the JCC early on, though not without emphasizing that the company acted out of humanitarian motives, not in acknowledgment of guilt.[125] Farben, meanwhile, faced claims from Auschwitz survivor Norbert Wollheim who had been a witness for the prosecution in Case 6. In what became one of the Federal Republic's first private litigation cases dealing with Nazi crimes, Farben and its successors paid a large team of lawyers, among them a number of Nuremberg veterans, who reiterated the defense arguments, notably the necessity motif: Farben had been a mere executive—and an unwilling one at that—of the regime's policies and had tried to improve the camp inmates' living and working conditions by all means, in fact protecting them from the SS murderous treatment rather than exploiting them.[126]

As the gospel ain't gospel until it is spread, additional efforts were required to bring the message home to a greater public beyond the courtrooms. The result was the publication of several eye-witness accounts by Nuremberg's industrialists, many of them helped by their defense counsel and prominent ghostwriters such as Eduard Wahl, Otto Kranzbühler, and Ernst Rudolf Huber, another student of Schmitt's. Huber was one of the authors of *Warum wurde Krupp verurteilt?*, published by Tilo von Wilmowsky, Gustav Krupp's brother-in-law and former member of the supervisory board. The slim volume revisited all the familiar places of the Nuremberg defense line, concluding that the trial had failed to account for the realities of a totalitarian regime.[127] Only slightly more subtle were those books which did not bear the names of defendants and attorneys on their dust jacket but were commissioned from professional writers. Among these were August Heinrichsbauer, who had served as a go-between of NSDAP and heavy industry in the 1930s, the mediocre but prolific playwright Gert von Klass, and Pulitzer-prize winning Louis Lochner whose title *Tycoons and Tyrant* gave away the message; the voluminous account mostly presented an elaborate version of the totalitarianism narrative which Lochner's clients had been laboring on for nearly a decade.[128]

In comparison to this massive PR wave, the output of the former prosecution staff remained fairly limited, and their writings were usually not translated into German as was true of most of Taylor's books or of Josiah DuBois's *The Devil's Chemists*, 350 pages born out of angry disappointment.[129] Still, books and essays such as DuBois's and Zeck's perpetuated the negative myths of Krupp and Farben, fostering a specific brand of populist literature which (mis)took them as impartial evidence of big business's key role in bringing about Nazism, war, and the Holocaust.[130] Nor was historical research immune to the grand narratives of the NMT. Relying strongly on the evidence collected and arranged by the prosecution, historiographical misperceptions resulted such as the widely assumed identity of IG Farben and Four Year Plan.[131] It was left to business historians from the late 1980s onwards to come up with non-exculpatory, nuanced, and precise accounts of the relations between business and regime. That the primacy debate of the 1960s, sparked by Tim Mason's critical view on both the totalitarianism and fascism paradigms, is still going strong four decades later (though with little significant heuristic progress)[132] attests to the power of the narratives which have emanated from the Palace of Justice at Nuremberg.

## Notes

1. [Celia Goetz], "Telford Taylor Panel: Critical Perspectives on the Nuremberg Trial," *New York Law School Journal of Human Rights* 12 (1995): 516. See also Celia Goetz, "Impressions of Telford Taylor at Nuremberg," *Columbia Journal of Transnational Law* 37 (1999): 669–72.
2. Christian Tomuschat, "The Legacy of Nuremberg," *Journal of International Criminal Justice (JICJ)* 4 (2006): 830–44; Hans-Heinrich Jescheck, "The General Principles of International Criminal Law Set Out in Nuremberg, as Mirrored in the ICC Statute," *JICJ* 2 (2004): 38–55.
3. For the uneasy discussion on Nuremberg's legal legacy, see *The Nuremberg Trials. International Criminal Law Since 1945/Die Nürnberger Prozesse. Völkerstrafrecht seit 1945*, eds. Herbert R. Reginbogin and Christoph J.M. Safferling (Munich, 2006); Annette Weinke, "'Von Nürnberg nach Den Haag'? Das Internationale Militärtribunal in historischer Perspektive," in *Leipzig—Nürnberg—Den Haag: Neue Fragestellungen und Forschungen zum Verhältnis von Menschenrechtsverbrechen, justizieller Säuberung und Völkerstrafrecht*, ed. Helia-Verena Daubach (Düsseldorf, 2008), 20–33. A polemic but rather ill-informed stand has recently been taken by John Laughland, *A History of Political Trials. From Charles I to Saddam Hussein* (Oxford, 2008).
4. William Allan Zeck, "Nuremberg: Proceedings Subsequent to Goering et al.," *North Carolina Law Review* 26 (1947–1948): 350–89. The best known and most disgruntled comment by a prosecutor is to be found in Josiah DuBois, *The Devil's Chemists*.

*24 Conspirators of the International Farben Cartel Who Manufacture Wars* (Boston, 1952), esp. 338–56. DuBois thought the sentences delivered in the Farben case "were light enough to please a chicken thief," ibid., 339.

5.  *Nazi Conspiracy and Aggression*, vol. 1, ed. Office of United States Chief of Counsel Prosecution of Axis Criminality (Washington, DC, 1946), x; cf. Donald Bloxham, *Genocide on Trial. War Criminals and the Formation of Holocaust, History and Memory* (Oxford, 2001), 18.

6.  For the reactions to the IMT which oscillated broadly between disinterest and consent, cf. *Public Opinion in Occupied Germany. The OMGUS Surveys, 1945–1949*, eds. Anna J. and Richard L. Merritt (Urbana, 1970), 93f., 121f.

7.  Brief Survey Concerning the Records of the War Crimes Trials held in Nurnberg, Germany, 3.1.1949, NARA RG 238, Entry 159, Box 7; Table of Length of the Twelve Nuremberg Trials before Tribunals Established Pursuant to Ordinance No. 7, *Trials of War Criminals before the Nuernberg Military Tribunals under Control Council Law No. 10 (TWC), Nuernberg October 1946–April 1949*, 15 vols (Washington, DC, 1951), vol. 15, 451.

8.  Robert P. Burns, "The Distinctiveness of Trial Narrative," *The Trial on Trial, Vol. 1. Truth and Due Process*, eds. Antony Duff, Lindsay Farmer, Sandra Marshall and Victor Tadros (Oxford and Portland, 2004), 158f. For the trials' quality as "dramas of didactic legality," see Lawrence Douglas, *The Memory of Judgement. Making Law and History in the Trials of the Holocaust* (New Haven, 2001), 3.

9.  Burns, "Distinctiveness," 176f.; quote from: Devin Pendas, *The Frankfurt Auschwitz Trial, 1963–1965. Genocide, History, and the Limits of the Law* (New York, 2006), 22.

10. Robert G. Moeller, *War Stories. The Search for a Usable Past in the Federal Republic of Germany* (Berkeley, 2001), 13.

11. The Bomber's Baedeker (Guide to the Economic Importance of German Towns and Cities), 2nd edn, 1944, NARA, RG 226, Entry 16, Box 1036, Doc. 89972; John K. Galbraith et al., The Effects of strategic bombing on the German war economy ([Washington, DC:] Overall Economic Effects Division, 1945); cf. Petra Marquardt-Bigman, *Amerikanische Geheimdienstanalysen über Deutschland 1942–1949* (Munich, 1995), 36–38.

12. Henry Morgenthau, *Germany is Our Problem* (New York, 1945); Lord Vansittart, "The Problem of Germany: A Discussion," *International Affairs* 21 (1945): 313–24, here: 322; Walter L. Dorn, "The Debate over American Occupation Policy in Germany in 1944–1945," *Political Science Quarterly* 72 (1957): 481–501, here 484–86.

13. Cf. Arieh J. Kochavi, *Prelude to Nuremberg. Allied War Crimes Policy and the Question of Punishment* (Chapel Hill, 1998), 19–63; Daniel Marc Segesser, *Recht durch Rache oder Rache durch Recht? Die Ahndung von Kriegsverbrechen in der internationalen wissenschaftlichen Debatte 1872–1945* (Paderborn, 2010), 314–61.

14. Cf. *History of the United Nations War Crimes Commission and the development of the laws of war* (London, 1948). In Raphael Lemkin, *Axis Rule in Occupied Europe. Laws of Occupation, Analysis of Government, Proposals for Redress*, 2nd ed. (Clark, NJ, 2008), three out of eight main sections deal with economic subject matters.

15. Ralf Ahrens, *Die Dresdner Bank 1945–1957. Konsequenzen und Kontinuitäten nach dem Ende des NS-Regimes* (Munich, 2007), 33. From late 1943 to 1945, the OSS created a vast number of personal files on German businessmen which focused on their complicity in Nazi crimes but did not suggest how these individuals would be dealt with, e.g. Zangen, Wilhelm, 11.4.1945, Cornell Law Library (CLL), Donovan Nuremberg Trial Collection (DNTC), Vol. XVII, Section 53.106; Quandt, Günther, 18.4.1945, CLL, DNTC, Vol. XVII, Section 53.051, http://library.lawschool.cornell.edu/WhatWeHave/SpecialCollections/Donovan/index.cfm (accessed August 2010).

16. For example, List of Names of Industrial Leaders Recommended to Be Detained for Interrogation Purposes, 27.11.1944 [26.4.1945], NARA, RG 226, Entry 192, Box 4, Folder 56A; Friedrich Flick K.G., Düsseldorf, no date [December 1945], NARA, RG

226, Entry 19, Box 281, Doc. XL 18998; Memorandum Lt. Albert Edelman to Col. B. Bernstein, Subject. Meeting of FIAT Advisory Council on July 11, 1945, 13.7.1945, NARA, RG 260, Entry 232 (A1), Box 19. Cf. Telford Taylor, *Final Report to the Secretary of the Army in the Nuernberg War Crimes Trials under Control Council Law No. 10* (Washington, DC, 1949), 65, 58f.; Ahrens, *Dresdner Bank*, 80f.; Axel Drecoll, "Flick vor Gericht: Die Verhandlungen vor dem alliierten Militärtribunal 1947," in *Der Flick-Konzern im Dritten Reich,* eds. Johannes Bähr, Axel Drecoll, Bernhard Gotto et al. (Munich, 2008), 577, 581.

17. Cf. Ahrens, *Dresdner Bank*, 81.
18. Letter from Nixon to Taylor, 14.12.1945, NARA, RG 238, Entry 159, Box 1.
19. Subject: Arrest and Trial of German Business Leaders, 30.1.1946; Subject: Status of Compilation of Lists of German Industrialists for Consideration as War Criminals, 3.9.1946, both NARA, RG 260, Office of the Adjutant General/General Correspondence, Box 4.
20. "Deutsche Schwerindustrie unter Anklage," *Allgemeine Zeitung*, no. 29, October 12, 1945.
21. For example, Statement Submitted by Leo T. Crowley (FEA) before the Sub-Committee on War Mobilization of the Senate Military Affairs Committee on the subject: "Germany's Economic Basis for Destruction," 26.6.1945, CLL, DNTC, Vol. VII, section 13.14; Testimony [by Herbert Wechsler] presented to the Subcommittee on War Mobilization of the Senate Military Affairs Committee, 28.6.1945, CLL, DNTC, Vol. VII, section 13.17, part 1; List of Kilgore Hearing Exhibits (Part 10), 24.10.1946, NARA, RG 238, Entry 159, Box 5, Folder 5.
22. For the development of the conspiracy concept and its link to the charge of aggressive war, cf. Bradley F. Smith, *The Road to Nuremberg* (New York, 1981), 50–52, 61f., 75–77, 233f.; Jonathan A. Bush, "'The Supreme ... Crime' and Its Origins: The Lost Legislative History of the Crime of Aggressive War," *Columbia Law Review* 102 (2002): 2324–423.
23. See, for instance, FEA, German-Austrian Branch. The Reich Ministry of Armament and War Production (Speer Ministry), February 1945, CLL, DNTC, Vol. VII, section 13.13.
24. Memorandum on Trial preparation (approved by Chief of Counsel, May 16, 1945), NARA, RG 238, Entry 159, Box 1, Folder 4.
25. R&A No. 3114, Nazi Plans to Dominate Europe, 12.6.1945, NARA, RG 238, Entry 45, Box 2; R&A No. 3113.2, Principal Nazi Organizations Involved in the Commission of War Crimes. Nazi Spoliation of Property in Occupied Europe. Draft for the War Crimes Staff, 24.7.1945, NARA, RG 238, Entry 45, Box 1 (quotes identical with draft from 12.6.1945).
26. Franz Neumann, *Behemoth. The Structure and Practice of National Socialism, 1933–1944* (Reprint Chicago, 2009), 361. However, other correlations—of both autochthon and émigré provenance—played key roles as well.
27. Marquardt-Bigman, *Geheimdienstanalysen*, 71–95; Barry M. Kätz, "The Criticism of Arms. The Frankfurt School Goes to War," *Journal of Modern History* 59 (1987): 439–78.
28. Neumann, *Behemoth*, 288–91, 589–96, 600f., 611–14.
29. Tentative Memorandum for Mr. Justice Jackson, 23.7.1945, printed in Bähr et al., *Flick-Konzern*, 880–84. For the trust-busting background of Jackson and some of his staff, cf. Drexel A. Sprecher, *Inside the Nuremberg Trial. A Prosecutor's Comprehensive Account*, vol. 1 (Lanham, 1999), 38f.; for a broader if less succinct account, see Elizabeth Borgwardt, "Re-examining Nuremberg as a New Deal Institution: Politics, Culture and the Limits of Law in Generating Human Rights Norms," *Berkeley Journal of International Law* 23 (2005): 401–62.
30. Tentative Memorandum, for Mr. Justice Jackson, 23.7.1945, printed in Bähr et al., *Flick-Konzern*, 881–83.

31. *Trial of the Major War Criminals before the International Military Tribunal (IMT), Nuremberg 14 November 1945–1 October 1946,* 42 vols (Nuremberg, 1947), here vol. 1, 124–47; Telford Taylor, *The Anatomy of the Nuremberg Trials. A Personal Memoir* (Boston, 1992), 90–94; Ann Tusa and John Tusa, *The Nuremberg Trial* (New York, 1984), 138–40.

32. The British delegation had refused Jackson's suggestion of a last-minute substitution of the ailing Gustav Krupp by his son Alfried as "a grotesque absurdity" and felt compelled to agree to a follow-up trial; Arguments for and against substituting Alfried Krupp for Gustav Krupp, undated [October 1945], NA (PRO), FO 1019/101; Trial of German Industrialists before an International Military Tribunal. Sargent to Atlee, 31.7.1946, NA (PRO), PREM 8/391.

33. The British position on the war crimes issue was less than coherent, and most accounts so far have emphasized British expediency in the second phase of decision-making rather than their contributions to the first; cf. Donald Bloxham, "British War Crimes Trial Policy in Germany, 1945–1957: Implementation and Collapse," *Journal of British Studies* 42 (2003): 91–118; Donald Bloxham, "'The Trial That Never Was': Why there was no Second International Trial of Major War Criminals at Nuremberg," *History* 87 (2002): 41–60.

34. Evidence of war crimes of leading executives of I.G. Farbenindustrie Aktiengesellschaft (Hermann Schmitz, Georg von Schnitzler, Max Ilgner, Karl [sic] Krauch), undated, NA (PRO), FO 371/57584; dossiers on Krupp, Röchling, et al. in NA (PRO), FO 371/57585.

35. Sargent to Atlee, 31.7.1946, NA (PRO), PREM 8/391; War Criminals. The German Industrialists & Bankers, 24.10.1946, NA (PRO), LCO 2/2989.

36. Report to the President by Mr. Justice Jackson, June 6, 1945, *Report of Robert H. Jackson, United States Representative, to the International Conference on Military Trials, London, 1945* (Washington, DC, 1949), 46; cf. Bloxham, *Genocide*, 30f.

37. Preliminary Draft of a Possible Indictment against Eight leading Economic and Political Leaders of Nazi Germany, 4.6.1946 [Sprecher], TGP, Box R, Doc. 9, fol. 124–45. The Gantt Papers have been accessed at http://wwwnew.towson.edu/nurembergpapers/Conservation%20and%20Digitization/Catalogue%20of%20Holdings.htm (accessed August 2010).

38. Cf. Taylor, *Final Report*, 54, 70–74; Bloxham, *Genocide*, 37–52.

39. C.[abinet] M.[eeting] (46). Conclusions, 4.11.1946, NA (PRO), PREM 8/391; Extradition of Probable Defendants in I.G. Farben Case, 8.4.1947; Extradition of Probable Defendants in Krupp Case, 8.4.1947, both in NA (PRO), WO 309/1457.

40. For example, List of names on which research is to be undertaken immediately, [April 1946], NARA, RG 238, Entry 203, Box 5; Leading Industrialists, Financiers and Economic Figures in Nazi Germany who may be subject to prosecution under Control Council Law No. 10, 1.8.1946, NARA, RG 238, Entry 165, Box 2.

41. The trial was prepared in close cooperation with Taylor's staff and the indictment and the judgment were to be included in the Green Series: *TWC*, vol. XIV, 1061–143; Memorandum for the Secretary of the Army, 4.1.1949 [Taylor], NARA, RG 238, Entry 159, Box 1; cf. Sprecher, *Inside the Nuremberg Trial*, vol. 2, 1446.

42. Summary of points covered in an OCC-OMGUS meeting, 28.5.1946, both NARA RG 238, Entry 159, Box 1; cf. Ralf Ahrens, "Der Exempelkandidat. Die Dresdner Bank und der Nürnberger Prozess gegen Karl Rasche," *Vierteljahrshefte für Zeitgeschichte* 52 (2004): 637 f., 650–52.

43. Interoffice Memorandum, 23.10.1946 [Brilliant], TUA, GNP, Vol. R, Doc. 6, fol. 89. Drecoll, "Flick," 576, shows that these misconceptions were adopted from the preceding OSS reports.

44. OCCPAC, Subsequent Proceedings Division, re Ernst Poensgen, 12.6.1946, NARA, RG 238, Entry 165, Box 1.

45. Digest of Revised 1947 Budget Estimates, undated [1947], NARA, RG 260, Office of the Adjutant General/General Correspondence, Box 3; Taylor, *Final Report*, 35,

80–82; Norma Ervin to Frederick Taylor, 4.2.1947, NA (PRO), WO 309/1456; Bloxham, *Genocide*, 49–51; Ahrens, *Dresdner Bank*, 97–99.

46. Report of Trip Undertaken by Messrs. Marcu and Stone of Trial Team II, 8.4.1947, Staatsarchiv Nürnberg (StAN), Rep. 502, KVA, Handakten, B-58.

47. For a detailed description of individual memoranda and notes, see Jonathan A. Bush, "The Prehistory of Corporations and Conspiracy in International Criminal Law: What Nuremberg Really Said," *Columbia Law Review* 109 (2009): 1094–262.

48. Neumann, *Behemoth*; Lemkin, *Axis Rule*; Otto Nathan, *The Nazi Economic System* (Durham, 1944); Sheldon Glueck, *War Criminals: Their Prosecution and Punishment* (New York, 1944), 39; John H.E. Fried, *The Exploitation of Foreign Labour by Germany* (Montreal, 1945).

49. Inter-Office Memorandum, 5.6.1946, NARA, RG 238, Entry 202, Box 2, Folder 2; cf. Bush, "Prehistory," 1181f.

50. Pomerantz's lack of subtlety has recently been used for an unsubstantiated attack on the Industrialist Trials by Frank Gausmann, arguing that these were nothing but a Morgenthau-inspired, anti-capitalist plot against German industry. However, Pomerantz may have been critical of big business but qualified by no means as anti-capitalist ("I love the buck"), nor did his colleagues, see "Milestones," *Time Magazine*, No. 23, December 6, 1982. Bush, "Prehistory," 1149–57, is much better informed, pointing out that Pomerantz's support for introducing corporate liability into international law was innovative if unsuccessful. He overestimates, though, the differences between Pomerantz and his colleagues who, on the same day, filed a brief which had much in common with his outline but used more careful language; Inter-Office Memorandum [Pomerantz], 20.8.1946, TUA, GNP, Box U, Doc. 14, fol. 360–62; Inter-Office Memorandum [Pomerantz], 22.8.1946, NARA, RG 238, Entry 202, Box 6, folder 4; Preliminary Memorandum-Brief on Support of the NSDAP by Industrialists, 22.8.1946 [Sprecher et al.], USHMM, RG 06.005.02*01; cf. Frank Gausmann, "Vergangenheitsbewältigung durch Recht? Kritische Anmerkungen zur Anklagestrategie in den Nürnberger Industriellenprozessen," *Leipzig—Nürnberg—Den Haag*, 48–65.

51. Memorandum to all research analysts the Farben and Krupp cases, 13.8.1946 [S. Zeck], NARA, RG 238, Entry 203, Box 1; Indictment of the Industrialists, 28.9.1946 [Drachsler], NARA, RG 238, Entry 165, Box 1. For discussions of Drachsler's memo, cf. Priemel, *Flick*, 619–21, and Bush, "Prehistory," 1157–60.

52. Intra-Office Memorandum, 2.10.1946, NARA, RG 238, Entry 202, Box 2, Folder [3]. However, understanding of what precisely 'institutional' meant, varied, cf. Subject: Progress of Work of the Berlin Branch, 21.9.1946, NARA, RG 238, Entry 202, Box 2, Folder [3].

53. Intra-Office Memorandum, 2.10.1946 (as above); Memorandum for Mr. Pomerantz, 4.10.1946 [Taylor], NARA, RG 238, Entry 159, Box 7; in contrast to: Bush, "Prehistory," 1160.

54. Case 6, Opening Statement for the Prosecution, 27.8.1947, *TWC*, VII, 206.

55. Lyon to Ervin, re: Selection of Defendants in the Flick Case, January 17, 1947, reprint in Bush, "Prehistory," 1258.

56. Case 6, Closing Statements Schmitz and Hörnlein, *TWC*, VIII, 1057f., 1064.

57. Statement of the Evidence, Miscellaneous War Crimes and Crimes against Humanity, 21./28.10.1946, NARA, RG 238, Entry 159, Box 5, Folder 5.

58. Case 6, Indictment, *TWC*, VII, 60–79.

59. Case 6, Opening Statement for the Prosecution, 27.8.1947, *TWC*, VII, 106, 114.

60. Preliminary Outline Brief on The Structures and Functions of Government Economic Agencies in the Third Reich, 30.11.1946, NARA, RG 238, Entry 165, Box 1; Cooperation of I.G. Farben officials in Nazi preparation for war through the Four Year Plan and other governmental and semi-governmental agencies, undated, NARA, RG 238, Entry 192, Box 2, Folder 3; Case 6, Indictment, and Opening Statement for the Prosecution, *TWC*, vol. VII, 23–25, 109.

61. Cf. the references in fn. 43 and Joseph Borkin/Charles A. Welsh, *Germany's Master Plan: The Story of Industrial Offensive* (London, 1943).

62. Case 6, Indictment, *TWC*, VII, 31–34, and Proceedings, 648–745; see also the account of chief prosecutor Josiah DuBois, *The Devil's Chemists* (Boston, 1952), 54, 80, 84–87, 142f., 145f., 325–27.

63. Cf. Ludolf Herbst, *Der Totale Krieg und die Ordnung der Wirtschaft. Die Kriegswirtschaft im Spannungsfeld von Politik, Ideologie und Propaganda 1939–1945* (Stuttgart, 1982), 127–44; Adam Tooze, *The Wages of Destruction. The Making and Breaking of the Nazi Economy* (London, 2006), 385–91.

64. Case 6, Opening Statement, *TWC*, VII, 173–89, and Proceedings, 1392–485, quote from 176.

65. Protokoll, 16.12.1947, Zentrum für Antisemitismusforschung (ZASF) Berlin, Fall X, Prot. (d), December 15–16, 1947, fol. 675f.; Case 10, Extract from Prosecution's Answer to Defense Motion for Acquittal on Charges of Crimes Against Peace, *TWC*, IX, 364–89, here 366, 375.

66. Verlesung der Anklageschrift, 8.12.1947, ZASF, Fall X, Prot. (d), November 17 and December 8, 1947, fol. 18, 25f.

67. Ibid., 110f.; Protokoll, 17.12.1947, ZASF, Fall X, Prot. (d), December 17 and 19, 1947, 683, 745–47.

68. Bernhard Menne, *Krupp. The Lords of Essen* (London, 1938); Case X, Opening Statement for the Defendant Alfried Krupp [Wecker], 22.3.1948, *TWC*, IX, 144.

69. For a brief overview, see Kim C. Priemel, "Heldenepos und bürgerliches Trauerspiel. Unternehmensgeschichte im generationellen Paradigma," *Generation als Erzählung. Neue Perspektiven auf ein kulturelles Deutungsmuster*, eds. Björn Bohnenkamp, Till Manning, Eva-Maria Silies (Göttingen, 2009), 107–28.

70. Dokumentenbuch I, ZASF, Fall X, VDB (d) 1, K 2.

71. Memorandum Friedrich Flick, [1946; Marcu], StAN, Rep. 502, KVA, Handakten, B-4.

72. Ibid.

73. Outline of Trial brief on Flick, 23.12.1946 [Pomerantz], StAN, Rep. 502, KVA, Handakten, B-75; "German Steel Men Indicted for Crimes 'on a Vast Scale'," *New York Times*, February 9, 1947; Case 6, Opening Statement for the Prosecution, 19.4.1947, *TWC*, VI, 81.

74. "Aryanization" also tested the scope of CCL 10 when it came to pre-1939 crimes against German nationals and thus was of immense importance to the prosecution.

75. Case 6, Opening Statement for the Prosecution, 19.4.1947, *TWC*, VI, 82.

76. The pioneering study is Jonathan Wiesen, *West German Industry and the Challenge of the Nazi Past, 1945–1955* (Chapel Hill, 2001), 8.

77. For detailed accounts, see Klaus-Dietmar Henke, *Die amerikanische Besetzung Deutschlands* (Munich, 1995), 530, 560f., 565–67; Werner Plumpe, *Vom Plan zum Markt. Wirtschaftsverwaltung und Unternehmerverbände in der britischen Zone* (Düsseldorf, 1987), 89–92; Gerhard Hetzer, "Unternehmer und leitende Angestellte zwischen Rüstungseinsatz und politischer Säuberung," *Von Stalingrad zur Währungsreform. Zur Sozialgeschichte des Umbruchs in Deutschland*, eds. Martin Broszat, Klaus-Dietmar Henke and Hans Woller (Munich, 1988), 51–91.

78. The so-called "Dustbin" prison was reserved for businessmen, scientists, and public officials whereas "Ashcan" detained mostly members of Party and Military; lists in NARA, RG 331, Entry 11, Box 6, and Memorandum Edelman to Bernstein, Subject. Meeting of FIAT Advisory Council on July 11, 1945, 13.7.1945, NARA, RG 260, Entry 232 (A1), Box 19.

79. Cf. Wiesen, *Industry*, 94.

80. Volker Berghahn, *Unternehmer und Politik in der Bundesrepublik* (Frankfurt, 1985), 188. Henke, *Besetzung*, 502f., 533, discerns a business-as-usual mentality.

81. Henke, *Besetzung*, 492–96.

82. Ibid., 521–24, 526–28; for the case of Siemens, see Wiesen, *Industry*, 22–33.

83. Wiesen, *Industry*, 17–51, quote on p. 30.
84. Vermerk, 27.6.1945 [Kaletsch] StAN, Rep. 502, KVA, Handakten, B-15; Persönliche Angelegenheiten Kaletsch, StAN, Rep. 502, KVA, Handakten, B-7; the folder contains several English translations.
85. Reinhard Mehring, *Carl Schmitt. Aufstieg und Fall. Eine Biographie* (Munich, 2009), 322; Carl Schmitt, *Das internationalrechtliche Verbrechen des Angriffskrieges und der Grundsatz 'Nullum crimen, nulla poena sine lege'*, ed. Helmut Quaritsch (Berlin, 1994), 125–28.
86. Lebensdarstellung Friedrich Flick, 20.8.1945, BArch, R 8122/80898; Lebensdarstellung Friedrich Flick, ca. November 1945, StAN, Rep. 502, KVA, Handakten, B-17; Ergänzungen (Politischer Teil), undated [1945], BArch, R 8122/80899; zur Schilderung der Persönlichkeit von F., undated [1945], ibid.; Entwicklung der von Dr. Friedrich Flick geführten Unternehmungen seit 1933, undated [1945], StAN, Rep. 502, KVA, Handakten, B-48.
87. Memorandum, re Dr. Friedrich Flick. Friedrich Flick Kommanditgesellschaft, Düsseldorf, and its enterprises situated in the four zones of occupation, undated [Autumn 1945], StAN, Rep. 502, KVA, Handakten, B-92.
88. The question of forced labor, however, was conspicuously absent in the document.
89. Memorandum [as fn. 87].
90. Ibid.
91. For the intellectual origins, consult William David Jones, *The Lost Debate. German Socialist Intellectuals and Totalitarianism*, (Urbana, IL, 1999), and Tim B. Müller, "Die gelehrten Krieger und die Rockefeller-Revolution. Intellektuelle zwischen Geheimdienst, Neuer Linken und dem Entwurf einer neuen Ideengeschichte," *Geschichte und Gesellschaft* 33 (2007): 198–227.
92. Notiz, 11.4.1947 [Steinbrinck] StAN, Rep. 502A, KVV, Handakten, Flächsner-2.
93. Cf. Wiesen, *Industry*, 70f.; Ahrens, *Dresdner Bank*, 105; Kim C. Priemel, *Flick. Eine Konzerngeschichte vom Kaiserreich bis zur Bundesrepublik* (Göttingen, 2007), 632–34.
94. For example, Document books VIIA, VII B, XI, ZASF, Fall X, VDB (d), 7A/B, 8–10, 11–12, K9–12, K16.
95. *TWC*, VII, 7–9; *TWC*, IX, 6; *TWC*, XIV, 1075; cf. Priemel, *Flick*, 634.
96. Plädoyer [Dix], 29.11.1947, StAN, Rep. 501, KVP, Fall 5, A 131–133, fol. 10634f.; Opening Statement for Alfried Krupp [Kranzbühler], *TWC*, vol. IX, 139.
97. Case 10, Opening Statement for Alfried Krupp, *TWC*, IX, 139; cf. Susanne Jung, *Die Rechtsprobleme der Nürnberger Prozesse dargestellt am Verfahren gegen Friedrich Flick* (Tübingen, 1992), 4, 65f., 181f.
98. For example, Eröffnungsrede Siemers, 18.7.1947, StAN, Rep. 501, KVP, Fall 5, A 50–53, fol. 3924; Plädoyer Kranzbühler, 25.11.1947, ibid, A 129–30, fol. 10171–87.
99. Eröffnungsrede Siemers, ibid., A 50–53, fol. 3918; Case 10, Opening Statement for Jannssen [Schilff], *TWC*, IX, 166.
100. Kreuzverhör Evlokia V., 1.5.1947, StAN, Rep. 501, KVP, Fall 5, A 9–11, fol. 695f.; Kreuzverhör Emil M., 5.5.1947, ibid., A 12–13, fol. 703–24; Frantisek D., 9.5.1947, ibid., 16–18, fol. 946–60; 1295–97. Cf. Jung, *Rechtsprobleme*, 84.
101. Jung, *Rechtsprobleme*, 67–69; Drecoll, "Flick," 635–41.
102. For example, Case 6, Testimonies of Defendants Krauch, Ter Meer, and Dürrfeld, *TWC*, VIII, 697, 706, 804; Verhör Burkart, 3.9.1947, StAN, Rep. 501, KVP, Fall 5, A 81–83, fol. 6396f.
103. Case 10, Opening Speech for Löser, *TWC*, IX, 148–51; Case 5, Eröffnungsrede für Flick, 2.7.1947, StAN, Rep. 501, KVP, Fall 5, A 37–39, fol. 3135f.; Case 6, Schnitzler, Affidavit, *TWC*, VII, 1514; Testimony of Defendant Ilgner, ibid., 1598.
104. Case 10, Opening Statement for Bülow, 23.3.1948 [Pohle], *TWC*, IX, 212; Plädoyer Dix, 29.11.1947, StAN, Rep. 501, KVP, Fall 5, A 131–33, fol. 10685–88; Eidesstattliche Versicherung Hermann Reusch, 28.7.1947, StAN, Rep. 501. KVP, Fall 5, E-7,

fol. 296f.; Case 6, Closing Statement for Defendants Schmitz and Häfliger, 2.6.1948, *TWC*, VIII, 951, 1066.

105.  Lebensdarstellung Friedrich Flick, 20.8.1945, BArch, R 8112/80898.

106.  Rückverhör Flick, 17.7.1947, StAN, Rep. 501, KVP, Fall 5, A 47–49, fol. 3861; Vernehmung Steinbrinck, 31.7. and 5.8.1947, ibid., A 37–39, fol. 4571, 4669, 4912; Vernehmung Flick, 7.7./8.7.1947, ibid., A 40–42, fol. 3250–3260, 3365–68.

107.  Case 6, Opening Statement for Defendant Ambros, 18.12.1947, *TWC*, VII, 274, and Final Statement Hörlein, *TWC*, VIII, 1064f.

108.  Case 6, Opening Statement for Defendant Krauch [Böttcher], 18.12.1947, *TWC*, VII, 213; Opening Statement for Defendant Hörlein, 18.12.1947 [Nelte], ibid., 245.

109.  Case 6, Final Statement Krauch, *TWC*, VIII, 1056; Friedrich Jähne used the same term whereas Ernst Bürgin professed his will "to serve technology;" cf. their respective closing statements, ibid., 1072, 1065.

110.  Case 10, Opening Statements for Defendants Houdremont and Müller, 28.3.1948, *TWC*, IX, 155, 160.

111.  Case 10, Opening Statement for Buelow, *TWC*, IX, 216, 190; cf. Affidavit and Testimony of Defense Witness Kurt Biegl, Defense Exhibit 438, ibid., 618f.; Schluß-Schriftsatz zur Verteidigung des Angeklagten Alfried von Bohlen und Halbach, June 1948, ZASF, Fall X, VDB (d), 21–23, K21.

112.  Case 6, Concurring Opinion of Judge Hebert on the Charges of Crimes against Peace, 28.12.1948, *TWC*, VII, 1212, 1305f.

113.  Case 10, Special Concurring Opinion of Judge Wilkins on the Dismissal of the Charges of Aggressive War, 31.7.1948, *TWC*, IX, 456f.; Concurring Opinion of Presiding Judge Anderson on the Dismissal of the Charges of Aggressive War, 7.7.1948, ibid., 449, 434.

114.  Cf. Lawrence Douglas' chapter in this volume; Kochavi, *Prelude*, 168f.

115.  Cf. Ahrens, "Exempelkandidat," 658–64; Bernd Boll, "Fall 6: Der IG-Farben-Prozeß," *Der Nationalsozialismus vor Gericht. Die alliierten Prozesse gegen Kriegsverbrecher und Soldaten 1943–1952*, ed. Gerd R. Ueberschär (Frankfurt, 1999), 141.

116.  Case 6, Concurring Opinion of Judge Hebert on the Charges of Crimes against Peace, 28.12.1948, *TWC*, VII, 1310, 1317–1325.

117.  Case 10, Opinion and Judgment of Military Tribunal III, 31.7.1948, *TWC*, IX, 1438–46, quote on p. 1146.

118.  Ferencz to Glueck, 16.4.1948, http://wwwnew.towson.edu/nurembergpapers/exhibit%20main/panel%203/Glueck.htm (accessed May 2012).

119.  Letter IHK Essen, Mülheim (Ruhr) and Oberhausen to Sir Brian H. Robertson, 10.8.1948, Rheinisch-Westfälisches Wirtschaftsarchiv, 130-40010145/166; Kaletsch to H. Reusch, 22.10.1948, ibid.; quote: Ludwig Kastl to H. Reusch, 11.8.1948, ibid.

120.  Cf. Thomas A. Schwartz, "Die Begnadigung deutscher Kriegsverbrecher. John McCloy und die Häftlinge von Landsberg," *Vierteljahrshefte für Zeitgeschichte* 38 (1990): 375–414; Norbert Frei, *Vergangenheitspolitik. Die Anfänge der Bundesrepublik und die NS-Vergangenheit*, 2nd edn (Munich, 2003), 195–266.

121.  Reprint in *Die Neuordnung der Eisen- und Stahlindustrie im Gebiet der Bundesrepublik Deutschland. Ein Bericht der Stahltreuhändervereinigung* (Munich, 1954), 329–35.

122.  Cf. Kim C. Priemel, "Unternehmensgeschichte Reloaded: Der Umgang der Friedrich Flick KG mit der NS-Vergangenheit in Öffentlichkeitsarbeit, Enflechtung und Restitution nach 1945," *Flick-Konzern*, 665–67.

123.  Ibid., 678–714.

124.  Ferencz to Katzenstein, 28.11.1972, USHMM, RG 12.004.08*12.

125.  Cf. Benjamin B. Ferencz, *Lohn des Grauens. Die verweigerte Entschädigung für jüdische Zwangsarbeiter. Ein Kapitel deutscher Nachkriegsgeschichte* (Frankfurt, 1979), 80, 200–12, 264f.

126.  Wolfgang Benz, "Der Wollheim-Prozeß. Zwangsarbeit für die I.G. Farben in Auschwitz," in *Wiedergutmachung in der Bundesrepublik Deutschland*, eds. Ludolf

Herbst and Constantin Goschler (Munich, 1989), 303–26; Joachim R. Rumpf, *Der Fall Wollheim gegen die I.G. Farbenindustrie AG in Liquidation: Die erste Musterklage eines ehemaligen Zwangsarbeiters in der Bundesrepublik Deutschland. Prozess, Politik und Presse* (Frankfurt a.M., 2010).

127. August v. Knieriem, *Nürnberg. Rechtliche und menschliche Probleme* (Stuttgart, 1953); Tilo von Wilmowsky, *Warum wurde Krupp verurteilt*, 3rd edn (Düsseldorf, 1962); for a detailed analysis, see Wiesen, *Industry*.

128. August Heinrichsbauer, *Schwerindustrie und Politik* (Essen, 1948); Louis P. Lochner, *Tycoons and Tyrant* (Chicago, 1954).

129. Joseph Borkin, *The Crime and Punishment of I.G. Farben* (New York, 1978), was published in German in 1979. Borkin had been a member of the OMGUS decartelization branch.

130. For example, Tom Bower, *Blind Eye to Murder. Britain, America and the Purging of Nazi Germany. A Pledge Betrayed* (London, 1995); and the introductory chapters in: *OMGUS. Ermittlungen gegen die Deutsche Bank*, ed. Dokumentationsstelle zur NS-Sozialpolitik (Nördlingen, 1985); *OMGUS. Ermittlungen gegen die Dresdner Bank*, ed. Hamburger Stiftung für Sozialgeschichte des 20. Jahrhunderts (Nördlingen, 1986); *OMGUS. Ermittlungen gegen die I.G. Farbenindustrie AG*, ed. Dokumentationsstelle zur NS-Sozialpolitik (Nördlingen, 1986).

131. Cf. Dietmar Petzina, *Autarkiepolitik im Dritten Reich. Der nationalsozialistische Vierjahresplan* (Stuttgart, 1968).

132. See the recent debate between Peter Hayes on the one hand and the late Christoph Buchheim and Jonas Scherner on the other in the *Bulletin of the German Historical Institute* 45 (Fall 2009).

## CHAPTER 7

# FROM CLEAN HANDS TO
# *VERNICHTUNGSKRIEG*

## HOW THE HIGH COMMAND CASE SHAPED THE
## IMAGE OF THE WEHRMACHT

*Valerie Hébert*

The first steps toward the revival of German militarism have already been taken. The German militarists know that their future strength depends on ... disassociating themselves from the atrocities they committed in the service of the Third Reich ... What about atrocities? The Wehrmacht committed none. Hitler's criminal orders were disregarded by the generals. Any atrocities which did occur were committed by other men such as Himmler and ... the SS ... The documents and testimony show that these are transparent fabrications. But here, in embryo, are the myths and legends which the German militarists will seek to propagate in the German mind. These lies must be stamped and labeled for what they are, now while the proof is fresh.[1]

**A**t the core of the Nuernberg Military Tribunals project, as Telford Taylor declared in 1947, was the goal to provoke among the German people a national self-examination of conscience for their responsibility and complicity in Nazi crime. Not every case was equally suited to the task. State organizations and institutions like the SS or the judiciary seemed to represent only a minority. The military trials, and chief among them the High Command case, allowed no such social or psychological distancing. The crimes charged in these proceedings implicated the many millions of "ordinary" Germans who had served in the ranks of the army. Even prior to the High Command case, Telford Taylor, Chief Prosecutor at the Nuernberg Military Tribunals (NMT), anticipated the tone and content of the defendants' claims which they would employ (having already heard them at the International Military Tribunal). He saw in them the seeds of an alternate, albeit false, memory of the war, but hoped that the evidence already being gathered for presentation at court would undermine these lies. Taylor understood that the narrative of crime and responsibility emerging from this trial would shape national identity for generations to come.

This article explains the early battle over the memory of the Wehrmacht in war. It describes the competing accounts presented by the prosecution and defense at trial, as well as the record confirmed in the judgment. Although the trial itself was successful, achieving convictions for war crimes and crimes against humanity on the basis of an incontrovertible documentary foundation, the image of a blameless army is what took root in the German public imagination in the postwar years. Tracing the American occupation authorities' post-trial decisions regarding clemency and parole for convicted war criminals, as well as their failure to publish the trial materials in German, accounts for how and why the truth of the army's crimes was submerged beneath the myth of the Wehrmacht's "clean hands" for three generations.

## From the End of the War to the High Command Case

If the Soviets, the British, or even American Secretary of the Treasury Henry Morgenthau, Jr. had had their way, there would not have been any trials at Nuremberg. According to their proposals, a punitive peace followed by summary executions of a greater or lesser number of Nazi leaders would have answered international calls for retribution. But other advisers within the American administration lobbied passionately for a judicial reckoning with Nazi crime. They argued that a trial designed to prove Nazi criminal planning and conduct would not only satisfy the desire for justice, but would educate the German people about their contested past. Upon a foundation of the regime's own records, prosecutors would show that Hitler and his followers had plunged Germany into war, had viciously violated all customary and formal laws of warfare, had attempted the destruction of entire peoples, and had obtained the complicity of millions in pursuit of these aims. The resulting rejection of the Nazi worldview and experience, so the trial advocates believed, would better prepare the ground in which to root the principles of peace and democracy.[2]

German reactions to the International Military Tribunal, the first Nuremberg trial, prosecuted jointly by the Americans, Russians, British, and French, seemed to validate the intent and goals of this project. According to public opinion polls, in December 1945, about a month after the trial began, 84 percent of respondents declared that they had learned something new from the proceedings. One month later, 78 percent of respondents had read press accounts of the trial. When the judgment was delivered, 78 percent believed the process had been just, and 76 percent believed that the sentences were either fair or too mild.[3] Perhaps these initial positive reactions reflected a certain sense of relief. After all, most of the defendants were top leaders of the state, remote in position and power from the average German. The logic of the IMT indictment pointed toward civil responsibility for Nazism and its crimes, and the trial itself was intended to provoke a national re-examination of conscience. However, the finality of the hangings and of the prison cells slamming shut in Spandau seemed to render this nascent period of introspection closed.

With the Americans' decision to pursue a subsequent set of proceedings, one that would probe more deeply into the complicity of all branches of the state in Nazi criminal plans and policies, the question of broadly-based responsibility for war crimes and crimes against humanity once again came to the fore. But there were early signs that education by trial was failing. In August 1947, polls revealed that only 35 percent of respondents believed Nazism was a bad idea. Intelligence analysts lamented that two years of occupation had "not made much progress in shaking many Germans loose from the past."[4] Not all of the NMT were equally suited to the task. The trials of Nazi doctors for their experiments on concentration camp prisoners, or of the SS-*Einsatzgruppen* who had shot hundreds of thousands of Jewish men, women, and children in the occupied Eastern territories certainly communicated the depth of Nazi depravity. But the perpetrators of these crimes were relatively few in number. The trials of industrialists or of high government officials revealed the crimes of the insatiably greedy and ambitious, which had caused the unprecedented suffering of millions of civilians. But these defendants, too, were not representative of the mass. It was the trials of military personnel (the High Command case in particular) that revealed the breadth of the German people's participation in Nazi crime. Twenty million citizens had served in the ranks of the Wehrmacht and many of them had participated in the crimes ordered or authorized by the men in the dock.

Three of the NMT proceedings pertained to the military. However, the case against Erhard Milch was concerned primarily with slave labor, and the case against the Wilhelm List et al., focused on the execution of hostages and partisans in the Balkans. The High Command case (US v. Wilhelm von Leeb et al., November 28, 1947–October 29, 1948) was the most thorough and comprehensive (in terms of personnel, geography, and scope of crimes concerned) of all the trials related to the military. The High Command case, called the *OKW-Prozess* in German, included both staff and field officers in the indictment. Crimes ranged from the invasions of countries contrary to treaties and conventions, the neglect, exploitation, and murder of prisoners of war, the terrorizing and murder of civilians in Nazi-occupied territories (especially, but not limited to Soviet civilians, Jews, Gypsies, and Communists), the carrying out of draconian anti-partisan and reprisal policies, and the deportation of civilians and POWs for slave labor. Many of these crimes had been mandated by illegal orders such as the Commissar, Commando, and the Barbarossa Jurisdiction Orders (BJO), all of which were examined in detail at trial. Victims could be counted by millions.

Four of the defendants were staff officers in the Wehrmacht High Command (*Oberkommando der Wehrmacht*, or OKW).[5] From their desks, they took Hitler's most fanatical and malicious aims and turned them into orders to be implemented by men in the field.[6] They included Walter Warlimont, who composed the infamous Barbarossa Jurisdiction Order, which gave soldiers free rein to murder men, women, and children with impunity; and Hans Reinecke, whose policies led to the deaths of 3.3 million Soviet prisoners of war from exposure, disease, starvation, exhaustion, and outright execution. The remaining defendants had served in the field from Norway to Greece and from the interior of France to the outskirts of Moscow. Having invaded, defeated, and occupied much of Europe allowed other Nazi state agencies access to the victims against whom to perpetrate ideologically motivated crimes. But the army's complicity in these offenses went much deeper. Among the defendants on trial were General Hans Reinhardt, in whose command area eleven teenagers had been executed for stealing bed sheets and shoes; Lieutenant-General Karl von Roques, who had issued decrees compelling Jews to wear the Star of David and live in ghettoes, and whose troops had murdered Jews and then looted their apartments, and Field Marshal Georg von Kuechler who, against his subordinate's own advice, had sent 150,000 civilians (including women and children) on a punitive march for forced labor.[7]

## Competing Narratives at Trial

The prosecution presented a compelling case based on an evidentiary record of the Wehrmacht's own creation. Counsel entered 1,778 exhibits into the record, including meeting minutes, as well as orders and directives emanating from the OKW and elsewhere in the top levels of the military. Reports, war diaries, and field correspondence proved that these plans and policies had been carried out. In arguing its case, the prosecution team required no interpretive or rhetorical embellishment. In language and in results, the evidence aligned with Nazi racial and political goals with such clear consistency and in such numbers that no one could deny the ideological purposes the Wehrmacht had served.[8]

Although the trial examined crimes committed in all European theatres and at all times during the war, the majority of the Wehrmacht's crimes had been perpetrated in the East. This stemmed from the Nazi leadership's conception of Operation Barbarossa (the invasion of the Soviet Union), which Hitler described as "a war of extermination."[9] Nazi propaganda described the campaign as a pre-emptive strike to save Germany from Communist aggression, but in truth, the battle was pre-meditated to crush Bolshevism and obtain "living space." SS, police, and military formations targeted all real and alleged Bolshevik leaders and adherents from among the intelligentsia, politicians, professionals, and military officers. Under a thin veneer of legitimate military functions such as the preservation of military security and the pacification of occupied areas, the army slaughtered countless Slavic and Jewish men, women, and children whom Nazi ideology had already identified as "sub-human."[10]

The indictment covered a vast array of offences, but four crimes are emblematic of the army's furtherance of Nazi racial and political goals. Foremost among these were the killings related to the June 1941 Commissar Order. Commissars were the ideological "morale-keepers" of the Red Army, responsible for the political instruction and oversight of Soviet soldiers. They were in all respects also regular soldiers: they wore the uniform, carried weapons, and fought at the front, and were entitled to the legal safeguards accorded to enemy belligerents and POWs. The order, drafted by the defendant Warlimont, instructed German troops that treating this "menace ... with consideration to leniency and international law is completely wrong" and that the commissars were to "be dealt with promptly and with the utmost severity."[11] In most cases, upon identifying commissars from among any POW population or in areas behind the front, the army handed them over to the SS or SD for execution. Frequently, however, regular German soldiers carried out the executions themselves. Hundreds of thousands of commissars were shot in accordance with this order.[12]

Another way in which the army served the racial and political policies of the state was in its treatment of Soviet POWs. Captured Soviet prisoners were frequently placed in barbed wire enclosures or rudimentary shelters, with no sanitary or cooking facilities, no protection from the elements, insufficient rations, and no medical care. Under these circumstances, disease was rampant, and millions (3.3 out of a total of 5.7 million in custody) died from neglect, starvation, and outright execution. The army also exploited POW labor for the most exhausting, dangerous (and illegal) forms of work: digging anti-tank ditches, clearing land mines, manning anti-aircraft guns, and locating booby-traps in abandoned buildings. POW camps located in General Karl von Roques' area of command reported mortality rates exceeding 80 percent.[13]

The Wehrmacht's treatment of civilian populations was equally savage. Army leaders issued dozens of orders to intimidate and terrorize non-belligerents in all occupied areas, but the most ferocious of these were reserved for the inhabitants of the East.[14] Foremost among them was the Barbarossa Jurisdiction Order (*Kriegsgerichtsbarkeitserlass Barbarossa*). Drafted in May 1941 by the defendants Warlimont and Rudolf Lehmann prior to the launching of Operation Barbarossa, and signed by Wilhelm Keitel, the horrific BJO legalized the killing of partisans and Soviet civilians suspected of hostile activities toward the German forces without trial of the civilians in question or evidence of their activities. It also permitted violent collective measures against communities where such activities took place, and released the army from any obligation to punish soldiers who committed crimes against civilians.[15] The prosecution presented dozens of evidence documents showing that the BJO resulted in a policy of near-indiscriminate killing of men, women, and children (even babies) on the flimsiest of pretexts. Activity reports originally submitted to Army Group North headquarters and then reproduced at trial showed that looking suspicious, listening to Radio Moscow, being stubborn, or having an "anti-German" attitude had been sufficient reasons to be shot or hanged.[16] Provoked by such brutal treatment, thousands of Soviets joined the partisan movement, which provided German forces with the excuse to intensify their policies of terror and reprisal, resulting in ever more civilian suffering and death.[17]

Wehrmacht activities toward racial "enemies" overlapped with their policies regarding political and military opponents. Jews, for example, could be murdered on a number of pretexts: because they were Communists, because they were partisans, or because they were commissars. The way in which orders were worded and the ideology which gave rise to them blurred the categories. Nonetheless, evidence produced in court showed clearly that the army's treatment of Jews had an exclusively racial motivation. Their participation in the events that later came to be called "the Holocaust" occurred at all levels. At a minimum, war provided the Nazi state the opportunity to enact the "Final Solution." Prior to the invasion of the Soviet Union, Quartermaster General Eduard Wagner, representing the OKW and OKH (*Oberkommando des Heeres*, or High Command of the Army) struck an unprecedented agreement with the head of the Reich Security Main Office Reinhard Heydrich allowing the SS *Einsatzgruppen* to work the army's operational areas. Following closely behind the troops, these mobile shooting squads would round up and execute all political and racial "enemies" (mainly Jews, Gypsies, and Communist leaders). Although their tactical orders would come from Heydrich, the agreement stipulated that they would remain subordinate to the army in terms of march, rations, and quarters. The *Einsatzgruppen* were instructed to report regularly on their activities to the local army commanders, who retained the authority to suspend or delay their work in the interests of military operations.[18] Reports attested that the army's relationship with the *Einsatzgruppen* exceeded tactical and administrative support. Relations were characterized as close and friendly, with frequent instances of direct participation by army personnel in the shootings. Further, the prosecution produced evidence that the army, and several of the defendants themselves, issued their own orders and directives to inflame antisemitic hatred among the troops, and to identify, isolate, and destroy Jews in their communities.[19]

The prosecution's stand did not remain unchallenged; rather, it prompted concerted argumentative action on the part of the defendants, their counsel, and the general public. In effect, the High Command case turned into a battleground for competing narratives about the conduct and character of the Wehrmacht during the war. In response to voluminous, incontrovertible evidence proving the complicity and participation of both individual defendants and the institution of the Wehrmacht in the ideologically motivated crimes of the Nazi state, the defense presented an alternate, albeit internally inconsistent, accounting of themselves and their comrades.[20] In court, the defendants described themselves and the officer corps as decent professional soldiers who were facing trial for no other reason than their rank and their defeat. All claimed ignorance of Hitler's aggressive and criminal ambitions until it was too late. The few instances of questionable behavior which may have transpired, they explained, could be blamed on the Soviets, who were the first to erase the boundary between belligerent and civilian.[21] It should be noted that the intensification of the Cold War proved a convenient and fertile context for these and other explanations. The defense repeatedly cited contemporary Soviet aggression in their postwar East European expansion to justify their treatment of Russia during the war.

The defendants resorted to two general strategies in answering specific evidence exhibits which directly implicated them in crimes: denial and justification. They would deny that an order or policy was criminal or illegal, or they would deny that they had seen, heard, known about, passed on, approved of, or received reports attesting to its implementation. When confronted with reports from their command areas detailing the execution of orders such as the Commissar Order or the murder of Jews, they denied that these were genuine and accurate—asserting instead that these were deliberately falsified documents concocted to deceive the higher-ups that their orders and policies were being obeyed. In other instances, defendants attempted to re-define language, insisting words like "shot" actually meant shot in battle, or shot but only wounded, or that "special treatment" in no way meant murder, and that "Jew" was synonymous with partisan. Regarding executed partisans, defendants avowed that all cases of suspected partisan activity had been thoroughly investigated and proven, that only true franc-tireurs had been executed, but that the findings of these proceedings were omitted from the record due to the frantic pace of warfare. They flatly denied all knowledge of the *Einsatzgruppen*'s exterminationist tasks.[22]

Repeatedly, defendants stated that their orders had been inescapable and issuing countermanding orders impossible. At other points, however, they claimed that they had indeed disobeyed orders and issued countermanding orders, but they had had to conceal their insubordination, so no records of their actions were made, and all corroborating witnesses had either gone missing or been killed in the fighting.[23] Occasionally, the prosecution presented orders or reports which the defendants admitted were questionable. In these instances, they denied all prior knowledge of them, but surmised that they must have come about because there had been no viable alternative. Further to that, the defendants staunchly insisted that they could not have resigned their posts, even in cases where their consciences might have warranted it. This, they declared, would have been tantamount to desertion. Resistance, they insisted, was futile. There were always others, less principled than them, who would have taken their place.[24]

Pressed further on the content of orders and reports documenting the Wehrmacht's criminal intentions and activities, defendants tried to lure attention away from their actions or their failures to act and to dilute the severity of their behavior by justifying their conduct. Their depictions of battle conditions in the East and the character of the Soviet opponent (the harsh climate, failing supply lines, allegations regarding Soviet torture and mutilation of captured German soldiers, their incitement of civilians to partisan warfare) cast Wehrmacht behavior as having been provoked and warranted, a response in kind, nothing more. Under those circumstances, so the reasoning went, traditional standards of warfare did not apply. For example, in the Opening Statements for the defendants Hermann Hoth and Hans Reinhardt, their counsel declared that "the battle in the East had its own character" and that "war in Russia had its own methods."[25] In responding to the many charges against them, defendants rarely quoted from documentary evidence (in stark contrast to the prosecution), relying instead on witness affidavits that uniformly attested to their humanitarian disposition and uncompromising attempts to do their best under impossible and unenviable circumstances. Having come from friends and colleagues, of course, these statements bore limited probative value.[26]

The tribunal found very little about the defense case convincing. Nonetheless, their judgment was measured and restrained in its interpretation of both the law and evidence, and much narrower in scope than the prosecution had hoped. The judges insisted that criminal culpability required personal action or omission, not just rank and command position, and in cases where evidence was unclear, they gave the defendants the benefit of the doubt. The judges were similarly generous in accepting the contention that no commander was all-knowing and all-powerful with regard to the conduct of his troops, and that no general presumption of knowledge of and acquiescence with criminal orders and policies was to be inferred.[27] Despite their conservative approach, however, the tribunal still found ample evidence to convict eleven of the thirteen defendants for having committed war crimes and crimes against humanity and sentenced them to prison terms spanning from time served to life.[28] Although sensitive to the predicament of the soldier, caught up in the chaos of battle, and integrated into a compelling command structure, the judges nonetheless saw the defendants' actions and omissions as unambiguously criminal. Moreover, the final verdict contained an implicit condemnation of the army as a whole. Since many of the defendants were found guilty because the men under their command had committed atrocities, it was clear that millions of "ordinary" Germans had served Nazi racial and political aims. Military men at all levels, from foot soldiers on the battlefield to high-ranking field and staff officers, had blood on their hands.[29] In view of the Americans' goal to use this trial to provoke a national re-evaluation of conscience, one would consider the High Command case a resounding success. But this would be mistaken.

Taken as a whole, the excuses and rationalizations woven together during the defense case provided an alternate image of the army in war, referred to in the time since as the myth of the Wehrmacht's "clean hands." The basic elements of this myth were that the Wehrmacht had been no servant of Hitler or his ideology; that it had accepted the war with the Soviet Union as a defensive strike against Communist aggression, that it had had no knowledge of or control over the SS destruction of the Jews; that whatever crimes might have occurred had been justified vengeance against an enemy whose conduct had been even worse, and that soldiers had merely done their duty, reluctantly followed orders, and ultimately had become victims of the state who had ruthlessly exploited their soldierly obedience and patriotic sense of duty. Despite mountains of evidence and an exhaustingly detailed judgment proving the contrary, it was the narrative that became fixed in the public imagination for generations.[30] This is hardly surprising, as this myth provided refuge and solace for a nation emerging from crushing defeat and facing worldwide moral contempt. Perhaps predictably, the conviction and imprisonment of eleven of the High Command case defendants set off a firestorm of controversy in West Germany. Perhaps less predictably, the fate of convicted soldiers became the fulcrum on which the legitimacy of the *entire* Nuremberg project turned. What had been a judicial matter transformed, in the period following proceedings, into a political problem.

## The Campaign to Free the Landsberg Soldiers

Once the trial concluded, the American occupation government assumed custody over the convicts and authority over the disposition of the trial records. However, these responsibilities soon came into conflict with new and pressing Cold War priorities. Despite the postwar Allied injunction against Germany ever again possessing arms, increasing hostility between East and West convinced Western powers of West Germany's strategic importance as a military force on the continent. West Germany's new-found political capital provided opponents of the trials (of which there were many) with an opportunity to pry convicted war criminals loose from Allied custody. In early Allied-West German negotiations over rearmament, the West German government made the release of convicted soldiers a clear condition for the reconstruction of their army. Moreover, the myth of the Wehrmacht's clean hands had freed the German people from the burden of guilt, and armed them with a narrative that called the whole notion of "war crimes" into question. The Churches, veterans' associations, the press, and ordinary citizens alike joined the government in its efforts to free soldiers convicted of war crimes.[31]

Shortly after the May 1949 foundation of the West German state, the Adenauer government announced its goal to request a general amnesty for persons sentenced by occupation government courts.[32] Notably, the law devised for the NMT had stipulated that issues of guilt were considered final and not subject to review. Consequently there was no formal appeals process through which the convicted could challenge the judgments issued against them. However, given America's desire to preserve political stability in Germany and its loyalty to the West, the US High Commissioner for Germany John J. McCloy felt obliged to make some concessions. While rejecting the demand for a general amnesty, in spring 1950 McCloy created an Advisory Board on Clemency for War Criminals which had a mandate to consider petitions and recommend sentence modifications, based on the convict's health, family conditions, or other mitigating factors.[33] Technically, because these revisions concerned themselves only with extenuating circumstances applicable to the sentences, they had no bearing on the original guilty verdicts.[34] That is, there would be no reversals of the judgments.

The Advisory Board was nicknamed the Peck Panel, after its chairman, David Peck, presiding judge of the New York Supreme Court's Appellate Division. Two others served on the panel: Brigadier General Conrad Snow of the State Department Legal Staff and Frederick Moran, chairman of the New York State Board of Parole.[35] None had had any prior dealings with the Nuremberg trial program. Apart from the injunction against reversing decisions of law or fact, the Peck Panel's instructions were vague. It was to try and harmonize sentences imposed for similar crimes, and in the interests of clemency, it could take a convict's health and family conditions into account. The form and procedure of the reviews were left to the Panel's discretion.[36] During spring and summer 1950, the three men studied the NMT judgments and read individual petitions from prisoners. Moran interviewed each NMT convict at Landsberg. Then, during eleven days in August, the panel heard 105 cases. Representatives of the convicted had thirty minutes each to speak, and an eight member panel of West German Ministry of Justice officials sat in to make recommendations. Not a single Nuremberg prosecutor was invited to take part, despite at least one offer to lend expertise on individual cases. The panel took fifteen minutes for deliberation before recording their decisions. No transcriptions of the proceedings were made.[37]

None of the High Command case convicts expressed any remorse or contrition in their applications. Rather, they repeated the claims they had raised in court: that they couldn't escape their oath of obedience, but they had nonetheless secretly subverted certain orders, that the current political situation validated their wartime approach toward the Soviets, and that no one could understand the pressures they had faced while in battle.[38] The Federal Ministry of Justice submitted summary sheets for all the applicants, highlighting their families' now dire financial straits in order to show that these men were badly needed back home.[39] The *Zentrale Rechtsschutzstelle* (Central Legal Defense Agency), a division of the Ministry of Justice and affiliate of the Red Cross and various Christian organizations, gathered allegedly "new" and exculpatory evidence to submit to the panel and paid for the High Command case convicts' legal representation before the panel.[40] Appeals from individual citizens described the High Command case convicts as kind and compassionate, family-oriented Christian men, well-meaning and honorable, used and abused by Hitler, who had exploited the "chaotic times" and their sense of soldierly duty.[41]

The prisoners themselves, their counsel, their relatives and friends, professional associates, clergy, church and school groups, public officials, and notably, former soldiers bombarded High Commissioner McCloy with petitions as well during the period of the clemency board's work. For example, retired Admiral Gottfried Hansen declared: "An end [must] be put to defamation by releasing the numerous innocent German soldiers who are still being held in confinement."[42] Aimed at more than securing early release, these appeals attacked the foundation and results of the trial program itself. However, occupation officials had already decided that they would not revisit the materials and conclusions of the trial, since they knew that this would only "open the door to an endless rehash of the ... arguments, ... cast doubt upon the validity of the findings, ... [and] undermine ... the policy and position of the United States in sponsoring and undertaking the program as a whole."[43]

Unfortunately, and contrary to their (admittedly imprecise) instructions, the Peck Panel departed from this policy. In explaining their sentence recommendations, the panel declared that they had felt themselves bound only by the facts established by the evidence, but not by the conclusions the tribunals had drawn from them. They intimated that they believed that individuals had been unfairly sentenced for the crimes of the group and justified their sometimes "sharp reductions" in 84 of the 105 sentences they reviewed as "due and proper recognition of differences in authority and action among defendants" and their connection to the programs in which they had participated.[44] The High

Commission's General Counsel, Robert Bowie, was deeply troubled by the clemency board's recommendations and communicated his concerns to McCloy. He surmised that the board's reliance on only the judgments had skewed and limited their understanding of the cases, since these did not reference all the incriminating evidence presented at court. Further, he felt that the panel's insistence on proof connecting individual defendants with specific crimes undermined the prosecution's assertion of guilt by omission, which had been upheld in the tribunal's judgment. It also seemed to suggest that the board had grievously underestimated the power and responsibility these army officers had wielded on the field.[45]

In responding to advocates on behalf of imprisoned soldiers, McCloy endeavored to set the record on military men straight. To retired admiral Hansen, he wrote:

> No one aware of the facts can possibly say that these men observed either the ethics of their profession or the fundamental principles of humanity and law ... I cannot believe that allowance should be made for a professional soldier who either connived or participated in [the] slaughter of Jews because they were Jews, communists, parachutists, aviators, commandos, and other "undesirables." Such connivance and participation took place and there can be no doubt of it.[46]

McCloy was indignant at the German people's refusal to acknowledge the truth of their past and declared that they should confront the enormity of the crimes. Nonetheless, McCloy hedged a bit when in other communications, he averred that in no way did the trials impugn the honor of the regular soldier.[47] These efforts to smooth over the public's bitterness over the imprisonment of soldiers was no doubt linked to the re-emergence of the rearmament question, kindled by the Americans' recent reverses in the Korean War. The US desire for West German rearmament would prove a persistent vulnerability in their dealings with the West Germans.[48] For its part, West Germany was clear and direct in exploiting their new-found political capital. In October 1950, under the supervision of Adenauer's foreign policy advisor, several former Wehrmacht officers met to discuss the nature and scope of a new German military at a monastery in Himmerod. The resulting declaration, endorsed by the Adenauer government, declared that the psychological preconditions for any German contribution to Western defense included an Allied declaration that the Germans had acted honorably during the war and the release of all "alleged" war criminals being held in prison.[49] Although McCloy claimed not to have allowed this pressure to sway his decisions, it became increasingly clear in later years that the Allied powers were unwilling to wager the West's military security on the war criminals' issue.

In January 1951, on the basis of the Peck Panel's recommendations, McCloy reduced the prison sentences for the vast majority of Nuremberg convicts, including three of the remaining eight High Command case convicts held at Landsberg.[50] In the brief written report on his decisions, which was distributed widely among German political, religious, and institutional leaders, McCloy made a special point of explaining his position vis à vis the military men in prison. Contrary to the common view that the sentences against them maligned the German military profession as a whole, McCloy was at pains to remind the West German public that the judgments were based on charges of excess far surpassing anything that could be considered militarily necessary. He declared that he understood the bitter realities of partisan warfare and that when "the heat of battle" or "true military considerations" could be convincingly argued, he moderated the sentences. However, regarding the High Command case convicts, he concluded that there remained "an area of real guilt which ... a professional soldier ... cannot countenance."[51] Despite McCloy's efforts at explaining the war criminals situation, however, German opponents remained unmoved. Analyzing over 1,000 letters written to McCloy in response to the Landsberg decisions, High Commission officials noted that over 95 percent favored further sentence revisions. Notably, 60 percent of those who wrote were former soldiers or family members of soldiers.[52]

The negotiations to end Allied occupation and for the proposed West German contribution to the planned European Defense Community (EDC), which were formalized in the 1952 Bonn Convention, reinvigorated the war criminals question and provided added leverage to those seeking early release of soldiers convicted of war crimes. Capitalizing on the Allies' desire to secure West German commitment to this supranational West European army, Chancellor Adenauer, with the backing of almost the entire parliament and at the insistence of many veterans' associations, once again raised the issue of a general release of war criminals. Erich Mende, the Chairman of the Foreign Policy Committee of the Free Democratic Party (part of Adenauer's coalition) wrote to McCloy: "[I]f our common purpose of keeping Germany in the Western orbit ... is to be achieved, it is essential to make further visible progress toward getting rid of the *rankling complex* of Landsberg."[53] Writing as chairman of the Association of German Soldiers and backed by another ten POW and veterans' groups (altogether representing about 80,000 people), Gottfried Hansen forwarded a resolution to the High Commission which declared "no German can be expected to don a military uniform again until the question of 'war criminals' has been satisfactorily settled."[54]

It should be noted that by mid-1952, only thirty-five out of an original 142 men convicted by the NMT remained at Landsberg.[55] Moreover, the rhetoric employed by groups lobbying for their release obscured the even smaller number of imprisoned soldiers. In the first place, all incarcerated war criminals were referred to as soldiers, even though many had had no connection to the Wehrmacht at all. Secondly, the term "war criminals" appeared only in quotation marks or preceded by the qualifier "so-called." Lastly, lobbyists conflated the category of "war criminals" with prisoners of war, identifying them with the POWs still held in foreign (particularly Soviet) custody. The German press echoed and encouraged these sentiments and demands. High Commission officials noted the almost daily appearance of articles campaigning for the release of war criminals, focusing particular attention on former soldiers. Their arguments tended to fall along the following lines: (1) that there had been no war crimes and therefore no basis for trials; (2) that the Allies had applied victors' justice and *ex post facto* law; and (3) that soldiers had only followed orders. Moreover, the newspapers rarely referenced facts, and because they lumped all prisoners into the category of soldiers and all common crimes into the now dubious category of "war crimes," American analysts concluded that they had been able to "thoroughly mislead and confuse the German public."[56] Indeed, a 1952 poll revealed that 62 percent of respondents did not believe that German generals held as war criminals were actually guilty and only 10 percent supported the war crimes program as a whole.[57] In a letter addressed to all US Congressmen and Senators, the Association of German Returnees, POWs and Family Members of Missing Germans (*Verband der Heimkehrer, Kriegsgefangenen und Vermisstenangehörigen Deutschlands*, VdH) wrote:

> Again and again we had hoped that the US Government would make a quick and overall decision for the solution of this burning "war criminals issue" by deciding to grant *amnesty* for all so-called "war criminals." ... We ask you to do all in *your* power to ... consent to the clear principle that those Germans sentenced for *supposed* war crimes ... should have the benefit of Clemency ... We appeal for the release of *all* German Prisoners of War who acted by order or out of the cruel necessities of an extra-ordinary situation in modern warfare ... 'How to win friends for the States? OPEN THE LANDSBERG PRISON GATES.'"[58]

In response, American officials repeatedly insisted that these men had been found culpable for offenses ranging from assault to murder and therefore could be classified as common criminals. They tried striking back at the apparent West German consensus which sought to trade military support for the release of war criminals. In an article entitled "A Necessary Clarification," US authorities warned the Germans not to make the war criminals question a political issue and declared that "during World War II things had taken place in the German Wehrmacht that until then had been absent from the armies of all civilized countries" and proclaimed that the United States would not purchase Germany's military commitment with concessions on war criminals.[59] Privately, however, US occupation authorities realized that the continued incarceration of Wehrmacht generals ensured the persistence of a "war criminals problem."[60]

In time, American occupation authorities accepted a significant share of the responsibility for why the German people had not understood the reasons for and findings of their war crimes trials. A July 1952 memorandum prepared for the US High Commission lamented that an absence of available trial records had caused the "grief" experienced with the present political/military negotiations and other prior war criminals issues, and had prevented these problems from having been more satisfactorily resolved. The author noted that the original purpose of the trials "was to document the Nazi period and bring before the world generally and the Germans particularly a working knowledge of the Nazi state." He declared pointedly that had American authorities honored their goal of education by ensuring the timely availability of the trial materials, then the present "scandalous deterioration" in the German public's understanding of war criminals and their crimes might have been avoided.[61] Indeed at that time there were only seven sets of trial records available in German in all of Germany, and most of these were incomplete.[62] American High Commission officials concluded that since they had not made the facts of the trials available to the German people, the press, politicians, and other institutional leaders had been able to exploit the situation to their own advantage.[63]

Moreover, other officials believed that the key historical moment for penetrating German public consciousness had already passed. A confidential brief reporting on the "Political Aspects of the War Criminals Question" observed, with regret, that since the problem had become an "irrational one," it could neither be eliminated nor managed by a public relations campaign. In any case, the United States had to consider its new political priorities. The brief's author predicted that the war criminals problem would continue to imperil any form of military cooperation and would act as a constant irritant in relations between West Germany and the United States.[64]

The inescapable conclusion was that the United States now found itself in two irreconcilable roles: occupier and executor of occupation justice and Germany's would-be ally and "friend."[65] They would have to choose one. Disappointed by their own failings, worn down by the uncertainty of the West's military security and from relentless pressure from the West Germans, and worn out by what was now the eighth year of occupation, the Americans ultimately opted in 1953 to end the war criminals problem via the formation of an interim mixed US–German Parole and Clemency Board which would implement a more lenient system of sentence reduction and parole. The High Commission advised the speedy release of those prisoners "whose retention will continue to occasion major outcry." At the top of this list were the High Command generals.[66]

Technically, parole was a continuation of punishment, only under different circumstances. The parolee would be closely supervised, prohibited from political activity and from speaking or writing publicly, and limited in terms of residence, employment, and travel.[67] The granting of clemency could either reduce a life term or a death sentence to a shorter prison sentence, or it could end the prisoner status altogether. The circumstances surrounding the formation of the Interim Mixed Clemency and Parole Board made clear that its goal was to empty Landsberg of convicted war criminals. However, the High Commission attempted—at least on paper—to protect the integrity of the war crimes trial program. They insisted that neither parole nor clemency constituted a critique of the trials, and forbade the board from reviewing the applicant's guilt. These original decisions, they insisted, were to be considered "final and incontestable."[68] Rather, the issues to be assessed were whether the offense in question was a single action or committed repeatedly over a long period of time, the applicant's rank and authority at the time of the crime, whether he had shown personal initiative in the commission of the crime, whether similar crimes had been given similar sentences, and the applicant's health, conduct in prison, and overall "character."[69]

When the Interim Mixed Parole and Clemency Board began its work, only three of the original High Command case convicts (Herman Hoth, Walter Warlimont, and Hans Reinecke) remained in prison. The others had either completed their sentences, died, or been released on medical or compassionate parole. Their applications consisted of their prison record (which detailed their comportment and activities at Landsberg), the prison director's evaluation of whether they were likely to adjust well to civilian life, and a summary of the case in which the applicant had been convicted. The case summary was a one page précis indicating the name of the trial, all previous clemency actions, and the projected release date. The description of the applicant's crimes was limited to two paragraphs. These paragraphs were devoid of any sense of the scope and scale of the suffering the convict had caused, and included no explanation of the extent and reliability of the evidence. Decisions were made on the basis of written records alone: neither the applicant nor his counsel appeared before the board. Members of the public as well as government and religious institutions submitted documents on the High Command case convicts' behalf. Private citizens (former colleagues, subordinates, and friends) submitted statements attesting to the applicants' honorable and upstanding characters. Leaders from religious organizations volunteered to act as parole sponsors. The federal pension office issued statements certifying the amount to which the applicants were entitled upon their release. A prominent veterans' and POW association mounted a campaign to elicit from members promises of jobs to be offered to parolees, in order to demonstrate to occupation authorities that these men would pose no financial strain to society if let go.[70]

Landsberg officials described the three High Command case convicts as excellent parole candidates. They had unblemished prison records, had carried themselves with dignity—even "good humor," in Reinecke's case—and had been cooperative and productive workers in the prison laundry, garden, school, or hospital. One of the prerequisites for parole was that the applicant should have made clear through his behavior that he regretted the acts for which he had been judged. There is no indication, however, that any had such regret. Warlimont declared that he felt no personal sense of guilt, and saw his conviction as a function of his rank. Reinecke also asserted that his senior position in the OKW alone had led to his "fate" as a convicted war criminal. Hoth went further, denying that he had committed any crime, and then warning prison Director E.C. Moore that his status as a parolee would grate on German public opinion. The German people, he continued, expected the stigma of criminality to be removed altogether. He added that this disappointment would no doubt reflect badly on their proposed military cooperation with the West. Still, the generals' lack of remorse proved no impediment to their release.[71] Overall, American authorities regarded these men as well-behaved and harmless. Within thirteen months of the Interim Board's foundation, the Americans returned the last High Command case convicts to their homes and their families. Their communities celebrated their homecoming, the government restored their pensions, and the generals lived out their days in peace.

For the remaining Landsbergers and parolees, parole and clemency hearings continued, in time under the auspices of a new board: the Mixed Clemency and Parole Board, which included members from Britain, France, the United States, and Germany. Here again, the Americans' intentions were clear. The Embassy in Bonn declared that the US member "will be as lenient as possible in dealing with the remaining US cases."[72] From 1955 to 1957, the board disposed of all of the British and French cases of imprisoned war criminals, imposing no conditions on the convicts' release. By May of the following year, all war criminals convicted by American courts had either had their paroles cancelled or were released unconditionally from Landsberg. What had started as a protest against imprisoning soldiers led to a series of parole and clemency programs that applied to all war criminals in American custody, including the hundreds of convicts of the army-led Dachau trials, and even former leaders of the *Einsatzgruppen*.

## Conclusion

Although the Americans never consented to the amnesty of war criminals (which was repeatedly demanded), nor retracted the verdicts passed against them, the premature release of the Landsberg generals had an analogous effect. In the ongoing struggle to define the memory of the Wehrmacht in war, the Americans' political calculation undermined the magnitude of the crimes which earned the sentences, and lent credence to the persistent and resolute German claims that there were no crimes for which to atone. Subsequent historical research restored the discussion to a truthful foundation, and vindicated the record of Wehrmacht crime created during the High Command case. However, it was not until the 1990s that this history gained wide acceptance.[73]

In the intervening decades, there were moments of honesty and clarity. Notably, the man who defined the institutional philosophy of the West German *Bundeswehr*, the veteran Count Wolf von Baudissin, was provoked to reform by the Wehrmacht's ethical collapse under Nazism. He believed that the reason why so many soldiers had become accomplices to Hitler's crimes was that they had had little understanding of democracy, and were bound in an institutional cult of obedience. They therefore had little to arm themselves against the National Socialist temptation. Von Baudissin believed that public institutions should be guided by Christian ethical principles, that soldiers should identify with the society they would be asked to defend, and that they should be political—a stark contrast to the Wehrmacht culture where officers did not even vote. The guiding idea behind the new military was called *"Innere Führung"* (internal leadership) and presented an image of citizens in uniform (*"Staatsbürger in Uniform"*). To be sure, a great number of veterans were hostile to the reform program, seeing in it an implied reproach of the Wehrmacht.[74] But the West German government's endorsement of the *Innere Führung* philosophy did not entail a formal public critique of the Wehrmacht, nor did it translate into support for the punishment of military war criminals. Their paradoxical approach fits in with the overall Janus-faced pattern of addressing the past. At the same time that President Theodor Heuss was decrying Germany's eternal shame for the Holocaust, and the West German government was paying reparations to Israel, the state, the churches, and other public and private institutions were harassing occupation officials to release convicted war criminals from prison.[75]

Despite the eventual adoption and implementation of *Innere Führung*, the Wehrmacht myth remained intact well into the 1990s. This was due in part to the fact that the Bundeswehr's internal historiography tended to gloss over all controversies, as the so-called *Traditionserlasse* (guidelines on the interpretation and preservation of German military tradition) indicated. Although the first, issued in 1965, lauded the military's involvement in the July 1944 assassination plot, it avoided comment on its conduct in the war as a whole. In fact, it did not even mention the Wehrmacht by name, even as it called for intergenerational comradeship between former and contemporary German soldiers. For the next two decades the Wehrmacht's role in the Third Reich would be characterized as patriotic, dutiful, and brave, endorsing the view that these eternal values had been exploited by the Nazi regime. A more determined revision of the *Traditionserlass* in 1982 by a Social Democrat, Hans Apel, provoked immediate, heavy criticism from within the military. Apel's successor, the conservative politician and NATO secretary-to-be Manfred Wörner, first renounced the reform but media pressure led him to moderate his position. President Ronald Reagan's visit to the Bitburg military cemetery in 1985 soon overshadowed Wörner's equivocation, and public discussion again focused on honoring the memory of those Germans who had fought in the war. A major overhaul of the *Bundeswehr*'s *Traditionspflege* therefore remained in the waiting.[76]

This background at least partially accounts for the shock of 1995 when the Hamburg Institute for Social Research launched a public exhibition called "War of Extermination: Crimes of the Wehrmacht 1941–1944," which documented, largely by photographs, the army's crimes against POWs, Jews, and other civilians on the Eastern front. The exhibition toured Germany and Austria, attracting 1.2 million visitors and the designation as "THE contemporary history exhibit in the Federal Republic."[77] The public's response was shock, dismay, and in some places, violent rage. In Munich, Vienna, and Dresden, there were street demonstrations against the exhibit's opening. Protesters fire-bombed the Saarbrücken exhibition site. If nothing else this response showed that the High Command case had made no lasting impression on public memory of the war, even though the trial had laid bare the truth of these crimes decades earlier, on an irrefutable documentary basis, covering a much larger geographical and temporal framework than the exhibit. As the exhibit moved from city to city, charged and painful debates about the responsibility of the "ordinary soldier" for racial and political crimes, and on the national heritage of the Third Reich ignited newspapers, radio, and even the German parliament. Ultimately the exhibit provoked what the trial had attempted and failed to bring about: a national confrontation with the Nazi past and a refutation of the "clean hands" myth.[78]

Perhaps the High Command case was doomed to fail as an educative exercise. The psychological cost of accepting the trial's message of broadly-shared complicity and participation in unprecedented atrocity might have been too much to bear, particularly in the immediate aftermath of defeat and division. But tracing the story from the American perspective reveals numerous identifiable moments when US officials made specific decisions that deliberately subordinated the educative goal to political interests. Although the trials laid a foundation for an ongoing discussion of guilt and responsibility, occupation authorities made, as Taylor wrote, "access to the truth difficult."[79] Because the United States did not test the didactic limits of the Nuremberg trial program, we will never know the extent of its rehabilitative potential.

## Notes

1. This chapter is based largely on research originally conducted for the book: *Hitler's Generals on Trial: the Last War Crimes Tribunal at Nuremberg*, published by University Press of Kansas, 2010.

   Epigraph from: Telford Taylor, "The Meaning of the Nuremberg Trials," Columbia University Law School, Arthur Diamond Law Library (CULS-ADLL), Telford Taylor Papers, Speeches, Box 53, 57 "The Meaning of the Nuremberg Trials," Address delivered to the International Association of Democratic Lawyers at the Palais de Justice, Paris, April 25, 1947.

2. For this early phase, see the now classic accounts by Bradley Smith, *The Road to Nuremberg* (New York, 1981); Ann Tusa and John Tusa, *The Nuremberg Trial* (London, 1984), and the more recent study by Arieh J. Kochavi, *Prelude to Nuremberg. Allied War Crimes Policy and the Question of Punishment* (Chapel Hill, 1998).

3. *Public Opinion in Occupied Germany: The OMGUS Surveys, 1945–49*, eds. A. Merritt and R. Merritt (Urbana, IL, 1970), 34–35.

4. OMGUS Survey Report #68: "The Trend in Attitudes Toward National Socialism," October 10, 1947, NARA 260, Entry 16 (A1)/9: Records Relating to Public Opinion 1945–1949, Box 153, Folder: Opinion Survey Reports 61–80. See also Merritt and Merritt, *Public Opinion*, 32.

5. Lieutenant-Generals Rudolf Lehmann, Hermann Reinecke, and Walter Warlimont served in the OKW, Admiral Otto Schniewind served in both the OKW and was a commander at sea.

6. The field commanders on trial were: General Johannes Blaskowitz, General Karl Hollidt, General Hermann Hoth, General Hans Reinhardt, General Hugo Sperrle, Field Marshal Georg von Kuechler, Field Marshal Wilhelm von Leeb, Lieutenant-General Karl von Roques, General Hans Salmuth, and Lieutenant-General Otto Wöhler.

7. Prosecution Memorandum of Law and Facts, "Responsibility of Hans Reinhardt under Counts Two and Three of the Indictment," August 26, 1948, NARA, M-898, Roll 57, 84; Prosecution Memorandum of Law and Facts, "Responsibility of Karl von Roques under Counts Two and Three of the Indictment," August 20, 1948, NARA, M-898, Roll 58, 55, 59; Prosecution Memorandum of Law and Facts, "Responsibility of Georg von Kuechler under Counts Two and Three of the Indictment," August 12, 1948, NARA, M-898, Roll 57, 67–68 and Prosecution Rebuttal Exhibit 24, NOKW-3379, NARA, M-898, Roll 27.

8. For the latest scholarship on this, see Dieter Pohl, *Die Herrschaft der Wehrmacht. Deutsche Militärbesatzung und einheimische Bevölkerung in der Sowjetunion 1941–1944* (Munich, 2008).

9. Closing Statement for the United States of America, August 10, 1948, NARA, M-898, Roll 57, 106 and Prosecution Exhibit 1359, NOKW-3140, NARA, M-898, Roll 24.

10. An indispensable guide to the vast German and English historiography of the Wehrmacht's war in the East is *Hitler's War in the East: A Critical Assessment*, eds. Rolf-Dieter Müller and Gerd Ueberschär (New York, 2002). Seminal works include Omer Bartov, *Hitler's Army: Soldiers, Nazis, and War in the Third Reich* (New York, 1992); Manfred Messerschmidt, *Die Wehrmacht im NS-Staat: Zeit der Indoktrination* (Hamburg, 1969). Hannes Heer and Klaus Naumann have edited an excellent collection of more recent scholarship, entitled *War of Extermination: The German Army in World War II, 1941–1944* (New York, 2000). Also, since 1979 the Militärgeschichtliches Forschungsamt (Military History Office, formerly of Freiburg, now based in Potsdam) has been publishing a massive ten-volume series on the Third Reich and World War II entitled *Das Deutsche Reich und der Zweite Weltkrieg* (Stuttgart, 1979–2008). The series is available in English translation up to volume 9:1 as *Germany and the Second World War* (Oxford, 1990–2008). See, especially, vol. 4, *The Attack on the Soviet Union* (1998) for the background and course of Germany's war against the Soviet Union, and the army's role in this unprecedented campaign of annihilation.

11. Prosecution Exhibit 57, NOKW-1076, NARA, M-898, Roll 12.

12. One of the very first pieces of historical writing on the Wehrmacht and Nazi crimes was a report on the Commissar Order by Hans-Adolf Jacobsen of the *Institut für Zeitgeschichte*. He wrote it for the 1964 Auschwitz trial. See "Kommissarbefehl und Massenexekutionen sowjetischer Kriegsgefangener," in *Anatomie des SS-Staates: Gutachten des Instituts für Zeitgeschichte*, vol. 2, eds. Hans Buchheim, Martin Broszat, Hans-Adolf Jacobsen, and Helmut Krausnick (Munich, 1965). For more recent

discussion of the Commissar Order, see Felix Römer, *Der Kommissarbefehl: Wehrmacht und NS-Verbrechen an der Ostfront 1941/42* (Paderborn, 2008).

13. Prosecution Memorandum, von Roques, 40–41. On the Wehrmacht's treatment of Soviet POWs, see Christian Gerlach, *Kalkulierte Morde: die deutsche Wirtschafts- und Vernichtungspolitik in Weißrussland 1941 bis 1944* (Hamburg, 1999); Alfred Streim, *Die Behandlung sowjetischer Kriegsgefangener im "Fall Barbarossa:" Eine Dokumentation* (Heidelberg, 1981); Christian Streit, *Keine Kameraden: Die Wehrmacht und die sowjetischen Kriegsgefangenen* (Stuttgart, 1978).

14. Karel Berkhoff describes life under German occupation in Ukraine in *Harvest of Despair: Life and Death in Ukraine under Nazi Rule* (Cambridge, 2004). See the work of Dieter Pohl for recent (and impressively accurate) figures for Wehrmacht atrocities committed in the East, *Herrschaft der Wehrmacht*.

15. Prosecution Memorandum of Law and Facts, "Responsibility of Wilhelm von Leeb under Counts Two and Three of the Indictment," July 1948, NARA, M-898, Roll 57, 102–103 and Prosecution Exhibit 594, C-50, NARA, M-898, Roll 16.

16. See these and numerous other examples in: Prosecution Memorandum, von Leeb, 110–19 and Prosecution Memorandum, von Kuechler, 83–89.

17. On the Wehrmacht's anti-partisan campaign, see Hannes Heer, "The Logic of the War of Extermination: The Wehrmacht and the anti-Partisan War," in *War of Extermination*, eds. Heer and Naumann, 92–126; Ben Sheperd, "The Clean Wehrmacht, the War of Extermination, and Beyond," *The Historical Journal* 52 (2009): 455–73.

18. Prosecution Memorandum, von Leeb, 72–73 and Prosecution Exhibit 847, NOKW-2080, Roll 18. On the Wehrmacht's complicity in crimes against Jews, see especially: Andrej Angrick, *Besatzungspolitik und Massenmord. Die Einsatzgruppe D in der südlichen Sowjetunion 1941–1943* (Hamburg, 2003); Hannes Heer, "Killing Fields: The Wehrmacht and the Holocaust in Belorussia, 1941–1942," *Holocaust and Genocide Studies* 7 (1997): 79–101; id., *Tote Zonen: die deutsche Wehrmacht an der Ostfront* (Hamburg, 1999); Walter Manoschek, *"Serbien ist Judenfrei": militärische Besatzungspolitik and Judenvernichtung in Serbien 1941/42* (Munich, 1993); id. (ed.), *Die Wehrmacht im Rassenkrieg: Der Vernichtungskrieg hinter der Front* (Vienna, 1996); Jürgen Förster, "Wehrmacht, Krieg und Holocaust," in *Die Wehrmacht: Mythos und Realität*, eds. Rolf-Dieter Müller and Hans-Erich Volkmann (Munich, 1999), 948–66; Ralf Ogorreck, *Die Einsatzgruppen und die "Genesis der Endlösung"* (Berlin, 1996); Edward Westermann, "Partners in Genocide: The German Police and the Wehrmacht, in the Soviet Union," *Journal of Strategic Studies* 31 (2008): 771–96; Wolfram Wette, *Wehrmacht: History, Myth, Reality* (Cambridge, 2006); Hans-Heinrich Wilhelm, *Rassenpolitik und Kriegführung: Sicherheitspolizei und Wehrmacht in Polen und der Sowjetunion* (Passau, 1991); Helmut Krausnick and Hans-Heinrich Wilhelm, *Die Truppe des Weltanschauungskrieges: Die Einsatzgruppen der Sicherheitspolizei und des SD 1938–1942* (Stuttgart, 1981).

19. Prosecution Exhibit 956, L-180, NARA, M-898, Roll 20; Prosecution Memorandum, von Leeb, 79–81, 9–94; Prosecution Memorandum, von Roques, 55–56, 67. In November 1941, Hermann Hoth instructed his troops that: "[The Jews'] annihilation is a law of self-preservation." See Prosecution Opening Statement, NARA, M-898, Roll 1, 137. Similarly, an order from within Reinhardt's 3rd Panzer Army from October 1943 declared: "[The Jews are an] eternal tribe of parasites ... and which now, through Bolshevist evil, is probably committing its last work of decomposition. The brave German western individual is still not energetic enough with their hellish monsters. He still treats the Jewish monster too much in accordance with decent concepts, instead of releasing his entire hatred and will of destruction against the breed of a 1000 year old infernal world ... I expect all ... commanders indefatigably to use the appearance of the Jewish–Bolshevist propaganda in order to open the eyes of our brave German soldiers at every possible opportunity to fill their hearts with deep hatred and will of destruction." See Prosecution Memorandum, Reinhardt, 99–100.

20. See, e.g., Manfred Messerschmidt, "Forward Defense: the 'Memorandum of the Generals' for the Nuremberg Court," in *War of Extermination*, eds. Heer and Naumann, 381–99.

21. See, e.g., Hans Surholt, Opening Statement for Hermann Reinecke, NARA, M-898, Roll 61, 5 and 8; Heinz Müller-Torgow, Closing Brief for Hermann Hoth, NARA, M-898, Roll 61, 21; Friedrich Frohwein, Closing Statement for Hans Reinhardt, NARA, M-898, Roll 62, 21; Hans Laternser, Opening Statement for Wilhelm von Leeb, NARA, M-898, Roll 61, 21.

22. See, e.g., Frohwein, Closing Brief for Hans Reinhardt, NARA, M-898, Roll 62, 98; Müller-Torgow, Closing Brief for Hermann Hoth, NARA, M-898, Roll 61, 98–99; Georg von Kuechler, Testimony, Transcript, NARA, M-898, Roll 4, 2962.

23. Kurt Behling, Opening Statement for Georg von Kuechler, NARA, M-898, Roll 61, 5–6; Paul Leverkühn, Opening Statement for Walter Warlimont, NARA, M-898, Roll 61, 14.

24. See, e.g., Paul Leverkühn, Opening Statement for Walter Warlimont, NARA, M-898, Roll 61, 12.

25. Heinz Müller-Torgow, Opening Statement for Hermann Hoth, NARA, M-898, Roll 61, 10 and Friedrich Frohwein, Opening Statement for Hans Reinhardt, NARA, M-898, Roll 61, 8.

26. For example, in testimony given on behalf of the defendant Hans Reinhardt, former subordinates claimed that he possessed "the highest principles of humanity," that his attitude was "chivalrous," that his conduct had been "irreproachable," and that he regarded both Soviet prisoners and civilians with kindness and goodwill. See Otto Heidkämper, Testimony, Transcript, NARA, M-898, Roll 5, 3852 and Maximillian Himmel, Testimony, Transcript, NARA, M-898, Roll 5, 3745. The trial records contain dozens more similar statements for other defendants. In the post-trial review of the cases, these witnesses continued to provide affidavits attesting to the convicts' good character and blameless conduct.

27. Judgment, Transcript, NARA, M-898, Roll 24, 10 108, 10 114–10 116.

28. Johannes Blaskowitz committed suicide on the day that the indictment was read. Hugo Sperrle and Otto Schniewind were found not guilty on all counts.

29. The responsibility and complicity of millions of men who served in the ranks of the Wehrmacht was implicit in how the tribunal interpreted the evidence presented in the High Command case. See Valerie Hébert, "Presiding Judge John Carlton Young and the High Command Case Judgment," *Hitler's Generals on Trial: the Last War Crimes Tribunal at Nuremberg* (Lawrence, 2010), 128–53, esp. 149.

30. On the "clean hands" myth, see among many others, Hannes Heer, *The Discursive Construction of History: Remembering the Wehrmacht's War of Annihilation* (New York, 2008); Manfred Messerschmidt, *Militarismus, Vernichtungskrieg, Geschichtspolitik: zur deutschen Militär- und Rechtsgeschichte* (Paderborn, 2006); *Wehrmacht*, eds. Müller and Volkmann; Klaus Naumann, "The 'Unblemished' Wehrmacht: the Social History of a Myth," in *War of Extermination*, eds. Heer and Naumann, 417–29; Wette, *Wehrmacht*.

31. On the campaign to exonerate soldiers convicted of war crimes, see Frank Buscher, *The U.S. War Crimes Trial Program in Germany* (New York, 1989); Norbert Frei, *Adenauer's Germany and the Nazi Past: The Politics of Amnesty and Integration* (New York, 2002); Hébert, *Hitler's Generals*; Robert Moeller, *War Stories: The Search for a Usable Past in the Federal Republic of Germany* (Berkeley, 2003); Kerstin von Lingen, *Kesselring's Last Battle: War Crimes Trials and Cold War Politics, 1945–1950* (Lawrence, 2009).

32. German Federal Government, letter, to the High Commissioners, no date, in BArch, B 305/141: Auswärtiges Amt, Deutsche Kriegsverurteilte in Landsberg 1949–1952.

33. John J. McCloy, letter to Mr. C.M. Bolds, Office of the Land Commissioner for Bavaria, March 1950, NARA 238, Entry 213: Correspondence and other Records, 1950, Box 2, Folder: Clemency Committee, General File; HICOG Staff Announce-

ment No. 117: "Establishment of Advisory Board on Clemency for War Criminals," July 18, 1950, ibid.; Major Joseph L. Haefele, Headquarters, European Command, Office of the Judge Advocate (JAG), Memorandum on war crimes for Colonel Stanley W. Jones, Acting JAG, August 3, 1950, NARA 549, Entry 2237: Records Relating to Post Trial Activities 1945–1947, Clemency Files 1947–1950, Box 2, Folder: Clemency Files 1949–1950 General Administration.

34  HICOG, Letter to Colonel Damon Gunn, JAG, May 22, 1950, NARA 238 Entry 213: Correspondence and other Records, 1950, Box 2, Folder: Clemency Committee, General File.

35. John Bross, Assistant General Counsel, HICOG, Memorandum for Gerald Fowlie, "Clemency Committee Program," May 18, 1950, ibid.

36. Office of the HICOG, Staff Announcement No. 117: "Establishment of Advisory Board on Clemency for War Criminals," July 18, 1950, ibid.

37. Office of the HICOG, "Landsberg: A Documentary Report," January 31, 1951, NARA 466, Entry 17: Publications Relating to the US's Occupation of Germany, 1945–1953, Displaced Persons thru The Special Projects Program, Box 3, Folder: Landsberg: A Documentary Report January 31, 1951; Gerald Fowlie, Letter to Peck, Moran and Snow, July 24, 1950, NARA 466, Entry 49: General Records, Box 36, Folder W.C. Clemency Board—Operational History; Fowlie, Letter re. board hearings to Peck, Snow, and Moran, July 20, 1950, NARA 238, Entry 213: Correspondence and Other Records, 1950, Box 1, Folder: Research for the Board; Office of the US HICOG, "Rules of Procedure in Clemency Board Hearings," July 22, 1950, NARA 466, Entry 49: General Records, Box 36, Folder: War Crimes Clemency Board—Operational History; Robert Bowie, Memorandum for John McCloy, "War Crimes Clemency Program," August 3, 1950, NARA 238, Entry 213: Correspondence and Other Records, Box 2, Folder: Clemency Committee, General File; Kai Bird, *The Chairman: John J. McCloy—the Making of the American Establishment* (New York, 1992), 336.

38. One sees these themes echoed in the German officer memoir literature of the post-war era as well. See Friedrich Gerstenmeier, "Strategische Erinnerungen—Die Memoiren deutscher Offiziere," in *Vernichtungskrieg: Verbrechen der Wehrmacht 1941–1944*, eds. Hannes Heer and Klaus Naumann (Hamburg, 1995), 620–29; Franz Halder, *Hitler als Feldherr* (Munich, 1949); Heinz Guderian, *Erinnerungen eines Soldaten* (Neckargemünd, 1977, c.1950); Erich von Manstein, *Lost Victories* (Novato, 1982, c.1958).

39  Bundesminister der Justiz, letter for the Clemency Board: "Investigations in the cases of Germans sentenced to confinement in the prison of Landsberg by American Tribunals in Nürnberg," July 28, 1950, NARA 238, Entry 213: Correspondence and Other Records, 1950, Box 2, Folder: General File concerning all cases.

40. "Einleitung," no date, in BArch, Findbuch B305: Zentrale Rechtsschutzstelle; Gerhard Rauschenbach, letter to the Zentrale Rechtsschutzstelle, August 4, 1950, BArch, B305/4775: Zentrale Rechtsschutzstelle, Otto Woehler.

41. Georg von Kuechler, letter to the US HICOG, June 26, 1950, NARA 466, Entry 53: Petitions for Clemency or Parole and Related Records of Persons convicted by the US Military Tribunals at Nuremberg 1947–1957, Box 37, Folder: von Kuechler, Georg, Case No. 12, Folder: #3 Petitions; Niedersächsisches Landvolk, Kreisverband Burgdorf, Petition for an earlier release of former general Otto Woehler, May 30, 1950, NARA 466, Entry 53: Petitions for Clemency or Parole and Related Records of Persons convicted by the US Military Tribunals at Nuremberg 1947–1957, Box 39, Folder: Woehler, Otto, Case No. 12, Folder: #3 Petitions; Otto Bitthorn, statement for the Clemency Board on behalf of Hermann Reinecke, June 12, 1950, NARA 466, Entry 53: Petitions for Clemency or Parole and Related Records of Persons convicted by the US Military Tribunals at Nuremberg 1947–1957, Box 27, Folder: Reinecke, Hermann, Case No. 12, Folder: #2 Petitions.

42. Admiral (Ret.) Gottfried Hansen, Letter to John J. McCloy, December 31, 1950, NARA 466, Entry 1: Classified General Records, 1949–1952, 1951 #1-134, Box 24, Folder: January 1951—D(51) 126 War Crimes.

43. Jonathan B. Rintels (Administration of Justice and Prisons Division), Secret Memorandum with proposals for C.A. McLain, Subject: Clemency for Nuremberg War Crimes Prisoners, December 28, 1949, NARA 466, Entry 48: Security Segregated Records of the Prisons Division, Box 10, Folder: War Crimes Trials—War Crimes Clemency Program.

44. Office of the HICOG, "Landsberg: A Documentary Report"; Bird, *The Chairman*, 361.

45. Robert Bowie, Secret Office Memorandum, Office of the HICOG, for John J. McCloy, "Report of Advisory Board on Clemency for War Criminals," October 31, 1950, NARA 466, Entry 10A: Security-Segregated Records, 1949–1952, Box 28, Folder 321.6: German War Criminals—General.

46. John J. McCloy, letter to Gottfried Hansen, January 22, 1951, NARA 466, Entry 1: Classified General Records, 1949–1952, 1951 #1-134, Box 24, Folder: January 1951—D(51) 126 War Crimes.

47. In a meeting with members of the German parliament who were requesting clemency for convicted war criminals, McCloy "stressed the fact that the honor of the German soldier was in no way involved … The soldiers convicted were not convicted for what they did on the field of battle, but for their guilt in participating and fostering programs designed to further the Nazi racial policies and to liquidate and suppress all political resistance to national socialism whether by the extermination of men, women and children or otherwise." Draft Memorandum: Meeting between Mr. McCloy and Delegation from Bundestag, January 9, 1951, NARA, RG 466, Entry 1, Box 24, Folder: January 1951—D(51) 126 War Crimes.

48. On the role of the rearmament debate in the reviews of the Nuremberg trials, see Buscher, *U.S. War Crimes*; Frei, *Adenauer's Germany*; Hébert, *Hitler's Generals*; Thomas Alan Schwartz, "John J. McCloy and the Landsberg Cases," in *American Policy and Reconstruction of West Germany*, eds. Jeffry M. Diefendorf, Axel Frohn, and Hermann-Josef Rupieper (New York, 1993), 433–54.

49. David Clay Large, *Germans to the Front: West German Rearmament in the Adenauer Era* (Chapel Hill, 1996), 58, 97–98.

50. These three reductions were to shorter prison terms; none were to "time served" as in many other cases. Office of the US HICOG, "Landsberg: A Documentary Report."

51. Office of the US HICOG, "Landsberg: A Documentary Report."

52. B.R. Shute, Office Memo for John J. McCloy: "Analysis of Letters on Landsberg Decisions," March 9, 1951, NARA 466, Entry 1: Classified General Records, 1949–1952, Box 24, Folder: January 1951—D(51) 126 War Crimes

53. Erich Mende, Free Democratic Party, Letter to John J. McCloy, November 27, 1951, BArch, B 305/131: Deutsche Kriegsverurteilte in Landsberg, Allgemeines und Einzelfälle 1949–1952. Emphasis added.

54. Eli Whitney Debevoise, HICOG General Counsel, Report, "Summary Background War Criminal Information," September 6, 1952, NARA 466, Entry 10A: Security-Segregated Records, 1949–1952 (later: 1953–1955), Box 28, Folder: 321.6 German War Criminals—General and Admiral (ret.); Gottfried Hansen, letter to General Ridgway, Commander in Chief, Atlantic Pact Forces, Paris, August 10, 1952 and *Verband Deutscher Soldaten* and *Bund der Berufssoldaten*, "Resolution," September 6, 1952, both NARA 466, Entry 10A: Security-Segregated Records, 1949–1952 (later: 1953–1955), 321.4–321.6, Box 28, Folder: 321.6 German War Criminals—General. Copies of both the letter and the resolution were sent to the HICOG as well.

55. They were imprisoned alongside 318 men sentenced by the US Army-administered Dachau trials.

56. Eli Whitney Debevoise, "Summary Background War Criminal Information," September 6, 1952 and HICOG translation of an editorial by Adelbert Weinstein, "A

Mortgage of a Special Kind," *Frankfurter Allgemeine*, August 18, 1952, NARA 466, Series 10A: Security-Segregated Records, 1949–1952 (later: 1953–1955) 321.4–321.6, Box 28, Folder: 321.6 German War Criminals—General. This editorial mentioned the cases of two High Command case convicts and its representation of them, their circumstances, and their crimes illustrates the style and tone of press coverage that sought to elicit sympathy for the prisoners, and mislead the public about the scope of and personal responsibility for their wartime crimes. For example: "[H]ow is Mr. Donnelly (the new HICOG) going to deal with the case of Colonel General von Salmuth, whose wife had to earn her living as a cloakroom attendant? Salmuth is still imprisoned at Landsberg for offences committed on orders of his Chief of Staff ..., with whose name the orders were signed ... Would it not be best to strike out the term "war criminals" in Germany and open the prisons?"

57. Confidential-Security Political Brief Number 5, "Political Aspects of the War Criminals Question", undated but likely January 1953, NARA 466, Entry 48: Security Segregated Records of the Prisons Division, Box 10, Folder: War Crimes Trial—War Crimes—118, and Buscher, *U.S. War Crimes*, 91.

58. August Fischer, mayor of the town of Kempten and president of the "Association of Returnees, POWs and Family Members of Missing Germans," letter, November 10, 1952, in BArch, B 305/55: Tätigkeit des Gemischten Ausschusses, insb. für die Landsberger Häftlinge. Emphases in original.

59. *Die Neue Zeitung*, August 9–10, 1952, 5. Quoted in Frei, *Adenauer's*, 211.

60. Eli Whitney Debevoise, "Summary Background War Criminal Information," September 6, 1952, NARA 466, Entry 10A: Security-Segregated Records, 1949–1952 (later: 1953–1955) 321.4–321.6, Box 28, Folder: 321.6 German War Criminals—General and Confidential-Security Political Brief Number 5, "Political Aspects of the War Criminals Question."

61. F.G. Hulse, HICOG Office Memo for E. W. Debevoise: "Publication of the Records and Justments [sic]."

62. Eli Whitney Debevoise, "Summary Background War Criminal Information," September 6, 1952, NARA 466, Entry 10A: Security-Segregated Records, 1949–1952 (later: 1953–1955) 321.4–321.6, Box 28, Folder: 321.6 German War Criminals—General.

63. E.W. Debevoise, HICOG Office Memorandum for Assistant High Commissioner Reber, "Publication of the Records and Judgments Made and Given in the Trials conducted at Nuremberg under Control Council Law 10," undated but after July 22, 1952, NARA 466, Entry 48: Security-Segregated Records of the Prisons Division, Box 6, Folder: Control Council Law No. 10 (Exchange of information re. persons transferred pursuant to Control Council Law No. 10 1952). Initial American plans called for the publication in German and English of significant excerpts of all NMT proceedings for public consumption. However, as the debate over imprisoned war criminals intensified, occupation officials became concerned that publication of these records in German would only further inflame tensions between West Germany and the United States. Also, for reasons that are not entirely clear, the American army (which controlled the publication project's budget) withdrew funding of the German edition late in its preparatory stage. On the failed publication project, see Hébert, *Hitler's Generals*, 178–87.

64. Confidential-Security Political Brief Number 5, "Political Aspects of the War Criminals Question," undated but likely January 1953, NARA 466, Entry 48: Security-Segregated Records of the Prisons Division, Box 10, Folder: War Crimes Trial—War Crimes—118.

65. HICOG Office of Political Affairs Memorandum, "The War Criminals Question," December 22, 1952, NARA 466, Entry 10A: Security-Segregated Records, 1949–1952 (later: 1953–1955) 321.4–321.6, Box 28, Folder: 321.6 German War Criminals—General.

66. HICOG Office of Political Affairs, Memorandum for the Department of State, "The War Criminals Question," December 22, 1952, NARA 466, Entry 10A: Security-Segregated Records, 1949–1952, 31.4–321.6, Box 28, Folder: 321.6 German War Criminals—General.

67. Ibid. and James Conant, US HICOG for Germany, Order of Parole and Terms and Conditions of Parole, April 1, 1954, NARA 466, Entry 54: Administrative and Medical Records of Landsberg Prisoners, Box 5, Folder: Hoth, Hermann, Paroled April 7, 1954.

68. James Conant and Charles Bolte, Anordnung betreffend Interimistischer Ge mischter Parole- und Gnadenausschuss, August 31, 1953, in BArch, B 305/53: Zentrale Rechtsschutzstelle, Bereinigung der Kriegsgefangenenproblems 1951–1961, Ge mischte deutsche-alliierte Ausschüße zur Überprüfung der Urteile.

69. Edwin Plitt, American Embassy, Bonn, Foreign Service Despatch to State Department, "History of the Interim Mixed Parole and Clemency Board, with comments for the guidance of future bodies of similar assignment," September 15, 1955, NARA 466, Entry 10A: Security-Segregated Records, 1949–1952, 31.4–321.6, Box 28, Folder: 321.6 War Criminals—Mixed Board 1953–1955.

70. Statements for James Conant, US High Commissioner in support of Hans Reinecke's application for clemency by Hans Gontard, November 20, 1953; Ellen Conrad, November 13, 1953; Bruno Titschenk, November 6, 1953; A. Westhoff, November 11, 1953; Hans Friede, November 6, 1953; Paul Kropf, November 23, 1953; Hans Sommer, November 17, 1953, all NARA, RG 466, Entry 54: Administrative and Medical Records of Landsberg Prisoners, Box 12, Folder: Reinecke, Hermann Paroled October 1, 1954; Heinz Assmann, Secretary General of the State Church Office for Community Service (Innere Mission), declaration of parole sponsor, June 28, 1954 and Annuity Office Hamburg, certificate of pension, June 22, 1954, NARA, RG 466, Entry 54: Administrative and Medical Records of Landsberg Prisoners, Box 12, Folder: Reinecke, Hermann Paroled October 1, 1954; Landesversorgungsamt Niedersachsen Pensionabteilung, certificate of pension, December 11, 1953, BArch, B 305/4523: Zentrale Rechtsschutzstelle, Hermann Hoth; Verband der Heimkehrer, Kriegsgefangenen und Vermissten-Angehörigen, Rundschreiben, October 30, 1953, BArch, B 305/53: Zentrale Rechtsschutzstelle, Bereinigung des Kriegsgefangenenproblems 1951–1961—Gemischte deutsch-alliierte Ausschüsse zur Überprüfung der Urteile.

71. James Conant and Charles Bolte, Anordnung betreffend interimistischer gemischter Parole- und Gnadenausschuss, August 31, 1953, BArch, B 305/53: Zentrale Rechtsschutzstelle, Bereinigung des Kriegsgefangenenproblems 1951–1961, Gemischte deutsch-alliierte Ausschüsse zur Überprüfung der Urteile; E.C. Moore, Landsberg Prison Director, Institutional Record, Walter Warlimont, October 31, 1953, NARA, RG 466, Entry 54: Administrative and Medical Records of Landsberg Prisoners, Box 17, Folder Warlimont, Walter Paroled June 9, 1954; Application for Clemency for Hermann Reinecke, February 1, 1954, NARA, RG 466, Entry 53: Petitions for Clemency or Parole and Related Records of Persons Convicted by the US Military Tribunal at Nuremberg 1947–1957, Box 27, Folder: HRO 12-3 Reinecke, Hermann; E.C. Moore, Landsberg Prison Director, Institutional Record, Hermann Reinecke, August 1, 1954, NARA, RG 466, Entry 54: Administrative and Medical Records of Landsberg Prisoners, Box 12, Folder: Reinecke, Hermann, Paroled October 1, 1954; E.C. Moore, Landsberg Prison Director, Institutional Record, Hermann Hoth, November 25, 1953, NARA 466, Entry 54: Administrative and Medical Records of Landsberg Prisoners, Box 5, Folder: Hoth, Hermann Paroled April 7, 1954; Hermann Hoth, summary of interview with Landsberg Director Moore, October 30, 1953, BArch-MA N 503/86: Unterlagen zur Verteidigung Hoths.

72. American Embassy, Bonn, Foreign Service Despatch to State Department, "War Criminals," August 3, 1955, NARA, RG 466, Entry 10A: Security-Segregated Records, 1953–1955, 321.4–321.6, Box 164, Folder: 321.6 War Criminals—Mixed Board 1953–1955.

73. On early scholarship on Wehrmacht complicity and participation in war crimes, see Volker Berghahn, "NSDAP und 'Geistige Führung' der Wehrmacht," *Vierteljahreshefte für Zeitgeschichte* 17 (1969): 17–21; Jürgen Förster, "Wehrmacht and the War of Extermination against the Soviet Union," *Yad Vashem Studies* 14 (1981): 7–34; Jacobsen, "Kommissarbefehl und Massenexekutionen sowjetische Kriegsgefangener," in Klaus-Jürgen Müller, *Das Heer und Hitler: Armee und nationalsozialistisches Regime 1933–1940* (Stuttgart, 1969); Benjamin Segalowitz, "The Wehrmacht's Guilt," *Yad Vashem Bulletin* 21 (1967): 10–18, Streim, *Die Behandlung sowjetischer Kriegsgefangener*; Streit, *Keine Kameraden*.

74. David Clay Large, *Germans to the Front*, 179, 183, and 190.

75. I refer here to President Heuss's speech on November 30, 1952, on the occasion of the dedication of a memorial to the victims at Bergen-Belsen. For an overview of the West German campaign to free the Landsbergers, see Hébert, "The Debate over Imprisoned Soldiers and the Politics of Punishment, 1949 to 1952," *Hitler's Generals*, 154–87.

76. Detlev Bald, *Die Bundeswehr. Eine kritische Geschichte, 1955–2005* (Munich, 2005), 65f., 97f., 111f.

77. Hannes Heer, "The Difficulty of Ending a War: Reactions to the Exhibition 'War of Extermination: Crimes of the Wehrmacht 1941 to 1944,'" *History Workshop Journal* 46 (1998): 187–203.

78. On the Wehrmacht exhibition, see: *Crimes of War: Guilt and Denial in the Twentieth Century*, eds. Omer Bartov, Atina Grossman, and Mary Nolan (New York, 2002); *The German Army and Genocide: Crimes against War Prisoners, Jews, and other Civilians, 1939–1944*, ed. Hamburg Institute for Social Research (New York, 1999); Heer, "The Difficulty of Ending a War"; Bill Niven, *Facing the Nazi Past: United Germany and the Legacy of the Third Reich* (London, 2002); Omer Bartov, "Professional Soldiers," in *The German Army and Genocide*, 11–14.

79. Taylor, *Final Report*, 100.

CHAPTER 8

# THE POWER OF IMAGES
## REAL AND FICTIONAL ROLES OF ATROCITY FILM FOOTAGE AT NUREMBERG

*Ulrike Weckel*

⚜

The Nuremberg trials are among the very first court proceedings in which film footage was presented as evidence.[1] During the trial of the major war criminals before the International Military Tribunal (IMT), it was only the prosecutors who attempted to make use of the power of images; during the trials before the Nuremberg Military Tribunals (NMT), some defense counsels also deployed the new medium trying to find counter-images that favored their clients. The importance attributed to visual evidence can be recognized in the unorthodox way in which *Schwurgerichtssaal* 600 in Nuremberg's Palace of Justice was reconstructed for the IMT proceedings: in order that the screen be visible from all seats, the bench was relocated from its ordinary place at the front to the right side of the courtroom facing the dock on the left (Figure 8.1). None of the films screened, however, turned out to be decisive for the verdicts, as they could neither prove that individual defendants had committed the crimes for which they were indicted nor that they had not. But, although the legal practitioners at Nuremberg must have been well aware of the juridical weakness of the films they had at hand, they continued to present them. And, as a matter of fact, the films screened in the courtroom, especially the so-called atrocity films, received considerable public attention, at least during the IMT trial. Journalists commented in their reports on the shocking images and their presumed effects on the defendants, several memoirists later mentioned the showing of atrocity films in court, and both documentaries and fictionalized feature films on the Nuremberg trials regularly included atrocity film screenings. In the first part of this contribution, I will reconstruct which films were actually shown at which of the various Nuremberg trials and discuss both the effects that were expected from the atrocity films in particular and the effects commentators believed them to have had. In the second part, I will compare these findings with the invented effects atrocity films have in three quite different filmic representations: an episode of the CBS series *Twentieth Century* from 1958, the TNT miniseries *Nuremberg* from 2000, and the well-known feature film *Judgment at Nuremberg* from 1961. I will argue that these films about the Nuremberg trials are telling primary sources for historians, not although, but exactly because, they depart from the historical reality. The ways in which each of them does this reveals a lot, not only about the film's agenda, but also about wishful thinking regarding the past.

**8.1** View of the courtroom: bench on the right and dock on the left to make room for a screen at the front
*Bundesarchiv, Digitales Bildarchiv, Koblenz, #183-H27798.*

## Films in the Trials

As a rule, spectators take unstaged moving images to be truthful representations of what in fact took place in front of the camera at a certain
moment in the past. Since an event's reproduction as an image is largely
physical and chemical, the human being behind the camera seems to
have hardly any impact on the result no matter how purposefully he or
she might have operated the apparatus.[2] Knowing that most people recognize greater probative force in filmic documentation than in written
or oral eyewitness accounts, every Allied army towards the end of World
War II instructed their cameramen to film as many traces of German
war crimes and crimes against humanity as possible. Soon after the
liberation of Nazi concentration and death camps, parts of this film footage were publicized through newsreels and various compilation films
and, indeed, they did successfully dispel the last doubts among Allied
populations about whether earlier reports of unimaginable mass murder possibly had been exaggerated atrocity propaganda of the sort that
is common in times of war. The broad majority of Germans whom the
Allies confronted with these films in 1945–46 also took the images to be
authentic even if several, pointing at alleged or actual Allied war crimes,
critized the films as "one-sided."[3] However, the reason why Germans
did not question the images' veracity more often than they did was not
only the persuasive power of filmic representation but at least as much
the fact that most had known much more about Nazi crimes than they
were willing to admit in the immediate postwar period. Of course, this
was true to a yet higher degree of those whom the Allies planned to put
on trial at Nuremberg as major war criminals.

Despite the legal weaknesses of such evidence, both the American and
the Soviet prosecution teams at the IMT compiled their own extended
atrocity film from their army's footage shot during the liberation of the
camps (as affidavits at the beginning of both films confirm). Unfortunately, their calculations remain unclear. While the Soviets, who did
not share the Western democracies' ideas of how to conduct the trial,
seem just to have followed the American example in this respect,[4] we
can assume that the American jurists did make some strategic calculation on the possible juridical effect of screening such a film in the courtroom. Yet, it is difficult to understand what those calculations were. In
the first place, presenting Allied armies' footage was inconsistent with
the strategy, announced by chief prosecutor Robert H. Jackson in his
opening address, to convict the defendants, not "on the testimony of
their foes," but on the basis of records that the Germans themselves
had meticulously kept, and preferably ones that bore defendants' sig-
natures.[5] In the second place, the American attorneys must have been
well aware, on the one hand, of their task to prove the individual defendants guilty under the indictment, and, on the other hand, that pictures
shot in liberated camps by American or British army cameramen could

hardly serve this purpose. For, those pictures did not show any of the defendants at the scene of the crime. This was not only because, with few exceptions, Allied cameramen arrived at the camps after the SS personnel had fled but also because hardly any of the 21 major war criminals indicted had ever set a foot into a concentration camp let alone commanded one.

The Nazis had been careful not to record their murders on film. Filming (and still photography) was strictly prohibited both during mass shootings and in the camps. Therefore, the juridically ideal proof of the worst Nazi crimes, showing the perpetrators in the act, does not exist.[6] Nevertheless, in their memories of the trial, some commentators later filled this void. In 1969, the commandant of the Nuremberg prison, Burton C. Andrus, "recalled" seeing the by now iconic photograph from the Stroop Report, documenting the crushing of the Warsaw ghetto uprising, as a scene in the atrocity film of the American prosecution:

> I shall never forget the sight of a little boy of about seven coming out of the ruins with his mother; his arms were raised and he looked bewildered. A few moments later the camera panned down to the boy's body on the ground. He had been shot to death.[7]

In addition to providing the ideal proof that many seem to have dreamt of, such falsely remembered Nazi film recordings of their own crimes fit people's impressions of the Nazi criminals' shamelessness. "The strange thing is that you'd think they would have destroyed some of the most terrible evidence, but they hadn't destroyed a single thing," claimed Sylvia De La Warr, wife of the British prosecutor David Maxwell Fyfe at the time of the trial, in an interview in 1990.[8] Budd Schulberg, who worked on the team gathering film footage for the American prosecution, would later call the "discovery" that the Nazis "so coldbloodedly wanted to record" their crimes the team's "defining moment."[9]

On other occassions, Schulberg told the dramatic story of how, after a persistent search, he finally had found the Nazis' hiding place for this footage only to see them set the most incriminating evidence on fire in the last minute.[10] In light of the restrictions on filming mentioned above, it is clear that the story is too good to be true. The fact is that, instead of documenting mass murder, the Nazi footage that prosecutors at the IMT trial possessed included a three-and-a-half-minute-long fragment of a clandestinely shot eight millimetre film showing abuses in the ghetto of Lviv in 1941,[11] a propaganda film against the Free Masons entitled *Dunkle Mächte*,[12] a short filmic documentation of the destruction of Lidice in retaliation for Heydrich's assassination in 1942,[13] and an excerpt from a newsreel in which one could recognize the defendant Schacht greeting Hitler after the latter's triumphant return from defeated France in June 1940,[14] but the great majority of what the prosecutors had at hand was numerous German newsreels and Leni Riefenstahl's party rally film *Triumph of the Will*. From these last two, the Americans compiled the four-hour-long film *The Nazi Plan*.[15] However, the assessment of whether or not these propagandistic images of what the Nazis themselves viewed as demonstrations of their power and success incriminated the defendants depended on the viewer's perspective. While the American prosecutors regarded *The Nazi Plan* as evidence that the men in the dock had participated "as leaders, organizers, instigators, or accomplices" in "a common plan or conspiracy to commit ... crimes against peace, war crimes, and crimes against humanity,"[16] several of the defendants were observed to enjoy seeing themselves in the times of their former glory.[17]

The Nazi films screened in the courtroom, though, are not the ones most often mentioned in memoirs, scholarly literature, documentaries, and feature films on the IMT trial. These were the atrocity films consisting exclusively of Allied footage shot during the advance of Allied troops and the liberation of the camps. The American prosecution first presented their one-hour-long compilation *Nazi Concentration Camps* on November 29, 1945, the eighth day of the proceedings. Twelve weeks later, on February 19, 1946, the Soviet prosecution screened its equally long *Film Documents of the Atrocities by the German Fascist Invaders*[18] followed by two documentaries on the destruction the Germans had perpetrated in the USSR.[19] On May 7, 1946, during their cross-examination of Funk, the American prosecutors submitted a short film taken in the vaults of the *Reichsbank* in Frankfurt by staff members of the Office of US Chief of Counsel in late August 1945 showing loot, including wedding rings and gold teeth, from concentration camps.[20] In what follows, I am going to focus on *Nazi Concentration Camps* and *Film Documents of the Atrocities by the German Fascist Invaders* and the quite different effects that each had in the courtroom.

The screening of *Nazi Concentrations Camps* did not fit into the American prosecutors' presentation of their case at all. They had taken on the prosecution of Count 1 of the indictment, the defendants' participation in a conspiracy. Thus, the eighth day found Sidney Alderman in the middle of his presentation of evidence about the various German breaches of international treaties. He had just described the staging of Austria's annexation. But, rather than proceeding to his discussion of the campaign against Czechoslovakia as expected, Alderman announced the screening of the atrocity film. "We have had to change our plans somewhat from a strictly logical order," he explained to the court, and Telford Taylor later added in his memoir, "What came next was dictated not by logic but by felt necessity."[21] Why did the American prosecutors screen the film at this strange time? Exactly what necessity did they feel? *Nazi Concentration Camps* had just been completed,[22] and prosecutor Thomas Dodd introduced the film by saying it represented "in brief and unforgettable form an explanation of what the words 'concentration camp' imply." More evidence on the subject of concentration camps

would be offered later, Dodd continued, including evidence that all of
the defendants had known of their existence, that the camps had been
instrumental in their retaining of power, and that some of the organizations also charged in the indictment had been responsible for the
origination, control, and maintenance of the entire concentration camp
system.[23] Given the impressive nature of the pictures from twelve different camps[24], only a few observers wondered about the prosecution's
motivations in showing the film at this point, or showing it at all. They
suspected the American prosecutors had noticed that their long-winded
readings from dry documents had started to bore many of the hundreds
of international journalists who had come to Nuremberg for the opening of the proceedings but, it was thought, would probably leave soon.[25]
Picking up on such contemporaneous considerations, both Lawrence
Douglas and Christian Delage have concluded the American prosecution team primarily wanted to provide something spectacular with their
atrocity film and "reinfuse drama into the proceeding."[26] Though I agree
with them, I also think it is worth looking more closely into precisely
what that spectacle was.

Most of the people gathered in the courtroom on November 29, 1945
had almost certainly already either seen pictures from liberated concentration camps (even if never so many in one film before) or seen
camps in person. Most, therefore, no longer needed an "unforgettable ...
explanation of what the words 'concentration camp' imply." Yet, no one
had ever watched images of the camps and its victims while in the presence of those considered responsible for the crimes, which is to say that
nobody before had been able to observe how these men would respond
to the images.[27] This opportunity created the sensation of November 29.
The appearance of the once so powerful men in the dock already was a
very popular topic among the journalists[28]—all the more since there was
no chance of interviewing the defendants, and it would still be several
weeks before they would be heard in court. Some observers brought
opera glasses or binoculars eager to catch a revealing glimpse of the
defendants' emotions and states of mind. Realizing that the lights would
have to be switched off during the film screening and that the safety
lighting would not suffice for study of the defendants' facial expressions,
the American prosecution team ordered US Army technicians to install
neon tubes in the dock the evening before showing *Nazi Concentration
Camps*.[29] Thus, it does not come as a surprise that the media coverage
of the American atrocity film screening focused more on the defendants
than on the film itself.[30]

My thesis is that this focus upon the defendants' reactions to the
film followed an unuttered, intuitive, common understanding that the
screening of images of Nazi atrocities in the courtroom primarily served
to shame the twenty-one men in the dock publicly. The wish publically
to shame the defendants, all of whom had pleaded "not guilty," might
have been all the stronger as many felt that no legal sentence, no matter

how severe, could fit their crimes. Testing whether the defendants would show any indication of shame was taken to be telling, I believe, for the question of whether they had become monsters or could still be regarded as moral beings. After all, shame is an immediate and barely controllable human reaction to being knowingly observed or exposed violating (or having violated) a norm. Thus, it reliably indicates that the person who exhibits shame knows of the norm he or she has violated and shares it.[31] Whether or not a defendant would reveal shame when being confronted with the atrocity film while hundreds of people watched was legally irrelevant. But, the same was true for the atrocity film itself. It was particularly because *Nazi Concentration Camps* could not prove any individual defendant's involvement in the camp system and, therefore, was free of this juridical burden that it could help answer a question that the court was not to decide but that the unprecedented crimes had raised.[32]

The observers' answers varied, and many observations as well as interpretations of what was observed even contradicted one another. Some commentators reported having seen a certain defendant with an expression of shock, lower his head, close or cover his eyes, or use his handkerchief, behaviors taken as indications of shame, while others claimed that the very same defendant had remained unimpressed or, at least, had tried not to show any emotion whatsoever. Many wanted to detect some tears somewhere, but attributions of them differed as did the answers to the question of whether they could be trusted. Had they perhaps been merely crocodile tears? And, what did it mean when a defendant turned his head away from the screen? Could he no longer stand the shame of such images, was he uninterested, or did he want to demonstrate to the prosecutors that they could not shame him? One reason for so much variation in what was observed, I take it, is that the film ran for an hour and, consequently, different journalists had simply noticed different moments. Moreover, reports varied because reporters had different background information on, and therefore different expectations about, certain defendants, which they used to tell good stories. Finally, the fact that there are no unambiguous outer signs of emotional states permitted much speculation on what defendants felt. Yet, despite these differences, most commentators came to the same conclusion that the public shaming had been successful. With unmistakable satisfaction, nearly all of them reported that the judges had left the courtroom after the screening without a word, skipping even the usual announcement of when the tribunal would reconvene, and then the audience had looked the defendants over in silent contempt. At least some of the defendants, most commentators were sure, finally had realized in this moment how shameful their deeds were.[33]

When the Soviet prosecutors showed their atrocity film nearly three months later, the media coverage was significantly different. The Soviets prosecuted Counts 3 and 4 of the indictment—war crimes and crimes against humanity—insofar as they covered crimes committed in the

East.[34] Their *Film Documents of the Atrocities by the German Fascist Invaders* did not interrupt their presentation of evidence but pictured several of the places and events that already had been mentioned in written documents submitted to the court.[35] Also, the film was only one among many particularly gruesome exhibits that the Soviet prosecutors presented on those days in rapid succession. Unlike in late November, when all media reports centered on the screening of the American atrocity film, now several articles, especially in Western newspapers, did not even mention the Soviet film. Instead they focused on other exhibits, e.g., two bars of soap allegedly produced from human fat,[36] photographs of executions that German soldiers had carried in their breast pockets like talismans or trophies, and the Nazi footage of the levelling of Lidice. In part, this can be explained by the fact that during this time—so many weeks into the prosecutors' presentation and yet still before the long awaited cross-examinations of the defendants—many Western papers had temporarily withdrawn their own correspondents from Nuremberg and instead relied on news agencies' daily press reports. They apparently chose from these whatever sounded most spectacular. With so much to choose from, that was not yet another atrocity film shot, in this case, by Soviet cameramen whom many in the West mistrusted. However, those commentators who followed the proceedings on February 19 from the press gallery all agreed that *Film Documents of the Atrocities by the German Fascist Invaders* exceeded in its horror everything else that had been read, spoken, and shown in the Nuremberg courtroom up to that time. Most described scenes from the film in vivid detail, and several Eastern journalists, following the Soviet prosecutor's line, wrote of the film that it was as if through it the millions of victims had finally appeared in the courtroom as mute witnesses reminding the court of its duty to give them satisfaction.[37] The film's narration identified several of these victims by name, age, and profession, and even if none of the information could be verified, the film thereby personalized the million-fold suffering that the court had been dealing with for weeks. As with *Nazi Concentration Camps* previously, *Film Documents of the Atrocities by the German Fascist Invaders* could not prove any of the defendants' personal guilt for the crimes in question. But this was something the Soviet prosecutors were far less concerned with than their Western colleagues anyway since they took the guilt of all of the defendants for granted.[38] Interestingly, not just Eastern journalists, but also many Western writers, now focused much more on the victims shown on the screen than on the defendants sitting in the dock. Although the neon tubes on the dock's rail had once again been lit, hardly anybody now commented on the defendants' facial expressions or speculated about their moral feelings. When two East German journalists claimed to have discovered fear in the defendants' eyes, they saw it as fear of their certain death sentences and took pleasure in their supposed cowardice and suffering. [39]

When atrocity films were screened once again in some of the NMT trials, neither the strategy of publicly shaming the defendants as a spectacle for observers nor the concept of victims symbolically entering the courtroom to ask for retribution can have played an important role. First of all, far fewer journalists followed these twelve trials, and their reports hardly ever made it onto their newspapers' front pages. Furthermore, the altogether 185 defendants were much less well known both to international and German audiences. Thus, observations of their behavior could not be turned into sensational stories as easily as the reactions that men like Göring, Heß, Frank, von Schirach, or Streicher were alleged to have given away unintentionally. Along with considerably less public attention, prosecution and defense now started to fight over the juridical relevance of film in some of the NMT trials. Allied atrocity films documenting traces of the crimes committed in Nazi death and concentration camps made most sense in Case 4, the trial against the WVHA, the *Wirtschafts- und Verwaltungshauptamt* of the SS, which had managed the KZ system since 1942.[40] In this trial, the prosecutors once again screened *Nazi Concentration Camps* and, in addition, the two Soviet films *Auschwitz* and *Majdanek*,[41] all on the same day, April 12, 1947.[42] In the Doctors' trial (Case 1), only excerpts of *Nazi Concentration Camps* were screened on January 28, 1947, probably those sequences in which either the film's narrator or a witness described some of the medical experiments scientists, doctors, and nurses had carried out in Hadamar, Buchenwald, and Bergen-Belsen. As in the IMT trial, there is no indication that the atrocity films had much impact on the verdicts, but nobody seems to have dared question their relevance.[43] This changed in Cases 8 and 9. When in the trial against the *Rasse- und Siedlungshauptamt* of the SS (RuSHA) the prosecution once again submitted the Nazis' own short filmic documentation of the destruction of Lidice, defense counsel Carl Haensel raised the objection that none of the defendants had had anything to do with this retaliatory measure. Nevertheless, the film was shown in the courtroom on October 29, 1947, but on the next day the presiding judge sustained the objection and declared the film would not be regarded as evidence.[44] In the *Einsatzgruppen* trial, defense counsel Hans Gawlik had immediate success in arguing that the Soviet *Film Documents of the Atrocities by the German Fascist Invaders* had no probative value for the trial.[45] The film was not screened although it did contain footage of various opened mass graves in the Soviet Union, that is to say, traces of mass executions some of which, like the massacre at Babi Yar, had been carried out by *Einsatzgruppen*. During the Ministries trial (Case 11), a longer discussion evolved over the evidentiary value of the footage from August 1945 shot in the vaults of the German central bank in Frankfurt for the IMT trial showing among the booty from death camps that the SS had deposited there gold fillings poured out from a bag bearing the inscription *"Reichsbank,"* a scene that obviously had been staged for the camera. Defendant Emil

Puhl, vice-president of the *Reichsbank* from 1939 to 1945, already had been questioned about this short film as a witness during the IMT trial in May 1946.[46] At that time, the inquiry had centered on the question of who at the bank had known of the nature and origin of the SS's deposits. Now, in the Ministries trial, however, it seems that the defense counsels argued against the validity of the scene of gold fillings stored in the *Reichsbank's* vaults as evidence by pointing out that the emptying of the bag had been arranged by the American film crew.[47]

Interestingly, German propaganda films were presented by both sides in the NMT trials, which underlines the ambiguity of propaganda and its message's dependence on the viewer's point of view. During the I.G. Farben trial (Case 6), the Ministries trial, and the High Command trial (Case 12), prosecutors again used *The Nazi Plan* or parts from it as evidence that defendants had participated in a conspiracy to start aggressive war and commit related crimes.[48] The footage of the proceedings before the People's Court against the conspirators of July 20, 1944, which was shown in the Justice trial (Case 3), the Nazis themselves had not dared to publicize because they feared audiences would be appalled by Freisler's scornful humiliation of the defendants.[49] In the Krupp trial (Case 10), the prosecution presented a film entitled *Krupp Activities* that was, according to the records, a compilation from films found by British armed forces in the Krupp Works at Essen and German newsreels.[50] The footage showed high ranking Nazis visiting some company festivities, which were decorated with swastika flags, and guests making the Hitler salute, and prosecutor Irving Brilliant intended it to document the close ties between Krupp and the Nazi state and that the company was run in the "Nazi spirit." Judge Daly, however, questioned the images' juridical value.[51] Indeed, it seems highly unlikely that a film on a commercial enterprise produced as advertising by the firm itself would reveal anything incriminating about the company and its managers. Presumably, it was exactly this omission of anything critical in such films that gave defense counsels in the I.G. Farben and the Ministries trials the idea to copy the prosecution's use of the power of images. In order to exonerate I.G. Farben manager Wilhelm Rudolf Mann, his attorney showed a film entitled *Gespeicherte Sonnenenergie* (translated both as "Storage of Sun Energy" and "Plenty of Sunshine"), which was owned by Farbenfabriken Bayer, Leverkusen.[52] In favor of Paul Pleiger, director-general of Reichswerke Hermann Göring, who in the Ministries trial was accused among other things of exploitation of forced laborers, the defense counsel presented a film entitled *Building of the Hermann Göring Works* that, to be sure, gave no hint of forced labor. The only film screened by the defense that is still known today is *German Entry into Austria*, a UFA newsreel from 1938. It shows Austrian crowds cheering the German soldiers who march into their towns and enthusiastically welcoming Hitler and other Nazi leaders. The film was presented to exculpate Wilhelm Keppler, who had prepared the annexation from the

German embassy in Vienna. However, it also included a scene in which a frightened, well-dressed Jewish couple rushes into a train station and boards a train marked as going to Warsaw.[53] There is no indication that this sequence with its revealing antisemitic threat and *Schadenfreude* was cut from the newsreel before it was shown in the courtroom.

It is difficult to assess the impact these films had in the Nuremberg trials. Regarding the American atrocity film at the IMT trial, Telford Taylor concluded in hindsight: "The public showing of the film certainly hardened sentiment against the defendants generally, but it contributed little to the determination of their individual guilt."[54] This sounds plausible. In general, the films' weakness as juridical evidence appears not to have reduced their psychological effect. In the course of the NMT trials, consequently, defense counsels embarked on two opposite strategies: some objected to the lack of evidentiary force and tried to prevent the screening of films while others employed films in order to put their clients in a favorable light. However, while prosecutors became increasingly selective and cautious in their use of atrocity films during these trials, this perhaps was caused less by the objections of the defense than by the fact that the images had become less sensational over time.

## Films about the Trials

Since the end of the era of the Nuremberg trials, filmic representations of them, both documentaries and features, once again have regularly assigned a crucial role to an atrocity film screening in the courtroom. In this way, the atrocity films of the immediate postwar period have continued to find new audiences. One relatively early example is *Trial at Nuremberg*, an episode from 1958 of the CBS television series *The Twentieth Century*, which portrays the IMT trial—"the trial of the century" as moderator Walter Cronkite put it—as an absorbing spectacle.[55] In the course of twenty-five minutes, numerous aspects of the trial are illustrated with many images taken exclusively from historical footage and presented in very short cuts. In the style of a news broadcast, the episode attempts to cover the essentials of the trial while at the same time presenting particularly striking moments without paying much attention to the proceedings' chronology. The selection of scenes suggests that the trial centered on the crimes committed in concentration and death camps. With a duration of nearly four minutes, the sequence on the screening of an atrocity film in court is by far the longest of the whole episode. Two things are of particular interest. First, what is portrayed as a single atrocity film is actually a mixture of several films screened at Nuremberg, insinuating that it came close to an ideal proof. Second, the sequence constantly switches between scenes from the fictitious atrocity film and telling close-ups of the defendants, suggesting that the latter are actual responses to the former. However, none of those close-ups could have been taken during the screenings, for it was then too dark.[56] The episode thereby retroactively brings about what journalists reporting on the screening of the American atrocity film scene were so eager to find.

Surprisingly, the episode presents its atrocity film as an initiative of the Soviets. Probably, this tribute was paid to heighten drama: "As the Soviet prosecutor Rudenko bows to the court, agitation flares in the dock," Cronkite states. "'They should be trying the Russians,' the defendants seem to be arguing. Possibly in rebuttal, Rudenko offers in evidence a film of the Nazi justice for conquered peoples, much of it captured German footage. At this tense international moment, however, someone blunders in the projection room. The film comes on upside down."[57]

As viewers, we first see the courtroom, with the white screen in front, darkened. Then, to the sound of a running film projector that lets us assume we are facing the screen in *Schwurgerichtssaal* 600, typical test patterns with Cyrillic letters flicker over the full TV screen, followed by the famous image of Auschwitz prisoners standing behind a barbed wire fence now turned onto their heads.[58] Next, the noise of the running projector stops, and we see and hear Göring and some others in the dock giggle. Though artificially created here, such a mishap and Göring's amusement over it during the Soviets' showing of their *Film Documents of the Atrocities by the German Fascist Invaders* is indeed testified to by prison psychologist Gustave Gilbert. The journalists present on that day, however, seem to have agreed not to make the incident public.[59] The punchline in *Trial at Nuremberg* is that "the laughter subsides as reel after reel of the film compiled by each of the four powers unfolds."[60]

The fictitious atrocity film indistinguishably mixes pictures from both the American and the Soviet films of the camps' liberations as well as scenes from *The Nazi Plan*, the film fragment of a pogrom in Lviv, the documentation of the destruction of Lidice, and some additional material of unclear origin.[61] Thus, viewers of *Trial at Nuremberg* are intended to get the impression that they, like the people in the Nuremberg courtroom in 1945–46, are witnessing crimes recorded in the act and the miserable conditions in the camps during the time of their operation. Cronkite's narration in no way prevents this illusion. For example, the episode's putative atrocity film includes the only existing footage of Himmler visiting a camp—it was a POW camp in Minsk—which the narrator here claims to be a concentration camp, remarking that Himmler paid "special attention to the weak, the sick, the very old." As these words are spoken, the Nazi film of Himmler facing atypically well-fed Soviet prisoners of war behind a barbed wire fence cuts to images from Auschwitz: miserable prisoners in striped uniforms also behind barbed wire, old women in an overcrowded barrack, and young children walking between two fences.[62] This use of the conventions of continuity editing suggests that Himmler inspected all of these sites and that, accordingly, the pictures were shot by German cameramen while in fact all three motifs from Auschwitz were staged by Soviet cameramen after the liberation.

Cronkite's description of the laughter in the dock subsiding as more and more incriminating images appeared on the screen is confirmed by inserted close-ups of individual defendants' faces. He explains the good reasons each of them had to be concerned about certain filmic revelations. From pictures of forced laborers on a freight train, for example, the film switches to an embarrassed looking Sauckel and a thoughtful Speer; nervous Rosenberg and seemingly emotionless Frank are shown while allegedly watching the destruction of the Warsaw ghetto; we see Heß getting sick and leaving the room after witnessing a scene of a pogrom, we are told; and the image of gold fillings spilling out of the bank bag leads to a shot of Funk in the witness stand and the narrator's insinuating remark: "For Dr. Walter Funk, head of the *Reichsbank*, American prosecutor Thomas Dodd has a few questions ..." The episode repeats this editing technique a little later in its portrayal of the judgment. Filming was prohibited when the judges pronounced the sentence to each defendant seperately. The viewers of *Trial at Nuremberg*, however, supposedly watched eleven of the defendants receive the information that they were sentenced to death by hanging. The episode thus conveys the satisfying idea that the International Military Tribunal convicted the twenty-one defendants on the basis of overwhelming evidence that included indisputable visual proofs, which did not fail to impress even the defendants.

Forty-two years later, the TNT mini-series *Nuremberg* employed a different genre: it is a docudrama reenacting the IMT trial in color with professional actors. The only historical footage included in the four-hour-long program is a short, pointed excerpt from *Nazi Concentration Camps* accurately presented as the atrocity film of the American prosecution. In many respects, the series tries to stay close to the historical events. Yet, for analysis it is more interesting to see where it takes its greatest liberties and consider their purposes and effects. In line with the docudrama genre, the mini-series turns the trial into a personalized human interest story. The series builds suspense through its focus on the power struggle between Robert Jackson (Alec Baldwin) and Hermann Göring (Brian Cox). The two antagonists exchange belligerent glances in the courtroom while each prepares himself in his own way for the showdown, Jackson's cross-examination of Göring, which provides the plot with a double turning point. The first round goes to Göring. Jackson is devasted and ready to cable his resignation to President Truman.[63] But then his loving and understanding secretary (Jill Hennessy) restores his self-confidence, and his British colleague Maxwell Fyfe (Christopher Plummer), rather than taking over Göring's interrogation as in the real trial, here advises Jackson—over a cognac—to treat Göring as the villain he is and not as the statesman he pretends still to be. The next day, Jackson triumphs over Göring. One can read this departure from the historical facts as a little restoration of the reputation of the historical chief prosecutor, who indeed handled the cross-examination of Göring quite awkwardly. First and foremost, however, it serves to adjust the complex subject matter to the format of mainstream television entertainment.

More instructive for our understanding of the mini-series' interpretation of the trial and its use of it for educational purposes are the historical inaccuracies that suggest that the IMT trial dealt exclusively with the murder of the European Jews. At no point do viewers learn about the charge of crimes against peace and the attempt in 1945–46 to criminalize wars of aggression. In *Nuremberg*, the American prosecutors—and, since the Soviets are caricatures and the British and French insignificant, only the Americans—present one proof of genocide after another: an affidavit of mass shootings in the Ukraine, survivors of Dachau and Auschwitz testifying on medical experiments and the murder of children, and, finally, the atrocity film *Nazi Concentration Camps*, which here begins with scenes of a gas chamber.[64] Once again, the editing juxtaposes screen images of atrocities and the faces of viewers in the courtroom though these now include judges, secretaries, and interpreters along with the defendants. Accompanying the sound of a running film projector we hear a woman's constant sobs; everybody is shocked and taken by surprise; nobody seems ever to have seen such images before, not even the prosecutors who are presenting the film. *Nuremberg* represents *Nazi Concentration Camps* as inevitably eye-opening. In the mini-series' tendency to tell rather than show, Jackson reveals to his secretary that all of the documents and testimony he had read before had left him perplexed, while the film finally made him understand what had happened. Even supervillain Göring is suddenly less self-assured although he tries to convince his distressed co-defendants that the American prosecutors' film is pure propaganda: anybody could come up with something like that putting together some pictures from here, some pictures from there.[65] The mini-series portrays Göring as the vital, cunning, dangerous Nazi arch criminal.[66] Although Jackson is granted his fictitious triumph over Göring—significantly, by establishing that Göring "ordered" the "Final Solution"[67]—*Nuremberg* maintains its focus on Göring and his power to obstruct American interests. In line with the historical facts, he manages to win the admiration of a naive American prison guard and to escape his hanging by a timely suicide. Less historically, the series attributes to Göring an even greater negative role. As the camera peers into various prison cells, the audience learns that confessions of some of the major war criminals are in the air. Jackson works towards this goal, the psychologist Gilbert softly presses the most likely candidates, and Speer, who is presented as the good, repentant Nazi, assists him by pointing out who the most likely candidates are. But all these attempts fail because Göring, who dominates them all, succeeds in cowing them over and over again. The TV series presumably borrowed the idea of pointing out the remarkable absense of a comprehensive confession during the Nuremberg trials from the cinema classic *Judgment at Nuremberg* of 1961. However, that film handles the issue in a much more sophisticated way.

The feature film *Judgment at Nuremberg*, with its star cast under the direction of Stanley Kramer, was the second adaptation of a script by Abby Mann. In 1959, a television play with the same title became embroiled in public debate because the American Gas Association, one of the sponsors of the famous CBS series *Playhouse 90*, had gotten a technician to black out all utterances of the words 'gas' and 'gas chamber' during the play's live broadcast. Viewers easily could fill in the unmotivated gaps in the dialogue, and, consequently, the association of gas with the Holocaust was not successfully suppressed. However, public attention now focused on censorship, and what the play was about got more or less lost. Mann had written it out of indignation at learning that during the culmination of the Cold War the American Military Tribunals at Nuremberg had conducted the trials against Nazi Germany's political, military, economic, and professional elites with declining insistence and that by the end of the 1950s none of those who had received prison sentences were still confined. Following Telford Taylor's advice, Mann modeled the fictitious trial of his didactic play on the Justice trial.[68] Those defendants had studied law before 1933 and should have defended its rule after the Nazis took power. Instead they had helped to pervert the law by legalizing state terror. They least of all Nuremberg defendants could claim that they had not been able to tell right from wrong.

The Justice trial served as a source of inspiration for *Judgment at Nuremberg*, but the film does not pretend to be its realistic reenactment even if the courtroom constructed in a Hollywood film studio was made to resemble *Schwurgerichtssaal* 600.[69] Mann too took several liberties with the historical events in order to adjust the trial to the rules of filmic story telling; for example, he reduced the number of defendants from 16 to a distinctive four, and he invented dramatic examinations of witnesses that never took place. *Judgment at Nuremberg*—like the CBS episode before it and the TNT mini-series four decades later—presents its own atrocity film that mixes scenes from both the American and the Soviet IMT films, and it switches between this film and faces of its audience in the courtroom.[70] However, two specific departures from the historical Justice trial allow for much more than captivating drama. These inventions permit a morally preferable picture of the Nuremberg trials to evolve, a picture that—this paper contends—does not so much assuage viewers as point at the ethical deficiencies in the past.

The first of these two departures from reality is the delay of the Justice trial to 1948, which allows for the inclusion of the Cold War's escalation. In *Judgment at Nuremberg*, the Soviet blockade of Berlin prompts the US government to exert considerable pressure upon the

fictitious presiding judge, Dan Haywood (Spencer Tracy), not to upset
the German people, whose support it now needs, by rendering a harsh
judgment on "their leaders." Given that American leniency toward Nazi
crimes induced by the Cold War had motivated Mann to write his play,
it is all the more remarkable that Haywood withstands these attempts
at political influence and sentences all four defendants to life imprisonment. Produced after the end of the McCarthy era, *Judgment at Nuremberg* celebrates an independent judiciary.[71] Still, historical reality comes
into play in the form of a wager German defense counsel Hans Rolfe
(Maximilian Schell) offers Haywood: in five years, Rolfe predicts, the
men Haywood sentenced to life imprisonment will be free.[72] Haywood
declares that he does not make wagers, though he grants the German
attorney that what he suggests may very well happen: "It is logical in
view of the times in which we live." Yet, he adds, "But to be logical is
not to be right." The film concludes with the following insert: "The
Nuremberg trials held in the American zone ended July 14, 1949. There
were ninety-nine defendants sentenced to prison terms. Not one is still
serving his sentence."[73]

Even more remarkable is the film's second crucial departure from
historical reality: one of the four defendants, Emil Janning (Burt Lan-
caster), makes a full confession to the court. This is dramatically staged.
Janning, one of the authors of Germany's democratic constitution of
1919, has served the Nazi regime as minister of justice for some time
and has signed various verdicts that led to the deaths of the convicted.
By keeping silent in court from the first moment, he demonstrates that
he does not recognize the American military tribunal's authority to try
him. His defense counsel, Rolfe, zealously portrays him as a patriot who
remained at his post continuing to serve his fatherland in bad times and
preventing worse from happening. To make Janning's verdicts appear
justified, the defense counsel mercilessly interrogates two of those formerly convicted. In the case of baker's helper Rudolf Petersen (Mont-
gomery Clift), Rolfe tries to show that the ruling in favor of Petersen's
forced sterilization was not based on the fact that he was a Communist
but that he was feeble-minded.[74] And in re-examining a case of supposed
"race defilement" (*"Rassenschande"*), he sets out to substantiate that
the relationship between the 65-year-old Jew Lehmann Feldenstein
and the 16-year-old Gentile Irene Wallner had been, indeed, a sexual
one—as if such a proof would show that Feldenstein's death sentence
was not juridical murder. As Rolfe presses the adult Irene Wallner (Judy
Garland) with more and more insolent allegations, Janning suddenly
stands up and for the first time speaks in the courtroom. "Herr Rolfe,"
he sternly rebukes his defense counsel, "are we going to do this again?"

Now Janning wants to make a statement. Although he pleads for
leniency toward a humiliated German people who had followed Hitler
in the hope that he would restore national greatness, Janning insists
that—contrary to what Rolfe had tried to make the court believe—

Germans in the Third Reich knew very well of the disfranchisement and persecution of those considered political or racial enemies. The existence of concentration camps was no secret. Janning accuses his three co-defendants—stereotypes of a conservative die-hard, an anxious opportunist, and a fanatical true believer—of corruption, callousness, and wickedness and himself of being the worst of all for the reason that he knew what kind of people they were and still went along with them. Out of his misunderstanding of the love of country he had not protested against injustice and had played an active part in a criminal regime. Hanno Loewy has argued that, as a coutroom drama, *Judgment at Nuremberg* needs this invented confession to reach closure: the defendant returns to the morality shared by his audience.[75] Loewy clearly has a point in referring to the conventions of the genre. But, the wishful invention of a confession is historically significant as well. Many people certainly had hoped to hear words of remorse from the defendants at Nuremberg—however unrealistic (for various reasons) this might have been. Janning's unusual statement in the feature film can remind viewers of how such relentless self-criticism was missing in the real Nuremberg courtrooms.[76] Juridically knowledgable viewers can discover even more in Janning's confession. His admission of having been aware of the immoral and illegal nature of his deeds confirms that calling him to justice is not applying laws *ex post facto*.

The atrocity film presented to the court by prosecutor Tad Lawson (Richard Widmark) might have contributed to Janning's decision to finally make his statement.[77] However, it is the way that Rolfe conducts his interrogations, reminiscent of Nazi show trials, and not the earlier film screening that triggers Janning's intervention and induces him to confess his guilt. The atrocity film does not appear as a "wonder weapon."[78] On the contrary, *Judgment at Nuremberg* uses it to introduce its viewers to various German strategies for immunizing themselves against an Allied atrocity film.

Firstly, defendant Werner Lampe takes refuge in disbelief. During the lunch recess in the prison, he asserts that what the film claimed was simply impossible. Nobody could kill millions of people. Since his co-defendants maintain an embarrassed silence, Lampe turns to fellow prisoner Oswald Pohl for support. As someone who ran those concentration camps, he should tell the others that it was impossible. Pohl, with a full mouth and not the slightest sign of emotion, states that it was possible. It only depended on the facilities, he explains. "It is not the killing that is the problem. It's the disposing of the bodies."[79] Lampe, with a whiny expression on his face, is forced to abandon his professed disbelief.

The second immunizing strategy is represented by defense counsel Rolfe. We can see him biting his lips during the screening. When, on the next morning, he addresses the court, it first seems as if the passionate defender of the German people in general and Janning in particular has had some second thoughts. He is calmer than ususal, his voice is lower, and his speech is halting when he talks about the "shocking films," the "devastating films" that the prosecutor had shown the day before. "As a German," Rolfe states, "I feel ashamed that such things could have taken place in my country." Never could there be a justification for them, he goes on, "not in generations, not in centuries." At this point, starting with a "but," his posture stiffens, Rolfe raises his voice, and he glances challengingly around the courtroom: "But it was wrong," he insists, "indecent, and terribly unfair of the prosecution to show such films in this case, in this court, at this time, against these defendants." Now yelling, he claims that atrocity films can in no way prove that the German people as a whole had been aware of the Nazi crimes and therefore was responsible for them. "None of us," Rolfe shouts self-confidently, pointing at the dock, "knew what was happening in the places shown on these films." It is this statement that Janning later contradicts in his confession.

Before Janning rejects the notorious German contention not to have known, Mrs Bertholt (Marlene Dietrich) asserts it in a different tone and manner and under conditions more apt to impress judge Haywood. Mrs Bertholt is an elegant, cultivated, handsome woman, the widow of a German general who was hanged after another military tribunal had found him guilty on all charges.[80] Haywood has been assigned accommodations in her commandeered mansion and, as a humble man and a hick from Maine, feels quite uncomfortable about it. He has taken an immediate liking to the worldly widow who recommends tasty German wines in fluent English; invites him to a piano concert given by an exilee from Nazi Germany whom she and her "rebuilding committee" had persuaded to return; and tries to convince the judge in their conversations that not all Germans were monsters, as she puts it. In contrast to Lampe's and Rolfe's immunizing strategies against the atrocity film, which are openly rejected in the course of the film, Mrs Bertholt's attitude is undermined by subtle filmic means that can easily be overlooked.

The editing technique of cutting back and forth between images of the atrocity film and the faces of characters who supposedly are watching them in the courtroom has the consequence that the viewers in *Judgment at Nuremberg* are shown more images of the camps than is *Judgment at Nuremberg*'s audience. One of the images that the audience does not see but only hears described by prosecutor Lawson—who, now a sworn witness as one of the liberators of various concentration camps, narrates the atrocity film to the court—is the infamous Buchenwald lampshade allegedly made of human skin, put on display for forced German visitors (Figure 8.2). Since the audience of *Judgment at Nuremberg* does not get to see the image of this lampshade, they are all the more free to correlate it with the small kitschy table lamp that, shortly afterwards, they see judge Haywood thoughtfully sitting in front of. He is in a folksy restaurant dimly lit by such lamps on all of the tables. A heavy tenor is singing a sentimental German folk-song, and Haywood is waiting for Mrs. Bertholt, who soon appears and sits down opposite him.

The lamp stands between them (Figure 8.3). Haywood has no appetite. Mrs Bertholt notices immediately that he is more serious and reserved than usual, and she has her guess as to why. She has been told that they saw "those pictures" in court this day, "Colonel Lawson's favorite pictures." "He drags them out at any pretext, doesn't he?," she asks as bitterly as rhetorically. Lawson has prosecuted her husband; she therefore hates him and speaks disparagingly of the atrocity film as his "private chamber of horrors." Haywood does not believe that all Germans knew of "those things," does he? He could not possibly think that all Germans "wanted to murder women and children!" While Mrs Bertholt insistently assures him that neither she and her husband nor most Germans knew of the Nazi crimes, the band in the restaurant switches to a more spirited song. In reply to Haywood's remark that nobody in the whole country seems to have known anything, Mrs Bertholt speaks of "things" that "happened on both sides." As she now explains, when her request that her husband be executed in the military tradition by firing squad was rejected, she took to drink and began to hate all Americans. But one can not live with hate, she tells Haywood: "We have to forget if we are to go on living." The audience does not hear what Haywood thinks of Mrs Bertholt's suggestion. It sees only his doubtful face and then—as the camera pans across the restaurant—the German patrons surrounding Haywood and Mrs Bertholt who, having heartily joined in the band's song, *schunkeln* and bang their beer mugs on the tables to the rhythm of the music. The camera zooms in on one of these tables: the little lamp and its lampshade quake with each beat (Figure 8.4). The

**8.2** Film still from the movie *Judgment at Nuremberg* (1961)
*MGM Media Licensing, Metro-Goldwyn-Mayer Studios, Los Angeles*

**8.3** Film still from the movie *Judgment at Nuremberg* (1961)
*MGM Media Licensing, Metro-Goldwyn-Mayer Studios, Los Angeles*

**8.4** Film still from the movie *Judgment at Nuremberg* (1961)
*MGM Media Licensing, Metro-Goldwyn-Mayer Studios, Los Angeles*

policy of forgetting that Mrs Bertholt recommends is already very well established in Germany, undisturbed by the ongoing Nuremberg trials and the reminders of Nazi atrocities.

## Conclusion

From the beginning, high hopes have centered on the power of images of Nazi atrocities. Visual evidence of these unprecedented crimes should achieve what written and oral eyewitness accounts and experts' studies have often failed to achieve. This expectation led to the orders for military cameramen to document traces of Nazi crimes; it probably prompted the production of films to be shown in the Nuremberg trials despite their questionable juridical value; it convinced observers of the trials that defendants, in their confrontation with these atrocity films, had felt shame although there were no unambiguous outer indications for that; and it induced filmmakers to grant atrocity films a prominent place in the stories their films tell about the Nuremberg trials. And it is true that filmic images of the conditions the liberators encountered in Nazi concentration and death camps have impressed millions of people. Yet, however powerful in their effects, atrocity films are no "wonder weapon." For juridical purposes, they do not provide the ideal proof as they do not show any defendant in the act of comitting one of the crimes of which he was indicted of. More importantly, atrocity films, like written documents, have their limits in reaching and convincing their audiences, in changing people and changing the world. Their screenings in and outside of courtrooms have not altered the fact that most perpetrators showed little or no remorse, not to mention empathy with their victims; that people who wanted to doubt Nazi crimes have continued to do so; and that despite the many who in all sincerity aver that such crimes should "never again" be allowed to happen subsequent genocides have not been prevented.

Filmic representations of atrocity film screenings in the Nuremberg courtrooms often "repair" some of these limitations. What is presented as a film in a film regularly includes historical footage of different origins frequently edited so that viewers get the impression that the Nazis in fact filmed their crimes and their miserable victims. This false impression is made all the easier, for it fits people's ideas of Nazi shamelessness. In addition, many films about Nuremberg remove the historical difficulties courtroom observers had in glimpsing defendants' reactions to the atrocity films and in deciphering what they did glimpse. Instead of ambiguous gestures and cryptic expressions of twenty-one men in the dimly lit dock, viewers are shown carefully selected, telling close-ups of individual faces accompanied by unequivocal narration. When thusly presented, atrocity films not only constitute ideal proof of the worst Nazi crimes but also serve as a litmus test for whether those responsible for the crimes feel shame for their deeds when publicly exposed. Through such editing technique some films, like the *Twentieth Century* episode of 1958, insinuate that the filmic evidence in particular was so overwhelming that at least some of the defendants were unable to immunize themselves against its power. Nuremberg feature films can be even more inventive in showing effects of an atrocity film screening. Both the cinematic *Judgment at Nuremberg* and the television docudrama *Nuremberg* depict expressive reactions. However, while in the mini-series of 2000 Jackson and his secretary talk about their responses and thereby explain them to the audience, movie-goers of 1961 were left to speculate about the atrocity film's effects on the protagonist Janning. He seems moved—but what are his feelings and thoughts? The actual uncertainty of how to read defendants' faces does not get resolved at this point, and this sustains suspense until the film's climax of Janning's confession.

At the same time, *Judgment at Nuremberg* depicts three different strategies to avoid, divert, or reduce the impact of atrocity films, all of which were in fact common among Germans in the immediate postwar period. Lampe's outright denial is the least sustainable strategy since the mass murderers themselves did not deny the mass murder as such but only their personal responsibility for it. The attitudes acted out by Rolfe and Mrs Berthold appear to have been more effective. Rolfe declares the American prosecutor's use of the film to be an unjust accusation of collective guilt.[81] Most Germans, he claims, knew nothing about the acts of a few criminals and therefore cannot be accused of having acquiesed to them. Mrs Berthold even goes a step further. By pointing at Allied war crimes, she denies the Allies the right to call any Germans to account. By this argument—a clearly invalid *tu quoque*—she strives to rid her plea for a policy of forgiving and forgetting of its German self-servingness and, thus, make such a policy appear as a wise compromise to end a period of evenly balanced hardships.

In the last decades, several scholars have critized Allied atrocity films, including *Nazi Concentration Camps* and *Film Documents of the Atrocities by the German Fascist Invaders*, for not emphasizing the murder of the European Jews as the Nazis' central crime.[82] Here is not the place to discuss filmmakers' different possible motivations for primarily identifying victims as political opponents to Nazism and listing them by their many nationalities. Still, one can say that it would be rash to suspect all of these decisions as being rooted in antisemitism. In addition, studies of audience reception of atrocity films show, at least for German viewers, that many took the portrayed victims to be Jewish even if the film's narration made no mention of Jews.[83] Subsequent filmmakers also have understood the victims shown in the early atrocity films primarily to be Jews and have used the footage accordingly in their films on Nuremberg. The genocide against European Jews figures prominently in narration or characters' comments or both. These Nuremberg films make the old images of liberated camps known once again, this time to audiences that, with the wave of Holocaust films since the 1980s, have a better idea of the victimization of Jews than they have of other victim groups. Because of documentary and feature films of the Nuremberg trials, the focus of these trials has considerably shifted in the public's perception. The charge of conspiracy and the attempt to criminalize aggressive war are mostly forgotten, and many believe that the Nuremberg processes were the first Holocaust trials.[84] The power of atrocity images seems to have played a leading role in this shift.

# Notes

1. Prior to the IMT trial, atrocity footage was shown in the Belsen Trial at Lüneburg on September 20 and October 15, 1945. Since several defendants had worked in Auschwitz before coming to Bergen-Belsen, the prosecutors screened both British footage from the liberation of Belsen and the Soviet film *Auschwitz. Trial of Josef Kramer and Forty-Four Others: The Belsen Trial*, ed. Raymond Phillips (London, 1949), 56f., 231.

2. See, e.g., the seminal works on filmic realism by André Bazin, *What is Cinema?* trans. Timothy Barnard (Montreal, 2009), esp. 3–20; Siegfried Kracauer, *Theory of Film: The Redemption of Physical Reality* (New York, 1960).

3. See Ulrike Weckel, *Beschämende Bilder. Deutsche Reaktionen auf alliierte Dokumentarfilme über befreite Konzentrationslager* (Stuttgart, 2012).

4. A memo from Andrej Vyshinskij to I.G. Bolshakov, chairman of the SNK's Committee for Cinematography, from October 23, 1945, suggests this. Archives of the Foreign Office of the Russian Federation (AVP RF), Fond 07, Opis 13, Papka 41, Delo 9, List 26–27. I thank Claudia Weber for this information,

5. International Military Tribunal (Blue Series), II, 130.

6. The only filmic exception is a two-minute-long sequence showing a mass execution in Liepaja, Latvia, in June 1941. The German NCO, who as an onlooker clandestinely shot this scene, hid the footage to prevent its confiscation. It became known only after it was handed over to Yad Vashem in 1974. The filming in both Theresienstadt and Westerbork was arranged to produce propaganda films intended to deceive audiences about the nature of those camps. See Joshua Hirsch, "Posttraumatic Cinema and the Holocaust Documentary," *Film & History* 32 (2002): 9–21, here 9; Karel Margry, "Das Konzentrationslager als Idylle: *'Theresienstadt'—Ein Dokumentarfilm aus dem jüdischen Siedlungsgebiet,*" in *Auschwitz. Geschichte, Rezeption und Wirkung*, ed. Fritz Bauer Institut (Frankfurt a.M./New York, 1996), 319–52.

7. Burton C. Andrus, *I Was the Nuremberg Jailer* (New York, 1969), 134f. The Stroop Report was entered as an exhibit on December 14, 1945, and some photographs were projected on the screen. Neither film footage of the events nor a second photograph of the boy showing him dead exists. Presumably, the boy survived. See Richard Raskin, *A Child at Gunpoint: A Case Study in the Life of a Photo* (Aarhus, 2004).

8. Hilary Gaskin, *Eyewitnesses at Nuremberg* (London, 1990), 99.

9. Quoted in Gene Warner, "Presenting *Nazi Plan* on Film," *Buffalo News*, January 27, 2004.

10. Schulberg relates this story, e.g., in Christian Delage's documentary *Nuremberg— Les nazis face à leurs crimes* of 2006.

11. The film was screened on December 13, 1945 as Document 3052-PS. IMT, III, 536f., and XXXI, 520–24; it is accessible online via the film collection of the USHMM, RG-60.0441, Tape 402.

12. Screened by the French prosecution on February 5, 1946 as Document RF-1152. IMT, VII, 14–22.

13. Screened by the Soviet prosecution on February 22, 1946 as Document USSR-401. IMT, VIII, 122.

14. Screened during the cross-examination of Schacht on May 3, 1946 as Document US-835. IMT, XIII, 31f.

15. Screened on December 11, 1945 as Document 3054-PS. IMT, III, 400–02 and XXXI, 524–636; the list of newsreels used can be found in the Donovan Collection at the Law Library of Cornell University: Newsreels from 1933 to 1944 Showing How the Nazis Prepared, Started and Prolonged the Second World War, no date, DNTC, Vol II, section 6.19.

16. Quotation from Count 1 of the indictment, IMT, I, 29.

17. The observations of many in the courtroom are confirmed by the reports of both prison psychologist Gilbert and defense counsel von der Lippe. Gaskin, *Eyewitnesses*, 79–81, 91–93; Gustave M. Gilbert, *Nuremberg Diary* (New York, 1947), 64–67; Viktor Freiherr von der Lippe, *Nürnberger Tagebuchnotizen November 1945 bis Oktober 1946* (Frankfurt a.M., 1951), 61.

18. Both atrocity films are included in the DVD-copy of Delage's film *Nuremberg*.

19. *The Destruction of Art and Museums of National Culture Perpetrated by the Germany on the Territory of the U.S.S.R.* was screened on February 21, 1946 as Document USSR-98, *Destruction Perpetrated by Germans on the Territories of the Soviet Union*, on the following day as Document USSR-401. IMT, VIII, 100, 124.

20. IMT, XIII, 166–69, 172.

21. IMT, II, 431; Telford Taylor, *The Anatomy of the Nuremberg Trials: A Personal Memoir* (New York, 1992), 186.

22. Or not even that. The part of the film on Mauthausen remained without narration. The production seems to have been rushed.

23. IMT, II, 431f.

24. These were Thekla, near Leipzig; Penig; Ohrdruf; Hadamar; Breendonck; Ahlem, near Hannover; Arnstadt; Nordhausen; Mauthausen; Buchenwald; Dachau and Bergen-Belsen in that order.

25. In the gallery, 240 seats were reserved for the international press; more journalists could follow the proceedings via loudspeakers in a large adjoining room. In peak periods, e.g., during the prosecutors' opening addresses, the cross-examination of Göring, and the defendants' final statements, almost 400 journalists came to Nuremberg. *Der Nürnberger Lernprozess. Von Kriegsverbrechern und Starreportern*, ed. Steffen Radlmaier (Frankfurt a.M., 2001), 12f.

26. Delage speaks of a psycho-dramatic dimension or "dimension 'vivante'." Christian Delage, "L'Image Comme Preuve. L'Expérience du Procès de Nuremberg," *Vingtième Siècle. Revue d'Historie* 72 (2001), 63–78, here 63; Lawrence Douglas, *The Memory of Judgment. Making Law and History in the Trials of the Holocaust* (New Haven/London, 2001), 21. The article by Yvonne Kozlovsky-Golan can be neglected since it includes too many errors and unfounded speculations. Yvonne Kozlovsky-Golan, "The Shaping of the Holocaust Visual Conscience by the Nuremberg Trials. Birth of the Holocaust in Hollywood-Style Motion Pictures: The Impact of the Movie *Nazi Concentration Camps*," *Search and Research* 9 (2006): 7–50.

27. One exception is to be noted here. It was never mentioned during the trial that this was not the first time that most of the defendants had seen an atrocity film. According to press reports, interrogators had confronted them with such footage in July 1945 in the prison of Mondorf-les-Bains. Yet, the literature on the interrogations provides no information about the responses of any of the later defendants at Nuremberg.

28. See Anneke de Rudder, "'Ein Prozess der Männer'. Geschlechterbilder in der Berichterstattung zum Nürnberger Hauptkriegsverbrecherprozess 1945/46," in *"Bestien" und "Befehlsempfänger". Frauen und Männer in NS-Prozessen nach 1945*, eds. Ulrike Weckel and Edgar Wolfrum (Göttingen 2003), 38–65.

29. Budd Schulberg's brother Stuart, who in 1948 produced the film *Nuremberg—Its Lesson for Today*, described the installation at length saying that the prosecution team had suddenly realized that without additional light "we were to be robbed of

the most interesting and even valuable ... experience." Whether or not Schulberg's anecdotal report is true in all of its details, his phrasing confirms that the prosecution understood the defendants' reactions to be an important part of their screening. Stuart Schulberg, "An Eyewitness Reports," *Hollywood Quarterly* 2 (1947): 412–14, quote on p. 413.

30. Correspondents probably assumed that their audiences too had already seen visual evidence of Nazi atrocities.
31. On shame and shaming see Hilge Landweer's instructive study *Scham und Macht. Phänomenologische Untersuchungen zur Sozialität eines Gefühls* (Tübingen, 1999).
32. Thus, I do not share Lawrence Douglas' reproach of the commentators that they asked their readers "to see the film voyeuristically through the eyes of ... those allegedly responsible for the very atrocities captured on film." Douglas, *Memory*, 26.
33. For more details, see Weckel, *Beschämende Bilder*, 200–26.
34. Previously, the French prosecutors had presented these two charges in regard to the West.
35. The Soviet film shows 38 places where the Red Army, during the counter-offensive that began in winter 1941, had come across traces of German crimes. Only a third of these places were German POW, work, concentration, or death camps or prisons, Majdanek and Auschwitz among them. All of the other places were villages and towns in the Soviet Union, and the victims therefore were civilian "Soviet citizens" as the narration repeatedly points out. The sequences on Majdanek and Auschwitz are the longest; together they amount to 15 minutes. However, the two sequences are placed neither at the beginning nor at the end of the film. They occur in a long chronology of discoveries as yet another variation of Nazi annihilation policies.
36. On the origins of these exhibits, see Joachim Neander, "The Danzig Soap Case: Facts and Legends around 'Professor Spanner' and the Danzig Anatomic Institute 1944–1945," *German Studies Review* 29 (2006): 63–86.
37. See, e.g., *Pravda*-correspondent Boris Polewoi later in his memoir or the two East German special correspondents at the IMT trial in their articles: Boris Polewoi, *Nürnberger Tagebuch,* 4th edn (Berlin, 1971), 140; Max Keilson, "Ein Film rollt ab in Nürnberg," *Deutsche Volkszeitung*, February 21, 1946; Bernt von Kügelgen, "Menschenhaut," *Berliner Zeitung*, February 22, 1946.
38. This becomes obvious in the Soviet prosecutors' condemning labels of the defendants as "German fascist criminals," "Hitlerite hangmen," etc. throughout the trial. Several anecdotes also illustrate their attitude. Telford Taylor, for example, reports that during a dinner in November 1945, Andrey Vyshinsky, who was responsible for the Soviet preparations for the IMT trial, proposed a toast to the defendants: "May their paths lead straight from the courthouse to the grave." Since most drank before the translation was completed, Western lawyers were troubled when they learned what they had drunk to. Taylor, *Anatomy*, 211; see also Francis Biddle, *In Brief Authority* (Garden City, 1962), 428.
39. Keilson, "Film rollt ab"; von Kügelgen, "Menschenhaut".
40. See Jan Erik Schulte's chapter in this volume.
41. In my view, screening these two films, each about 20 minutes long, instead of the 15 minutes on Auschwitz and Majdanek included in *Film Documents of the Atrocities by the German Fascist Invaders* is all the more remarkable, for in the film produced for the IMT trial the narration is quite matter-of-fact, while both *Auschwitz* and *Majdanek* are accompanied by propagandistic narration as well as dramatic music.
42. All of this information on the various films' screenings is according to the memos gathered in the folder "Films", NARA RG 238, OCCWC, Entry 145, Box 2. I wish to thank Alexa Stiller who found this folder in the archives and kindly provided me with copies.
43. According to one of the archived lists of films presented during the NMT trials, which is dated November 4, 1948, two new short films, presumably containing Allied footage, were screened during the Hostages trial (Case 7): *From the Tragedy of our*

*Country*, submitted by the Greek government, and *Finnmark*, submitted by the Norwegian government. Ibid.

44. Minutes of the RuSHA Trial, NARA RG 260, Entry 195, Box 141. Once again I thank Alexa Stiller for this information.

45. Einsatzgruppen Trial Transcript, October 6, 1947, NARA, M-895, Einsatzgruppen Trial Transcript, Roll 2, 257–64. I thank Hilary Earl for this information.

46. See IMT, XIV, 41–61.

47. So far, researchers of the Ministries trial have not commented on this detail. In the preface to a new edition of IMT defendant Hans Fritzsche's memoir, the right-wing publisher gloats over the German attorneys' revelation in "one of the later Nuremberg trials" that the scene with "sacks full of jewellry and dental gold" had been staged. Hildegard Springer, *Vor dem Tribunal der Sieger. Gesetzlose Justiz in Nürnberg* (Preußisch Oldendorf, 1981), 19.

48. In the I.G. Farben trial, the film was presented as exhibit 824 on October 7, 1947, in the Ministries trial as exhibit 376 on January 26, 1948, and in the High Command trial as exhibit 1232 on March 2, 1948. For the Ministries trial, the archival material also mentions a film entitled *Nazi Rise and Power* presented as exhibit 1435 on March 10, 1948. The film's title suggests that it was an excerpt from *The Nazi Plan* and not, as noted, from *Nazi Concentration Camps*, which did not include any footage of the Nazis' rise to power.

49. The film was presented on March 29, 1947 as exhibit 192.

50. The film was presented on February 7, 1948 as exhibit 928, Doc. No. NIK-13440.

51. Case 10, Protokoll, 7. and 9.2.1948, Zentrum für Antisemitismusforschung, Berlin, Prot. (d), 3489–92. I thank Kim C. Priemel for this information.

52. Bayer's ownership is documented by the fact that the court returned the film to the firm. B. Mandellaub to I.G. Farben Control Offices, March 31, 1949, NARA, RG 238, OCCWC, Entry 145, Box 2, Folder Films. The film was presented on March 31, 1948 as Mann Exhibit 1.

53. See UFA Anschluss footage, Story RG-60.0741, Tape 500, USHMM, Film and Video Archive.

54. Taylor, *Anatomy*, 187.

55. *The Twentieth Century: Trial at Nuremberg*, March 2, 1958; all quotations from the narration are my own transcriptions.

56. An additional indication is that none of the defendants turns his face to his left, where the screen was.

57. General Roman Andreyevich Rudenko was the Soviet Chief Prosecutor at the IMT.

58. The image became iconic because it suggests that the survivors were desparately watching for their liberators. Of course, these shots grouping survivors behind barbed wire fences as impressively as possible were staged after the liberation. See Detlef Hoffmann, "Menschen hinter Stacheldraht," in *Representations of Auschwitz. 50 Years of Photographs, Paintings, and Graphics*, ed. Yasmin Doosry (Oświęcim, 1995), 87–94.

59. "Goering is tickled at the false start, as the film starts upside down and has to be readjusted; he covers his laugh with his hand, but looks around to see if the audience is laughing ... The film starts again." Gilbert, *Nuremberg Diary*, 161.

60. Several journalists used the same punchline in their coverage of November 29, 1945. Referring to Göring's and other defendants' pleasure during the morning session over the cunningly orchestrated annexation of Austria, they remarked that with *Nazi Concentration Camps* in the afternoon, the defendants' good mood was spoiled (in German: *das Lachen sei ihnen vergangen*).

61. It is well possible that the origin was often not even clear to the filmmakers. Much of the footage for the whole episode is obviously taken from Stuart Schulberg's film *Nuremberg—Its Lesson for Today* from 1948, which already undistinguishably mixes Nazi and Allied footage. Here one finds a filmed photograph of a car whose exhaust is piped into a house in order to gas people. The image documents early experiments

with carbon monoxide in 1941 in Mogilev. See Peter Longerich, *Politik der Vernichtung. Eine Gesamtdarstellung der nationalsozialistischen Judenverfolgung* (Munich
1998), 403f., 442.

62. The clip mentioned last is an excerpt from the famous scene of twins who survived
medical experiments approaching the camera and rolling up their sleeves to show the
numbers tattooed on their arms.

63. Among the many descriptions of this "duel," see especially Ann and John Tusa, *The
Nuremberg Trial* (London, 1984), 269–93; Bradley F. Smith, *Reaching Judgment at
Nuremberg* (London, 1977), 108–10; Robert Conot, *Justice at Nuremberg* (New York,
1983), 333–46.

64. These scenes relate to the testimonies of Friedrich Gräbe, Anton Pachelogg, and
Marie-Claude Vaillant-Couturier. The latter is not identified as a gentile member of
the French resistance and therefore is most likely taken to be a Jewish Auschwitz
survivor by twenty-first-century audiences. Later, the mini-series also re-enacts
Rudolf Höß's statement as a witness for the defense.

65. *Nuremberg* combines Göring's different reactions to the American and the Soviet
atrocity films. According to Gilbert's diary, on the evening of November 29, Göring
complained to him that "that awful film" had "spoiled everything," referring to how
the report on his staging of Austria's annexation had earned him much laughter
in the courtroom that morning. The Soviet film, however, he dismissed outright as
propaganda. Gilbert, *Nuremberg Diary*, 49, 162.

66. Göring himself contributed considerably to such a perception. He assumed that he
would be sentenced to death and was eager to give an impressive performance as the
mightiest Nazi ever tried. See Tusa and Tusa, *Nuremberg Trial*, 275–77.

67. In what is probably a reply to this invented film scene, the American prosecution's
chief interpreter Sonnenfeldt describes the exact opposite in his recent memoir. Jackson could have proven Göring's responsibility for the "Final Solution" if only he had
gotten Sonnenfeldt's translation of the letter to Heydrich right. Richard Sonnenfeldt,
*Witness to Nuremberg* (New York, 2006), 58–61.

68. Abby Mann, "Introduction," in *Judgment at Nuremberg. A Play by Abby Mann* (New
York, 2002), vii–xxii.

69. The Justice trial was held in another courtroom in the Nuremberg Palace of Justice.
However, since *Schwurgerichtssaal* 600 had become emblematic of all Nuremberg
trials, it was most recognizable to the film's audiences.

70. The screening of an atrocity film is also an invention since in the real Justice trial
only the Nazi footage of the *Volksgerichtshof* proceedings was shown.

71. Ironically, the Cold War's influence on the perception of Nazi crimes, which is
resisted in the film, dominated the film's reception after its premiere in West Berlin
in December 1961. The premiere was held not far from the recently erected wall
which many of the famous cast demonstratively visited. See Ulrike Weckel, "Amerikanischer Traum von einem deutschen Schuldbekenntnis. Der Spielfilm *Judgment
at Nuremberg* (1961) und seine Rezeption in der deutschen Presse," in *Das Gericht
als Tribunal, oder: Wie der NS-Vergangenheit der Prozess gemacht wurde*, ed. Georg
Wamhof (Göttingen, 2009), 163–85.

72. Rolfe starts the conversation by informing Haywood that the verdict in the I.G. Farben trial, which had just been delivered that morning, was very different from his:
"Most have been acquitted and the others received light sentences."

73. In fact, the number was even higher. Also those defendants whose sentences to
death or life-long imprisonment had been revised were released by 1958. See Frank
M. Buscher, *The US War Crimes Trial Program in Germany, 1946–1955* (New York
1989); Thomas A. Schwartz, "Die Begnadigung deutscher Kriegsverbrecher. John
J. McCloy und die Häftlinge von Landsberg," *Vierteljahrshefte für Zeitgeschichte* 38
(1990): 375–414.

74. For the dealing with forced sterilizations and medical experiments at Nuremberg see
Paul Weindling's chapter in this volume.

75. Hanno Loewy, "Zwischen *Judgment* and *Twilight*. Schulddiskurse, Holocaust und das Courtroom Drama," in *Die Shoah im Bild*, ed. Sven Kramer (Munich, 2003), 133–69, here 148.
76. The Janning character borrows from the historical defendant Franz Schlegelberger only insofar as his career is concerned, not in regard to his behavior in court. In Robert Kempner's view, the only Nuremberg defendant who ever showed sincere remorse was Ernst Wilhelm Bohle, indicted in the Ministries trial. Robert M.W. Kempner, *Ankläger einer Epoche. Lebenserinnerungen* (Frankfurt a.M., 1983), 90, 391.
77. At the beginning of the screening, Janning sadly stares straight ahead. He seems to listen to Lawson's words, but he does not look at the screen. Later, he turns his head toward the front of the courtroom, which suggests that in the long run Janning cannot (or does not want to) elude the images.
78. Jeffrey Shandler claims that it is the atrocity film that brings about Janning's confession in the television play. However, in this earlier version, too, Janning remains silent after the film screening and speaks up only when Rolfe humiliates the witness Irene Wallner. Jeffrey Shandler, *While America Watches. Televising the Holocaust* (New York, 1999), 69–79. The television play can be watched at the Paley Center for Media, New York, T: 43627.
79. 'Pohl' is the only historically accurate name. For Pohl's trial and background information on his career, see Jan Erik Schulte's chapter.
80. It is vaguely suggested that it was the IMT trial. Mann claims to have modeled the character of Mrs Berthold, who does not appear in the television play, after Luise Jodl *née* von Benda; Mann, "Introduction," xi–xii.
81. For the curious phenomenon that Germans heard this Allied accusation much more often than it was in fact uttered, see Norbert Frei, "Von deutscher Erfindungskraft oder: Die Kollektivschuldthese in der Nachkriegszeit," *Rechtshistorisches Journal* 16 (1997): 621–34.
82. Among many others, see Douglas, *Memory*, 11–37; Tony Kushner, *The Holocaust and the Liberal Imagination. A Social and Cultural History* (Oxford, 1994), 205–25; Deborah E. Lipstadt, *Beyond Belief: The American Press and the Coming of the Holocaust, 1933–1945* (New York, 1986), 250–63.
83. All of this in more detail in Weckel, *Beschämende Bilder*, 181–86 and 540.
84. Perhaps this shift suggests that the first two counts of the indictment did not outweigh the attention to war crimes and crimes against humanity as much as Donald Bloxham has argued. Donald Bloxham, *Genocide on Trial. War Crimes Trials and the Formation of Holocaust History and Memory* (Oxford, 2001).

## CHAPTER 9

# THE FATE OF NUREMBERG

## THE LEGACY AND IMPACT OF THE SUBSEQUENT NUREMBERG TRIALS IN POSTWAR GERMANY

*Devin O. Pendas*

 $\mathcal{C}\!\mathit{s\!f\!s}$ 

The collapse of efforts to establish a second International Military Tribunal in the summer and fall of 1946 meant that many of the major goals the Americans had had for the international Nuremberg trial were now transferred to the Subsequent Proceedings.[1] The two most important of these were the development of an international legal regime that could help contain the threat of major global wars, and the democratization of Germany. For Germans, who were both the object and most immediate audience for the Subsequent Trials, it was this second goal that mattered most.

In the very first of the Subsequent Proceedings (the Medical case), the new head of the Office of the US Chief of Counsel for War Crimes, Telford Taylor, outlined what he took to be the "larger responsibilities" of the Americans in these trials.[2] Among the chief of these was the need to offer "public proof" of Nazi atrocities and to explain how such things could occur. "It is incumbent upon us to set forth with conspicuous clarity the ideas and motives which moved these defendants to treat their fellow men as less than beasts." Otherwise, the "perverse thoughts and distorted concepts which brought about these savageries" might return and spread like a "cancer in the breast of humanity." The Subsequent

Proceedings were, according to their guiding architect, as much forward looking as retrospective in orientation. They were prophylactic, not just retributive. Historical truth would prevent a resurgence of National Socialism or similar world-threatening ideologies. The successor trials were to be, above all, forums for moral and political pedagogy, history lessons in judicial robes.

It was the Germans who were to be the main pupils. It was they more than anyone else who had to be protected from a relapse of moral and political cancer. The material consequences of war and defeat were abundantly clear to all Germans, Taylor noted. Yet how would they understand this devastation? "To what cause will these [German] children ascribe the defeat of the German nation and the devastation that surrounds them?" If they attributed their defeat merely to material causes, to the superior numbers or better technology of the Allies, it would be "a sad and fatal thing for Germany and for the world." Such a response, Taylor insisted, would lead to revanchism and a revival of German militarism, as it had done after the World War I. The result could well be yet another global war. "This [Medical] case, and others which will be tried in this building, offer a signal opportunity to lay before the German people the true cause of their present misery." It was not so much Allied bombs as Nazi ideology that had destroyed German cities like Nuremberg. "The insane and malignant doctrines that Nuernberg [sic] spewed forth account alike for the crimes of these defendants and for the terrible fate of Germany under the Third Reich." It was imperative that the Americans use the Subsequent Proceedings to teach the Germans the proper lessons to be gleaned from the history of the Third Reich, lessons they might be reluctant to learn. "I do not think the German people have as yet any conception of how deeply the criminal folly that was nazism [sic] bit into every phase of German life, or of how utterly ravaging the consequences were. It will be our task to make these things clear."[3]

The Subsequent Trials were, of course, not the only component in the American (and more broadly Allied) effort to teach Germans the proper lessons of the World War II. Criminal trials were one leg of a triad that also included the denazification of German institutional life and formal programs for re-education.[4] Still, trials, the Nuremberg trials in particular, had distinct advantages over the other two mechanisms for reorienting Germany and curing it of its presumed moral cancer. They attracted a good deal of publicity, and thus reached a wider audience than did the formal programs for re-education.[5] In contrast to the mass denazification proceedings before so-called *Spruchkammern*, staffed by Germans themselves and dealing only indirectly with the actual crimes of the regime, prominent criminal trials were ideally suited to the kind of pedagogical function Taylor advocated. By systematically prosecuting representatives of different segments of Germany's governing elite, the trials were explicitly designed to demonstrate the breadth and depth of

Nazism's impact on German society. Taylor and many others hoped the Nuremberg trials would teach Germans the truth about Nazism and in the process transform Germany's political culture. Along the way, Nuremberg was also intended to reveal to the whole world the evils of international aggression, racism, authoritarianism, and contempt for the rule of law. That was a lot to ask of twelve criminal trials.

Trials, by their nature, are procedures for determining and producing "truth" or more accurately "truths," for trials are of course venues for adjudicating competing truths, those of the defense and the prosecution, of various, often mutually contradictory witnesses, even, in political cases such as these, between mutually antagonistic political ideologies.[6] Consequently, the truths produced by trials are never as straightforward or unambiguous as attorneys and judges sometimes make them out to be. Nor is it clear in advance how people watching a trial or reading about it in the press will respond to these various truths. They may accept the "wrong" one or they may reject all of them. It is doubtful that any trial ever produces an unambiguous, uncontested, homogeneous truth and, even if it did, it seems unlikely that such a truth would be universally accepted among the trial's audience. Yet a trial's multiple and contested "truths" remain socially powerful for all that, if for no other reason than the social legitimacy that attaches to legal procedures in modern, juridified societies. The law operates through narratives, and trials are powerful mechanisms for producing cogent and potentially persuasive stories. Moreover, because criminal trials in particular operate with a language of judgment that is simultaneously legal, moral, and political (think, for instance, of the term "guilt"), they not only tell stories, they offer ready made idioms for judging and evaluating those stories.[7] This is why some scholars of what has come to be called "transitional justice" share Taylor's enthusiasm for—in Mark Osiel's words—"liberal show trials."[8]

Yet do show trials, liberal or otherwise, work? Can courtrooms be transformed into classrooms? As anyone who has ever been at the front of a class knows, simply teaching a lesson is no guarantee the students will learn or accept it. Certainly, in the case of the Nuremberg Military Tribunals (NMT), there is good reason to think that in the short to medium term, their pedagogical lessons by and large failed to stick. Until well into the 1960s, a sizable majority of Germans rejected the Nuremberg trials (both the IMT and the Subsequent Proceedings) as biased examples of "victor's justice."[9] Much to the consternation of the American occupation authorities, the percentage of those viewing "the" Nuremberg Trial, i.e. the IMT, as "fair" fell from 78% in 1946 to 38% in 1950, while 30% felt the trial was "unfair" by the later date.[10] Such data seem to call into question Taylor's high hopes for the pedagogical potential of the NMT.

Of course, as Norbert Frei and others have pointed out, one needs to understand this skepticism concerning the fairness of the IMT in a broader context.[11] The positive evaluation of the IMT trial in 1946 concerned the trial of a small handful of elites from the highest levels of the Nazi regime, while the same question at the later date necessarily evoked the much broader spectrum of Allied reorientation policies, including not only the Subsequent Proceedings, but also the much more extensive trials for Nazi crimes taking place in German courts, the tremendously unpopular denazification program, perhaps even the delayed release of German POWs, especially from Soviet custody. This is not to mention the highly coordinated campaign by political, judicial, and religious leaders within Germany to discredit and undermine the entire program—German and Allied—of trying Nazi criminals.[12] In other words, it was not necessarily just (or mainly) the Nuremberg trials program that had become unpopular in Germany by 1950, but the whole panoply of Allied policies designed to transform and reorient Germany. Whatever political lessons the Americans were trying to teach in the Subsequent Proceedings, they were doing so in an unruly classroom full of disruptive, distracted pupils who were being seduced by other teachers offering reassuring lessons about German victimhood and innocence.

In this context, the pedagogical efforts of the NMT confronted an increasingly recalcitrant audience. More specifically, I argue that the juridical nature of the Subsequent Proceedings, which in some respects increased their potential legitimacy, in fact helped undermine the historical lessons they hoped to convey. To the extent that attention focused on the real or imagined procedural inequities of the proceedings, the abundant evidence of Nazi malfeasance could be rejected or ignored. To the extent that the evidence of wrongdoing was evaluated in terms of the demonstrated ("beyond a reasonable doubt") legal guilt of individuals, it could be relativized, minimized, or distorted. Great wrongs which did not meet the high and peculiar standards of legal proof could be reinterpreted as not having been wrong at all. The acquittal of individuals could be generalized as an exoneration of German society, while convictions could be dismissed as procedurally flawed acts of revenge. In this respect, jurists set the tone for German responses to the NMT. The dominant attitude in the German legal press regarding the trial series could be best described as revisionist. For the most part, the trials were not openly condemned or rejected in the legal press in the late-1940s. Germany was, after all, still an occupied country and the press subject to Allied control.[13] There were limits to what could be said openly. But if it was rare for the Subsequent Proceedings to be rejected entirely in the German legal press, it was common for them to be reinterpreted to teach lessons that in many cases were the direct opposite of what Taylor and others had in mind when they stressed the pedagogical significance of the trials.

## Responses and Defense Tropes in the German Legal Press

Most of the German legal press responded with conspicuous silence to the successor trials.[14] This silence itself speaks volumes regarding German reluctance to learn the lessons of Nuremberg. One leading German legal journal, the *Neue Juristische Wochenschrift*, broke ranks and published a number of articles dealing with the successor trials, virtually all of them written by defense counsel from the trials. These articles were intended to both summarize and analyze the judgments, focusing in particular on the legal questions that arose, as opposed to the evidence against individual defendants or the portrait that emerged of the Third Reich as a whole. Already in their very format, these articles were well positioned to shift attention from the historical or political lessons of Nuremberg and to instead focus on legal technicalities that were often beside the point. But these articles turned out to be more than mere distractions from the historical lessons of the Nuremberg trials. In many cases, they articulated subtle but clear counter-interpretations that actively rejected the portrait of the Third Reich painted by the prosecution or the courts. This is hardly surprising, nor was it likely unintended. In turning to defense counsel to take the lead in interpreting the successor trials for a broader legal audience, the *Neue Juristische Wochenschrift* in effect became a mouthpiece for the defense in the Subsequent Proceedings.

It is true that, on one occasion, the *Neue Juristische Wochenschrift* published an article about one of the successor trials written by a jurist who had not served as defense counsel, but this was little more than a cursory summary of the court's judgment in the Medical case.[15] Similarly, one of the articles by a defense attorney, Herbert Thiele-Fredersdorf's purely descriptive account of the verdict in the Justice case, could hardly be described as a brief for the defense.[16] Yet most of the *Neue Juristische Wochenschrift* articles were exercises in what can only be described as, at best, creative reinterpretation, at worst, egregious and ideological misreading.

Helmuth Dix, who served as defense counsel in the Farben case and who had been a member of the rightwing *Deutscher Herrenklub* during the Weimar Republic, offered a careful but skeptical assessment of the three economic cases among the NMT (IG Farben, Flick, and Krupp).[17] In a pattern noticeable throughout these articles, he praised the court when it rejected prosecution arguments, acquitted defendants, and generally agreed with positions advocated by the defense, without thereby embracing the legitimacy of the broader project of prosecuting Nazi criminality. With regard to the Farben Trial, for instance, he praised the court for acquitting all of the defendants on the charge of crimes against peace, since they did not have a "demonstrable relationship to Hitler's actual attack plans."[18] He went out of his way to applaud the tribunal for restricting the sphere of those who could be prosecuted even for waging (as opposed to planning) aggressive war. The court, he noted, had parsed the London Charter and the Moscow Declaration in such a way that only "major war criminals" could be convicted of waging aggressive war. He cited approvingly the court's conclusion that, "[i]t is, of course, unthinkable that the majority of Germans should be condemned as guilty of committing crimes against peace. This would amount to a determination of collective guilt to which the corollary of mass punishment is the logical result for which there is no precedent in international law and no justification in human relations."[19] If Albert Speer had been acquitted of crimes against peace by the IMT, then the defendants in the Farben case who had played even less of a role in the formulating of German military and foreign policy could likewise not be convicted. "To find the defendants guilty of waging aggressive war would require us to move the mark without finding a firm place in which to reset it," the court had determined. "We leave the mark where we find it, well satisfied that individuals who plan and lead a nation into and in an aggressive war should be held guilty of crimes against peace, but not those who merely follow the leaders."[20] Such a narrow interpretation of the sphere of responsibility for the waging of aggressive war was quite agreeable to Germans who had been taught to fear allegations of collective guilt since the last years of the war.[21]

Similarly, Dix was pleased that the courts in the Flick and Farben cases had acquitted a majority of defendants on the charge of war crimes and crimes against humanity for their use of forced labor, based on a necessity defense.[22] By contrast, he was quite critical of the court in the Krupp case, which had reached a rather different interpretation of the necessity defense and had consequently issued more stringent verdicts. Of the Krupp court's finding that resistance to the use of forced labor would likely not have entailed "considerable danger" for the defendants, Dix states laconically, "these findings do not, in my opinion, take into sufficient consideration the circumstances under the national socialist regime during the war."[23]

In defending the use of slave labor by the accused in the economic cases, Dix did not shy away from openly legitimating Nazi policy. Protective custody, he noted, "was, after the suspension of constitutional guarantees in 1933 and under the international laws of war, in itself purely legal."[24] Furthermore, the use of slave labor was part of the German war effort, and as such, was a "necessary" obligation to the state. Not only was enslavement thus legal, on Dix's reading, it also constituted an act of mercy. The defendants in the Farben case had simply hoped to improve the living conditions of concentration camp prisoners by offering them "employment."

The logic of Dix's argument is quite striking. First, in asserting the legality of protective custody, he legitimated the Nazi suspension of individual rights as an act of law. Second, he articulated a position that would become a recurring defense trope in later Nazi trials—that using concentration camp inmates as slave labor was doing them a favor, a way to save their lives, not exploit them. Finally, he reiterated an understanding of necessity so broad as to preclude any possibility of convicting anyone of anything under international criminal law, so long as there was the slightest government interest in the act in question. Dix recapitulated the Nazi ideological justification for the creation of concentration camps in the first place, while simultaneously undermining the premise behind the entire effort to develop international criminal law in the second. The rejection of the specific political pedagogy of the Nuremberg trials aimed at German re-education (slave labor is bad), here led to a rejection as well of the other major American goal at Nuremberg, the development of international law.

Still, Dix was not entirely hostile to the Nuremberg economic trials. They had done some good, he concluded on a positive note. The mass of evidence turned up in the economic trials, together with the broad latitude of discovery and cross-examination granted the defense under American criminal procedure, meant that these trials had been very instructive in historical terms. They had revealed an important truth: "Through these trials the myth of culpability (*Mitschuld*) on the part of German industry and its most important representatives for the outbreak of the war and its inhumanity was destroyed and the way made clear for their peaceful reconstruction."[25] The great historical lesson of the Nuremberg trials, according to Dix, was the innocence of German big business. This was hardly the lesson Taylor had had in mind in his Opening Statement.

If Dix had to creatively (mis)read the necessity defense to undermine the American project of individualizing international criminal legal responsibility, other defense counsel could simply latch onto sympathetic American judges to make essentially the same argument. Carl Haensel, lead counsel for Gustav Steengracht von Moyland in the Ministries case, wrote an assessment of that trial that managed to focus almost entirely on the dissenting opinion of Judge Leon Powers, as opposed to the actual judgment in the case.[26] Powers, it will be recalled, had insisted that the prosecution had failed to prove the direct, personal responsibility of the individual defendants, and had instead painted a portrait of Nazi atrocities in broad brushstrokes.[27] This was inadequate, given that the court had declined to apply the conspiracy charge for war crimes or crimes against humanity, and had found insufficient evidence of conspiracy for crimes against peace. Only demonstrable individual responsibility would suffice for a conviction. "The question," according to Haensel, "is simply whether it is possible using state files to convincingly demonstrate this [direct culpability] for individual defendants who acted not for themselves but as functionaries."[28] One would have to be "a legal magician, to speak with Judge Powers," to demonstrate such international criminal legal guilt, "except for the members of Hitler's inner circle." International law, because it was universal, had to be "generous" and restrict its competence to "the greatest, most serious, internationally significant crimes and exclude all smaller, more local misdemeanors."[29] Haensel thus deployed the authority of the American judge to argue for an extremely restrictive reading of international criminal law. By implication, the IMT had been acceptable because it had focused on a very small number of (for the most part) very high-ranking representatives of state and party, Hitler's "inner circle." But trials like the Subsequent Proceedings that proposed to punish second order officials, mere generals and ministry undersecretaries, exceeded the proper limits of international law.

Haensel did not bother to explain how this interpretation differed from the traditional doctrine of acts of state, which would, after all, have granted sovereign immunity to the head of state as well as his inner circle.[30] It is possible that Haensel was tacitly following the argument advanced by Carl Schmitt in his brief for the Flick case. According to Schmitt, if one granted that aggressive war could be illegal as such (something Schmitt very much doubted on *ex post facto* grounds), one would still have to determine the "real responsibility for the political decision to wage war" on the basis of the "internal constitutional situation of the state" when deciding who could be held responsible under international law.[31] On this view, only those with direct "access to the top" could be held liable under international law, at least for crimes against peace.[32] Whether or not Haensel was familiar with Schmitt's then unpublished brief, the logic of the two arguments is quite similar. The upshot of both was that even if there was no sovereign immunity for acts of state, the sphere of culpability was narrowly determined by political authority.

Haensel also did not bother to note that it was highly unlikely that second tier offenders could (or would) be prosecuted on the basis of domestic law, since as government agents, they had typically operated in bureaucratically prescribed ways and thus only rarely violated domestic law. State agents are hard to convict under the laws of the state that authorized their crimes in the first place. The exclusion of international law would mean an end to the prosecution of mid- to high-ranking government officials. This was exactly what happened after 1950 when Germans assumed sole responsibility for the prosecution of Nazi crimes and abandoned the use of the specific international law categories of Control Council Law No. 10 for the prosecution of Nazi crimes.[33]

If in some cases, it was possible for German jurists to creatively misread the Nuremberg judgments or to adopt the positions of dissident American judges in order to draw what Jackson, Taylor, and others would surely have felt were the "wrong lessons" from the Nuremberg trials, in other cases, it was possible to deploy the Nuremberg judgments as instruments of critique against *German* courts that were perceived as being excessively harsh in their own treatment of Nazi crimes. Attorney V.H. Ruff contrasted the jurisprudence of the *Oberste Spruchgerichtshof* in Hamm unfavorably with that of the Military Tribunals in Nuremberg in matters pertaining to the crime of belonging to an organization declared criminal by the IMT.[34] The IMT had declared certain organizations within the Nazi party and the German state to be in and of themselves criminal (the SS, the SD, the Gestapo, and the leadership corps of the Nazi party). Anyone who had voluntarily joined or remained in such an organization and who knew of its criminal character could be held liable. *Spruchgerichte* were special courts set up in the British zone to try charges of membership in a criminal organization, and are not to be confused with *Spruchkammern*, which were denazification commissions in the American zone. The *Oberste Spruchgerichtshof* was the appeals court for the *Spruchgerichte* in the British zone.[35] As such, it was responsible for crafting a consistent and coherent jurisprudence concerning membership in a criminal organization.

Ruff noted that the Nuremberg courts and the *Oberste Spruchgerichtshof* had developed very different interpretations of the charge of crimes against humanity as defined in CCL No. 10 and the IMT charter. "The determination of this concept, however, is the key to understanding organizational crimes overall."[36] In order to convict someone of membership in a criminal organization, it was necessary to demonstrate that they had knowledge of its criminal character. According to Ruff, this meant *Spruchgerichte* had to first determine that "acts of a certain type" had been committed of which the defendant had been aware and, secondly, that these acts were "criminal in the sense of the statute." In other words, you had to know what a crime against humanity was in order to determine if a defendant charged with criminal membership had been aware of one.[37] For this reason, the different understandings of crimes against humanity that emerged in the jurisprudence of the Nuremberg courts and the *Oberste Spruchgerichtshof* undermined the "unified legal foundation" that the Allies had sought to create in occupied Germany. According to Ruff, the Americans, who seemed to be more restrictive in their interpretation of crimes against humanity than the German court, were right and the Germans should adjust their jurisprudence accordingly.

On Ruff's reading, the American courts had interpreted crimes against humanity as being a crime only under international law. "Only acts that extend beyond the borders of a state can be viewed as crimes against humanity. Crimes committed by Germans against Germans, by French against French etc. are in the first instance to be judged according to the national law of the affected country. This is a self-evident demand of sovereignty."[38]

This was a tendentious reading of international law, but, as Ruff rightly noted, one not without some basis in the jurisprudence of the IMT and successor trials. In international law as it was developed in the London Charter, crimes against humanity were "simply an extension of war crimes, because the category of protected persons is the same in the

two laws [i.e. non-combatants], the difference being whether the viola-
tors were of the same or another nationality."[39] The concept of crimes
against humanity was grounded on the older category of war crimes in
part as a way to vitiate the criticism that prosecuting a newly developed
legal category violated the so-called principles of legality, the prohibition
on *ex post facto* law in particular. For the Allies, crimes against humanity were viewed as a common law evolution of war crimes. This was
why the definition of crimes against humanity in the London Charter—
unlike Control Council Law No. 10—explicitly linked crimes against
humanity to "any crime within the jurisdiction of the Tribunal," i.e.,
to crimes against peace and war crimes.[40] Most of the proscribed acts
were identical between the war crimes and crimes against humanity
(e.g., murder, deportation, enslavement, etc.) as defined in both the IMT
charter and CCL 10. The latter did add imprisonment and rape to the
enumerated crimes, but these would have been subsumed under "other
inhumane acts" in the London Charter, and so did not really expand
the definition. The principle difference between war crimes and crimes
against humanity was that the former had to be committed against the
"civilian population of or in occupied territory" or "prisoners of war,"
while the latter comprised such acts "committed against any civilian
population, before or during the war."[41] Thus, in the 1940s, POWs were
covered by war crimes, while civilians in occupied territories were covered by both war crimes and crimes against humanity. German civilians
could only be covered by the latter.[42]

Yet crimes against humanity remained ambiguous in definitional
terms. The chief difficulty stemmed from the linkage between crimes
against humanity and war crimes/crimes against peace. In its judgment,
the IMT decided that this linkage deprived it of jurisdiction over crimes
against German citizens prior to the outbreak of the war. "To constitute
crimes against humanity, the acts relied on before the outbreak of war
must have been in execution of, or in connection with, any crime within
the jurisdiction of the Tribunal." However "revolting and horrible" prewar Nazi crimes against Germans may have been, they fell outside the
court's jurisdiction because they were unrelated to war crimes/crimes
against peace.[43] "Inhumane acts" committed after the outbreak of war,
"insofar as [they] … did not constitute war crimes," were held to be
linked to aggressive war and hence to constitute crimes against humanity and fell within the court's jurisdiction.

The IMT's interpretation arguably violated the spirit, though not
the letter, of the London Charter.[44] In any case, it seems that the Allied
Control Council sought to overturn the IMT's restrictive ruling on
crimes against humanity through legislative amendment. The definition of crimes against humanity in Control Council Law No. 10 differs
from that of the London Charter in two significant respects, though it
otherwise adopts the language of the London Charter verbatim. CCL
10 removes any reference to "other crimes" under Allied jurisdiction

in its definition of the concept.[45] Secondly, CCL 10 explicitly states that German courts may be granted jurisdiction over crimes "committed by persons of German citizenship or nationality against other persons of German citizenship or nationality, or stateless persons."[46] Since war crimes could only be committed against civilians "from occupied territory" or POWs, and since Germans could hardly wage aggressive war against Germany, this clearly meant crimes against humanity. The British, the French, and the Soviets, in authorizing German trials in their respective zones explicitly authorized such cases to be tried as crimes against humanity. They also explicitly approved the prosecution of pre-1939 crimes. Only the Americans declined to authorize such jurisdiction, perhaps to remain consistent with the jurisprudence of the IMT.

The prosecutors in the successor trials certainly thought that the changed statutory language implied a more expansive definition of crimes against humanity. As Telford Taylor noted in his Opening Statement in the Flick case:

> The definition of crimes against humanity certainly comprehends such crimes when committed by German nationals against other German nationals. It is to be observed that all the acts (murder, imprisonment, persecution, etc.) listed in the definition of crimes against humanity would, when committed against populations of occupied countries, constitute war crimes. Consequently, unless the definition of crimes against humanity applies to crimes by Germans against Germans, it would have practically no independent application.[47]

By removing the linkage between crimes against humanity and war crimes/crimes against peace, CCL 10 posed greater challenges in terms of the principles of legality, particularly with regard to the *ex post facto* issue, than had the London Charter.[48] There would have been little reason to create such additional difficulties, unless the point was to try to expand the definition to unambiguously cover prewar crimes against German citizens. Yet the preamble, which incorporated the London Charter and Moscow Declaration into CCL 10, offered a way to bring the more restrictive interpretation back in. The Moscow Declaration referred repeatedly to war crimes, but not to crimes against humanity, and the London Charter bound crimes against humanity to war crimes and crimes against peace. Thus the Nuremberg tribunals adopted the IMT's more restrictive interpretation of crimes against humanity, which was what Ruff wanted the *Spruchgerichte* to do as well.

Ruff noted, quite rightly, that in the Doctors' trial, for instance, the court was careful to demonstrate the commission of crimes against non-Germans in cases of both inhumane medical experiments and so-called euthanasia killings.[49] Ruff also emphasized that the court deliberately side-stepped the question of whether a state could legally authorize the euthanasia killing of its own citizens, since the killing had included foreign nationals and therefore was an international crime. Similarly, Ruff

cited the court in the Pohl case to the effect that Germans had a right
to set up a police state for themselves, but that attempts to apply police
state measures "extraterritorially" against "non-Germans" infringed
upon international law.[50] Consequently, Ruff insisted, "only ... such
acts that extend beyond the territory of a state or its citizens and impose
suffering upon the citizens of foreign nations" could be crimes against
humanity.[51] In the absence of demonstrable knowledge of such acts,
membership in a criminal organization ought not to be punishable.

Ruff's reliance on the language of the American military tribunals
to make his case was of questionable legal relevance. He was, after all,
addressing the jurisprudence of German courts in the British, not the
American, occupation zone. The British military government had issued
directives granting German courts jurisdiction over crimes against humanity against German citizens, quite specifically including those before the
outbreak of the war.[52] Given the traditionally limited role of judicial precedent in German law, Ruff's real goal was clearly political. The point was
not that the American judgments were binding on German court—for
they were not—but that they offered a more palatable interpretation.

Ruff contrasted the jurisprudence of the *Oberste Spruchgerichtshof*
for the British Zone unfavorably with the American tribunals. The
*Oberste Spruchgerichtshof* had consistently held that "even acts of a
purely intra-German and domestic-political character could be seen as
crimes against humanity" and that therefore knowledge of such acts
sufficed for a conviction for membership in a criminal organization. The
court had ruled, for instance, that placing political opponents in protective custody in the concentration camps or the introduction of the mandatory Star of David for Jews within Germany had constituted crimes
against humanity. Such an interpretation ran counter to the "sense of
these international legal norms," according to Ruff.[53]

However tendentious Ruff's legal interpretations were, in political
terms, they were highly significant. "It is not a question," Ruff insisted,
"of whether or not ... such reprehensible acts by Germans against Germans can be punished."[54] The issue was whether they could be punished
under international criminal law, which Ruff denied. Instead, they would
have to be punished under German law. "The German criminal legal
order is a closed and sophisticated legal order that in principle covers
and promises to punish all crimes recognized by western civilization
and actionable under the continental legal tradition." The "domestic
political purification" of Germany would have to be done by German,
not international law.[55] This argument, which was quite widespread in
conservative German legal circles in the late 1940s, was a deliberate red
herring. The same circles that argued most vociferously that Nazi crimes
should be handled under German, rather than international, law were
the ones most vocally advocating a general amnesty for Nazi offenses and
putting pressure on the western Allies to terminate their own war crimes
prosecution programs and release all incarcerated "war condemned."[56]

Ruff was equally critical of the divergence between the American courts at Nuremberg and the *Oberste Spruchgerichtshof* when it came to legally defining "consenting participation" in organizational crimes. The Americans, Ruff noted approvingly, had defined this concept as requiring a direct and active participation in the crimes of the organization. Simply knowing about and not opposing crimes committed by others was insufficient to prove consent, in the absence of any evidence that a defendant had a "direct, causal relationship to the crime." In Ruff's opinion, the *Oberste Spruchgerichtshof* had wrongly diverged from the Americans in this area as well. The *Spruchgerichtshof* had ruled consistently that consenting participation meant "that someone became or remained a member of an organization, although he knew that this organization was being deployed for criminal purposes."[57] This was an excessively broad definition of consent, on Ruff's view, one that "seemed to cross the line separating [criminal membership] from collective responsibility."

Here too there was an exculpatory political agenda at work. If consenting participation meant only acts which directly caused criminal outcomes, then the entire concept of organizational criminality as developed at Nuremberg would fall apart. The initial impetus to prosecute certain Nazi organizations as in and of themselves criminal arose from the insight that in cases of state-sponsored mass criminality, the individuating impulse of ordinary criminal law was bound to fail. Many Nazi crimes, including both aggressive war and genocide, were of such a nature that they could not be committed by individuals as such, but only by organized groups. There were, of course, serious limitations to the paradigm of organizational criminality as established at Nuremberg. It marked a significant departure from the tradition of individual responsibility under criminal law. As initially conceptualized by the Americans, although not as implemented by the IMT, it also shifted the burden of proof from the prosecution to the defense. In part as a consequence, this approach was abandoned, not only in the successor trials, but in the subsequent development of international criminal law. Ruff, however, choose not to challenge the legitimacy of the concept of criminal organizations head on, since the *Spruchgerichte* were created to prosecute such cases, but rather to use the jurisprudence of the successor trials to undermine it from within. Politically, this was a far more promising strategy. It mobilized the moral authority of the Americans, clearly the dominant partner among the three western Allies for purposes which, if articulated in a more purely German idiom, might seem suspiciously pro-Nazi. It also attacked one Allied priority (punishing membership in a criminal organization) in the name of another (creating a unified legal structure for at least western Germany). As such, it could frame what was in fact a radical assault on one of the basic premises of the Allied war crimes trials program as simply a concern for legal consistency and fairness. Ruff sought to seize the moral high ground, to critique Nazi trials in the name of justice.

Given that Ruff's critique marked, in effect, a wholesale rejection of organizational criminality and, consequently, of the *Spruchgericht* system, it is unsurprising that it prompted a rebuttal from the chief prosecutor for the *Spruchgericht* in Stade, one Dr Strunck.[58] Strunck rightly stressed the expansive character of crimes against humanity, in contrast to the more restrictive nature of war crimes. In contrast to Ruff's almost common law appeal to the precedent of the American military tribunals, Strunck took a more traditional German approach and parsed the language of Control Council Law No. 10 with some care. He asserted that "in place of atrocities committed against civilians in or from occupied territory [i.e. war crimes], crimes against humanity apply to atrocities against any civilian population whatsoever, including those from Germany." He also pointed out that CCL 10's provision allowing German courts to be granted jurisdiction over crimes against Germans would make no sense whatsoever, were Ruff's interpretation of the statute correct. On these grounds, Strunck had a strong legal case. Yet politically, such narrow parsing of statutes could hardly hope to compete with the moral authority of an American court.

Consequently, Strunck tried to interpret the successor trials as articulating an expansive definition of crimes against humanity. Strunck cited as evidence for his interpretation the "view of Military Tribunal 4 in the Flick case" that "acts committed by Germans against other Germans are punishable as crimes under Law No. 10."[59] The problem is that the passage quoted by Strunck came not from the court's verdict, but rather from the prosecution's Opening Statement.[60] The court itself, in fact, had come to exactly the opposite conclusion. Noting that the London Charter—incorporated into CCL 10 in the preamble—referred persistently to "war crimes," the court inferred that crimes not connected directly with the war lay outside its jurisdiction. "We can see no purpose nor mandate in the chartering legislation of this Tribunal requiring it to take jurisdiction of such cases [crimes by Germans against Germans prior to the outbreak of the war]."[61] Strunck was either sloppy or dishonest. Either way, he played into Ruff's hands, because he granted American jurisprudence priority, and then got it wrong.

Whether the Nuremberg tribunals were right to adopt such a narrow interpretation of crimes against humanity is a matter of legal debate. In historical terms, what matters is that they provided cover for German critics, like Ruff, who sought to undermine the entire project of Nuremberg, both as a model for legal prosecution and as an exercise in democratic pedagogy. Far from conveying a democratizing message, as Taylor had wished, in this instance the American Military Tribunals emboldened the critics of the Allies' reorientation strategy for Germany.

It was not just with regard to legal matters that Germans reinterpreted Nuremberg in ways that ran counter to American expectations. History and politics were likewise reconfigured. One of the key historical points Jackson, Taylor, and others hoped to make in the trials was that the Nazi regime had enjoyed deep and broad popular support. Nuremberg defense counsel again were among the most vocal and articulate public critics of this interpretation. Otto Kranzbühler, who represented Karl Dönitz at the IMT and several clients in the successor trials, was particularly interested in what he took to be Nuremberg's historical lessons. In his 1949 book on the trials, Kranzbühler began by noting that it was unlikely that such a volume of historical documentation could have been gathered had it not been for the trials. However valuable these documents would be for future historians, they had to be used with "great caution." Because of the antagonistic character of Anglo-American legal procedure, the courts, unlike their German counterparts, had no capacity to independently (and objectively) investigate the past. Moreover, the prosecution, again in contrast to German prosecutors, had no obligation to seek exculpatory evidence or even to present any such mitigating evidence as it discovered. "This system might nonetheless come to a result approaching near the truth in instances where both parties disposed of equal resources. It must of necessity, however, function so much the worse, the more one party predominates over the other."[62] This was, he maintained, clearly the case at Nuremberg, especially in the IMT trial, but also to a lesser extent in the successor trials. Inadequate personnel and greatly restricted access to archival materials, especially those of the Allies themselves, meant that the defense had been unable to present an adequate counterweight to the prosecution's one-sided narrative. The secret agreement between Germany and the Soviet Union regarding the attack on Poland was only the most glaring omission of this sort in the trials.

Nonetheless, Kranzbühler ventured a cautious assessment of what he took to be the key historical lessons of the Nuremberg trials. The first of these—and the only one in accordance with the message the Americans had hoped to convey—was that the invasion of Poland was unambiguously an act of aggression on Germany's part. "With respect to the ensuing wars and campaigns, the results are neither so clear nor so convincing."[63] The invasions of both Norway and the Soviet Union could be seen as preventative wars, whatever the court said to the contrary. Equally important "for our political position," was the fact that the Nuremberg courts concluded that the wars against France, England, and the United States had not been wars of aggression. "Among the many bitter droughts that the Nuremberg judgment holds for us, we should also take in the good. We should know, and should disseminate this knowledge among the western Allies, that, according to their own tribunal, we did not attack any of them."[64] The significance of this claim in the context of the burgeoning Cold War would not have been lost on Kranzbühler's audience.

With regard to German atrocities, Kranzbühler was able to note with evident pride that the naval war had been exonerated, in no small part due to his efforts. As far as the land war was concerned, he admitted there had been serious irregularities on the German side. He pointed to the Commissar Order and the "worst discovery" of the Nuremberg trials, "the extermination measures against real or imagined political enemies," including the Polish intelligentsia and the Jews. The evidence for these atrocities was overwhelming and anyone who recognized this "would never overcome the shame that Germans, albeit only a very few Germans, did such things."[65] One of the great services of the Nuremberg trials, however, was to demonstrate that most Germans had known nothing of these crimes, whatever the prosecution might have claimed. This was the true significance of the need to ascertain direct knowledge of criminal acts in order to convict individuals for membership in criminal organizations. The inability to do so in many cases showed how narrow the sphere of culpability really was. Altogether, the historical knowledge generated by the Nuremberg trials was, according to Kranzbühler, a mixed bag. It was "historically illuminating but also historically obfuscating."[66] It needed to be treated with great caution, lest it become a "dangerous weapon in the hands of demagogues."

Kranzbühler was equally skeptical of the trials' efficacy with regard to international law and order. "Is war in our contemporary global political order really nothing more than a criminal conspiracy of a few whom one can deter by threat of punishment? One glance at the current state of affairs demonstrates the opposite."[67] The conflict between the United States and the Soviet Union was only the most obvious counterexample. The founding of the state of Israel provided another demonstration of the truism that war was a necessity. In one breath, Kranzbühler here managed to combine a blatant appeal to Cold War anxieties with a none-too-subtle inversion of antisemitic tropes about Jewish power into their philosemitic opposite.[68]

## Nuremberg and Nazi Trials in German Courts

The Subsequent Proceedings by and large failed to live up to the expectations set for them as political pedagogy by their American architects. As legal precedent for the prosecution of Nazi atrocities, their record was unfortunately little better. Unlike trials for Nazi atrocities in German courts after 1950, which were held under ordinary statutory law, during the occupation period, German courts outside the American Zone prosecuted Nazi crimes as crimes against humanity. Control Council Law No. 10 had authorized the occupation authorities to grant German courts jurisdiction for Nazi crimes against Germans or stateless persons.[69] We have already seen how German jurists used the Nuremberg jurisprudence concerning crimes against humanity to both exonerate major segments of German society under the Nazis and to criticize the practices of German *Spruchgerichte*. How did ordinary German criminal courts handle crimes against humanity?

The Americans declined to grant German courts jurisdiction over Nazi crimes under CCL 10. Instead, they had the *Land* governments in their zone pass identical laws authorizing the prosecution of Nazi crimes against Germans under German statutory law. The British, the French, and the Soviets all authorized German trials for crimes against humanity. Although German courts in the Soviet Zone prosecuted Nazi crimes against humanity—after August 1947 in conjunction with denazification under Soviet Military Government Order 201—the Nuremberg successor trials, as American institutions, had very little influence in eastern Germany. The trials in the German courts of the Soviet Zone were reasonably fair, at least initially, although they became increasingly instrumentalized for contemporary political purposes as the Soviets gradually came to accept a permanent division of Germany and the SED consolidated its dictatorial control over the emerging German Democratic Republic.[70] Before they were fully Stalinized in 1950, German courts in the Soviet Zone developed a surprisingly sophisticated jurisprudence of Nazi atrocity, one that deviated from the individuating and restrictive jurisprudence of Nuremberg and western Germany to embrace the kind of broadly systemic understanding of Nazi criminality Taylor advocated.

In contrast to the Nuremberg defense attorneys, German courts in the Soviet Zone were largely unconcerned by the vague quality of the crimes against humanity charge. As one superior court judge put it, discerning a crime against humanity was "in the end a question of conscience ... where it is less a matter of subsuming events under certain principles and statutory provisions than it is a matter of the ethical sensibilities of those affected."[71] More important than any attempt to specify the concrete actions that constituted a crime against humanity was CCL 10's proviso that any persecution on racial, religious, or ethnic grounds constituted such a crime. Consequently, virtually any action could conceivably be construed as a crime against humanity, so long as it violated what the Superior Court in Dresden called the "ethical minimal existence" (*Existenzminimum*) characteristic of civilized communities.[72]

Obviously, this led to a very broad definition of crimes against humanity. For instance, the Superior Court in Dresden overturned a lower court verdict acquitting a man for divorcing his Jewish wife in 1944, whereupon she was deported to Auschwitz and subsequently died in Bergen-Belsen in early 1945. Divorce was obviously legal at the time and not in and of itself a violation of civilized moral standards. Consequently the defendant had a "legally protected interest" in his decision to divorce. Yet because divorcing a Jewish partner led to her being deprived of the relative safety of living in a "mixed marriage," her murder was a foreseeable result of the divorce. The Superior Court held this act to therefore constitute a crime against humanity.[73] The same court ruled that even the victim of a theft by a forced laborer working in his house ought to have suppressed his "in itself not unjustified sense of injury" and not reported the theft to the police, given the inevitable consequences, the execution of the alleged thief.[74] The defendant's report was held to constitute a crime against humanity.

In the western zones, by contrast, German courts failed to, in Taylor's words, demonstrate "how deeply the criminal folly that was nazism [sic] bit into every phase of German life."[75] Quite the opposite in fact. Far from expanding the definition of crimes against humanity, as their eastern colleagues had done, judges in the western courts narrowed it. Taking up restrictions already noticeable in the judgments in the Subsequent Proceedings, western German courts quickly constructed a jurisprudence that restricted the sphere of responsibility for Nazi crimes, isolated these from broader social forces, and relativized Nazi atrocities as exemplars of the universal horrors of war.

One can take an influential ruling by the State Court in Konstanz from 1947 as typical in this regard. In 1942, the defendant had gone on vacation with a friend, during the course of which the friend had made disparaging remarks about the Nazi party and predicted Germany's eventual defeat in the war, looking forward to the summary execution of at least some party officials. Upon their return to Konstanz, the defendant had denounced her friend to the Gestapo. The friend was convicted and sentenced to nine months imprisonment and a fine. In this case, the state court found the defendant innocent. While recognizing that in principle, even factually true denunciations could be crimes against humanity, i.e., could be a form of political persecution per CCL 10, the court denied that was the case in this instance. The court cited a statement from Telford Taylor's discussion of crimes against humanity in the Flick case. Taylor had noted that not every rape or murder could be considered a crime against humanity, since these "unfortunately occur" in every society. "Nor, we believe, are localized outbursts of race hatred, or petty discriminations, covered by the word 'persecutions.'"[76]

Taking up Taylor's suggestion, the Konstanz court maintained that only participation in "gigantic crimes" directed by the state and affecting whole populations constituted crimes against humanity. The contrast with the eastern German jurisprudence could not be clearer:

> In keeping with these views and in recognition of the fact that political denunciations are an uncanny consequence of political power that make an appearance in every time period, in every nation, under every governmental system and, in particular, in cases of fundamental political transformation, the court comes to the conclusion that not every political denunciation from the period of national socialist domination can be viewed as a punishable crime against humanity.[77]

There was nothing unusual about denunciatory practices during the Third Reich, the court found, not even in comparison with democratic regimes.

What then would make a denunciation a crime against humanity? A denunciation was only a crime against humanity when it was done on the basis of an "inhumane sensibility," was "in itself illegal," and was designed to serve the Nazis' "will to power that was oriented against human dignity (*Menschenwürde*)."[78] Illegality (*Rechtswidrigkeit*) alone did not define crimes against humanity; they had to comprise "inhumane illegality." And how might one determine whether a given defendant had had the requisite "subjective inhumanity"? It would be "unjust" to decide the question on the basis of "retrospective observation" from "a newly won vantage point enriched by experience gained since the act in question." Rather, the question could only be properly addressed from the perspective of the "time of the event in question" and on the basis of an understanding of the "defendant's state of mind and spirit at the time," as well as what the defendant could actually have known and anticipated during the Third Reich. In other words, one had to judge the subjective inhumanity of a defendant in cases of political denunciations on the basis of Nazi standards. However morally regrettable the defendant's actions in this particular case may have been, they were not crimes against humanity.

The jurisprudence of the Konstanz court in this case was quite typical of the German courts of the three Western zones.[79] It functioned to narrow the sphere of responsibility for Nazi crimes, to protect ordinary Germans from any association with the regime, while in fact validating the regime's own perspective. It was a way of denying large-scale culpability for the systematic criminality of the Third Reich. It was also a form of what might be called sham-distancing from Nazi values. Rhetorical tricks were used to modestly decry Nazi atrocities, while protecting their perpetrators; the defendant's actions were to be "morally decried" but not criminally punished.[80] One could only evaluate the inhumanity of an act on the basis of the values in place at the time of its commission and these were, of necessity, Nazi values. Though the courts never went so far as to actually declare that only acts the Nazis themselves would have condemned should be punished, it was implicit in much of the jurisprudence of the western German courts in the late 1940s.

The *Oberlandesgericht* in Kiel reached an even more dramatic variant of the same conclusion in a 1947 case where a teacher, an active member of the NSDAP, had denounced the local barber for defeatism based on second-hand reports from his students. The judges upheld a lower court's decision not to arraign the defendant, on the grounds that "it is not clear that [the defendant's] actions constitute 'persecution' in the sense of CCL 10, since the accused, as a member off the [Nazi] party, was obligated to obey the directives of his district leader and nothing was demanded of him that was not legal at the time."[81] Consequently his denunciation, which had led to the arrest and imprisonment of the barber, did not constitute crimes against humanity. The court in effect accepted a defense of superior orders, despite the fact that this was explicitly disallowed in CCL 10.

Earlier in 1947, the Kiel court had upheld the conviction of a defendant for *resisting* the Nazis. The accused, a young Wehrmacht deserter,
had gravely injured a police officer while escaping custody to avoid a
death sentence. Returning to Germany after the war, he was convicted
of assault. Upholding this conviction, the superior court in Kiel rea-
soned that "the international illegality of the war does not contravene
the legality of the actions" by the state officers in support of the war.
"The breach of international agreements by international criminal
offenses fundamentally grounds only a responsibility of states and not
individual persons, since only states are subjects of international law."[82]
The "exceptions," such as the Nuremberg judgments, "cannot be generalized." A more explicit valorization of Nazi legal practices in contra-
vention of Nuremberg precedents would be difficult to imagine. If one
of the key lessons the Americans hope to convey at Nuremberg was the
depth of Nazi criminality, the fundamental illegality of the war, and
the political bankruptcy of Germany for embracing the Nazis, then the
jurisprudence of the Kiel court must have been bitterly disappointing.

## Long-term Impact

In the context of the occupation period, then, the Nuremberg Subsequent Proceedings fundamentally failed to live up to the high expectations set for them. They led to neither a historical appreciation for the
"deep bite" of Nazism on German society nor, in the western zones, to
a sustainable and far reaching German jurisprudence of crimes against
humanity. But if the Nuremberg trials failed to have a significant trans-
formative impact in the near term, might they have had a more substantial impact in the long run? This question is difficult to answer with any
certainty. Clearly, West Germany liberalized and democratized quite
successfully in the postwar period, though it seems fair to agree with
Ulrich Herbert that this was a long-term "learning process" that only
settled in comfortably in the 1970s or even 1980s.[83] The contributions
of the Subsequent Trials to this long-term process were mainly indirect
and were, in some cases, ambivalent at best.

Because German courts stopped prosecuting Nazi crimes as crimes
against humanity in the early 1950s, the NMT had no direct precedential value for later German trials. The decision to prosecute Nazi
crimes under ordinary German criminal law was predictable, given the
substantial and ever increasing hostility toward using crimes against
humanity charges in Nazi cases throughout the occupation period.[84]
This meant, however, that West German trials for Nazi crimes from
the 1950s onward faced substantially different legal and jurisprudential
challenges from those confronting the American military tribunals or
the German courts of the occupation period.[85] In any direct legal sense,
the Subsequent Proceedings were simply irrelevant to Nazi trials in

Germany after 1950. Still there were some elements of long-term continuity, both legal and political, most of which tended toward the exculpatory and apologetic.

In the first instance, the NMT (as well as the IMT) served as an important training ground for a number of attorneys who would go on to have significant careers as defense counsel in numerous later German Nazi trials. Among the most prominent of these were Rudolf Aschenauer, Hans Laternser, and Alfred Seidl, though one should not forget Eichmann's defense attorney Robert Servatius. Seidl had defended Heß and Frank at the IMT and several defendants in the successor trials, including Oswald Pohl in Case 4, Hans Lammers and Otto Meissner in the Ministries case, and several defendants in the Medical case. Later, Seidl would represent the notorious Ilse Koch, the so-called "Kommandeuse of Buchenwald."[86] Aschenauer, who served as defense counsel in the Farben, Justice, and *Einsatzgruppen* cases was one of the more aggressive of the defense attorneys in the Frankfurt Auschwitz trial of 1963–65.[87] Laternser, who served as defense counsel in the Farben, High Command and Hostages cases, was an even more prominent figure in the Auschwitz trial.[88] Otto Kranzbühler worked for German corporations, including IG Farben, defending them against civil claims for compensation from former forced laborers.[89]

More striking than such instances of personnel continuity, though, are the continuities in defense strategy and interpretation between the Subsequent Proceedings and later Nazi trials in West German courts. In the Auschwitz trial, for instance, Laternser developed Helmuth Dix's idea that the use of concentration camp prisoners by German businesses constituted a form of rescue even further.[90] Dix had argued the defendants in the Farben case had thought they were helping prisoners by giving them employment, claiming this would improve their living conditions within the concentration camps and save them from liquidation.[91] Laternser in the Auschwitz trial went Dix one better. In his closing arguments, Laternser argued that it was a "historical fact" that all Jews under German domination were slated to die, including those sent to Auschwitz. It was in this context that one had to understand the notorious selections at the ramp in Auschwitz, where arriving prisoners were sorted into those to be admitted to the camp and worked to death and those to be sent directly to the gas chambers to be murdered immediately.

> If there had not been a selection at the Ramp in Birkenau, that is the choosing of a previously determined number of persons capable of working, then in every case, the entire transport would have been exterminated. Without the selection of those capable of work for an always well-determined purpose, then more Jewish people would have been murdered than was actually the case ... The selections thus meant preserving the persons selected from being murdered immediately upon arrival. Choosing which persons were admitted to the camp could thus not constitute participation in murder ... because the persons chosen were not murdered."[92]

Both Dix and Laternser fundamentally refused to acknowledge that the Nazi's use of slave labor, especially Jewish slave labor, was part of a general process of annihilation in which "extermination through work" had been one element alongside more direct mechanisms of murder.

Such arguments rarely met with direct legal success, in the sense of winning acquittals for their clients. Nor is it clear that that was their main purpose. Certainly the Frankfurt court rejected Laternser's argument that selection equaled rescue. The point of Laternser's arguments in Frankfurt was similar to that of earlier defense arguments in Nuremberg, to win the battle of public opinion, even if the struggle in the courtroom was a lost cause. Moreover, even though these kinds of overt trivializing and minimizing arguments rarely resulted in acquittals, they helped create a climate of opinion favorable to the development of the "jurisprudence of accessories" (*Gehilfenjudikatur*).[93]

This was part of a larger apologetic tendency in postwar West German society to restrict the sphere of responsibility for Nazi atrocities as narrowly as possible.[94] While this trend extended well beyond the Nuremberg defense counsel, they went out of their way to foster such an interpretation of the Nazi past. The defense may have lost more cases than it won at Nuremberg, but when it came to the battle for public opinion in (West) Germany, they scored a clear victory that persisted for twenty years or more. In this, they may have served as the prototype for what Dirk Moses has called "German Germans," postwar intellectuals who "warded off" the "stigma" of Nazism by "denationalizing" it, that is, by ascribing the "Nazi catastrophe" to "non-German causes."[95]

The Nuremberg trials, designed in their comprehensive and typological structure to counter such a trend, proved incapable of overcoming this tendency and were even made to abet it in the creative reinterpretation of German jurists. In the aftermath of World War I, a toxic "stab-in-the-back" legend had grown up in Germany that held that Germany had been defeated not on the battlefield but on the home front, by socialists, war profiteers, and Jews.[96] Part of the point of the Nuremberg trials had been to prevent a recurrence of this kind of militaristic mythology. It is true that, after the World War II, Germans did not deny their total military defeat as they had done after the first. Instead, they developed a narrative of themselves as the first and most prominent of Hitler's victims. Yet, this was but a different kind of stab-in-the-back legend. Germany had not been betrayed into losing the war; instead, it had been betrayed into starting it. Kranzbühler, for instance, posited as one of the key revelations of Nuremberg that there was "not one of the big, real crimes that cannot be traced back to a personal decision by Hitler."[97] Far from vitiating a narrative of German victimization, Nuremberg was transformed in German public discourse into a confirmation of it.

The transformations in German attitudes toward the Nazi past that became noticeable beginning in the 1960s have to be attributed mainly to factors outside the realm of law: generational change, the rise of a critical media sphere, cultural imports from abroad like the American TV mini-series *Holocaust*, pressure from East German propaganda, the political success of the SPD, among others. Neither Nuremberg nor the subsequent trials for Nazi crimes in German courts were able to foster such a critical stance toward the past. Indeed, they frequently reinforced the opposite perspective.

If the impact of the Allied successor trials within Germany thus has to be regarded as disappointing, it is possible that, viewed more globally, their legacy appears in a different light. There can be no doubt that the advocates of revived international legalism in the 1990s looked to "Nuremberg" for both legal precedents and political examples. While there has doubtless been a good deal of naïveté on the part of international law boosters, the return of the Nuremberg paradigm is nonetheless preferable to a continued stagnation of international criminal law and the blatant application of *realpolitik*.[98] Efforts to apply law to mass violence and armed conflict may never domesticate violence in ways analogous to what happened on a national level with the development of the modern state, but it does articulate a set of (potentially) consensual norms that can serve a culturally regulative function in the international arena. If Carlyle's "Everlasting No" could transform in the end to an "Everlasting Yea," we can yet hope that the refusal to accept atrocity as a human norm can have some affect on the human predicament.[99]

## Notes

1. Donald Bloxham, "'The Trial that Never Was': Why there was no Second International Trial of Major War Criminals at Nuremberg," *History* 87 (2002): 41–60.
2. Case 1, Opening Statement of the Prosecution by Brigadier General Telford Taylor, December 9, 1946, *Trials of War Criminals before the Nuernberg Military Tribunals under Control Council Law No. 10* (Washington, DC, 1949) [TWC], I, 27–29.
3. Ibid., 29.
4. On denazification, see Lutz Niethammer, *Mitläuferfabrik. Die Entnazifizierung am Beispiel Bayerns* (Berlin, 1982); Clemens Vollnhals with Thomas Schlemmer, *Entnazifizierung. Politische Säuberung und Rehabilitierung in den vier Besatzungszonen 1945–1949* (Munich, 1991). On re-education, see Karl-Heinz Füssl, *Die Umerziehung der Deutschen: Jugend und Schule unter den Siegermächten des Zweiten Weltkriegs, 1945–19. Die Bildungspolitik der Besatzungsmächte in Deutschland und Österreich* (Stuttgart, 1981); Gaspar von Schrenck-Notzing, *Charakterwäsche:. Die Re-Education der Deutschen und ihre bleibenden Auswirkungen*, exp. edn (Graz, 2004).
5. See, e.g., *Holocaust und NS-Prozesse: Die Presseberichterstattung in Israel und Deutschland zwischen Aneignung und Abwehr*, eds. Jürgen Wilke, Birgit Schenk, Akiba A. Cohen and Tamar Zemach (Cologne, 1995).
6. Devin O. Pendas, "Truth and its Consequences: Reflections on Political, Historical and Legal 'Truth' in West German Holocaust Trials," *traverse: Zeitschrift für Geschichte/Revue d'histoire* 11 (2004): 25–38.
7. Robert Cover, "Nomos and Narrative," in *Narrative, Violence and the Law: The Essays of Robert Cover*, eds. Martha Minow, Michael Ryan and Austin Sarat (Ann Arbor, 1995), 95f.

8. Mark Osiel, *Mass Atrocity, Collective Memory, and the Law* (New Brunswick, NJ, 1999). Other transitional justice scholars have developed an antipathy toward criminal trials in transition settings because of the procedural problems that tend to plague them and prefer the alternate route of truth commissions. See Martha Minow, *Between Vengeance and Forgiveness: Facing History after Genocide and Mass Violence* (Boston, 1999).

9. For a forceful argument to this effect regarding the IMT, see Werner Maser, *Nürnberg: Tribunal der Sieger* (Dusseldorf, 1977).

10. *Public Opinion in Occupied Germany: The HICOG Surveys, 1949–1955*, eds. Anna J. and Richard L. Merritt (Urbana, 1980), 11, 101.

11. Norbert Frei, *Adenauer's Germany and the Nazi Past: The Politics of Amnesty and Integration* (New York, 2002), 83–95. See also Peter Reichel, *Vergangenheitsbewältigung in Deutschland: Die Auseinandersetzung mit der NS-Diktatur von 1945 bis heute* (Munich, 2001), 70.

12. Frei, *Adenauer's Germany*, 230–33.

13. Norbert Frei, *Amerikanische Lizenzpolitik und deutsche Pressetradition. Die Geschichte der Nachkriegszeitung Südost-Kurier* (Munich, 1986).

14. Outside the *Neue Juristische Wochenschrift*, the principle exception is Gustav Radbruch, "Des Reichsjustizministeriums Ruhm und Ende: Zum Nürnberger Juristen-Prozess," *Süddeutsche Juristen-Zeitung* 3 (1948): 57–64.

15. See Siegfried Wille, "Grundsätze des Nürnberger Ärzteprozesses," *Neue Juristische Wochenschrift* 10 (1949): 377.

16. Herbert Thiele-Fredersdorf, "Das Urteil des Militärgerichtshofes Nr. III im Nürnberger Juristen-Prozeß," *Neue Juristische Wochenschrift* 4 (1947): 122–26.

17. Helmuth Dix, "Die Urteile in den Nürnberger Wirtschaftsprozessen," *Neue Juristische Wochenschrift* 17 (1949): 647–52. On the Herrenklub, see Manfred Schoeps, "Der Deutsche Herrenklub: ein Beitrag des Jungkonservatismus in der Weimarer Republik," Ph.D. diss. (University of Erlangen-Nuremberg, 1974).

18. Dix, "Urteile," 647.

19. Dix, "Urteile," 648; Case 6, Decision and Judgment, *TWC*, VIII, 1126.

20. Case 6, Decision and Judgment, *TWC*, VIII, 1126.

21. Jeffrey K. Olick, *In the House of the Hangman: The Agonies of German Defeat, 1943–1949* (Chicago, 2005).

22. See the chapter by Kim C. Priemel in the present volume.

23. Dix, "Urteile," 649.

24. Ibid.

25. Ibid., 652.

26. Carl Haensel, "Der Ausklang von Nürnberg," *Neue Juristische Wochenschrift* 10 (1949): 367–70. Haensel had also served as lead counsel for defendants in the Justice, RuSHA, and Pohl cases.

27. See the chapter by Lawrence Douglas in the present volume.

28. Haensel, "Ausklang," 370.

29. Ibid.

30. This position was articulated most forcefully by Hans Kelsen in his critique of the IMT. See Hans Kelsen, "Will the Judgement in the Nuremberg Trial Constitute a Precedent in International Law?" *International and Comparative Law Quarterly* 1 (1947): 153–65. See also Andrea Gattini, "Kelsen's Contribution to International Criminal Law," *Journal of International Criminal Justice* 2 (2004): 795–809.

31. Carl Schmitt, *Das international-rechtliche Verbrechen des Angriffskrieges und der Grundsatz "Nullum crimen, nulla poena sine lege,"* ed. Helmut Quaritsch (Berlin, 1994), 64.

32. See the discussion in Reinhard Mehring, *Carl Schmitt: Aufstieg und Fall. Eine Biographie* (Munich, 2009), 440–42.

33. For the marked class bias in German prosecutions for Nazi crimes, where high officials were scarcely prosecuted, while low-ranking soldiers and police bore the brunt

of efforts to try Nazi offenses, see Kerstin Freudiger, *Die juristische Aufarbeitung von NS-Verbrechen* (Tübingen, 2002).

34. V.H. Ruff, "'Einheitliche Rechtsgrundlage': Zur abweichenden Rechtsprechung des Obersten Spruchgerichtshofes in Hamm und der Nürnberger Militärgerichte," *Neue Juristische Wochenschrift* 1 (1947/48): 283–86.

35. Sebastian Römer, *Mitglieder verbrecherischer Organisationen nach 1945: Die Ahndung des Organisationsverbrechens in der britischen Zone durch die Spruchgerichte* (Frankfurt, 2005). More generally, see Henri Meyrowitz, *La Répression par les Tribunaux Allemands des Crimes contre L'Humanité et de L'Appartenance a une Organisation Criminelle en Application de la Loi No. 10 du Conseil de Contrôle Allié* (Paris, 1960).

36. Ruff, "'Einheitliche Rechtsgrundlage,'" 283.

37. Ruff did not explain why one had to know about crimes against humanity, as opposed to war crimes or crimes against peace, raising the suspicion that his core concern was less with the charge of criminal membership and more with the category of crimes against humanity itself.

38. Ruff, "'Einheitliche Rechtsgrundlage,'" 283.

39. M. Cherif Bassiouni, *Crimes against Humanity in International Criminal Law*, 2nd rev. edn (The Hague, 1999), 10.

40. "London Agreement of 8 August 1945", *TWC*, I, xii.

41. Ibid., xi–xii.

42. The status of civilian citizens of Axis Allies, such as Italy or Hungary, was complicated. Prior to their nation's surrender, such individuals would have been in the same category as Germans, since they were not in occupied territory. After their nation's surrender, they would have been covered by the category of war crimes as well.

43. *Trial of Major War Criminals before the International Military Tribunal, Nuremberg, 14 November 1945–1 October 1946 [IMT]* (Nuremberg, 1948), XXII, 498.

44. M. Cherif Bassiouni argues that the drafters of the London Charter intended a narrow definition of crimes against humanity, an interpretation somewhat difficult to square with the subsequent, more expansive definition in CCL 10. See Bassiouni, *Crimes against Humanity*, 14–25. Certainly, the subsequent development of international law jurisprudence, for instance before the ad hoc tribunals for Yugoslavia and Rwanda, has trended in precisely the opposite direction, expanding the protections of crimes against humanity to civilian populations independent of both international and internecine war.

45. "Control Council Law No. 10," *TWC*, I, xvii.

46. Ibid.

47. Case 5, Taylor, "Opening Statement," *TWC*, VI, 81.

48. Bassiouni, *Crimes against Humanity*, 33–37.

49. Ruff, "'Einheitliche Rechtsgrundlage,'" 283. On Allied jurisprudence concerning German medical crimes, see the chapter by Paul Weindling in the present volume. See also Patricia Heberer, "Early Postwar Justice in the American Zone: The 'Hadamar Murder Factory' Trial," in *Atrocity on Trial*, eds. Patricia Heberer and Jürgen Matthäus (Lincoln/London, 2008), 25–47 and Michael Bryant, *Confronting the "Good Death": Nazi Euthanasia on Trial, 1945–1953* (Boulder, 2005).

50. Ruff, "'Einheitliche Rechtsgrundlage,'" 284.

51. Ibid.

52. See Devin O. Pendas, "Retroactive Law and Proactive Justice: Debating Crimes against Humanity in Germany, 1945–1950," *Central European History* 43 (2010): 428–63.

53. Ruff, "'Einheitliche Rechtsgrundlage,'" 285.

54. Ibid., 284.

55. Ibid., 285.

56. Frei, *Adenauer's Germany*, 97–120.

57. Cited in Ruff, "'Einheitliche Rechtsgrundlage,'" 286.

58. Dr Strunck, "Zur Rechtsprechung des Obersten Spruchgerichtshofes in Hamm. (Nochmals: Einheitliche Rechtsgrundlage)," *Neue Juristische Wochenschrift* 1 (1947/48): 685–86.
59. Ibid., 686.
60. Case 5, "Opening Statement for the Prosecution," *TWC*, VI, 82.
61. Case 5, "Opinion and Judgment," *TWC*, VI, 1213.
62. Otto Kranzbühler, *Rückblick auf Nürnberg* (Hamburg, 1949), 6.
63. Ibid., 7f.
64. Ibid., 8.
65. Ibid., 9.
66. Ibid.., 10.
67. Ibid., 19.
68. This was a commonplace maneuver in postwar Germany. See Frank Stern, *The Whitewashing of the Yellow Badge: Antisemitism and Philosemitism in Postwar Germany* (Oxford, 1992).
69. "Control Council Law No. 10," *TWC*, I, xvi–xix.
70. *Die Waldheimer "Prozesse": fünfzig Jahre danach. Dokumentation der Tagung der Stiftung Sächsische Gedenkstättten am 28. und 29. September 2000 in Waldheim*, eds. Norbert Haase and Bert Pampel (Baden-Baden, 2001); Christian Meyer-Seitz, *Die Verfolgung von NS-Straftaten in der Sowjetischen Besatzungszone* (Berlin, 1998); Annette Weinke, *Die Verfolgung von NS-Tätern im geteilten Deutschland: Vergangenheitsbewältigung oder eine deutsch-deutsche Beziehungsgeschichte im Kalten Krieg* (Paderborn, 2002); Bettina Weinreich, *Strafjustiz und ihre Politisierung in SBZ und DDR bis 1961: Auswertung von Dokumenten und Urteilen unter Berücksichtigung des historischen Zusammenhangs* (Frankfurt, 2005).
71. Dr Ledig, "Zum Kontrollratsgesetz Nr. 10," *Neue Justiz* 2 (1948): 191.
72. OLG Dresden, Urteil 11.5.1948, 21 ERKs 112/48, *Neue Justiz* 2 (1948): 115.
73. OLG Dresden, Urteil 5.9.1947, 20. 167/47, *Neue Justiz* 1 (1947): 196.
74. OLG Dresden, Urteil 12.9.1947, 20. 188/47, *Neue Justiz 1 (1947)*: 195.
75. Case 1, "Opening Statement," *TWC*, I, 27–29.
76. Case 5, Taylor, "Opening Statement," *TWC*, VI, 83.
77. LG Konstanz, Strafkammer II (KLs 22/47), September 2, 1947, *Monatsschrift für deutsches Recht* 1 (1947): 305.
78. Ibid.
79. Cf., e.g., OLG Freiburg, Urteil, *Deutsche Rechts-Zeitschrift* 3 (1948): 259.
80. LG Konstanz, 305.
81. OLG Kiel, Urteil 3.10.1947, Ws 67/47, *Monatsschrift für deutsches Recht* 1 (1947): 307.
82. OLG Kiel, Urteil 26.3.1947, Ss 27/47, *Monatsschrift für deutsches Recht* 1 (1947): 71.
83. Ulrich Herbert, "Liberalisierung als Lernprozeß: Die Bundesrepublik in der deutschen Geschichte—eine Skizze," in *Wandlungsprozesse in Westdeutschland: Belastung, Integration, Liberalisierung 1945–1980*, ed. U. Herbert (Göttingen, 2002), 13.
84. Pendas, "Retroactive Law and Proactive Justice."
85. The literature on German Nazi trials in the period after 1950 has grown substantially in recent years. For a historiographic overview, see Devin O. Pendas, "Seeking Justice, Finding Law: Nazi Trials in the Postwar Era, 1945–1989," *Journal of Modern History* 81 (2009): 347–68.
86. Alexandra Przyrembel, "Transfixed by an Image: Ilse Koch, the 'Kommandeuse of Buchenwald,'" *German History* 19 (2001): 369–99. On Seidl's role in the Eichmann trial, see the authoritative account by Hannah Yablonka, *The State of Israel vs. Adolf Eichmann* (New York, 2004).
87. On the Auschwitz trial in general, see Rebecca Wittmann, *Beyond Justice: the Auschwitz Trial* (Cambridge, MA, 2005); Devin O. Pendas, *The Frankfurt Auschwitz Trial, 1963–1965: Genocide, History, and the Limits of the Law* (Cambridge, 2006).

88. Laternser was very concerned to publicize his legal arguments. See, e.g., Hans Laternser, *Verteidigung deutscher Soldaten: Plädoyers vor alliierten Gerichten* (Bonn, 1950).

89. Cf. Joachim R. Rumpf, *Der Fall Wollheim gegen die I.G. Farbenindustrie AG in Liquidation: Die erste Musterklage eines ehemaligen Zwangsarbeiters in der Bundesrepublik Deutschland. Prozess, Politik und Presse* (Frankfurt a.M., 2010).

90. Christian Dirks, "Selekteure als Lebensretter: Die Verteidigungsstrategie des Rechtsanwalts Dr. Hans Laternser," in *"Gerichtstag halten über uns selbst...": Geschichte und Wirkung des ersten Frankfurter Auschwitz-Prozesses*, ed. Irmtrud Wojak (Frankfurt, 2001), 163–67.

91. Dix, "Urteile," 649.

92. Hans Laternser, *Die andere Seite im Auschwitz-Prozeß, 1963/65* (Stuttgart, 1966), 186.

93. Axel von der Ohe, *Das Gesellschaftsbild der Bundesgerichtshofs: Die Rechtsprechung des BGH und die frühe Bundesrepublik* (Frankfurt, 2010).

94. Robert G. Moeller, *War Stories: The Search for a Usable Past in the Federal Republic of Germany* (Berkeley, 2001); Jeffrey K. Olick, *House of the Hangman*; *A Nation of Victims? Representations of German Wartime Suffering from 1945 to the Present*, ed. Helmut Schmitz (Amsterdam, 2007).

95. Dirk Moses, *German Intellectuals and the Nazi Past* (Cambridge, 2007), 37.

96. Boris Barth, *Dolchstoßlegenden und politische Desintegration: Das Trauma der deutschen Niederlage im ersten Weltkrieg, 1914–1933* (Düsseldorf, 2003).

97. Kranzbühler, *Rückblick*, 10.

98. Donald Bloxham and Devin O. Pendas, "Punishment as Prevention? The Politics of Punishing Génocidaires", in *The Oxford Handbook of the History of Genocide*, eds. Donald Bloxham and A. Dirk Moses (Oxford, 2010), 617–37.

99. Thomas Carlyle, *Sartor Resartus: The Life and Opinions of Herr Teufelsdröckh in Three Books* (Berkeley, 2000).

## CHAPTER 10

# FROM IMT TO NMT
## THE EMERGENCE OF A
## JURISPRUDENCE OF ATROCITY

*Lawrence Douglas*

⟨ℰ§§⟩

**T**he fabric of international law has been radically and irrevocably changed as a result of its contact with atrocity—first in the form of Nazi crimes, and more recently in the shape of atrocities in the Balkans and genocide in Rwanda. At the most basic level, this has led to a shift in the basic model of criminality. In the familiar domestic national model, law views criminal behavior as a deviant act, characteristically committed by a discrete individual, harmful of community norms and interests. The state, in this account, intervenes as the accuser and as the agent for enforcing and defending violated norms of community order. As such, the state serves as the locus of legality—in certain positivist accounts, such as the Hobbesian, this is true by definition; and this strong connection between state power and legal efficacy informs the theory of sovereignty and the prerogatives of immunity that generally have insulated the state from legal interference.[1]

The contact with Nazi crimes revolutionized law by creating the exigent need, if not the theoretical apparatus, for puncturing this shield of sovereignty. Today we accept without argument the idea that state actors responsible for atrocities should have to answer for their conduct in courts of criminal law—be they domestic, international, or of a hybrid character. But we run the risk of forgetting how deeply radical this idea was before the trial of the major Nazi war criminals before the International Military Tribunal (IMT) in Nuremberg. Sovereignty—the plenary power of the nation state, articulated in the political theory of Hobbes, enshrined in the Peace of Westphalia—was widely seen prior to the IMT as erecting a bar to international prosecutions.[2] As a practical matter, the shield of sovereignty has hardly lost its luster: sixty plus years after the IMT proceeding, it remains mighty strong—from the perspective of the human rights lawyer, frustratingly so. The very trope of *puncturing* sovereignty has its limits, as it overlooks how the contact with atrocity has also rendered state power more fluid and extended its reach, by authorizing the exercise of such unorthodox practices as universal jurisdiction.[3] Nonetheless, the conceptual shift has been dramatic. In the wake of Nuremberg, Karl Jaspers framed the term *Verbrecherstaat*, the criminal state, a notion meant to name and denote a phenomenon that lay beyond the ken of the standard model of the criminal law and was nonsensical to it.[4] Jaspers' formulation demanded that the state be seen not as the defender of order but as the principal perpetrator of crimes, as the very agent of criminality.

The trial of the major Nazi war criminals is rightly credited with establishing this breakthrough in international criminal law. Indeed, it would be no exaggeration to claim that international criminal law was an *invention* of the IMT—this notwithstanding the fact that the international community had condemned actions such as piracy and war crimes well before the advent of the twentieth century.[5] If Nuremberg did not discover, then it firmly established the principle of individual criminal responsibility in international law. Whatever doubts jurists might have had about the IMT at the time, these have now been largely answered by history. If the IMT once struggled against the taint of "victors' justice," six decades after its original staging the trial's prestige has never been greater. Jurists, legal scholars, and historians—groups that often find much to disagree about—appear unified in viewing the IMT as by far the most important single event in the development of international criminal law. Conferences staged to coincide with the sixtieth anniversary of the trial often had a celebratory, even hagiographic quality.[6] Law students around the globe now dutifully study the so-called "Nuremberg Principles," the norms of international law, which insist, among other things, that "acts of state" and "superior orders" supply no defense against the charge of perpetrating international crimes.[7]

By contrast, the twelve so-called "subsequent proceedings" staged by American jurists before the Nuremberg Military Tribunals (NMTs) have been long considered nothing more than footnotes to the IMT—and unhappy ones at that.[8] No conferences were staged to consider, much less to celebrate, the anniversary of the NMT trial program. The trials often warrant no more than brief mention in textbooks on international criminal law and are seen to have delivered little by way of precedent. Admittedly the Justice case recently experienced a vogue of attention in

the United States as lawyers trawled for possible precedents for bringing charges against the authors of the "torture memos" in Bush's Justice Department.[9] But even this brief renaissance of interest quickly
waned as the precedential relevance of the Justice case appeared smaller
than hoped.[10]

The fact that the NMT program has long been treated as nothing
more than a footnote to the IMT does, of course, have its logic. Telford
Taylor, the chief NMT prosecutor, came himself to think of the trial
program as a failure—in his insightful, though hardly definitive memoir
cum history, *Anatomy of the Nuremberg Trials*, Taylor barely mentions
the trials that he oversaw, this despite the insertion of the plural term
in his book's title.[11] Some of the problems had to do with the "talent
gap" that plagued the NMT. The decision of Fred Vinson, Chief Justice of the US Supreme Court, to bar Federal Judges from serving as
NMT judges—a decision largely motivated by a desire to avoid the kind
of backlog of cases caused by Justice Jackson's tenure at the IMT[12]—
meant that NMT cases were presided over by state court judges, jurists
lacking the prestige and often the competence of their federal court
counterparts.[13] Congress's dreadfully short-sighted decision to slash
the budget of the NMT while the program was in mid-course made
it difficult if not impossible for the trial program to "get its message
out"—about which, more later. As a result of these cuts, the judgment
in the High Command case, an impressive document that lay bare the
complicity of the Wehrmacht in crimes of genocidal sweep and which
anticipated the "revelations" of Wehrmacht criminality that gripped
Germany in the mid-1990s, could not be translated into German, a
failure that Taylor lamented.[14] Most fatally tarnishing the reputation
of the NMT program was the commutation of sentences of those convicted. As has been amply documented, war criminals and perpetrators
of atrocity found their sentences reduced and commuted in an American
effort to secure Germany as a reliable ally in the escalating Cold War.
To Taylor's great and understandable frustration, by 1958 the last of
the NMT convicts found themselves free men. The premature release
of Nazi criminals contributed, however, not only to Taylor's prosecutorial despair, but also to a larger perception that the trial program had
been a waste of time and money. That the commutation policy was the
consequence of political calculations completely beyond the purview and
control of the hundreds of jurists involved in the trial program seems
largely to have been lost on those observers who saw the post hoc release
of the Nazis as an indictment of the trials themselves.[15]

These shortcomings have led jurists and historians to overlook the
accomplishments of the NMT. In this essay, I want to try to rescue,
however modestly, the NMT program from its decades of comparative
neglect. My point is less to argue that the NMT trials achieved specific
successes that can now be better appreciated with historical hindsight.
Rather, I will be more interested in showing that the NMT program,

more than the IMT, anticipated, if not paved the way to, more recent developments in international criminal law. Put somewhat differently, I believe our contemporary paradigm of international criminal law—what I will call a "jurisprudence of atrocity"—bears more similarities to the jurisprudential profile of the NMT than the IMT. Though following directly on the heels of the IMT, the NMT proceedings already began dismantling the jurisprudential paradigm that guided the trial of the major war criminals, delivering in its place the template for the future development of international criminal law. Ostensibly building on the fresh IMT precedent, the NMT in fact reoriented the newly established paradigm of international criminal law.

## The IMT and the Aggressive War Paradigm

As we recall, the twenty-one defendants who appeared before the international tribunal stood trial for three substantive crimes—crimes against peace, war crimes, and crimes against humanity—and also for a fourth offense, conspiracy, which sought to link a disparate group of state actors to a larger common plan to perpetrate the three substantive crimes. Genocide, now considered the gravest offense in international law, was, at the time of the trial, still a freshly minted neologism, a descriptive term that named certain atrocities enfolded with war crimes and crimes against humanity; genocide did not come to name an independent crime in international law until the Genocide Convention of 1948.[16]

If we examine the IMT's charge sheet from sixty-five years of hindsight, the incrimination that clearly appears most problematic is "crimes against peace." It was the charge that at the time invited vehement charges of "victors' justice" and that seemed most vulnerable to the charge of violating the foundational norm of *nulla poena sine lege*.[17] In the years since the trial before the IMT, "crimes against peace" has shown the least durability and utility as a term of legal art. While the concept of the "crime against peace" has played some role in authorizing the use of military force—most notably in the Korean War and in the war to liberate Kuwait from Iraqi invasion—it has largely disappeared from the charge sheet in more recent war crimes trials. It is revealing, for example, that when Iraqi prosecutors (with the aid of American jurists) prepared their cases against Saddam Hussein, the invasion of Kuwait—Hussein's most obvious offense against the international community, the action that led to the first and most unified military response to his aggression—played no role in the legal proceedings against him.[18] The fledgling International Criminal Court, the permanent international criminal tribunal that came into effect on July 1, 2002 with jurisdiction over genocide, crimes against humanity, and war crimes, also, in principle, claims jurisdiction over aggressive war, though this latter jurisdiction remains entirely speculative, and even recent successes toward framing a satisfactory definition of the crime leave unsettled whether the crime will ever be included in the charge sheet of ICC prosecutors.[19]

But if we turn the clock back to Nuremberg, crimes against peace was the gravamen of the prosecution's case—it was understood as *the* principal international crime. The history of how this came to be is vexed, and we need not review the involved story of the roles variously played by Professor Glueck, Colonel Chanler, Colonel Bernays, President Roosevelt, Secretary Stimson, Justice Jackson, and Baron Shawcross that led to framing the trial around the crime of aggressive war.[20] As Jonathan Bush has demonstrated, the decision made for sharp disagreements not only among the Allied powers—the French in particular never accepted this stratagem—but also between members of the American team, which pioneered the idea.[21] Allied jurists notably failed to frame an adequate definition of crimes against peace—the description of "aggressive war" in Article 6(a) of the IMT charter is startlingly imprecise, a fact made all the more glaring in light of the relatively well-framed definitions of war crimes 6(b) and crimes against humanity 6(c).

And yet, however anomalous "aggressive war" may appear today and however controversial it was at the time, the incrimination made sense from the perspective of the classic theory of sovereignty. By criminalizing the unprovoked attack of one nation on another, the crime against peace can be seen as less a radical if not futile effort to juridify the logic of war, and more as a conservative gesture, an attempt to safeguard and not usurp the system of sovereign nation-states. I would thus express the jurisprudential theory of the IMT in this way: on certain rare occasions, such as in the case of transparently unprovoked warfare, it may be necessary to puncture the shield of sovereignty in order to protect the larger system of sovereign nation-states. From this perspective, the decision to treat aggressive war as the paradigmatic international crime made perfect sense in 1945. Indeed, the *international* character of the crime was beyond question. The IMT could thus be seen as protecting the Westphalian system from the destabilizing effects of unprovoked warfare, not as a tool for supplanting it.[22]

This jurisprudential understanding informed the construction and interpretation of the two other substantive crimes adjudicated at Nuremberg: war crimes and crimes against humanity. As is well known, the tribunal interpreted the conspiracy charge to apply only to the crime of waging a war of aggression; conspiracy to commit war crimes and crimes against humanity was deemed not a justiciable offense. This reinforced the centrality of crimes against peace, and solidified the logic that plausibly insisted that war crimes occur only in times of war; eliminating war would thus eliminate the crimes it gives rise to. Moreover, the international character of war crimes is not open to question, except, perhaps, in circumstances of civil war. Like crimes against peace, war crimes permit the international community to shatter sovereignty for the ultimate purpose of preserving it; it is a regulation meant to forestall the possibility that warring sovereigns will annihilate one another, particularly in an age in which the technologies of war-making make possible slaughter on a scale unimaginable at an earlier period of history.

The IMT's conceptualization of crimes against humanity, a crime first recognized at Nuremberg, also fits this paradigm. By now it is familiar that the IMT concluded that only those crimes against humanity that demonstrated a nexus to aggressive war were deemed justiciable. As a result of this holding, the tribunal refused to consider German on German crimes perpetrated before the Wehrmacht crossed the Polish frontier on September 1, 1939. The practical consequences of this ruling might have been negligible as the overwhelming majority of the Nazis' most egregious crimes against humanity occurred after the start of the war (most but not all—examples of prewar atrocities, such as forced sterilizations and the November pogrom, abound). But the *conceptual* importance of the nexus requirement remains. Certainly Jackson, who acknowledged, "[w]e have some regrettable circumstances at times in our own country in which minorities are unfairly treated," was concerned that the absence of a nexus requirement could potentially open Jim Crow laws to the scrutiny of some future international jurist.[23] Yet more to the point, the nexus requirement reflected the larger jurisprudential vision of Nuremberg that conceived of *international* crimes in the quite literal and altogether convincing sense as crimes *between* legal entities called nation-states. If the IMT empowered international law and international courts to shatter the prerogatives of the sovereign, it was toward the conservative end of preserving, not supplanting, the larger system of sovereign nation-states.

## The NMT Atrocity Trial: Supplanting the Nuremberg Paradigm

The NMT trials, by contrast, represent an unmistakable, if not always fully articulated, shift away from the IMT aggressive war paradigm and towards what I will call the "atrocity paradigm." By this I mean that the NMT trials focused far more explicitly on what may be called crimes of atrocity: acts of extermination, genocide, systematic murder of civilian populations, and other crimes against humanity. This is not to say that the IMT aggressive war paradigm entirely vanished from the subsequent proceedings. In the IG-Farben trial (Case 6), the Krupp trial (Case 10), the Ministries trial (aka the Wilhelmstraße trial, Case 11) and High Command trial (Case 12), crimes against peace remained the organizational focal point of the proceedings.[24] Indeed, as Kevin Jon Heller notes, the Ministries trial actually expanded the notion of aggression to include the *Anschluss* of Austria and the invasion of Czechoslovakia.[25] Still, the shift toward the atrocity paradigm can be clearly seen. Of the twelve NMT trials, crimes against peace appear as a formal charge in only the four cases just listed. By contrast, crimes against humanity appear as a charge in *all* twelve. In the IMT proceeding, crimes against humanity were treated as interstitial offenses, covering a relatively narrow range of crimes that technically could not be enfolded within the ambit of war crimes. Before the NMT, by contrast, crimes against humanity emerge as the principal crime in the Medical trial (Case 1), the RuSHA proceedings (Case 8) and the *Einsatzgruppen* trial (Case 9). Even in those trials nominally organized around the IMT paradigm of aggressive war, such as the High Command case, crimes against humanity came to play a central role in the proceeding, as acts of atrocity came to the fore of the prosecutors' case.[26] The same pattern can be seen in the NMT judgments. As Taylor noted:

> The great majority of the convictions in the trials under Law No. 10 were based upon charges relating to war crimes and crimes against humanity, involving atrocities and offenses such as slave labor, economic spoliation, the killing of hostages, and persecution and extermination of Jews, and other racial, religious, or national groups. No defendant was convicted of conspiracy, and only 5 of the 52 defendants tried for war-making were convicted.[27]

In small part, this shift in focus can be explained in terms of the law that controlled the subsequent Nuremberg proceedings, Control Council Law no. 10 (CCL 10). This Allied document, signed on December 20, 1945, less than five months after the promulgation of the IMT charter and while the trial of the major war criminals was only entering its third month, already supplied a definition of crimes against humanity that differed from the definition framed by the IMT in two notable respects.[28] First, CCL 10 expanded the range of crimes against humanity to include "atrocities and offenses" such as "imprisonment," "torture," and "rape," acts not mentioned in 6(c) of the IMT charter. Second, and perhaps more significantly, CCL 10 severed the nexus requirement that conditioned the justiciability of crimes against humanity to their link to crimes against peace. The practical significance of the severance of the nexus requirement should not be overstated. It appears that many of the NMT judges failed to appreciate the significance of this change and continued to hew narrowly to the IMT precedent. As Robert Wolfe has observed, the tribunals in the Medical, Flick, and Ministries (Weizsäcker) cases all "reaffirmed the IMT opinion that crimes against German nationals antedating September 1939 and not directly connected to aggressive war, ... however deplorable, were not ... punishable under international law."[29] Taylor himself underscored this point in his *Final Report*, diplomatically noting, "For the most part, the tribunals established under Law No. 10 were reluctant under any circumstances to adopt a broader construction of these definitions than the IMT had applied in its judgment."[30]

On the other hand, the change wasn't entirely lost on the subsequent tribunals. In his Opening Statement in the *Einsatzgruppen* case, Benjamin Ferencz specifically called attention to the difference:

> The London Charter restricted the jurisdiction of the International Military Tribunal to crimes against humanity connected with crimes against peace or war crimes. This restriction does not appear in the Control Council enactment, which recognizes that crimes against humanity are, in international law, completely independent of either crimes against peace or war crimes. To deny this independence would make the change devoid of meaning.[31]

And judges in both the *Einsatzgruppen* case and the Justice case "deliberately went out their way," pace Wolfe, to recognize and endorse CCL 10's new construction of crimes against humanity. As the tribunal in the Justice case insisted:

> The grim fact of worldwide independence, and the moral pressure of public opinion have resulted in international recognition that certain crimes against humanity committed by Nazi authority against German nationals constituted violations not alone of statute but also of common international law.[32]

The practical consequences of the tribunals' pronouncements in the *Einsatzgruppen* and Justice cases should not be exaggerated; both cases ultimately dealt with crimes against humanity committed during and not before the war. Still, their dicta reflect an important conceptual appreciation of the rapidly changing contours of the meaning and application of crimes against humanity.

The reasons for the shift from the aggressive war to the atrocity paradigm are, then, multiple. Obviously NMT prosecutors could afford to place greater emphasis on crimes against humanity inasmuch as they could now rely on the IMT case as precedent. Yet this explanation goes only so far, as it can be applied with equal weight in the case of aggressive war: just as the judgment of the IMT offered a basis for subsequent prosecutions for crimes against humanity, it also supplied a precedent for trials against perpetrators of aggressive war. And yet the NMT program makes clear that prosecutors were already pulling away from aggressive war while aggressively pressing forward with trials based on crimes against humanity.

No doubt NMT prosecutors were sensitive to the fact that criticisms of the crime against the peace had hardly abated with the conclusion of the IMT case. Controversial from its first insertion in the IMT charter, the crime of aggression remained contested by prominent international jurists in the wake of the conclusion of the trial of the major war criminals. These critiques issued not only from questionable figures, such as Carl Schmitt,[33] but also from leading voices in liberal legal positivism. In 1947, the great Austrian Jewish legal thinker Hans Kelsen, himself an escapee of Nazi terror, published an influential critique of the IMT proceeding which predicted—perhaps in self-fulfilling fashion given the renown of the commentator—that trials based on the crime of peace would have deservedly little future in international law.[34]

But it would be misleading to say that NMT prosecutors focused on crimes against humanity solely because of doubts about the legal coherence of crimes against peace. Also at play was a dawning understanding among prosecutors of the novel character of Nazi atrocities. This trend was already apparent in the IMT case, where one clearly finds a shift in prosecutorial emphases as the trial moves into its later stages; it is as if the IMT prosecutors themselves only came to appreciate the full nature and meaning of Nazi criminality in the course of trying the case.[35] Although crimes against peace remained the formal gravamen of the case, as prosecutors mastered the learning curve of Nazi criminality, they came to place ever greater emphasis on crimes against humanity.[36]

A further sign of this is the greater reliance that NMT jurists placed on the concept of genocide. As we recall, the term genocide was the creation of Raphael Lemkin, a Polish-Jewish jurist who, long before the Nazi extermination of the Jews, had agitated for international legal recognition of Turkish atrocities perpetrated against the Armenians, and who, in 1943, coined the neologism to name the Nazis' techniques of administrative massacre directed against the Jewish population of Europe.[37] The term made its first appearance in a legal document in the IMT indictment—albeit as a description of war crimes, not as a crime against humanity—and found scant mention during the trial (though it did surface in the statements of both British and French prosecutors). The neologism gains far greater circulation in the NMT trials. In the RuSHA case, prosecutor James McHaney uses the term as the sharpest way to characterize and designate the Nazis' most extreme crimes against humanity, although McHaney's formulations still hark back, in part, to the IMT paradigm—"... genocide was part of the Nazi doctrine of total warfare."[38]

More revealing is the use of "genocide" in the *Einsatzgruppen* case, where it gains even wider currency. Judge Michael Musmanno, in his judgment, speaks sardonically of the "development of the fine art of genocide."[39] And Benjamin Ferencz, in his Opening Statement for the prosecution, describes the "crime of genocide"[40]—though the term had yet to gain independent legal status—and specifically decouples it from the logic of warfare:

> Genocide, the extermination of whole categories of human beings, was a foremost instrument of the Nazi doctrine. Even before the war the concentration camps within the Third Reich had witnessed many killings inspired by these ideas. During the early months of the war the Nazi regime expanded its plans for genocide and enlarged the means to execute them.[41]

In Ferencz's narrative, genocide is not a consequence of war, but war an instrument and pretext for pursuing genocide. Ferencz returns to this point, noting, "… the killing of defenseless civilians during a war may be a war crime, but the same killings are part of another crime, a graver one if you will, genocide—or a crime against humanity. This is the distinction we make in our pleading. It is real and most significant."[42]

The shift, then, was ultimately conceptual, borne of an emerging understanding among prosecutors and jurists that Nazi crimes *were* in the first instance crimes of atrocity—extermination, annihilation, genocide. Taylor's experience is emblematic. In *Anatomy of the Nuremberg Trials*, Taylor recalls, "Like so many others, I remained ignorant of the mass extermination camps in Poland, and the full scope of the Holocaust did not dawn on me until several months later, at Nuremberg."[43] During his tenure as chief prosecutor of the NMT program, his thinking changed dramatically. Prodded by Lemkin, he considered organizing an NMT trial that would concern itself exclusively with the destruction of European Jewry, which he acknowledged as "the most important and sinister item in the entire Nazi history";[44] if this effort failed, it was more a result of thorny logistical problems than misplaced juridical priorities.[45] Taylor made clear his own understanding of the juridical importance of the NMT in a speech delivered at the *Palais de Justice* in Paris, on April 25, 1947:

> I suggest, in conclusion, that it is in the field of crimes against humanity that international criminal law can make its most valuable contribution to the safeguarding of human dignity and to the peace of the world. So, too, it is in connection with crimes against humanity that we can best realize the hope, so well expressed by Monsieur le Professeur Donnedieu de Vabres, that international penal [sic] should not remain a law imposed only by victors against vanquished.[46]

Here we find the clearest expression of the paradigm shift, away from the IMT's focus on crimes against peace (note Taylor's implicit critique in his mention of victors' justice) and toward the atrocity paradigm focused on crimes against humanity. This, of course, is not to claim that the understanding of atrocity presented at the NMT trials was entirely adequate, nuanced, and complete. As a number of other chapters in this volume make clear, the shortcomings were at times grave, especially in hindsight. Yet when viewed as a whole, the NMT program, by focusing on crimes of atrocity, produced a thicker and richer understanding of the meaning and processes of extermination and genocide than did the IMT. In this regard, the NMT represents a substantial improvement over the IMT.

In moving toward an atrocity paradigm, the NMT trials anticipated and arguably influenced the subsequent development of international criminal law. If we shift our attention forward by several decades, and examine the ongoing work of the International Criminal Tribunal for the Former Yugoslavia (ICTY) and the International Criminal Tribunal

Rwanda (ICTR), as well as the early operations of the permanent International Criminal Court (ICC), we clearly see the predominance of the NMT atrocity paradigm. The IMT's focus on aggressive war remains largely an irrelevancy despite recent efforts at resuscitation[47]; what now dominates international criminal law is the NMT's focus on crimes of atrocity such as genocide, systematic extermination, and ethnic cleansing. The principle first articulated in Control Council Law no. 10, that international law no longer required a nexus between crimes against humanity and aggressive war—a principle imperfectly understood by many NMT judges—is now well settled in international criminal law.[48]

The ascendency of the atrocity paradigm—exemplified in the severing of the IMT's nexus requirement, the eclipse in the importance of the crime of aggression, and in the development of a free-standing jurisprudence of crimes against humanity and genocide—finds further elaboration in the recent jurisprudence of war crimes. In the IMT paradigm, war crimes stood second to the crime of aggression as the paradigmatic *international* crime, as such offenses arose in the context of armed conflict between sovereign nations (as we recall, by the terms of its Charter, the IMT had jurisdiction only over war crimes committed by Axis powers). More recently, however, rulings by international tribunals have again abandoned the IMT paradigm, essentially severing war crimes from any connection to hostilities between nation-states. In its important ruling, the ICTY concluded in its Tadić decision that a conflict need not be strictly international in character to give rise to violations of the laws of war justiciable in an international court.[49]

Perhaps the most dramatic example of the rejection the IMT paradigm is supplied by the NATO air war waged against the Federal Republic of Yugoslavia in the spring of 1999. The war, as we recall, was launched without authorization of the United Nations' Security Council, and thus, under the terms of the UN Charter, arguably constituted an act of aggression. NATO, of course, argued that military intervention was necessary in order to stop Serbian acts of ethnic cleansing tantamount to crimes against humanity and genocide. However we might feel about the particulars of the case, it represents the clearest triumph of the NMT paradigm over the IMT approach, or to put it somewhat differently, of the atrocity paradigm over the aggressive war paradigm. Indeed, the NATO air war does not simply represent the priority of atrocity over aggressive war in contemporary international law. Rather, it stands for the more remarkable proposition that acts of atrocity arguably warrant the waging of aggressive war.[50]

The rise of the atrocity paradigm is further visible in the evolution of the role of victims and victim groups in international criminal law. Following the strategy outlined by Justice Jackson, IMT prosecutors structured their case around captured documentary evidence, material considered harder and more reliable than eyewitness testimony. By the conclusion of the trial, Jackson was able to report to President

Truman, "the case … against the defendants rests in large measure on documents of their own making, the authenticity of which has not been challenged."[51] The IMT's aggressive war paradigm supported the "trial by document," as few witnesses, let alone members of victims groups, could offer any insight into the motives, planning, and preparations of the war of aggression, while highly incriminating official Nazi documents abounded. As a consequence, the prosecution unfolded largely absent the testimony of witnesses, depriving the trial of an "affirmative human aspect" and turning it into, to borrow Rebecca West's memorable formulation, a "citadel of boredom."[52] The failure of the prosecution to call more than a token number of victims, and the virtual absence of testimony from Jewish survivors, disappointed victims' groups and eroded support for the trial within victim communities.

The atrocity paradigm, by contrast, came to place narratives and testimony of the survivor-victim at the center of the legal proceeding. The most outstanding example of this remains the Eichmann trial, perhaps the greatest of all atrocity trials. However much Arendt might have lamented Gideon Hausner's courtroom histrionics,[53] the Israeli Attorney General and lead prosecutor succeeded in his aim of capturing the hearts and minds of the public by organizing the prosecution's case around survivor testimony.[54] If the Eichmann trial perfected the victim-centered jurisprudence of the atrocity paradigm, the NMT proceedings again demand to be seen as constituting a critical moment of transition. Our claims need to be modest and respectful of the differences between the distinct NMT cases. The *Einsatzgruppen* trial, the case that most explicitly focused on the crimes of the Holocaust, disappoints in this respect. Conducted with untoward haste, the prosecution presented its entire case in three days, and, hewing to the IMT approach, relied almost exclusively on documentary evidence and the statements of perpetrators.[55] Taylor himself acknowledged that most of the NMT cases "rested primarily on documents assembled prior to the trials and only secondarily on the testimony of witnesses."[56] Indeed, the majority of witnesses called before the NMT appeared at the behest of the defense. Still, we find some notable exceptions to this pattern. The Medical trial took a different approach, one that would be repeated in future atrocity trials. Prosecutors used advertisements to search for victims willing to testify, and, after a process of vetting to select the sturdiest and most articulate survivors, organized their cases, at least in part, around survivor testimony.[57] Prosecutors even discussed the creation of a fund meant to compensate witnesses; although this came to naught, it anticipated more recent international tribunals.

If we jump ahead to the work of the ICTY and the ICTR, we see that it now becomes possible to speak of victims' *rights* in international cases. These latter rights include matters of voice and control, and embrace everything from protecting the interest that victims have in telling their stories told in court; to a relaxation of the norms that conventionally protect the defendant's rights of confrontation; to a recognition of the right of civil interveners to represent victims groups in the trial process.[58] The ICC, as Amnesty International recognizes, goes further still, specifically enshrining three key principles relating to victims' rights: "(1) victim participation in the proceedings, (2) protection of victims and witnesses and (3) the right to reparations."[59] To strengthen this latter right, the ICC statute formally creates the novel device of a victims' trust fund. Here again, I do not want to claim the ICC has followed the precedent established in the Medical case. The NMT's innovations were more conceptual than causal. And compared to the Eichmann trial, the NMT's reliance on victim testimony remained quite modest. That said, the NMT program still deserves to be seen as emblematic of a larger shift toward privileging the voice and testimony of survivors in the atrocity paradigm.

Let us for a moment stand back and take stock. The IMT, we have observed, saw the crime of aggression as constituting *the* international crime. This, I argued, made perfect sense in terms of a classic theory of sovereignty, and turned the IMT, a radical legal innovation, into a tool for conserving, not usurping the system of sovereign nation-states. When we shifted our focus to the NMT program, we noticed something surprising. Although ostensibly building on the precedent freshly established by the IMT, the NMT in fact began to abandon the core orientation, shifting international criminal law to what I have called the "atrocity paradigm." This shift, I have argued, anticipated more recent developments in international law. The crime of aggressive war—the focus of the IMT and the incrimination with the clearest connection to international conduct—has become largely a dead letter, and in its stead we find the development of a rich jurisprudence of three international crimes—crimes against humanity, genocide, and war crimes—and the rise of a victim-centric jurisprudence. We have arrived then at the surprising result that the NMT program, long considered no more than a footnote to the IMT, more powerfully anticipated, if not contributed to the creation of, the atrocity paradigm that now dominates international criminal law.

## Retribution and Didactic Legality

Finally we should note that even the failures of the NMT demand to be seen as emblematic of problems that have vexed the atrocity paradigm. These failures specifically involved the retributive and didactic functions of the trials, and the complex relationship between the two. As I observed at the outset, the commutation of sentences of those convicted by the NMT dramatically compromised the prestige of the trial program, conferring an aura of failure upon the entire endeavor. At its most basic, criminal justice is a retributive exercise, in which justice demands the imposition of an adequate punishment. The failure to punish, or the failure to punish adequately, suggests a failure of justice itself. In this regard, the effects of commutation can be seen as far more deleterious than the effects of acquittal. Acquittal is a judicial act that results when the prosecution does not follow proper procedures or cannot shoulder its evidentiary burden of proof. In the context of atrocity trials, the occasional acquittal can serve as a legitimating device, demonstrating the neutrality and independence of the tribunal, its capacity to remain faithful to the rule of law even in the face of extreme charges that create a pressure to convict.

Commutation, by contrast, is an executive decision, that applies to persons already found guilty through the trial process. While commutation, when prudently administered, may be seen as an act of mercy, it appears profoundly problematic when offered in blanket fashion— especially in the context of atrocity trials, involving the most horrific crimes. Blanket commutation extends a pall back over the entire trial program. It suggests either the original process was so flawed that none of those convicted deserve continued punishment, or the interests of justice have been cynically subordinated to political goals, such as, in this case, appeasing an ally. The failure to punish acts of atrocity in a commensurate fashion strongly undermines the cause of justice.[60]

And yet the problem of adequate punishment was not peculiar to the NMT but has vexed all atrocity trials. At the time of the IMT proceeding, Hannah Arendt famously wrote to Karl Jaspers, "The Nazi crimes, it seems to me, explode the limits of the law; and that is what constitutes their monstrousness. For these crimes, no punishment is severe enough."[61] Arendt, prescient as ever in her thinking, saw the IMT in a manner different from the trial's own self-understanding. She understood the IMT as an atrocity proceeding whose greatest contribution to international law was the adumbration of the crime against humanity, a point she explicitly made years later in *Eichmann in Jerusalem*. Indeed, in her book, Arendt faults the Israeli court for failing to build on the one distinctive achievement of the IMT—the juridical recognition of crimes against humanity.[62] Yet here, too, she returned to the retributive dilemma of the jurisprudence of atrocity: that no punishment appears proportional to crimes of atrocity. In his summation before the court, Israeli Attorney General and lead prosecutor Gideon Hausner himself conceded, "It is not always possible to apply a punishment which fits the enormity of the crime."[63]

This issue continues to vex the work of the ICTY and ICTR, and will most certainly plague the ICC, as well. As Mark Drumbl has painstakingly documented, the sentencing practices of international and quasi-international tribunals reveal the absence of any clear guidelines, standards, or logic;[64] in conversations with numerous participants associated with ICTY, I heard time and again concerns raised about the unseemliness of sentencing a convicted perpetrator of crimes against

humanity to, say, eleven years in prison. Needless to say, these dispari-
ties appear all the more grotesque when compared to sentences meted
out by domestic national courts in trials involving conventional crimes,
particularly those in the punishment-happy United States: how can we
reconcile, for example, the sentencing of a juvenile killer to a mandatory
life term with the twenty-five-year term given a perpetrator of genocide?

The most satisfactory way to solve the dilemma of retribution is to
link the atrocity trial more firmly to its didactic function. Punishment,
in this calculus, serves more a symbolic end, helping to communicate
the pedagogic or tutelary lessons of the trial.[65] The atrocity trial can
serve as a tool of political-legal legitimation by making visible the sober
operation of the rule of law; it can serve the ends of history and memory
in communities overcoming the legacy of atrocity by clarifying a history
of horror often obscured in rumor, denial, and silence; it can establish a
baseline account that may serve the interests of democratic transition;
and it can confer public recognition upon the memories of survivors and
honor upon the memory of victims.

While some scholars have expressed serious doubts about the value
of atrocity trials as tools of historical instruction and memory construction,[66] I would insist that legal didactics are a necessary feature of the
justificatory logic of any jurisprudence of atrocity. Indeed, it is no coin-
cidence that many principal participants in atrocity trials have openly
embraced the didactic function of such proceedings. Robert M.W. Kempner memorably defended the Nuremberg trials as the "world's greatest
research institute,"[67] and Michael Musmanno, in his judgment in the
*Einsatzgruppen* case, likewise saw the trial as a pedagogic exercise:

> Judicial opinions are often primarily prepared for the information and guid-
> ance of the legal profession, but the Nuremberg judgments are of interest to
> a much larger segment of the earth's population. It would not be too much
> to say that the entire world itself is concerned with the adjudications being
> handed down in Nuremberg.[68]

Taylor himself offered the strongest defense of the NMT program as a
didactic exercise:

> Nowhere can these records be put to more immediate or better use than in
> German schools and universities, and in German books and magazines. It is
> true, to be sure, that the reorientation of German thought along democratic
> lines must ultimately be accomplished by the Germans themselves. But the
> least we can do is to insure that the documents which expose the true nature
> of the Third Reich are circulated throughout Germany. The Nuremberg
> documents must be utilized to the full in writing German history, if the Ger-
> mans of today are to grasp the truth about the past.[69]

Didactic legality, of course, has its risks, and few would claim that the
NMT program succeeded in its didactic ambition. But here again the

failures remain emblematic. The NMT experience makes clear that an atrocity trial cannot succeed as a didactic exercise in the absence of a commitment of resources and supporting acts of political will. An atrocity tribunal itself can only go so far toward the goal of "getting the word out." Taylor was painfully aware of this, and his concluding remarks in his summary report betray his frustration with the absence of coordinated support for the NMT program. Though his words are phrased in the rhetoric of anticipatory warning, his tone clearly betrays his awareness that his government will not marshal the support required to achieve didactic success:

> In my judgment, failure to complete the publication of the Nuremberg trial records in both English and German would tend strongly to defeat the objectives of the United States in the field of war crimes as originally developed by Mr. Stimson and approved by Presidents Roosevelt and Truman, and would result in waste of most of the time, money, and effort invested over the past 10 months in the preparation of this material for publication.[70]

He returns to this point later in this *Final Report*:

> A failure to disseminate the Nuremberg records and judgments in Germany, accordingly, is not only a failure to make use of their contents to promote the positive aims of the occupation. It is a failure to put the necessary 'ammunition' in the hands of those Germans who can make use of the documents presented and testimony given during the trials in reconstituting a democratic German society.[71]

Had the United States invested the requisite money and energy toward disseminating the NMT records and judgments, there is no way of knowing whether Taylor's didactic ambitions would have met with success. History by counterfactual is always a tricky enterprise, and there is no clear recipe for orchestrating the successful reception of an atrocity program. But if we cannot confidently chart the path to success, we certainly know the way to failure. The unwillingness or inability to use political tools to support the juridical lessons of an atrocity trial will certainly doom its reception, especially given the opposition that such proceedings inevitably arouse. In this case, the failure to "get the word out" played into the hands of a well-organized campaign of opposition within Germany that was able to cast the NMT program as a tool of victors' justice.[72] Indeed, this campaign to discredit was successful in no small part precisely because it was able strategically to ignore, in the absence of the dissemination of contradicting material, the deeper meaning of the NMT program. German opposition was thus able to cast the NMT proceedings as a continuation of the IMT's aggressive war paradigm. The German public never came to understand the NMT's shift from aggressive war to atrocity. The commutation of sentences, arguably justified for perpetrators of aggressive war, unseemly in the case of perpetrators of crimes of atrocity, only strengthened the Germans' self-serving misapprehension of the NMT. The failure aggressively to support the retributive functions of punishment permitted a spurious narrative to frustrate and usurp the intended didactic message of the trial program.

However much atrocity trials may contribute to a reckoning with the past and to a transition to a more democratic present, they cannot by themselves create the socio-political conditions for their own reception. Even the most even-handed trials, even those that supply the most balanced and nuanced historical narrative, cannot magically transform perpetrator societies. Atrocity trials can contribute to justice and a reckoning with the past, but their success also depends crucially on acts of political will and networks of social support. This difficult lesson, made vivid in the rejection of the NMT by Germany at the time, is another legacy of the trial program, one that must be absorbed by the fledgling International Criminal Court.

## Notes

1.  The classic treatments are Thomas Hobbes, *Leviathan* (Cambridge, 2004) and Jean Bodin, *On Sovereignty* (Cambridge, 1992).
2.  On the barriers that sovereignty posed to the development of international criminal law, see J.L. Brierly, *The Law of Nations: An Introduction to the International Law of Peace* (Oxford, 1954). For a discussion of precedents to the IMT, see Arieh J. Kochavi, *Prelude to Nuremberg: Allied War Crimes Policy and the Question of Punishment* (Chapel Hill, 2005).
3.  See, e.g., Luc Reydams, *Universal Jurisdiction: International and Municipal Legal Perspectives* (Oxford, 2004).
4.  Karl Jaspers, *Wohin treibt die Bundesrepublik?* (Reprint, Munich, 1988).
5.  See Ilias Bantekas and Susan Nash, *International Criminal Law* (London, 2007).
6.  See, e.g., the papers collected in *Die Nürnberger Prozesse: Völkerstrafrecht seit 1945/ The Nuremberg Trials: International Criminal Law Since 1945: Internationale Konferenz zum 60. Jahrestag/60th Anniversary International Conference*, eds. Herbert R. Reginbogin and Christoph Safferling (Munich, 2006).
7.  See "Report of the International Law Commission covering its Second Session, 5 June–29 July 1950, Document A/1316," reprinted in *Yearbook of the International Law Commission* II (1950): 374–78.
8.  In his widely used textbook on international criminal law, former ICTY president Antonio Cassese fails to mention the NMT cases; Antonio Cassese, *International Criminal Law*, 2nd ed. (Oxford, 2008).
9.  See, e.g., the "Grievance Project": http://grievanceproject.wordpress.com/2008/05/07/professor-john-yoo-and-the-justice-case/ (accessed August 2010).
10. The Justice case never reached the question of the liability of legal officials in international law for legal advice. See the discussion by Kevin Jon Heller, "John Yoo and the Justice Case," http://balkin.blogspot.com/2008/05/john-yoo-and-justice-case.html (accessed August 2010).
11. See Telford Taylor, *The Anatomy of the Nuremberg Trials: A Personal Memoir* (London, 1993). Admittedly Taylor had planned to write separately about the NMT trials, though died before the completion of the manuscript that he was preparing with Jonathan Bush.

12. See James E. St. Clair and Linda C. Gugin, *Chief Justice Fred M. Vinson of Kentucky: A Political Biography* (Lexington, 2002).
13. Annette Weinke, *Die Nürnberger Prozesse* (Munich, 2006), 63.
14. See Valerie Hebert, *Hitler's Generals on Trial: The Last War Crimes Tribunal at Nuremberg* (Lawrence, 2010), 178–81.
15. See Peter Reichel, *Vergangenheitsbewältigung in Deutschland: Die Auseinandersetzung mit der NS-Diktatur in Politik und Justiz* (Munich, 2007); Norbert Frei, *Adenauer's Germany and the Nazi Past* (New York, 2002); Jörg Friedrich, *Die Kalte Amnestie: NS-Täter in der Bundesrepublik* (Berlin, 1994); and Ulrich Brochhagen, *Nach Nürnberg: Vergangenheitsbewältigung und Westintegration in der Ära Adenauer* (Berlin, 1999).
16. See Samantha Power, *"A Problem from Hell": America and the Age of Genocide* (New York, 2002).
17. See Robert K. Woetzel, *The Nuremberg Trials in International Law* (New York, 1960), 226–32. Also Carl Schmitt, *Das internationalrechtliche Verbrechen des Angriffskrieges und der Grundsatz "Nullum crimen, nulla poena sine lege,"* edited with notes and afterword by Helmut Quaritsch (Berlin, 1994).
18. See Michael A. Newton and Michael P. Scharf, *Enemy of the State: The Trial and Execution of Saddam Hussein* (New York, 2008).
19. See Matthew Weed, "International Criminal Court and the Rome Statute: 2010 Review Conference" Congressional Research Office 7-5700, R41682, March 10, 2011. See also, William Schabas, *An Introduction to the International Criminal Court*, 3rd edn (Cambridge, 2008). See also *The International Criminal Court and the Crime of Aggression*, eds. Mauro Politi and Giuseppe Nesi (Surrey, 2004) and Larry May, *Aggression and Crimes against Peace* (Cambridge, 2008).
20. See, generally, Bradley F. Smith, *The Road to Nuremberg* (New York, 1981). Also Telford Taylor, *The Nuremberg War Crimes Trials: War Crimes and International Law* (New York, 1949) and Robert Jackson, "The Significance of the Nuremberg Trials to the Armed Forces: Previously Unpublished Personal Observations by the Chief Counsel for the United States," *Military Affairs* 10 (1946): 2–15.
21. Jonathan A. Bush, "'The Supreme … Crime' and Its Origins: The Lost Legislative History of the Crime of Aggressive War," *Columbia Law Review* 102 (2002): 2324–424.
22. See Lawrence Douglas, *The Memory of Judgment: Making Law and History in the Trials of the Holocaust* (New Haven, 2001), 41–53.
23. *Report of Robert H. Jackson, United States Representative to the International Conference on Military Trials, London, 1945* (Washington, DC, 1949), [henceforth: *Jackson Report*], 333.
24. See the contributions by Valerie Hébert and Kim C. Priemel in the present volume.
25. See Kevin Jon Heller, *The Nuremberg Military Tribunals and the Origins of International Criminal Law* (Oxford, 2011), 180-183.
26. The use of forced labor, a crime against humanity, also played a key role in the three industrialists trials; experiments and slave labor also stood at the heart of the *Milch* case.
27. Telford Taylor, *Final Report to the Secretary of the Army on the Nuernberg War Crimes Trials Under Control Council Law No. 10* (Washington, DC, 1949) [henceforth: *Final Report*], 92.
28. For a full text of CCL 10, see Taylor, *Final Report*, Appendix D.
29. Robert Wolfe, "Flaws in the Nuremberg Legacy: An Impediment to the International War Crimes Tribunals' Prosecution of Crimes against Humanity," *Holocaust and Genocide Studies* 12 (1998): 444.
30. Taylor, *Final Report*, 107.
31. Case 9, Opening Statement for the Prosecution, *TWC*, IV, 49.
32. Case 3, Opinion and Judgement, *TWC*, III, 979.
33. Schmitt, *Das internationalrechtliche Verbrechen*.

34. Hans Kelsen, "Will the Judgment in the Nuremberg Trial Constitute a Precedent in International Law?," *International Law Quarterly* 1, 2 (1947): 153–77.
35. See Lawrence Douglas, *Memory of Judgment*, 65–94.
36. This was perhaps nowhere more vividly captured than in the closing statement of British chief prosecutor Hartley Shawcross. Whereas Jackson's Opening Statement for the prosecution clearly focused on crimes against peace, Shawcross's summation focused on crimes against humanity, and specifically crimes against Europe's Jewish population. See Douglas, *Memory of Judgment*, 91–94.
37. Raphael Lemkin, *Axis Rule in Occupied Europe: Laws of Occupation—Analysis of Government—Proposals for Redress* (Washington, DC, 1944), 79. See Alexa Stiller's contribution to this volume.
38. Case 8, Opening Statement of the Prosecution, *TWC*, IV, 622.
39. Case 9, Opinion and Judgment, *TWC*, IV, 450.
40. Case 9, Opening Statement for the Prosecution, *TWC*, IV, 32.
41. Ibid., 30.
42. Ibid., 48.
43. Taylor, *Anatomy*, xi.
44. Telford Taylor, "Memorandum of 6 February 1947," printed in Jonathan Bush, "The Prehistory of Corporations and Conspiracy in International Criminal Law: What Nuremberg Really Said," *Columbia Law Review* 109 (2009): 1262.
45. See Bush, "Prehistory," 1178–88.
46. Taylor, "The Meaning of the Nuremberg Trials," 19. Unpublished manuscript. Papers of Robert H. Jackson, Library of Congress, Manuscript Division, Box 110, N6 War Crimes Trial, Office File, US Chief of Counsel, Subsequent Trials folder 2.
47. Here I am referring to amendments on the crime of aggression adopted at the Review Conference of the Rome Statute that convened in Kampala, Uganda, from 31 May to 11 June 2010. See note 19.
48. See, e.g., Gerhard Werle, *Principles of International Criminal Law*, 2nd edn (The Hague, 2009).
49. See Louis G. Maresca, "Case Analysis: The Prosecutor v. Tadić, The Appellate Decision of the ICTY and Internal Violations of Humanitarian Law as International Crimes," *Leiden Journal of International Law* 9 (1996): 219–33.
50. Of course, those defending humanitarian intervention would argue that such acts can never be considered aggressive. For a critical comment on this novel doctrine of intervention, see Tzvetan Todorow, "Right to Intervene or Duty to Assist?" in *Human Rights, Human Wrongs*, ed. Nicholas Owen (Oxford, 2002), 28–48.
51. *Jackson Report*, 6.
52. Rebecca West, *A Train of Powder* (New York, 1955), 3.
53. Hannah Arendt, *Eichmann in Jerusalem: A Report on the Banality of Evil* (New York, 1963), 15f.
54. Douglas, *Memory of Judgment*, 104–13.
55. See Hilary Earl, *The Nuremberg SS-Einsatzgruppen Trial, 1945–1958: Atrocity, Law, and History* (Cambridge, 2009).
56. Taylor, *Final Report*, 86.
57. See Paul Weindling, *Nazi Medicine and the Nuremberg Trials* (Basingstoke, 2005), and his contribution in the present volume.
58. See M. Cherif Bassiouni, "International Recognition of Victims' Rights," *Human Rights Law Review* 6 (2006): 203–79.
59. "Victims' Rights": http://www.amnestyusa.org/international_justice/pdf/IJA_Factsheet_4_Victims_Rights.pdf, "Fact Sheet Four 2007–2008," Program for International Justice and Accountability, http://www.amnestyusa.org/international_justice (accessed August 2010).
60. Contemporaneous public opinion polls suggest that many Germans embraced McCloy's commutation policies as a de facto recognition of the unfairness of the trial program. See Brochhagen, *Nach Nürnberg*, 50–63.

61. *Hannah Arendt–Karl Jaspers Correspondence 1926–1969*, eds. Lotte Kohler and Hans Santer, trans. Robert Kimber and Rita Kimber (New York, 1992), 54.
62. Hannah Arendt, *Eichmann in Jerusalem*, 252.
63. *The Trial of Adolf Eichmann: Record of the Proceedings in the District Court of Jerusalem*, ed. State of Israel, Ministry of Justice (Jerusalem, 1992–95), vol. 5, 2214.
64. Mark Drumbl, *Atrocity, Punishment, and International Law* (Cambridge, 2007).
65. For an extensive discussion, see Lawrence Douglas, "The Didactic Trial: Filtering History and Memory into the Courtroom," in *Holocaust and Justice: Representation and Historiography of the Holocaust in Post-War Trials*, eds. David Bankier and Dan Michman (Jerusalem, 2010), 11–22. Also, generally, Douglas, *Memory of Judgment*.
66. See, e.g., Michael Marrus, "History and the Holocaust in the Courtroom," in *Lessons and Legacies IV: The Holocaust and Justice*, ed. Ronald Smelser (Evanston, IL, 2002). Also Donald Bloxham, *Genocide on Trial: War Crimes Trials and the Formation of Holocaust History and Memory* (New York, 2003).
67. Robert M.W. Kempner, "The Nuremberg Trials as Sources of Recent German Political and Historical Materials," *American Political Science Review*, 44 (1950): 447–59, 447.
68. Case 9, Opinion and Judgment, *TWC*, IV, 413.
69. Taylor, *Final Report*, 106.
70. Ibid., 102.
71. Ibid., 111.
72. See Frei, *Adenauer's Germany*.

# SELECT BIBLIOGRAPHY

Ahrens, Ralf, "Der Exempelkandidat. Die Dresdner Bank und der Nürnberger Prozess gegen Karl Rasche," *Vierteljahreshefte für Zeitgeschichte* 52 (2004): 637–70.
—— *Die Dresdner Bank 1945–1957. Konsequenzen und Kontinuitäten nach dem Ende des NS-Regimes* (Munich, 2007).
Andrus, Burton C., *I Was the Nuremberg Jailer* (New York, 1969).
Annas, George and Grodin, Michael, *The Nazi Doctors and the Nuremberg Code* (Oxford, 1992).
Arendt, Hannah, *Eichmann in Jerusalem: A Report on the Banality of Evil* (New York, 1963).
——, *The Origins of Totalitarianism* (New York, 1951).
Aronson, Shlomo, "Preparations for the Nuremberg Trial: The O.S.S., Charles Dwork, and the Holocaust," *Holocaust and Genocide Studies* 12 (1998): 257–81.
Aschenauer, Rudolf, *Landsberg. Ein dokumentarischer Bericht von deutscher Seite* (Munich, 1951).
Ash, Timothy Garton, "The Truth about Dictatorship," *The New York Review of Books* 45 (1998): 35–40.
Bartov, Omer, Grossman, Atina and Nolan, Mary (eds.), *Crimes of War: Guilt and Denial in the Twentieth Century* (New York, 2002).
Bassiouni, M. Cherif, *Crimes against Humanity in International Criminal Law*, 2nd rev. edn (The Hague, 1999).
——, "The History of Universal Jurisdiction and Its Place in International Law," in *Universal Jurisdiction. National Courts and the Prosecution of Serious Crimes under International Law*, ed. Stephen Macedo (Philadelphia, 2004), 39–63.
——, "International Recognition of Victims' Rights," *Human Rights Law Review* 6 (2006): 203–79.
Bellamy, Suzanne, *Hoosier Justice at Nuremberg* (Indianapolis, 2010).
Benz, Wolfgang, "Der Wollheim-Prozeß. Zwangsarbeit für die I.G. Farben in Auschwitz," in *Wiedergutmachung in der Bundesrepublik Deutschland*, eds. Ludolf Herbst and Constantin Goschler (Munich, 1989), 303–26.
Bickford, Louis, "Transitional Justice," in *Encyclopedia of Genocide: and Crimes against Humanity*, ed. Dinah L. Shelton (Detroit, 2005), 1045–47.
Biddle, Francis, *In Brief Authority* (Garden City, 1962).
*Biographisches Handbuch der deutschsprachigen Emigration nach 1933. Vol. 1, Politik, Wirtschaft, öffentliches Leben*, ed. Institut für Zeitgeschichte München (Munich, 1980).

Bird, Kai, *The Chairman: John J. McCloy—the Making of the American Establishment* (New York, 1992).

Bloxham, Donald, *Genocide on Trial. War Crimes Trials and the Formation of Holocaust History and Memory* (Oxford/New York, 2001).

——, "'The Trial that Never Was': Why there was no Second International Trial of Major War Criminals at Nuremberg," *History* 87 (2002): 41–60.

——, "British War Crimes Trial Policy in Germany, 1945–1957: Implementation and Collapse," *Journal of British Studies* 42 (2003): 91–118.

Bloxham, Donald and Moses, A. Dirk (eds.), *The Oxford Handbook of Genocide Studies* (Oxford, 2010).

Bloxham, Donald and Pendas, Devin O., "Punishment as Prevention? The Politics of Punishing Génocidaires", in *The Oxford Handbook of the History of Genocide*, eds. Donald Bloxham and A. Dirk Moses (Oxford, 2010), 617–37.

Borgwardt, Elizabeth, "Re-examining Nuremberg as a New Deal Institution: Politics, Culture and the Limits of Law in Generating Human Rights Norms," *Berkeley Journal of International Law* 23 (2005): 401–62.

Borkin, Joseph, *The Crime and Punishment of I. G. Farben* (New York, 1978).

Borkin, Joseph and Welsh, Charles A., *Germany's Master Plan: The Story of Industrial Offensive* (London, 1943).

Bower, Tom, *Blind Eye to Murder. Britain, America and the Purging of Nazi Germany. A Pledge Betrayed* (London, 1995).

Brierly, James L., *The Law of Nations: An Introduction to the International Law of Peace*, 5th edn (Oxford, 1955).

Brochhagen, Ulrich, *Nach Nürnberg: Vergangenheitsbewältigung und Westintegration in der Ära Adenauer* (Hamburg, 1994).

Brooks, Peter and Gerwitz, Paul (eds.), *Law's Stories. Narrative and Rhetoric in the Law* (New Haven, 1996).

Bryant, Michael, *Confronting the "Good Death": Nazi Euthanasia on Trial, 1945–1953* (Boulder, 2005).

Burns, Robert P., *A Theory of the Trial* (Princeton, 1999).

——, *The Death of the American Trial* (Chicago, 2009).

Buscher, Frank M., *The U.S. War Crimes Trial Program in Germany, 1946–1955* (New York, 1989).

Bush, Jonathan A., "Soldiers Find Wars: A Life of Telford Taylor," *Columbia Journal of Transnational Law* 37 (1999): 675–88.

——, "'The Supreme ... Crime' and Its Origins: The Lost Legislative History of the Crime of Aggressive War," *Columbia Law Review* 102 (2002): 2324–423.

——, "The Prehistory of Corporations and Conspiracy in International Criminal Law: What Nuremberg Really Said," *Columbia Law Review* 109 (2009): 1094–262.

Cassese, Antonio, *International Criminal Law*, 2nd edn (Oxford, 2008).

Clavero, Bartolomé, *Genocide or Ethnocide, 1933–2007. How to Make, Unmake, and Remake Law with Words* (Milan, 2008).

Conot, Robert E., *Justice at Nuremberg* (New York, 1983).

Cooper, John, *Raphael Lemkin and the Struggle for the Genocide Convention* (Basingstoke, 2008).

Cover, Robert, "Nomos and Narrative," in *Narrative, Violence and the Law: The Essays of Robert Cover*, eds. Martha Minow, Michael Ryan and Austin Sarat (Ann Arbor, 1995), 95–172.

Delage, Christian, "L'Image Comme Preuve. L'Expérience du Procès de Nuremberg," *Vingtième Siècle. Revue d'Historie* 72 (2001): 63–78.

Dix, Helmuth, "Die Urteile in den Nürnberger Wirtschaftsprozessen," *Neue Juristische Wochenschrift* 17 (1949): 647–52.

Dorn, Walter L., "The Debate over American Occupation Policy in Germany in 1944–1945," *Political Science Quarterly* 72 (1957): 484–86.

Douglas, Lawrence, "The Didactic Trial: Filtering History and Memory into the Court-room," in *Holocaust and Justice: Representation and Historiography of the Holocaust in Post-War Trials*, eds. David Bankier and Dan Michman (Jerusalem, 2010), 11–22.

———, *The Memory of Judgment. Making Law and History in the Trials of the Holocaust* (New Haven, 2001).

Drecoll, Axel, "Flick vor Gericht: Die Verhandlungen vor dem alliierten Militärtribunal 1947," in *Der Flick-Konzern im Dritten Reich*, eds. Johannes Bähr, Axel Drecoll, Bernhard Gotto, et al (Munich, 2008), 559–645.

Drumbl, Mark, *Atrocity, Punishment, and International Law* (Cambridge, 2007).

DuBois, Josiah, *The Devil's Chemists. 24 Conspirators of the International Farben Cartel Who Manufacture Wars* (Boston, 1952).

Duff, Antony, Farmer, Lindsay, Marshall, Sandra and Tadros, Victor (eds.), *The Trial on Trial*, 3 vols (Oxford, 2004–2007).

Earl, Hilary, "Confessions of Wrong-doing or How to Save Yourself from the Hangman? An Analysis of British and American Intelligence Reports of the Activities of Otto Ohlendorf, May–December 1945," in *Secret Intelligence and the Holocaust*, ed. David Banker (New York, 2006), 301–26.

———, *The Nuremberg SS-Einsatzgruppen Trial, 1945–1958: Atrocity, Law, and History* (Cambridge, 2009).

Eiber, Ludwig and Sigel, Robert (eds.), *Dachauer Prozesse. NS-Verbrechen vor amerikanischen Militärgerichten in Dachau 1945–1948* (Göttingen, 2007).

Ferencz, Benjamin B., "Nurnberg Trial Procedure and the Rights of the Accused," *Journal of Criminal Law and Criminology* 39 (1948): 144–51.

———, *An International Criminal Court: A Step Toward World Peace* (Oceana, VA, 1975).

———, *Less than Slaves: Jewish Forced Labor and the Quest for Compensation* (Cambridge, MA, 1979).

Finger, Jürgen, Keller, Sven and Wirsching, Andreas (eds.), *Vom Recht zur Geschichte. Akten aus NS-Prozessen als Quellen der Zeitgeschichte* (Göttingen, 2009).

Fraenkel, Ernst, *The Dual State. A Contribution to the Theory of Dictatorship* (New York, 1941).

Frei, Norbert, "Von deutscher Erfindungskraft oder: Die Kollektivschuldthese in der Nachkriegszeit," *Rechtshistorisches Journal* 16 (1997): 621–34.

———, *Vergangenheitspolitik. Die Anfänge der Bundesrepublik und die NS-Vergangenheit* (Munich, 1996) [*Adenauer's Germany and the Nazi Past: The Politics of Amnesty and Integration* (New York, 2002)].

Frei, Norbert, van Laak, Dirk and Stolleis, Michael (eds.), *Geschichte vor Gericht. Historiker, Richter und die Suche nach Gerechtigkeit* (Munich, 2000).

Freudiger, Kerstin, *Die juristische Aufarbeitung von NS-Verbrechen* (Tübingen, 2002).

Fried, John H.E., *The Exploitation of Foreign Labour by Germany* (Montreal, 1945).

———, "Nuremberg and the Holocaust," in *Toward a Right to Peace: Selected Papers of John H.E. Fried* (Northampton, MA, 1994), 15–32.

Friedman, Jonathan, "Law and Politics in the Subsequent Nuremberg Trials, 1946–1949," in *Atrocities on Trial. Historical Perspectives on the Politics of Prosecuting War Crimes*, eds. Patricia Heberer and Jürgen Matthäus (Lincoln, NE, 2008), 75–101.

Friedrich, Jörg, *Die Kalte Amnestie: NS-Täter in der Bundesrepublik* (Berlin, 1994).

Gaskin, Hilary, *Eyewitnesses at Nuremberg* (London, 1990).

Gattini, Andrea, "Kelsen's Contribution to International Criminal Law," *Journal of International Criminal Justice* 2 (2004): 795–809.

Gerlach, Christian, "Extremely Violent Societies: an Alternative to the Concept of Genocide," *Journal of Genocide Research* 8 (2006): 455–71.

Gerstenmeier, Friedrich, "Strategische Erinnerungen—Die Memoiren deutscher Offiziere," in *Vernichtungskrieg: Verbrechen der Wehrmacht 1941–1944*, eds. Hannes Heer and Klaus Naumann (Hamburg, 1995), 620–29.

Gilbert, Gustave M., *Nuremberg Diary* (New York, 1947).

Glueck, Sheldon, *War Criminals: Their Prosecution and Punishment* (New York, 1944).

——, "The Nuremberg Trial and Aggressive War," *Harvard Law Review* 59 (1946): 396–445.

——, *The Nuremberg Trial and Aggressive War* (New York, 1946).

Goschler, Constantin, *Wiedergutmachung. Westdeutschland und die Verfolgten des Nationalsozialismus 1945–1954* (Munich, 1992).

Haas, Peter M., "Introduction: Epistemic Communities and International Policy Coordination," *International Organizations* 46 (1992): 1–35.

Haensel, Carl, "Der Ausklang von Nürnberg," *Neue Juristische Wochenschrift* 10 (1949): 367–70.

Harris, Whitney R., *Tyranny on Trial. The Evidence at Nuremberg* (Dallas, 1954).

Heberer, Patricia and Matthäus, Jürgen (eds.), *Atrocities on Trial. Historical Perspectives on the Politics of Prosecuting War Crimes* (Lincoln, NE, 2008).

Hébert, Valerie G., *Hitler's Generals on Trial: the Last War Crimes Tribunal at Nuremberg* (Lawrence, KS, 2010).

Heer, Hannes, "The Difficulty of Ending a War: Reactions to the Exhibition 'War of Extermination: Crimes of the Wehrmacht 1941 to 1944,'" *History Workshop Journal* 46 (1998): 187–203.

——, *The Discursive Construction of History: Remembering the Wehrmacht's War of Annihilation* (New York, 2008).

Heer, Hannes and Naumann, Klaus (eds.), *War of Extermination: The German Army in World War II, 1941–1944* (New York, 2000).

Heller, Kevin Jon, *The Nuremberg Military Tribunals and the Origins of the International Criminal Law* (New York, 2011).

Henke, Klaus-Dietmar, *Die amerikanische Besetzung Deutschlands* (Munich, 1995).

Herf, Jeffrey, *Divided Memory. The Nazi Past in the Two Germanys* (Cambridge, MA, 1997).

Hilberg, Raul, *The Politics of Memory: The Journey of a Holocaust Historian* (Chicago, 1996).

Jackson, Robert, "The Significance of the Nuremberg Trials to the Armed Forces: Previously Unpublished Personal Observations by the Chief Counsel for the United States," *Military Affairs* 10 (1946): 2–15.

Jacobs, Steven L. (ed.), *Raphael Lemkin's Thoughts on Nazi Genocide. Not Guilty?* (Lewiston, ID, 1992).

Jescheck, Hans-Heinrich, "The General Principles of International Criminal Law Set Out in Nuremberg, as Mirrored in the ICC Statute," *Journal of International Criminal Justice* 2 (2004): 38–55.

Jung, Susanne, *Die Rechtsprobleme der Nürnberger Prozesse dargestellt am Verfahren gegen Friedrich Flick* (Tübingen, 1992).

Katz, Barry M., *Foreign Intelligence: Research and Analysis in the Office of Strategic Services 1942–1945* (Cambridge, MA, 1989).

Kelsen, Hans, "Will the Judgment in the Nuremberg Trial Constitute a Precedent in International Law?" *International and Comparative Law Quarterly* 1 (1947): 153–77.

Kempner, Robert M.W., "The Nuremberg Trials as Sources of Recent German Political and Historical Materials," *American Political Science Review* 44 (1950): 447–59.

——, *Eichmann und Komplizen* (Zurich, 1961).

——, *SS im Kreuzverhör. Die Elite, die Europa in Scherben schlug* (Munich, 1964).

——, *Das Dritte Reich im Kreuzverhör. Aus den unveröffentlichten Vernehmungsprotokollen des Anklägers Robert M.W. Kempner* (Munich, 1969).

——, *Ankläger einer Epoche. Lebenserinnerungen* (Frankfurt a.M., 1983).

Kirchheimer, Otto, *Political Justice. The Use of Legal Procedure for Political Ends* (Princeton, 1961).

Kittel, Manfred, *Nach Nürnberg und Tokio. "Vergangenheitsbewältigung" in Japan und Westdeutschland 1945 bis 1968* (Munich, 2004).

Knieriem, August von, *Nürnberg. Rechtliche und menschliche Probleme* (Stuttgart, 1953).

Kochavi, Arieh J., *Prelude to Nuremberg. Allied War Crimes Policy and the Question of Punishment* (Chapel Hill, 1998).

Kogon, Eugon, *Der SS-Staat. Das System der deutschen Konzentrationslager* (Munich, 1946).

Koskenniemi, Martti, *The Gentle Civilizer of Nations: The Rise and Fall of International Law 1870–1960* (Cambridge, 2001).

———, "Hersch Lauterpacht and the Development of International Criminal Law," *Journal of International Criminal Justice* 2 (2004): 810–25.

Kraft, Claudia, "Völkermorde im 20. Jahrhundert: Rafał Lemkin und die Ahndung des Genozids durch das internationale Strafrecht," in *Finis mundi: Endzeiten und Weltenden im östlichen Europa*, eds. Joachim Hösler and Wolfgang Kessler (Stuttgart, 1998), 91–110.

Krohn, Claus-Dieter, *Wissenschaft im Exil. Deutsche Sozial- und Wirtschaftswissenschaftler in den USA und die New School for Social Research* (Frankfurt a.M., 1987).

Kunz, Josef L., "The Future of the International Law for the Protection of National Minorities," *American Journal of International Law* 39 (1945): 89–95.

———, "The United Nations Convention on Genocide," *American Journal of International Law* 43 (1949): 738–46.

———, "The Present Status of the International Law for the Protection of Minorities," *American Journal of International Law* 48 (1954): 282–87.

Kushner, Tony, *The Holocaust and the Liberal Imagination. A Social and Cultural History* (Oxford/Cambridge, MA, 1994).

Large, David Clay, *Germans to the Front: West German Rearmament in the Adenauer Era* (Chapel Hill, 1996).

Laternser, Hans, *Verteidigung deutscher Soldaten: Plädoyers vor alliierten Gerichten* (Bonn, 1950).

*Law Reports of Trials of War Criminals. Selected and Prepared by the United Nations War Crimes Commission [LRTWC]*, 15 vols (London, 1947–1949).

Lemkin, Raphael, *Axis Rule in Occupied Europe: Laws of Occupation—Analysis of Government—Proposals for Redress* (Washington, DC, 1944).

———, "Genocide as a Crime under International Law," *The American Journal of International Law* 41 (1947): 145–51.

Lingen, Kerstin von, "Conspiracy of Silence: How the 'Old Boys' of American Intelligence Shielded SS General Karl Wolff from Prosecution," *Holocaust and Genocide Studies* 22 (2008): 74–109.

———, *Kesselrings letzte Schlacht. Kriegsverbrecherprozesse, Vergangenheitspolitik und Wiederbewaffnung: Der Fall Kesselring* (Paderborn, 2004) [*Kesselring's Last Battle: War Crimes Trials and Cold War Politics, 1945–1950* (Lawrence, KS, 2009)].

Lippe, Viktor von der, *Nürnberger Tagebuchnotizen November 1945 bis Oktober 1946* (Frankfurt a.M., 1951).

Lippman, Matthew, "A Road Map to the 1948 Convention on the Prevention and Punishment of Genocide," *Journal of Genocide Research* 4 (2002): 177–95.

Loewy, Hanno, "Zwischen *Judgment* und *Twilight*. Schulddiskurse, Holocaust und das Courtroom Drama," in *Die Shoah im Bild*, ed. Sven Kramer (Munich, 2003), 133–69.

Maguire, Peter, *Law and War. An American Story* (New York, 2001).

Mann, Abby, "Introduction," *Judgment at Nuremberg. A Play by Abby Mann* (New York, 2002).

Marquardt-Bigman, Petra, *Amerikanische Geheimdienstanalysen über Deutschland 1942–1949* (Munich, 1995).

Marrus, Michael R., *The Nuremberg War Crimes Trial 1945–1946: A Documentary History* (New York, 1997).

———, "The Holocaust at Nuremberg," *Yad Vashem Studies* 26 (1998): 5–41.

———, "The Nuremberg Doctor's Trial in Historical Context," *Bulletin of the History of Medicine* 73 (1999): 106–23.

———, "History and the Holocaust in the Courtroom," in *Lessons and Legacies IV: The Holocaust and Justice*, ed. Ronald Smelser (Evanston, IL, 2002), 215–239.

Maser, Werner, *Nürnberg: Tribunal der Sieger* (Düsseldorf, 1977).

May, Larry, *Aggression and Crimes against Peace* (Cambridge, 2008).

Mazower, Mark, "The Strange Triumph of Human Rights, 1933–1950," *Historical Journal* 47 (2004): 379–98.

Mendelsohn, John, *Trial by Document. The Use of Seized Records in the United States Proceedings at Nuernberg* (Phil. Diss., University of Maryland, 1974).

Meron, Theodor, "From Nuremberg to The Hague," in *War Crimes Law Comes of Age. Essays* (Oxford, 1998), 198–203.

Merritt, Anna J. and Merritt, Richard L. (eds.), *Public Opinion in Occupied Germany. The OMGUS Surveys, 1945–1949* (Urbana, IL, 1970).

———, *Public Opinion in Semisovereign Germany: The HICOG Surveys, 1949–1955* (Urbana, IL, 1980).

Messerschmidt, Manfred, "Forward Defense: the 'Memorandum of the Generals' for the Nuremberg Court," in *War of Extermination: The German Military in World War II, 1941–1944*, eds. Hannes Heer and Klaus Naumann (New York, 2000), 381–99.

Meyrowitz, Henri, *La Répression par les Tribunaux Allemands des Crimes contre L'Humanité et de L'Appartenance a une Organisation Criminelle en Application de la Loi No. 10 du Conseil de Contrôle Allié* (Paris, 1960).

Minow, Martha, *Between Vengeance and Forgiveness. Facing History after Genocide and Mass Violence* (Boston, 1998).

Mitscherlich, Alexander and Mielke, Fred (eds.), *Medizin ohne Menschlichkeit—Dokumente des Nürnberger Ärzteprozesses* (Frankfurt a.M., 2004).

Moeller, Robert G., *War Stories: The Search for a Usable Past in the Federal Republic of Germany* (Berkeley, 2001).

Morsink, Johannes, *The Universal Declaration of Human Rights: Origins, Drafting, and Intent* (Philadelphia, 1999).

Moses, A. Dirk, "The Holocaust and Genocide," in *The Historiography of the Holocaust*, ed. Dan Stone (New York, 2005), 533–55.

———, "Lemkin, Culture, and the Concept of Genocide," in *The Oxford Handbook of Genocide Studies*, eds. Donald Bloxham and A. Dirk Moses (Oxford, 2010), 19–41.

Müller, Tim B., "Bearing Witness to the Liquidation of Western Dasein: Herbert Marcuse and the Holocaust, 1941–1948", *New German Critique* 85 (2002): 133–64.

Musmanno, Michael A., *The Eichmann Kommandos* (London, 1962).

———, *Verdict! The Adventures of the Young Lawyer in the Brown Suit* (New York, 1963).

Nathan, Otto, *The Nazi Economic System* (Durham, NC, 1944).

Naumann, Klaus, "The 'Unblemished' Wehrmacht: the Social History of a Myth," in *War of Extermination. The German Army in World War II, 1941–1944*, eds. Hannes Heer and Klaus Naumann (New York, 2000), 417–429.

*Nazi Conspiracy and Aggression*, ed. Office of United States Chief of Counsel for Prosecution of Axis Criminality, 8 vols plus 2 suppl. (Washington, DC, 1946–1948).

Neumann, Franz L., "War Crimes Trials," *World Politics* 2 (1949): 135–47.

———, *Behemoth. The Structure and Practice of National Socialism, 1933–1944* (Reprint Chicago, 2009) [*Behemoth. Struktur und Praxis des Nationalsozialismus 1933–1944*, 4th ed. (Frankfurt a.M., 1993)].

Niven, Bill, *Facing the Nazi Past: United Germany and the Legacy of the Third Reich* (London, 2002).

Olick, Jeffrey K., *In the House of the Hangman: The Agonies of German Defeat, 1943–1949* (Chicago, 2005).

*OMGUS. Ermittlungen gegen die Deutsche Bank*, ed. Dokumentationsstelle zur NS-Sozialpolitik (Nördlingen, 1985).

*OMGUS. Ermittlungen gegen die Dresdner Bank*, ed. Hamburger Stiftung für Sozialgeschichte des 20. Jahrhunderts (Nördlingen, 1986).

*OMGUS. Ermittlungen gegen die I.G. Farbenindustrie AG*, ed. Dokumentationsstelle zur NS-Sozialpolitik (Nördlingen, 1986).

Oppitz, Ulrich-Dieter, *Medizinverbrechen vor Gericht. Das Urteil im Nürnberger Ärzteprozeß gegen Karl Brandt und andere sowie aus dem Prozeß gegen Generalfeldmarschall Milch* (Erlangen, 1999).

Osiel, Mark, *Mass Atrocity, Collective Memory, and the Law* (New Brunswick, 1999).

Pendas, Devin O., "Truth and its Consequences: Reflections on Political, Historical and Legal 'Truth' in West German Holocaust Trials," *traverse: Zeitschrift für Geschichte/Revue d'histoire* 11 (2004): 25–38.

———, *The Frankfurt Auschwitz Trial, 1963–1965: Genocide, History, and the Limits of the Law* (Cambridge, 2006).

———, "Seeking Justice, Finding Law: Nazi Trials in the Postwar Era, 1945–1989," *Journal of Modern History* 81 (2009): 347–68.

———, "Retroactive Law and Proactive Justice: Debating Crimes against Humanity in Germany, 1945–1950," *Central European History* 43 (2010): 428–63.

Perels, Joachim, "Fast vergessen: Franz L. Neumanns Beitrag zur Konzipierung der Nürnberger Prozesse. Eine Erinnerung aus Anlaß seines 100. Geburtstages," *Kritische Justiz* 34 (2001): 117–25.

Persico, Joseph E., *Nuremberg. Infamy on Trial* (New York, 1994).

Polewoi, Boris, *Nürnberger Tagebuch*, 4th edn (Berlin, 1971).

Politi, Mauro and Nesi, Giuseppe (eds.), *The International Criminal Court and the Crime of Aggression* (Surrey, 2004).

Pöppmann, Dirk, "Robert Kempner und Ernst von Weizsäcker im Wilhelmstraßenprozess. Zur Diskussion über die Beteiligung der deutschen Funktionselite an den NS-Verbrechen," in *Im Labyrinth der Schuld. Täter, Opfer, Ankläger*, ed. Irmtrud Wojak and Susanne Meinl (Darmstadt, 2003), 163–97.

———, "Der Wilhelmstraßenprozess als vergangenheitspolitischer Diskurs," in *Leipzig—Nürnberg—Den Haag. Neue Fragestellungen und Forschungen zum Verhältnis von Menschenrechtsverbrechen, justizieller Säuberung und Völkerstrafrecht*, ed. Helia-Verena Daubach (Düsseldorf, 2008), 99–116.

Power, Samantha, *"A Problem from Hell": America and the Age of Genocide* (New York, 2002).

Priemel, Kim C., *Flick. Eine Konzerngeschichte vom Kaiserreich bis zur Bundesrepublik* (Göttingen, 2007).

Prusin, Alexander V., "Poland's Nuremberg: The Seven Court Cases of the Supreme National Tribunal, 1946–1948," *Holocaust and Genocide Studies* 24 (2010): 1–25.

Rabinbach, Anson, "The Challenge of the Unprecedented—Raphael Lemkin and the Concept of Genocide," *Simon Dubnow Institute Yearbook* 4 (2005): 397–420.

Radbruch, Gustav, "Des Reichsjustizministeriums Ruhm und Ende: Zum Nürnberger Juristen-Prozeß," *Süddeutsche Juristen-Zeitung* 3 (1948): 57–64.

Radlmaier, Steffen (ed.), *Der Nürnberger Lernprozess. Von Kriegsverbrechern und Starreportern* (Frankfurt a.M., 2001).

Reginbogin, Herbert R. and Safferling, Christoph (eds.), *Die Nürnberger Prozesse: Völkerstrafrecht seit 1945: Internationale Konferenz zum 60. Jahrestag/The Nuremberg Trials: International Criminal Law Since 1945: 60th Anniversary International Conference* (Munich, 2006).

Reichel, Peter, *Vergangenheitsbewältigung in Deutschland: Die Auseinandersetzung mit der NS-Diktatur von 1945 bis heute* (Munich, 2001).

*Report of Robert H. Jackson, United States Representative to the International Conference on Military Trials, London, 1945* (Washington, DC, 1949).

Reydams, Luc, *Universal Jurisdiction: International and Municipal Legal Perspectives* (Oxford, 2004).

Ruff, V.A., "'Einheitliche Rechtsgrundlage': Zur abweichenden Rechtsprechung des Obersten Spruchgerichtshofes in Hamm und der Nürnberger Militärgerichte," *Neue Juristische Wochenschrift* 1 (1947–48): 283–86.

Salter, Michael, *Nazi War Crimes, US Intelligence and Selective Prosecution at Nuremberg* (Abingdon, 2007).

Schabas, William A., *Genocide in International Law: The Crimes of Crimes* (Cambridge, 2000) [*Genozid im Völkerrecht* (Hamburg, 2003)].

———, *An Introduction to the International Criminal Court* (Cambridge, 2001).

Schechtman, Joseph B., "Decline of the International Protection of Minority Rights," *The Western Political Quarterly* 4 (1951): 1–11.

Schmitt, Carl, *Das international-rechtliche Verbrechen des Angriffskrieges und der Grundsatz "Nullum crimen, nulla poena sine lege,"* ed. Helmut Quaritsch (Berlin, 1994).

Schmitz, Helmut (ed.), *A Nation of Victims? Representations of German Wartime Suffering from 1945 to the Present* (Amsterdam, 2007).

Schulte, Jan Erik, *Zwangsarbeit und Vernichtung: Das Wirtschaftsimperium der SS. Oswald Pohl und das SS-Wirtschafts-Verwaltungshauptamt 1933–1945* (Paderborn, 2001).

———, "Zur Geschichte der SS. Erzähltraditionen und Forschungsstand," in *Die SS, Himmler und die Wewelsburg*, ed. Jan Erik Schulte (Paderborn, 2009), XI–XXXV.

Schwartz, Thomas Alan, "John J. McCloy and the Landsberg Cases," in *American Policy and Reconstruction of West Germany*, eds. Jeffry M. Diefendorf, Axel Frohn, and Hermann-Josef Rupieper (New York, 1993), 433–54.

Searle, Alaric, "Revising the 'Myth' of 'Clean Wehrmacht': Generals' Trials, Public Opinion, and the Dynamics of Vergangenheitsbewältigung in West Germany, 1948–60," *German Historical Institute London, Bulletin* 25 (2003): 17–48.

Segesser, Daniel Marc, *Recht durch Rache oder Rache durch Recht? Die Ahndung von Kriegsverbrechen in der internationalen wissenschaftlichen Debatte 1872–1945* (Paderborn, 2010).

Segesser, Daniel Marc and Gessler, Myriam, "Raphael Lemkin and the International Debate on the Punishment of War Crimes (1919–1948)," *Journal of Genocide Research* 7 (2005): 453–68.

Selbmann, Frank, *Der Tatbestand des Genozids im Völkerstrafrecht* (Leipzig, 2003).

Seltzer, William, "Population Statistics, the Holocaust, and the Nuremberg Trials," *Population and Development Review* 24 (1998): 511–52.

Shandler, Jeffrey, *While America Watches. Televising the Holocaust* (New York, 1999).

Sheperd, Ben, "The Clean Wehrmacht, the War of Extermination, and Beyond," *Historical Journal* 52 (2009): 455–73.

Shklar, Judith N., *Legalism: Law, Morals and Political Trials* (Cambridge, MA, 1986).

Smith, Bradley F., *Reaching Judgment at Nuremberg* (London, 1977).

———, *The Road to Nuremberg* (New York, 1981).

———, *The Shadow Warriors. O.S.S. and the Origins of the C.I.A.* (New York, 1983).

Söllner, Alfons (ed.), *Zur Archäologie der Demokratie in Deutschland. Analysen politischer Emigranten im amerikanischen Geheimdienst, vol. 1: 1943–1945* (Frankfurt a.M., 1982).

Sprecher, Drexel A., *Inside the Nuremberg Trial. A Prosecutor's Comprehensive Account*, vol. 1 (Lanham, MD, 1999).

Stave, Bruce M., Palmer, Michele and Frank, Leslie (eds.), *Witnesses to Nuremberg. An Oral History of American Participants at the War Crimes Trials* (New York, 1998).

Stiefel, Ernst C. and Mecklenburg, Frank, *Deutsche Juristen im amerikanischen Exil (1933–1950)* (Tübingen, 1991).

Stiller, Alexa, "Die frühe Strafverfolgung der nationalsozialistischen Vertreibungs- und Germanisierungsverbrechen: Der 'RuSHA Prozess' in Nürnberg 1947–1948," in *Krieg und Verbrechen. Situation und Intention: Fallbeispiele*, ed. Timm C. Richter (Munich, 2006), 231–41.

————, "Die Volkstumspolitik der SS vor Gericht: Strategien der Anklage und Verteidi-
    gung im Nürnberger 'RuSHA-Prozess', 1947–1948," in *Leipzig—Nürnberg—Den
    Haag: Neue Fragestellungen und Forschungen zum Verhältnis von Menschen-
    rechtsverbrechen, justizieller Säuberung und Völkerstrafrecht*, ed. Helia-Verena
    Daubach (Düsseldorf, 2008), 66–86.
Stoltzfus, Nathan and Friedlander, Henry (eds.), *Nazi Crimes and the Law* (Cambridge,
    2008).
Stone, Dan, "Raphael Lemkin on the Holocaust," *Journal of Genocide Research* 7 (2005):
    539–50.
Taylor, Telford, *Final Report to the Secretary of the Army in the Nuernberg War Crimes
    Trials under Control Council Law No. 10* (Washington, DC, 1949).
————, *The Nuremberg War Crimes Trials: War Crimes and International Law* (New
    York, 1949) [*Die Nürnberger Prozesse. Kriegsverbrechen und Völkerrecht* (Zurich,
    1951)].
————, *Sword and Swastika* (New York, 1952).
————, *Nuremberg and Vietnam. An American Tragedy* (Chicago, 1970).
————, *The Anatomy of the Nuremberg Trials* (New York, 1992) [*Die Nürnberger Prozesse.
    Hintergründen, Analysen und Erkenntnisse aus heutiger Sicht* (Munich, 1994)].
"Telford Taylor Panel: Critical Perspectives on the Nuremberg Trial," *New York Law
    School Journal of Human Rights* 12 (1995): 453–544.
*The History of the United War Crimes Commission and the Development of the Laws of
    War*, compiled by UNWCC (London, 1948).
*The Trial of Adolf Eichmann: Record of the Proceedings in the District Court of Jerusalem*,
    8 vols (Jerusalem, 1992–95).
*The United Nations and Human Rights 1945–1995*, ed. United Nations (New York, 1995).
Thiele-Fredersdorf, Herbert, "Das Urteil des Militärgerichtshofes Nr. III im Nürnberger
    Juristen-Prozeß," *Neue Juristische Wochenschrift* 4 (1947): 122–26.
Tomuschat, Christian, "The Legacy of Nuremberg," *Journal of International Criminal
    Justice* 4 (2006): 830–44.
*Trial of the Major War Criminals before the International Military Tribunal, Nuremberg
    14 November 1945–1 October 1946*, 42 vols (Nuremberg, 1947–49).
*Trials of War Criminals before the Nuernberg Military Tribunals under Control Council
    Law No. 10 [TWC]*, 15 vols (Washington, DC, 1950–1953).
Tusa, Ann and Tusa, John, *The Nuremberg Trial* (New York, 1984).
Ueberschär, Gerd R. (ed.), *Der Nationalsozialismus vor Gericht. Die alliierten Prozesse
    gegen Kriegsverbrecher und Soldaten 1943–1952*, 2nd edn (Frankfurt a.M., 2000).
Vollnhals, Clemens and Schlemmer, Thomas, *Entnazifizierung. Politische Säuberung und
    Rehabilitierung in den vier Besatzungszonen 1945–1949* (Munich, 1991).
Vrdoljak, Ana Filipa, "Human Rights and Genocide: The Work of Lauterpacht and Lem-
    kin in Modern International Law," *European Journal of International Law* 20
    (2010): 1163–94.
Weckel, Ulrike, "Amerikanischer Traum von einem deutschen Schuldbekenntnis. Der
    Spielfilm *Judgment at Nuremberg* (1961) und seine Rezeption in der deutschen
    Presse," in *Das Gericht als Tribunal, oder: Wie der NS-Vergangenheit der Prozess
    gemacht wurde*, ed. Georg Wamhof (Göttingen, 2009), 163–85.
————, *Beschämende Bilder. Deutsche Reaktionen auf alliierte Dokumentarfilme über
    befreite Konzentrationslager* (Stuttgart, 2012).
Weckel, Ulrike and Wolfrum, Edgar (eds.), *'Bestien' und 'Befehlsempfänger': Frauen und
    Männer in NS-Prozessen nach 1945* (Göttingen, 2003).
Weindling, Paul, "'Tales from Nuremberg': the Kaiser Wilhelm Institute for Anthropol-
    ogy and Allied Medical War Crimes Policy," in *Geschichte der Kaiser-Wilhelm-
    Gesellschaft im Nationalsozialismus. Bestandsaufnahme und Perspektiven der
    Forschung*, 2 vols, ed. Doris Kaufmann (Göttingen, 2000), 621–38.
————, "From International to Zonal Trials: the Origins of the Nuremberg Medical Trial,"
    *Holocaust and Genocide Studies* 14 (2000): 367–89.

————, *Nazi Medicine and the Nuremberg Trials: From Medical War Crimes to Informed Consent* (Basingstoke, 2004).

Weinke, Annette, *Die Nürnberger Prozesse* (Munich, 2006).

————, "'Von Nürnberg nach Den Haag'? Das Internationale Militärtribunal in historischer Perspektive," *Leipzig—Nürnberg—Den Haag: Neue Fragestellungen und Forschungen zum Verhältnis von Menschenrechtsverbrechen, justizieller Säuberung und Völkerstrafrecht*, ed. Helia-Verena Daubach (Düsseldorf, 2008), 20–33.

Werle, Gerhard, *Principles of International Criminal Law*, 2nd edn (The Hague, 2009).

Westphalen, Tilman, *Ein Advokat für die Humanität. Verleihung der Ehrendoktorwürde an Robert M.W. Kempner* (Osnabrück, 1986).

Wiesen, S. Jonathan, *West German Industry and the Challenge of the Nazi Past, 1945–1955* (Chapel Hill, 2001).

Wilke, Jürgen, Schenk, Birgit and Cohe, Akiba A. (eds.), *Holocaust und NS-Prozesse: Die Presseberichterstattung in Israel und Deutschland zwischen Aneignung und Abwehr* (Cologne, 1995).

Wille, Siegfried, "Grundsätze des Nürnberger Ärzteprozesses," *Neue Juristische Wochenschrift* 10 (1949): 377.

Wilmowsky, Tilo von, *Warum wurde Krupp verurteilt*, 3rd rev. edn (Düsseldorf, 1962).

Wittmann, Rebecca, *Beyond Justice. The Auschwitz Trial* (Cambridge, MA, 2005).

Woetzel, Robert K., *The Nuremberg Trials in International Law* (New York, 1960).

Wojak, Irmtrud (ed.), *"Gerichtstag halten über uns selbst …" Geschichte und Wirkung des ersten Frankfurter Auschwitz-Prozesses* (Frankfurt/New York, 2001).

Wolfe, Robert, "Flaws in the Nuremberg Legacy: An Impediment to the International War Crimes Tribunals' Prosecution of Crimes against Humanity," *Holocaust and Genocide Studies* 12 (1998): 434–53.

Wrochem, Oliver von, *Erich von Mannstein: Vernichtungskrieg und Geschichtspolitik* (Paderborn, 2006).

————, "Die Stunde der Memoiren: Militärische Eliten als Stichwortgeber," in *Public History. Öffentliche Darstellungen des Nationalsozialismus jenseits der Geschichtswissenschaft*, eds. Frank Bösch and Constantin Goschler (Frankfurt a.M., 2009), 105–29.

Yablonka, Hannah, *The State of Israel vs. Adolf Eichmann* (New York, 2004).

Zeck, William Allan, "Nuremberg: Proceedings Subsequent to Goering et al.," *North Carolina Law Review* 26 (1947–1948): 350–89.

# NOTES ON CONTRIBUTORS

* C8/8*

**Lawrence Douglas** is James J. Grosfeld Professor of Law, Jurisprudence, and Social Thought, Amherst College, Massachusetts. He has published widely on the didactic function of trials and is the author of four books, including *The Memory of Judgment: Making Law and History in the Trials of the Holocaust* (Yale University Press, 2001). He is currently working on a history of the jurisprudence of atrocity.

**Hilary Earl** is Associate Professor of History, Nipissing University, North Bay, Canada. She has published widely on the *Einsatzgruppen* trial. Her monograph *The Nuremberg SS-Einsatzgruppen Trial, 1945-1958: Atrocity, Law, and History* was published by Cambridge University Press in 2009.

**Valerie Hébert** is assistant professor of history and interdisciplinary studies at Lakehead University at Orillia, Ontario, Canada. *Hitler's Generals on Trial*, her monograph on the Nuremberg High Command case, was published by University Press of Kansas in 2010. Her ongoing research concerns the social impact of atrocity trials, particularly those related to the Rwandan genocide.

**Michael R. Marrus** is Chancellor Rose and Ray Wolfe Professor Emeritus of Holocaust Studies and Adjunct Professor of Law at the University of Toronto. He is the author of several books, including *The Holocaust in History* (Penguin, 1989), *The Nuremberg War Crimes Trial 1945–46: A Documentary History* (Bedford Books, 1997), and most recently *Some Measure of Justice: The Holocaust Era Restitution Campaign of the 1990s* (University of Wisconsin Press, 2009).

**Devin O. Pendas** is Associate Professor at Boston College. His research focuses on war crimes trials after World War II, particularly on West German Holocaust trials. He has published widely on war crimes, their legal prosecution, and on the history of law and mass violence in the modern period. He is the author of *The Frankfurt Auschwitz Trial, 1963-1965: History, Genocide and the Limits of the Law* published by Cambridge University Press in 2006. He is currently completing a study of Nazi trials in German courts during the occupation period.

**Dirk Pöppmann** is a PhD candidate at the Ruhr University of Bochum, Germany. His dissertation sets out a political biography of Nuremberg attorney Robert M.W. Kempner, funded by the Jürg Breuninger Foundation, Fritz Bauer Institute, Frankfurt/Main, Germany. He has written several articles on the Ministries trial at Nuremberg.

**Kim C. Priemel** is Assistant Professor of History at Humboldt University Berlin, Germany. He has done research on German occupation of the Soviet Union, forced labor in the Third Reich, "Aryanization" policy, and the German war economy. He has also worked in the field of business history, the result of which is a book-length study of the Flick combine in the twentieth century.

**Jan Erik Schulte** is Senior Research Associate at the Hannah Arendt Institute for Research on Totalitarianism at the Dresden University of Technology, Germany. He has written widely on the history of the Nazi regime, concentration camps, Holocaust and the SS. His book *Das Wirtschaftsimperium der SS. Oswald Pohl und das SS-Wirtschafts-Verwaltungshauptamt 1933–1945* was published in 2001 by Schöningh. He is currently working on a research project on Canada and the politics of international peace-keeping in the twentieth century and a monograph on the history of the SS.

**Alexa Stiller** is Research Associate at the Department of Modern History and Contemporary History, University of Berne, Switzerland. She is currently completing a project titled, *Germanization and Genocide: Nazi Policy in the Annexed Territories, 1939–1945*. She has published several articles on Nazi occupation policy, the RuSHA trial, and the Nuremberg trials. She is also co-editor of a book on Nazi concentration camps.

**Ulrike Weckel** is Associate Professor in the History Department of the Ruhr University Bochum, Germany. Her research interests include gender history of the Third Reich, postwar cultural representations of National Socialism and the manifold audience responses to such representations. Her most recent book, *Beschämende Bilder. Deutsche Reaktionen auf alliierte Dokumentarfilme über befreite Konzentrationslager (Shameful Pictures: German Responses to Allied Documentaries on Liberated Nazi Concentration Camps)*, was published by Franz Steiner Verlag in 2012.

**Paul Weindling** is Wellcome Trust Research Professor in the History of Medicine, Oxford Brookes University, UK. Among his many books, *Nazi Medicine and the Nuremberg Trials: From Medical War Crimes to Informed Consent* was published by Palgrave Macmillan in 2004 and *John W. Thompson. Psychiatrist in the Shadow of the Holocaust* by Rochester University Press in 2010. He is currently working on a research project on the victims of Nazi human experiments and research atrocities involving a full reconstruction of the life histories of this victim group.

# INDEX

# U

Ukraine *see* Occupied Eastern Territories
and Soviet Union
United Kingdom
British zone of occupation, 49, 168,
183, 230, 257, 259–260
and war crimes trials, 8, 51–53, 75, 78,
81–82, 91, 108–109, 137, 164, 166–
167, 188n32–33, 195, 210, 223–224,
233–234, 243n1, 265, 284, 294n36
*see also individual prosecutors, and
individual trials*
United Nations, 14, 54, 78–79, 98, 104–
105, 117, 121, 126, 286
Commission on the Status of Women,
98
Educational, Scientific and Cultural
Organization (UNESCO), 98
Economic and Social Council, 78, 98
General Assembly, 14, 78, 100n23,
117, 121, 123, 129n56, 177
Human Rights Commission, 97
Secretary-General, 98
Security Council, 133n136, 286
War Crimes Commission (UNWCC),
105, 111
United States of America
Army, 48, 55, 64, 226
emigrants in the, 25–31
American zone of occupation, 41, 61,
126, 195, 202–203, 205, 207–212,
264–265
and international law after
Nuremberg, 279
Universal Declaration of Human Rights,
123
Universum Film Aktiengesellschaft
(UFA), 230
US-German Parole and Clemency Board,
208–209
USSR *see* Soviet Union

# V

Vaillant-Couturier, Marie-Claude, 247n64
Vatican, 41
Veesenmayer, Edmund, 38, 132n123,
155n29
Vereinigte Stahlwerke AG
Versailles Treaty, 41, 109, 164–165, 172
Vetter, Hellmuth, 96
victims' testimony *see* survivors
"victors' justice," 9, 41, 177, 207, 251, 279,
285

Viermetz, Inge, 138
Vietnam War, 14
Vinson, Fred M., 278
Volk, Leo, 144
Völkermord (term), 106, 127n16
Volksdeutsche Mittelstelle (VoMi), 112
Vyshinsky, Andrey, 177, 245n38

# W

Waffen-SS, 88, 96, 124, 134, 136, 138, 141,
144, 149–153, 158n95
Wagner, Eduard, 199
Wahl, Eduard, 184
Walton, Peter, 56, 63, 71n66, 72n109
Wannsee Conference, 105, 120
Protocol, 13, 38, 91
war crimes, xi, 1, 4, 6, 13–15, 16n3, 37,
39–40, 42, 47, 53, 55–56, 61, 65,
75–76, 78, 80–82, 91, 105, 108, 112,
119, 134, 139, 144, 165–166, 169,
171, 173–174, 176, 183, 195–196,
201, 203, 206–209, 223, 225, 227,
242, 254–255, 258–262, 277,
279–281, 286, 288
Warlimont, Walter, 197–199, 209–210,
213n5
Wehner, Bernd, 150–151
Wehrmacht, 10, 12–13, 52, 118–119, 124,
136, 144, 149, 153, 169, 171, 178,
194–212, 268, 278, 281
*see also* High Command, *and* General
Staff
myth of innocence of ("clean hands"),
13, 149–150, 195, 201–203, 212
exhibition (Wehrmachtsausstellung),
13, 212
Weichmann, Herbert, 32
Weinberg, Gerhard L., 13
Weizsäcker, Ernst von, 23, 37–41,
132n123, 155n29
Werner, Paul, 150
West Germany *see* Germany
"Westintegration" *see* Germany
Wilkins, William J., 180
Wilmowsky, Tilo von, 184
Woermann, Ernst, 132n123, 155n29
Wöhler, Otto, 213n6
Wolff, Karl, 138, 144, 154n21, 157n81
Wollheim, Norbert, 184
World Jewish Congress, 80
Wörner, Manfred, 211–212

www.ingramcontent.com/pod-product-compliance
Lightning Source LLC
Chambersburg PA
CBHW060026030426
42334CB00019B/2193